EDWARD WAGENKNECHT

AMERICAN PROFILE

1900-1909

THE UNIVERSITY OF MASSACHUSETTS PRESS

Amherst, 1982

Copyright © 1982 Edward Wagenknecht
All rights reserved
Printed in the United States of America
Designed by Mary Mendell

Library of Congress Cataloging in Publication Data
Wagenknecht, Edward, 1900–
American profile, 1900–1909.
Bibliography: p.
Includes index.
1. United States—Civilization—1865–1918.
2. United States—History—1901–1909—Biography.
3. United States—Biography. I. Title.
E169.1.W17   973.91   81–16510.
ISBN 0–87023–350–5   AACR2
ISBN 0–87023–351–3 (pbk.)

AMERICAN PROFILE, 1900–1909

Dear Philip Winsor,

*It seems a work of supererogation to dedicate this book to you;
since it would never have been written without your unselfish encouragement and cooperation, it belongs to you already. But because its value will be greatly enhanced in my eyes if I am permitted
to write your name here and acknowledge my obligation to you, I
hope you will indulge me for the sake of the friendship you have
served in so many ways.*

Edward Wagenknecht

Contents

Preface

THIS book is an attempt to survey American life in manifold aspects between 1900 and the close of Theodore Roosevelt's administrations. I hope to follow it with another volume covering the Taft years and the Wilson years up to our entry into World War I. It was that event, and not the close of Wilson's tenure, which marked the end of an era.

The volume is not essentially a book about Theodore Roosevelt, though since he, in so many ways, dominated the era, he could not be kept out of it. Neither is it a personal memoir in the sense in which that term may be applied to such a book as William L. Shirer's *20th Century Journey*. I do not at any point occupy center stage. But it does concern the world into which I was born and where I spent my formative years, and I have not hesitated to make use of personal memories where they seemed to fit in or to shed light on the subject under consideration.

In factual and fictional writing alike, there are two ways to write about the past. One may confine himself to the period under consideration (or try to), viewing the times through the eyes of a contemporary and permitting backward glances but none toward the future. Or one may remain where he is and view the past in the light of all he knows, from wherever it may have been derived. The latter is the way Sir Walter Scott wrote historical novels, and to compare small things with great, it is the way I have tried to write this book. For as nothing of the past that still has meaning for us has ever died, so nothing which has lost its meaning can possibly be of any significance. The reader will perhaps notice this aspect of my method primarily in the mini-portraits—obviously, if you are going to write about the life of a human being, you must view the whole life, not chop off one decade and ignore the rest—but the same thing appears less strikingly elsewhere. I hope, however, that I have everywhere brought my picture to focus upon the decade with which I am primarily concerned.

E.W.
West Newton, Massachusetts
May 25, 1981

AMERICAN PROFILE, 1900–1909

THOUGH every American capable of counting up to 100 must have known that 1900 was not the first year of the twentieth century but the last of the nineteenth, the change in the figures on the calendar made it hard to realize this. Press and pulpit alike devoted themselves to stocktaking and prophecy, and though the country was still struggling with the war in the Philippines and divided on the issues connected with it, everybody seemed to be bracing for a fresh start. The Reverend Newell Dwight Hillis saw art, industry, invention, literature, learning, and government all "captives marching in Christ's triumphant procession up the hill of fame," while the more worldly Chauncey M. Depew was sure every man in America felt 100 percent better in 1900 than in 1899. When, on January 1, 1901, the Philadelphia neurologist and novelist, S. Weir Mitchell, was to write words that it is now difficult to read without a shudder, most Americans must have felt that he was already a year out of date. "The new century," said Dr. Mitchell, "came in with God knows what in its hands and was welcomed. We may entertain devil or angel unawares."

The first volume of *Who's Who in America* was dated 1899–1900 and contained 8,602 entries, a number that would nearly double by the time Theodore Roosevelt left office. At the beginning of 1900 William McKinley still had more than a year left of his first term in the White House, and the federal government was spending half a billion dollars annually. There were forty-five states in the federal

A New Century

1

Union, and the center of a population in excess of 76 million, 60 percent of whom were still classified as rural, and with a preponderance of one and a half million men over women, lay near Columbus, Indiana. Most of the country west of the Alleghenies still lay as God had made it. Only Chicago and San Francisco had much place in the minds of dwellers on the eastern seaboard (Los Angeles had a little over 100,000 people and the whole Pacific Coast about 3 million), and only the most thoughtful persons had become aware that our natural resources were not inexhaustible.

Deaths were running 1,775 in 100,000, and the average life expectancy was slightly over forty-nine years. Typhoid and tuberculosis were still unconquered, and the incidence of fatalities from appendectomies was high. Few families expected to rear all their offspring; more than 108 out of every 100,000 babies died during their first two years.

The population included some 9 million Negroes, 227,000 Indians, and 114,000 Orientals, and the Spanish-American War had left us in control of 125,000 square miles in the West Indies and the Pacific populated largely by people of alien races, customs, and traditions. Except for the survival of the Napoleonic Code in Louisiana, British cultural institutions were still the most influential in America, but only 41 million among the whites had been here for a whole generation, and though northern European strains still predominated among the immigrants and their children, the influx from eastern and southern Europe was increasing rapidly. Nearly 450,000 immigrants arrived in 1900; by 1905 the number would rise to a million. The Spanish language predominated in portions of the Southwest, French in Louisiana, and a dialectal form of German in sections of Pennsylvania. In time the "new Americans" would notably widen and enrich our cultural heritage, but because they settled largely in cities and industrial centers and were herded into ghettos there, their immediate effect was to contribute to the growth of slums and help shift the balance of population from country to city, and because they were poor, unfamiliar with American institutions, and therefore easily exploitable by selfish interests, they were often involved, in spite of themselves, in political corruption and social degradation.

As for the minorities, under a Supreme Court decision of 1896, the Negroes had "separate but equal" facilities in the South, which

Immigrants arriving at Ellis Island

in practice turned out to be merely separate. Orientals were a problem only in California, and since the Indians had ceased to be a danger, nobody was worrying much about them. In 1905, in an article in the *Saturday Evening Post*, the Reverend Thomas Dixon, Jr. would advocate deporting all American Negroes to Liberia! Harvard's Albert Bushnell Hart replied in an article that knocked Dixon's thoroughly unscientific racist arguments into a cocked hat, and the *Post* ran other sympathetic articles by Joel Chandler Harris, Rebecca Harding Davis, and Paul Laurence Dunbar.

Though England's sympathy toward America during the Spanish-American War had done much to lessen traditional suspicion of "the old country," Americans were inclined to sympathize with the Boers in their struggle against the Empire. On January 1, 1900, Secretary of State John Hay made it known that he had persuaded the powers to support an "open-door" policy in China. Hay had saved China from being partitioned, but he had also won trading rights for Americans who might otherwise have been excluded from the Celestial Empire, and American troops would soon join with those of European powers to put down the Boxer uprising against foreigners.

At home too there was progress on every hand. On January 2, Chicago opened the Drainage Canal, which reversed the flow of the Chicago River, thereby protecting Lake Michigan, the source of the city's water supply, from contamination by waste; this would reduce Chicago's typhoid death rate from sixty-five to one per 100,000. New York City was planning a subway (Boston, often called slow, had stolen a march on her by opening the first in America three years before, but Chicago was to drag her own feet until the forties). In 1901 New York would build the Fuller ("Flatiron") Building, where Broadway crosses Fifth Avenue; Chicago had pioneered with the skyscraper, but New York would take to it with a vengeance. In 1901 too, Tulsa, Oklahoma, would strike oil and begin its phenomenal growth. Against such achievements not even disasters like the Galveston "flood" of September 8, 1900 (more accurately, the almost complete destruction of the city by a cyclonic hurricane from the Gulf of Mexico), made much impression, and indeed the calamity itself inspired a heroic and amazing engineering achievement, calculated to prevent a repetition of the calamity, that boosted the coming century's estimate of itself.

Industrial production increased after the Spanish war, unemployment declined, and farm products rose in value. The United States was producing more than half the world's cotton, corn, copper, and oil; more than one-third of its steel, pig iron, and silver; about a third of its coal and gold. The value of consumer goods sold, which had been some 12 billion annually in 1883, would increase to 25 billion early in the new century. Foreign investments and interests were increasing, and the newly organized National Association of Manufacturers was busy promoting exports. The United States Treasury had a surplus in excess of 46 million dollars.

There were no income taxes, and business practices were virtually unregulated. In theory, businessmen believed in unregulated competition, but in practice they were forever using "pools" and other devices to force their competitors out. Businesses that operated on the owner's own capital were managed quite at his discretion, and though stock market manipulations were increasing steadily in importance, minority stockholders were still often quite uninformed concerning policies and operations. Though many products were still being made, under deplorable sanitary conditions, in tenements, the factory system was developing rapidly and handcraftsmanship was declining. The tide was already turning against small businesses, individually managed, and J. P. Morgan and Company; Kuhn, Loeb, and Company; Kidder, Peabody, and Company; and Lee, Higginson, and Company were widening and extending their credit control. In 1899 and 1900 there were twenty-eight books and some 150 magazine articles about the "trusts."

Many saw the balance of power passing from statesmen to financiers; certainly there could be no doubt that clergymen, artists, and intellectuals were lagging far in the rear. Writing in the *Saturday Evening Post*, Russell H. Sage advised that boys be "turned into the active work of the world at fifteen or sixteen," prepared to work eighteen to twenty hours a day if necessary and never to spend a penny they could possibly save. Grover Cleveland's article in the same periodical three years later, though not so inhuman or anti-cultural, was still significantly entitled "Does a College Education Pay?"

Unfortunately, not all were sharing in the great American prosperity. The two-week summer vacation was just getting started, and the government itself had not yet adopted the eight-hour day.

Woman worker in a shoe factory in the early 1900s

In the textile mills the working week sometimes ran to sixty-two hours, in steel to eighty-four. Garment factories paid women pressers as little as eight cents an hour and men twenty-five. Miners began their underground work at dawn. In off-seasons industry could shut down without notice, leaving the workers without means of subsistance. Over one-fourth of the boys between ten and fifteen were employed and 10 percent of the girls. In southern cotton mills one-fourth of the employees were children, with six-year-old girls working as many as thirteen hours a day. In northern cities, small bootblacks, newsboys, and messengers froze in the streets and ran errands in saloons and brothels. Some states had no laws at all regulating the employment of children, and many suffered death or mutilation from machinery with no protection or compensation. Yet the American Federation of Labor had 500,000 members in 1900, which was just twice the number it had had four years earlier, and in Dayton, Ohio, there was enough alarm so that an employers' association was formed to fight the unions. In such a climate of opinion, it is hardly to be wondered at that the Industrial Workers of the World (IWW) should have been formed in 1905 on the premise that "the working class and the employing class have nothing in common."

Yet "agitators" were not the only forces behind the winds of change. Sometimes they were fanned much more powerfully by "intellectuals" who had no direct contacts with either capital or labor and whom the economic barons despised too much to fear. If Yale's William Graham Sumner was still the high priest of nineteenth-century social Darwinism, William James, John Dewey, Thornstein Veblen, Charles S. Peirce, Richard T. Ely, Albion W. Small, and other scientists, philosophers, and sociologists ("social science" was a challenging new word) were moving toward a more "open" conception of the universe as subject to changes in which the human will might have a part. In the election of 1900 the Socialist candidate Eugene V. Debs polled 87,000 votes, and this was to rise to 400,000 in 1904, 420,000 in 1908, and 900,000 in 1912. Here and there too Socialists were being elected to local offices; after 1910 thirty-three cities including Milwaukee, Butte, and Flint, Michigan, would opt for Socialist administrations, while both New York and Wisconsin would send Socialists to Congress. Yet some American reformers were chauvinists and racists, and some were suspicious of the people whose lot they were trying to improve. Some sponsored reform on the basis of simple, nonideological humanitarianism, and some were actuated by the fear that unless capitalism was reformed it would be destroyed and replaced by a monolithic state that would set up a ten times worse tyranny than the capitalists had ever dreamed of.

Utility franchises in cities were generally under the control of the state legislature, which might, however, be quite as corrupt as the city machine itself. Such United States senators as Matthew Quay in Pennsylvania and Thomas C. Platt in New York wielded great power as the tools of corporate interests. But the home rule movement was gaining ground, and with it a trend toward the city manager form of government. What a reform mayor could do was demonstrated in Toledo, Ohio, where a Welsh immigrant, the proprietor of an oil equipment factory, Samuel M. ("Golden Rule") Jones, was elected in 1897. Jones defied the local machine, took clubs away from the police, established a free lodginghouse and free kindergartens, set a minimum wage for common laborers employed by the city, and championed public ownership. Moreover, he held power until he died in 1904, when he was succeeded by Brand Whitlock, who continued his work. In 1901 too the like-minded Tom L. Johnson, an industrialist who had become a disciple of Henry George and an apostle of municipal ownership, became mayor of Cleveland and remained in office until 1910.

Robert M. La Follette, governor of Wisconsin from 1900 to 1906, when he moved on to the United States Senate, carried out a reform administration on a larger scale. La Follette advocated direct primaries and later the initiative and referendum. He opposed monopolies wherever they were not required by the nature of things and advocated government regulation elsewhere, along with regulation of railroads and lobbyists, competitive examinations for state civil service employees, and much besides. Though he was not the first reform governor (Roosevelt had been one in New York), he was the most successful, and his success not only lived after him in Wisconsin but inspired similar action elsewhere. In 1902 Oregon adopted the initiative and the referendum. For various reasons, including lack of support from the immigrants and fear of radical labor, reform movements often languished both in the East and in the Far West, but Hiram Johnson triumphed in California, and in

1905 Charles Evans Hughes became governor of New York after his magnificent exposure of life insurance abuses. In the Deep South the reformers improved the condition of the poor whites but did little for the blacks.

Many reforms, proposed or achieved, had nothing to do with politics save as they employed poltical means to achieve their ends. The first juvenile court was established in Chicago in 1900, but the most famous juvenile court judge was Ben B. Lindsey of Denver. In 1900 a Committee of Fifteen, including John D. Rockefeller, Jr., Jacob Schiff, and George Foster Peabody, explored the "lower depths" in New York City, and a New York state building law established minimum standards for lighting, sanitation, ventilation, and fire protection. Support for reform often appeared also in unexpected places. William Randolph Hearst's connection with the movement is touched upon elsewhere in this volume, and the Chicago *Tribune's* Joseph Medill Patterson, later the founder of the New York *Daily News,* became a Socialist and wrote *A Little Brother of the Rich* to propagate his views. One of the *Tribune's* own pet crusades was for the abolition or regulation of fireworks, which were killing and maiming many children every Fourth of July. The first victory came in St. Paul in 1903.

Of more widespread interest was the crusade against alcohol. In 1900 the liquor interests were riding high. Only four states—Maine, New Hampshire, Kansas, and North Dakota—were dry; there were 100,000 saloons; the brewing firm of Anheuser-Busch had just reported the best year in its history; the Anti-Saloon League was only two years old. Here was a crusade in which women could engage wholeheartedly, for they knew what happened to a family when the breadwinner squandered his small earnings in drink. Up to World War I the antiliquor forces gained steadily. In 1908 alone, for example, Georgia adopted statewide prohibition; Worcester, Massachusetts, became the largest city in the country to vote dry; and both the Baltimore and Ohio Railroad Company and the Henry C. Frick interests discouraged the use of liquor by employees. (That same year too both New York and Louisiana prohibited racetrack gambling.) In 1900 Frances E. Willard was already two years dead, but her long-effective Woman's Christian Temperance Union lived on after her, not only engaging in political propaganda but carrying on an important educational work in teaching young people the dangers of alcohol, and Carry A. Nation was just getting started on her spectacular saloon smashing.

But women still had plenty of reforming to do in their own behalf. They could vote in only five states—Idaho, Wyoming, Utah, Colorado, and Montana; worse still, three-fourths of the states prohibited a wife from holding property in her own name; in one-third she had no legal right to her own earnings; only one-fifth gave her equal rights with her husband in the guardianship of their children. Until now it had generally been assumed that unmarried girls of good family would live at home and be supported by their fathers. Teaching and nursing were respectable occupations, and those with special gifts found a way to exercise them, though often to the accompaniment of many raised eyebrows, and those who went into medicine were considered "odd." Education and technology were changing all this, however, and girls were becoming stenographers (100,000 by 1900) and telephone operators, though sometimes they earned only ten dollars a week. Many women who were not working were joining women's clubs (there were nearly a million members), and the Association of Collegiate Alumnae was also gathering strength.

In the field of transportation, the railroad, not yet equipped with oil-burning locomotives, was king, supplemented, sometimes even threatened, especially on short hauls, by interurban electric cars, which enthusiasts saw as soon girdling the nation. Many carried baggage as well as passengers, and some even put on dining cars; this business was destined to thrive up to about 1912 and decline rapidly thereafter. In the interest of the commuter trade, the railroads were encouraging city dwellers to move to the suburbs and the country, where, in the second half of the century, they would leave them stranded. There were few paved roads, and though the first American-made, gasoline-driven truck was produced in 1900 and the first tractors in 1902, neither was very important as yet in American life.

In the cities, the trolley car, drawing its power from overhead wires, was driving out the horsecars; some cities had elevated railroads also. Chicago had built its first elevated on the South Side in time to carry passengers from the Loop to the World's Columbian Exposition in 1893; in the early years of the new century New York was also dreaming of tunnels under the Hudson and East rivers. In the cities, traction companies ran open cars in summertime and, in the absence of other available forms of transportation, people often rode them in the evening to "cool off." Those who were able to afford them had carriages and buggies everywhere, and deliveries were made by horse-drawn wagons. Livery stable owners and black-smiths did a thriving business even in the city. Many sidewalks were still made of wood, some of them built high on wooden trestles on a level with the street, with a thriving rat population and other things underneath; I can still remember when both the cement sidewalks and the asphalt paving were laid along Chicago's Douglas Park on South California Avenue, where I lived. Before that, streets had been paved with wooden blocks, set close together and fastened with tar; if a hole got started, it was a great temptation to a small boy to kick it and make it larger for the pleasure of watching the wood shred. The first bicycle in America had been seen at the Philadelphia Centennial Exposition in 1876, but the "safety," with pneumatic tires, did not come in until just before 1890. During the last decade of the old century, bicycling had become a craze with both men and women, but the absence of modern paving in many localities was a handicap.

William Morrison of Des Moines is the reputed first maker of an electric automobile; in 1892 he drove it through the streets of Chicago. The automobile was essentially a European creation; the Americans merely combined elements and established quantity production. The first automobile show was held in Madison Square Garden in 1900. The previous year motors had been barred from Central Park; this year they were limited to nine miles an hour and required to carry a gong.

To us the most unbelievable thing about the 1900 show is that more than one-third of the cars shown were electrics and most of the rest steam cars. The first "taxicabs" did not arrive in New York until 1907, and at least up to the coming of Henry Ford's Model T the following year, the automobile, though steadily wedging its way in, was still regarded by the average American as something whose interest was confined to the rich and those who enjoyed tinkering with machinery.

Compared with what we have today, early motorcars were both uncertain in their performance and difficult to operate, and few women cared to risk a broken arm when the vehicle "kicked" while

Fifth Avenue, New York City, about 1905. Courtesy, New York Historical Society, New York City

being cranked. The high, open cars, running on what look to us like bicycle tires, seemed ideally calculated to throw the passenger out on his head in case of a collision or sudden stop. When breakdowns occurred, as they often did, passersby were likely to shout, "Get a horse!"; the "automobile joke" was staple in cartoons, popular songs, and vaudeville all through the early years. In the beginning, indeed, "coaching" was often preferred even by the wealthy, whose clubs centered about Madison Square and whose elegant four-in-hands were driven up Fifth Avenue to Central Park.

If the automobile was making its way, few serious persons believed at the beginning of the century that man would ever learn to fly. One of the exceptions was Professor Samuel P. Langley of the Smithsonian Institution, who enlisted the aid of the War Department and the scientist Charles M. Manly. Their second and final failure occurred on December 8, 1903, when, as the New York *Sun* gleefully reported, their "aerodrome did a flipflop" by "swooping" into the Potomac and "ducking" Professor Manly, to the accompaniment of considerable satisfaction and indignation on the part of those who resented public money's being spent on such nonsense. But only nine days later, the self-taught proprietors of a bicycle shop, Wilbur and Orville Wright, with no backing but their own, produced, as the *Virginian-Pilot* reported, a "flying machine" that flew "3 miles in teeth of high wind over sand hills and waves" with "no balloon attached to it." The *Virginian-Pilot* was one of the few papers impressed. Many did not trouble to report this fifth and at last successful try of the Wright brothers at Kitty Hawk, North Carolina, at all, and the New York *Tribune,* which did, put it on the sports page! Not until after 1908 and further experiments was the public made generally aware of what had occurred. I was eleven when I was taken to an aviation meet in Chicago's Grant Park on the lakefront; during the week or so that the show ran, two flyers were killed.

People worked harder in 1900 than they do today and, perhaps in consequence, led less active lives in other aspects. Croquet was "refined," but tennis had not yet taken a great hold, and golf was definitely "sissy." Taft would be the first American president to play it, and his sponsor TR feared the effect on his image. Some men went in for hunting and fishing, and horseback riding was popular among the wealthy, but football was still largely the monopoly of the great eastern colleges, with Harvard, Yale, and Princeton dominating the field, their big games being social as well as athletic events. The common assumption was still that sports were "kid stuff," and baseball was the only spectator sport that had really come into its own. The American League was organized in 1900, rivaling the twenty-four-year-old National League, which had had a stranglehold on the business. After three years, peace was made, a code was drawn up, and the first World Series was held in Boston.

Men were much given to wearing blue serge suits, which picked up all the lint in sight. All suits came with vests, and though it might be permissible to discard the vest in summer weather, the gentleman would still cling to his jacket. Bankers and business executives were still likely to wear frock coats and silk hats to work; in Oak Park, Illinois, where I then lived, some citizens of substance wore silk hats to church as late as World War I. Many shirts still opened in the back; shoes generally came up over the ankles and might be either tightly laced or buttoned. Collars were stiff, high, and starched, generally fastened to the shirt by collar buttons, and sometimes cuffs were detachable too; J. C. Leyendecker's pictures of the "Arrow Collar man" made him as famous as Charles Dana Gibson had made the "Gibson girl." In summertime, it was proper, under some circumstances, to wear white flannel or duck trousers.

Persons of both sexes who needed eyeglasses wore steel- or gold-rimmed spectacles, depending upon their· means, but "refined" people generally preferred rimless pince-nez, at least for dress occasions. If you were afraid of losing them, you might attach them to a slender gold chain, fastened behind your ear, but not even Theodore Roosevelt could make his countrymen believe that a black cord was not an affectation.

Both men and women were always hatted out of doors, many men still clinging to the stiff derby, except between May 1 and October 1, when they substituted a sailor-shaped straw hat (it was a serious gaffe to wear one at any other time) or, if they could afford it, a fine, fedora-shaped Panama. Women were likely to buy their clothes from dressmakers, most of whom operated in their own homes and designed to order, and their hats from the corner "millinery store." A man could get a suit for fifteen dollars, and three dollars was a good price for a pair of shoes, but hats were as elaborate and expensive as milady could afford, weighted down with lace, ribbon, artificial flowers and fruit, and dead birds and feathers, ranging all the way from ostrich plumes to aigrettes, to which women clung stubbornly and insensitively, despite the efforts of Mrs. Fiske, Edward W. Bok, and other humanitarians and conservationists, until fresh legislation took the feathers away from them.

Women held themselves together with stiff, whalebone- and steel-fortified corsets, which the more fashionable laced as tightly as possible, and often they wore boned collars too. The "hourglass figure" was much admired; the actress Anna Held was said to have achieved an eighteen-inch waist, and when she died people would say that she had laced herself to death. Skirts nearly touched the floor and the sidewalk (their bottoms were continually needing to be cleaned and rebound). Black clothes and hideous "mourning veils" were worn for a year after a death had occurred in any respectable family, during which period all amusements were taboo. Both girls and women generally wore long cotton or woolen stockings and an abundance of petticoats. Nearly everybody wore long underwear all the year round; when winter approached, you switched, generally under vain, vigorous protest, if you were a child, to your torturous flannels. All this was beginning to be modified, however, by the more active life that women were coming to lead, and daring people were already approving an ankle-length "rainy day skirt." Shirtwaists, beginning in the nineties, gained in popularity, despite the disapproval that increased notably with the introduction of the "peekaboo" variety in 1907. Freak fashions, like the "hobble" skirt and the slit skirt, were frowned upon, as was the "sheath dress," when it came in in 1908. Women still clung, however, to an abundance of false hair—pompadours, "rats," puffs, curls, and other accoutrements. Face powder was respectable, but "painting" was not.

Both sexes wore "dresses" for the first two or three years, but trousers of all kinds were a male prerogative at any age. In all strata of society, people dressed their children as well as they could afford, and even "poor people," whose children might look comparatively ill-kempt when they went to school, almost always "dressed them up" on Sundays, the girls in stiffly starched white dresses. Boys wore short pants, with long stockings, the trouser leg sometimes cut off just above the knee and sometimes fastened just below it. I never saw a boy wearing a Little Lord Fauntleroy suit, or curls either, but the "Buster Brown suit" had a great vogue after 1905, and candor forces me to admit that I wore one. The boom in summer "cottages," generally little shacks whose inhabitants were eaten by mosquitoes, was just beginning, but those who could afford it went in the summer to the big resort hotels, some of whose ghosts still dot the landscape, where they sat on the wide porches and fanned themselves, doing nothing between consuming elaborate meals in the dining room. If the hotel was near the water, some, to be sure, were tempted to "bathe," but women's bathing costumes tended to discourage that, for they included skirts that covered the knees and long black stockings; when Annette Kellerman appeared barelegged at Boston's Revere Beach in 1907, she was arrested.

In the country both boys and girls went barefoot and barelegged in summertime as a matter of course, but in the cities this was generally confined to the lower classes. Shorts of course were unknown, and comparatively few little girls even wore sox. It is true that foreigners or "bohemian" people sometimes allowed small children the luxury of running about naked in hot weather, but most "right-thinking" people were inclined to regard this as both indecent and "un-American." Boys were generally taught that their genitals were superlatively shameful and that masturbation, always described merely as "self-abuse," was not only a heinous moral offense but an imprudence capable of producing a variety of diseases. Often the price of innocence was high. Many a woman married in a now inconceivable state of ignorance, feeling in a vague way that it was her duty to yield to her husband's passion but improper to share it, and there is a still unsolved mystery of as late as 1916 in which a tormented girl was driven to what may well have been suicide because she imagined herself pregnant though the autopsy showed an unbroken hymen.

In the suburbs, some families were now living in "bungalows," and "apartment houses," as distinguished from the old two- or three-"flat" buildings, were beginning to be respectable in the cities. Even here, however, there were still many "cottages," some of them even with the outdoor privies still almost universal in the country.

In the "parlor" the old-fashioned horsehair had given way to three-piece upholstered "sets" (not yet "overstuffed"), comprising sofa, armchair, and "rocker." Rocking chairs of all kinds were much in vogue; they ranked with icewater, pie, chewing gum, and baseball among American institutions. Ingrain carpets with floral designs were still in use, but they were giving way to Wilton and Axminster rugs, the former generally with the famous red center. The Moorish vogue was passing, but many were going in for mission furniture and Morris chairs. Round oak extension tables were popular in dining rooms, as were padded "Turkish" leather couches, elevated at one end for the head, and there was a variety of sofa pillows, including burned leather and ribbon-woven. Green was the favorite color for glass lampshades, and Louis Tiffany was nearing the end of a lifetime during which he had created many beautiful glass objects for those who could afford them.

Old-fashioned music boxes were still being advertised, and there were player pianos whose records were perforated rolls. Thanks to the emerging phonograph, both were on their way out, but the great triumph of the latter was still in the future; its ultimate destiny was to make great music by great performers available to anybody who wanted it, at the same time tending to discourage the home music making that until then had prevailed. In 1900 no home with any pretensions to gentility could get along without a piano and "piano lessons" for the children, whether they had any talent or not, generally for fifty to seventy-five cents a hour from a teacher who accommodatingly called at the house to give them.

The housewife had a "carpet sweeper," operated by woman power, but no vacuum cleaner, electric stove, or electric iron. Electric power existed of course, but only one generating station exceeded 5,000 horsepower, and most homes were still lighted, if you could call it that, by gas, often a miserable open flame in the kitchen and a somewhat more effective "mantle" that was always burning out in the "front" rooms. Kerosene lamps were passé, but many households still kept them on hand for emergencies. Streets were lighted by gas also, and I used to love to watch the lamplighter making his rounds at dusk with a light on the end of a pole, which he would thrust through an opening at the bottom of the lamp, turn on the gas, ignite it, and pass on. Though there were a million telephones in use (the number would triple within five years), many of the humbler households were still without them. There might be a gas "plate" for light meals, but for the serious cooking Mother still relied on her kitchen "range," fired by wood and anthracite coal, which had to be polished laboriously by hand and—if she was thrifty—to have its ashes sifted in the alley, even in zero weather. She turned her washing machine by hand too and heated her heavy irons on the stove. Often she lived in a cold-water flat, without central heating ("furnace heat" was considered unhealthy by many), which meant that all the water for baths had to be heated on the kitchen stove. Bathtubs were made of tin or cast iron, with a rolled rim and claw-feet; the double-shell enameled bathtub did not replace these until about 1916. When the children were small, however, they were bathed on Saturday nights in winter in a portable tub before the kitchen stove, and when they jumped out of bed on a cold morning they grabbed their clothes and ran to the "base burner" in the dining room, where they dressed in the heat afforded by the red-hot coals shining gratefully through the isinglass on the iron doors. Mother did have a Singer sewing machine, however, and was much more inclined to use it than the woman of today. She ground her coffee fresh every day from "coffee beans," and in season she was much given to preserving fruits and vegetables and making ketchup and chili sauce and other delicacies, which filled the house with odors almost maddening in their delightsomeness. She was also very likely to bake her own bread, cakes, and pies; indeed "store-bought bread" was rather looked down upon, along with the lazy woman who used it.

The "department store" was well established; indeed, the pioneering enterprise, which was A. T. Stewart's in New York and which is credited with being the first to make it possible for milady to buy virtually everything she needed under one roof, dated back to 1846. The five-and-ten too was thriving; F. W. Woolworth had opened his first in Utica in 1879, and by 1909 he would have 250 (in 1913 he would build the Woolworth Building).

The "A & P" had 200 stores by 1900, but there were no supermarkets and no self-service, and housewives were inclined to buy in much smaller quantities than they do today, making the short trip to the neighborhood "grocery store" and "butcher shop" every day and carrying home their purchases on foot. Brand names were beginning to be important, and advertising was becoming more and more ingenious. Everybody in my generation must remember the pretty little girl, dressed to the nines, holding a bunch of violets and perched on a bar of Fairy Soap and the little boy who was showing his bare behind because his mother had forgotten to wash his shirt with Wool Soap, to say nothing of the enchantingly black Gold Dust twins, naked except for ballet skirts and devoted almost demoniacally to a variety of cleaning activities, or Aunt Jemima and her family. Yet even in city groceries many articles were still kept in open barrels or bins, and you could see whole carcasses of animals hanging up in the butcher shops. Fresh fruit and vegetables were scarce during the winter, however, and most people ate a diet much heavier in starch than is favored today. Prices of course were fantastically low by present-day standards; a Boston "boarding-house" (that late, lamented, now defunct institution) advertised a turkey dinner for twenty cents and supper and breakfast for fifteen cents each.

Of course you did not buy everything you needed in the shops. The milkman came to the house every day and delivered your milk at seven cents a quart, and in winter the cream sometimes froze up out of the bottle, making the finest kind of ice cream. In summer too the iceman came two or three times a week, whenever you put a sign in your window. Children watched eagerly for his coming and begged for chips of ice, which were unhygienically sucked. Mailmen were still called "letter carriers" (the parcel post was not established until 1913), and the mail was delivered three times a day in residential districts and four times in business areas. Letters cost two cents postage, cards a penny, including the card. When you had something to dispose of, you hailed the junkman, who came driving through the alley calling "Rags, old iron," generally in a strong foreign accent. Even the doctor came whenever you called him, charging three dollars for the service (when you went to his office, it cost only two).

Ice cream might be obtained at either the drugstore or one of the "ice cream parlors" that were now springing up everywhere; here either a soda or a sundae might be had for a dime, and if you had only a nickel you might settle for a Coca-Cola. A large part of the drugstore's profits still came out of patent medicines, which were in their last great period of unregulated prosperity before the passage of the Pure Food and Drug Act in 1906. Lydia Pinkham's Vegetable Compound, which survived into recent years, is now the best remembered; it was also one of the less dangerous ones, but Samuel Hopkins Adams called Peruna "the most conspicuous of all medical frauds." Not only were many of the proprietary remedies medically worthless; many fostered both alcoholism and drug addiction, and did so deliberately for greed of gold.

Drugstores sold a variety of other products also, including candy, chewing gum, and postcards. The Brownie dollar camera came out in 1900, one of the most popular gadgets of the new century. Chewing gum was not yet almost invariably Wrigley's; it was quite likely to be Zeno, which came in assorted flavors and was often retailed at a penny a stick out of slot machines. You put your penny in the slot and watched Foxy Grandpa or the Yellow Kid turn about while the gum was ejected. It was fascinating to wonder what flavor you would get but disappointing if it was not your favorite, in which case you were tempted to try again with another penny, which was probably the idea.

The first American mailing card seems to date from 1861, and the Post Office issued the first government mailing cards in 1873, but the interest in souvenir cards began with the World's Columbian Exposition of 1893. The great collecting craze started about 1900 and continued unabated until World War I, after which it sharply declined; nobody ever really found out why. During these years, postcards were big business in the United States, though a large number of the best cards were imported from Germany.

"View cards" celebrating particular places predominated (this tied in of course with the increasing mobility of the population), but almost everything that either happened or was dreamed of during the years in question appeared sometime on cards. Every cause and every national candidate were boomed, and every product was advertised. Theatrical folk and comic strip characters decorated the cards, and every holiday produced its own series. People bought cards in sets as well as singly and collected them in albums, and there were novelty cards of wood, leather, and other substances.

Some of these things probably interested women and children more than men, but the male was still lord and master of the American home. He shaved with a straight-edged razor, honed on a leather strop, and applied shaving soap out of a mug with a brush. Some men kept their own mugs at the local barbershop and went there to be shaved for fifteen cents (haircuts cost a quarter), but this custom was declining. The carved, wooden, painted Indian in front of tobacco shops was as familiar a sight as the barber pole is today. Men smoked pipes and cigars without reproach, and the filthy habit of chewing tobacco, which had so disgusted Dickens when he visited America, had carried over sufficiently from the nineteenth century so that many homes were still ornamented with cuspidors. Cigarettes, however, were widely regarded as dangerous and evidence of degeneracy, and smoking by women was generally thought of as belonging to brothels. When the habit began to come out into the open, New York City would be sufficiently alarmed to pass the Sullivan Ordinance of 1908, banning smoking by women in public places, which would have been an excellent law if only it had applied to both sexes.

I N the election of 1900 the incumbent president, William McKinley, was again pitted against William Jennings Bryan. Since it was the Republicans who had taken the country into the Spanish-American War, many regarded the election as a referendum on the war, and certainly the presence of Theodore Roosevelt, military hero of that war, as McKinley's running mate did not tend to play down that issue. McKinley had not particularly wanted Roosevelt, and his political mentor, Senator Hanna, regarded the "damned cowboy" as a "madman" and trembled at the idea of having only one life between him and the presidency. Yet the issue was never clearly drawn. Bryan had shocked the financial community and all conservatives by campaigning in 1896 on a platform calling for the free and unlimited coinage of silver in a ratio of sixteen to one, and though this might now have been overshadowed by other issues, Bryan was still committed to it. Moreover, though the Democrats denounced Republican "militarism" and land-grabbing, they still approved of expansion "by peaceful and legitimate means." The antimilitarist Carnegie supported McKinley while southern jingoes like Senator John T. Morgan were in Bryan's camp. Nobody, consequently, will ever know how many voted for McKinley because they approved of the war and how many were simply for what they saw as prosperity and "the full dinner pail."

McKinley conducted a front-porch campaign at Canton, Ohio,

Czolgosz' Beneficiary

2

while TR triumphantly barnstormed the country, and the Hearst press published a series of brilliantly vicious cartoons by Frederick Opper in which both McKinley and Roosevelt appeared as children in the care of "Nurse Hanna" and a bloated papa-figure labeled "The Trusts." Though Hanna and McKinley cannot possibly have enjoyed these cartoons in any other aspect, they must have heartily agreed that "Teddy" was under some apprehension as to who was the real candidate and that he was making far too much noise. The outcome, however, was never in doubt. In 1896 the Republicans had won by an electoral vote of 271 against 176 and a popular vote of 7,102,246 against 6,492,559; in 1900 the figures would be 292 against 155 and 7,212,491 against 6,356,734.

On September 6, 1901, McKinley was shot by a fanatical anarchist, Leon Czolgosz, at the Pan-American Exposition in Buffalo. Oddly enough, when a member of the welcoming committee had greeted him upon arrival, he had replied, "Yes, and I don't know whether I'll ever be able to get away." He had also done his best to discourage security: "No one would wish to hurt me." He called his assassin "a poor misguided fellow" and asked that he should not be hurt and even apologized to the director of the exposition: "I'm so sorry that this should have happened here." But the operation was bungled, performed in haste without proper sanitary precautions, and the wound was closed without providing for proper drainage. The president manifested patience and forbearance worthy of a saint, and until September 12 it seemed as though he might win his fight. Then came a sudden turn for the worse; heart and stomach failed, and he lost consciousness. He died on September 14. There followed the kind of sickish, macabre hysteria to which Americans are prone on such occasions. As for Czolgosz, the state of New York promptly electrocuted him and destroyed his body with sulfuric acid.

Roosevelt received the news of the attempted assassination at Isle La Motte, near Burlington, Vermont, where he had been addressing the Vermont Fish and Game League. He went at once to Buffalo, but upon receiving assurances that McKinley was likely to recover, retreated with his family to the Adirondacks, where, on the afternoon of September 13, he was notified by a guide that the wounded man was worse and that he must come. Through the night he risked his neck and the danger of leaving the country without a president by rattling at top speed over dangerous mountain roads

Theodore Roosevelt

by horse and wagon to the special train waiting for him at North Creek. Upon arriving at Buffalo, he refused, with characteristic gentlemanliness and thoughtfulness, to take the oath until after he had paid his respects to Mrs. McKinley. It was a terrible thing, he thought, to come to the presidency thus, but it would be worse to be morbid about it.

Theodore Roosevelt and his great antitype Woodrow Wilson were the dominating figures in American political life during the first quarter of the twentieth century, but Wilson did not become a part of the national consciousness until 1912; Roosevelt exerted his spell therefore over a much longer period, and the appeal he made was incomparably more vivid and personal. No other American president had ever been so pervasive; with the single exception of Jefferson, whom he did not admire, he was the most many-sided and variously gifted man who ever occupied the White House. He refers somewhere to "those who care intensely for both thought and action"; he assuredly was one of them. He was a phenomenal reader in several languages, and he seems to have possessed a photographic memory. His skill as a naturalist was manifested even in childhood, and such beautiful and eloquent writing as the forewords to *African Game Trails* and *A Booklover's Holidays in the Open*, the panegyric to the frontiersman in *Ranch Life and the Hunting Trail*, and the wonderful description of birdsong in *The Wilderness Hunter* all vibrate to the single note of passionate nature love. So he became the foremost authority on the big-game animals of North America, and his invasion of Africa, after his presidency, collected a larger and more intelligently chosen group of specimens than had elsewhere been assembled. His first historical work, *The Naval War of 1812*, which he began as a student at Harvard, is still standard, and his magnum opus, *The Winning of the West*, is the most Parkman-like work in American literature outside of the writings of Parkman himself. He did not confine himself to action nor even to political history as such but showed philosophical grasp, power of generalization, and an ability to describe the workings of vast historical forces. When he got fed up with the Brownsville controversy during his second administration, he did not go off to play golf; instead he recreated himself by turning out an article on "The Ancient Irish Sagas" for the *Century Magazine*. Less than two months after he had been defeated by Wilson in 1912, he delivered before the American Historical Society a trenchant and penetrating address, "History as Literature." Stefansson the explorer once remarked that since TR was human, there must be some areas in which he was ill informed, but that he himself had not been able to pin down any of them, and this is only one of many testimonies which might be cited from reliable authorities.

He was quite as alert in the arts as he was in science; only music seems always more or less to have eluded him. In 1911 he went to the famous Armory Show in New York and described it in an article for the *Outlook*. Coming from a man of generally conservative tastes, it was a remarkable paper, for while he was sure that Matisse had more pathological than artistic significance and that change might mean "death and not life, and retrogression instead of development," he knew too that "there can be no life without change, and that to be afraid of what is different or unfamiliar is to be afraid of life," and he praised the exhibition as a whole because "there was not a trace of simpering, self-satisfied conventionality to be found in it."

Roosevelt did not think his powers exceptional; instead he was inclined to believe that other men of ordinary endowments might have accomplished much more than they did had they cultivated the powers they were born with with something of his own zeal. Though he was capable of violent, sometimes unfair, often highly amusing denunciation of persons who disagreed with him or whom he found antipathetic, his reputation for impulsiveness in action is undeserved; no president ever consulted advisers more diligently, and even when he reached decisions swiftly, they had generally been carefully considered. Many have testified eloquently to his personal charm. "I wonder," says Sonyà Levien, who worked with him during his later years on the *Metropolitan Magazine*, "how a man so thick-set, of rather abdominal contour, with eyes heavily spectacled, could have had so much an air of magic and wild romance about him, could give one so stirring an impression of adventure and chivalry," and Woodrow Wilson, who certainly had no reason to love TR, was charmed when he came to see him and pleaded to be allowed to do a rerun of his Rough Rider act in World War I. "There is a sweetness about him that it very appealing," he told his secretary Tumulty. "You can't resist the man."

His acts of kindness and consideration, his gifts of time, money, and interest were many. He hated "to see humble people hurt," and during the coal strike the thought of suffering kept him awake at night. "It may be true that he travels farthest who travels alone; but the goal thus reached is not worth reaching." He often interceded for offenders to give them a second chance, and when he could not give financial assistance himself, he was likely to solicit it from wealthy friends. On a journey by train, he took a fretful baby from a strange woman's arms and walked the floor with her until she fell asleep so that her tired mother could rest, and when a little girl in Oyster Bay wanted a bowl of goldfish for Christmas and the express company refused to guarantee safe delivery on account of the weather, he carried them out to her from the city on the train.

His affectionate nature was seen at its best in his own family and with his own children; visitors at the White House were sometimes doubtful whether it was an executive mansion or a children's playground. To be sure, his elder daughter, his only child by his first marriage to Alice Lee, was not one of his great successes. "Princess Alice" was certainly the most famous nonprofessional young woman in America in her time, but it would be too much to say that she was universally admired, for Alice belonged to what would today be called the jet set, and her father was credited with saying that he could be president of the United States or look after Alice but that he could not do both. With the younger children, all except Ethel boys, his relations were very close. "You must always remember," said Sir Cecil Spring-Rice, "that the President is about six," and Mrs. Roosevelt herself is said to have remarked on one occasion, "For heaven's sake, don't put it into Theodore's head to go too; I should have another child to take care of." He manifested no eagerness to hurry his offspring out of their childhood; the boys took an array of stuffed animals to bed with them long after most fathers would have thought they should have outgrown such nonsense and kissed him good-night when they were at home together as long as he lived. He loved *Little Women* as much as any girl ever did, and he read children's books and popular women's magazines with the same zest that he read everything else. I do not know anything that shows the hold he had upon his countrymen in his nonpolitical aspects more strikingly than the still-continuing vogue of the Teddy bear, which began in 1902 with a cartoon by Clifford K. Berryman in the Washington *Post,* inspired by his refusal to shoot a cub on one of his hunting trips.

Theodore Roosevelt was born in a brownstone house at 28 East Twentieth Street, New York City, on October 27, 1858. The family had means and social position but was not "filthy rich" by the standards of the upstarts who were soon to elbow the old New York aristocracy from the center of the stage. Besides the Dutch ancestry that gave him his surname, he had Irish, Scottish, Welsh, English, French, and German forebears, and his mother was a Georgian whose relatives had been active in the Confederate cause.

Educated at Groton and Harvard, he began his political career as the youngest member of the New York State Assembly (1882–84), having been chosen by the "bosses" because it was thought necessary to have a candidate from the Twenty-first District who would appeal to respectable voters. As an assemblyman, he was, as William Henry Harbaugh has happily expressed it, "a bull on morality and a bear on social reform." He went after municipal corruption with zest, attacking Jay Gould as "part of that most dangerous of all dangerous classes, the wealthy criminal class," and achieved as much in this area as anybody could under the circumstances, but he was still too much under the spell of the laissez-faire economics on which he had been reared to be very keen for labor reform or social change. Nevertheless, he did begin to form the views concerning the dangers of monopoly that he was to carry into his presidency, championed limiting the work hours of women and children, and moved toward the abolition of tenement sweatshops. Defeated for the speakership, he conducted a fearless investigation of municipal corruption as chairman of a committee appointed to investigate the Public Works Department.

In September 1883 Roosevelt bought a ranch in the Bad Lands of Dakota, where he lived intermittently for the next three years. Though this venture was not a financial success, it contributed importantly to both his health and his legend. In those days the West was still "wild," and a "four-eyed" easterner inevitably confronted difficulties there. Roosevelt's rule was to obey the biblical adjuration, "If it be possible, as much as lieth in you, live peaceably with all men," but he never showed the white feather when faced with a challenge. As for the cowboys, though they never forgot he had once shouted "Hasten forward quickly there" during a roundup, their eager flocking to his standard as "Rough Riders" during the Spanish war shows how completely they finally accepted him.

He was defeated as candidate for mayor of New York in 1886 but served as civil service commissioner from 1889 to 1895. President Harrison, who appointed him reluctantly, gave him no real support, but the Democrat Cleveland, who succeeded Harrison, reappointed him. Roosevelt greatly increased the number of women appointees and attacked Postmaster General John Wanamaker, demanding an investigation of his conduct in office. Halfway through Cleveland's administration, he resigned to become police commissioner of New York, in which capacity he stood for strict law enforcement and against graft and inefficiency in the force. His midnight prowls, checking personally on patrolmen, and his attempt to enforce the Sunday closing law for saloons contributed toward strengthening his image as a reformer and fostered his growing national reputation but antagonized the German community as well as the vice and liquor interests. Labor too was estranged when he used the police power against violence in labor disputes. He was in many respects a hamstrung and frustrated commissioner when he resigned in 1897 to become assistant secretary of the Navy.

In this aspect he was a frank jingo, and as soon as war came he resigned to become lieutenant colonel (under his friend Leonard Wood) of the First United States Cavalry. Mr. Dooley said his book *The Rough Riders* ought to have been called "Alone in Cubia." His gallantry at San Juan Hill was not particularly important so far as the outcome of the war was concerned, but it caught the popular imagination, as did also his daring and insubordinate energy in trying to cut through army red tape to bring his troops home out of a fever-ridden area once the fighting was over. If military tactics should be modeled on Charge of the Light Brigade principles, Roosevelt was a brilliant leader, but casualties were high enough to lend reasonableness to Secretary of War Newton D. Baker's opposition to his being given a command in World War I.

The New York state "boss," Senator Thomas C. Platt, had never wanted Roosevelt as governor of New York but had accepted him because he needed a candidate who could be elected. He found Roosevelt an executive who treated him politely and was always willing to consult but who did not hesitate to take a stand on such matters as the appointment of a state insurance commissioner or the administrator of the canal system. The governor's victory in these confrontations sometimes fell short of completeness, but Platt did definitely get the idea that he was "a little loose on the relations of capital and labor, on trusts and combinations, and . . . the right of a man to run his business in his own way." State taxes were imposed on corporation franchises, a measure that importantly affected the street railway corporations and gas and electric companies and thus redistributed the tax burden. A good civil service law was passed, and there were new regulations in the interest of pure food and affecting the operation of factories, sweatshops, tenements, insurance companies, and savings banks. Wildlife was protected and prizefighting outlawed, and the state moved toward workmen's compensation and desegregation in the public schools.

Roosevelt afterward denied that Platt had opposed his renomination as governor in 1900 in the event of his refusing or being denied the vice-presidential nomination; however this may be, Platt must surely have been pleased to see him kicked upstairs out of New York State and the boss's own hair. Henry Cabot Lodge, alone among his friends and advisers, saw the vice-presidency as a stepping-stone toward the White House; at the outset Roosevelt repelled the suggestion; when he went to Washington to disavow candidacy, McKinley told him he thought he would be more valuable in New York, and Root, John Hay, and Henry Adams all made fun of him for refusing what he had not been offered. It soon became clear, however, that the country and especially the West emphatically wanted him on the national ticket.

The fresh life and vigor that TR brought into the White House made it a revitalized center of the nation's life. He worked a long day, seeing a vast number of persons, not only politicians and businessmen but educators, sociologists, writers, and others, and displaying alertness and a wide range of intellectual interests. He employed McKim, Mead, and White to restore the White House and Saint-Gaudens to design coinage. At the same time he played hard, sometimes taking absurd chances, displaying the boy in him and that side of his nature that made him such a glorious subject for caricature. In this aspect he dragged his friends on "point-to-point" walks across Rock Creek Park, during which no detours were permitted; if a huge rock stood in the way, it must be climbed over, and streams must be forded or swum.

The most sensational event during Roosevelt's early days in the White House was his invitation to the Negro educator Booker T. Washington to share his table. He seems to have been surprised by the hysteria that ensued; it had not occurred to him that he was doing anything unusual. This was not the kind of shock that upset the stock market, however. So far Mark Hanna's "damned cowboy" had shown no inclination to turn over the applecart, and even the conservative New York *Sun* had been reassured by his first message to Congress. Then, alas without warning, on February 18, 1902, he announced that the attorney general was ready to move against the Northern Securities Company.

The Sherman Act to end monopolies had been on the books since 1890, but only three suits had been brought under it during McKinley's administration. The Northern Securities Company, chartered on November 12, 1901, by the state of New Jersey, had grown out of the war between James J. Hill, who, in association with the Morgan interests, controlled the Northern Pacific and Great Northern railroads, and Edward H. Harriman, backed by Kuhn, Loeb & Company, who controlled the Union and Southern Pacific, and the battle that ensued produced a brief panic in May 1901, which almost wrecked the market and wiped out small investors before it was settled by the compromise of which the formation of Northern Securities was a part.

Morgan was both stunned and hurt by the administration move. Like other financiers, he had regarded the holding company as safe from prosecution under existing laws. He also considered Roosevelt a gentleman of his own class, and he felt genuinely aggrieved that the president should make such a move without consulting him. On March 14, 1904, the government action was upheld, five to four, by the Supreme Court.

During the next seven years, mostly during Roosevelt's second term, the administration would bring more than forty suits against Swift and Company, Standard Oil, the American Tobacco Company, the New Haven Railroad, the Du Pont Corporation, and others. When, after the move against Northern Securities, Morgan asked TR point-blank whether he planned to attack his other interests also, he replied, certainly not, unless it should appear that they had done something wrong, which was quite in accord with his principle of drawing the line "on conduct and not on size." In the characteristic balanced sentences he sometimes affected, he spelled out the distinction so carefully as to lay himself open to Mr. Dooley's ridicule.

"The trusts," says he, "are heejous monsthers, built up be th' inlightened intherprise iv th' men that have done so much to advance progress in our beloved counthry," he says. "On wan hand I wud stamp thim undher fut; on th' other hand not so fast."

Though this observation was both keen and amusing, it was not really devastating. After the 1902 elections a measure forbidding railroads to pay rebates on freight charges passed quickly, and opposition in Congress to the establishment of a Department of Commerce and Labor and within it a Bureau of Corporations to investigate commercial operations crumbled when Roosevelt pulled a fast one by telling the press that John D. Rockefeller had been notifying senators of his opposition (technically the telegrams had been signed by Standard Oil's chief counsel, John D. Archbold, but TR had never been one to stand on technicalities). It is true that before the election of 1904, like Br'er Rabbit, he showed a tendency to "lay low" on big business. Nevertheless, he had achieved a breakthrough in dikes that were never to be completely whole again, and the final word may well go to the Detroit paper which quipped, "Wall Street is paralyzed at the thought that a President of the United States would sink so low as to try to enforce the law."

Roosevelt's intervention in 1902 to settle a coal strike that had reduced supplies in eastern cities to famine level and sent prices soaring and which threatened to shut down industry and freeze people in their homes as winter came on was far more daring than what he had done about Northern Securities, for this time he ventured out into the shadowy land of "broad construction" or "the Jackson–Lincoln theory" of the presidency, which would be specifically rejected by the courts as late as 1952.

The anthracite mines that had been struck were owned largely by six railroads, for whom George F. Baer, president of the Philadelphia and Reading, was the spokesman. The issues were wages and working hours, payment by weight rather than carload, abolition of the company store and doctor system, compliance with the often disregarded requirement for semimonthly payment in cash, and (the hardest pill for management to swallow) recognition of the then only three-year-old union as a bargaining agent. The strike began on May 12, after the operators had refused to treat with the soft-spoken union leader, John Mitchell (whom Roosevelt was to describe as the only gentleman at the White House conference, not excepting himself), or to be bound by the impartial arbitration board he had suggested.

It is not true, as has often been stated, that the operators resented the intervention of the federal government. On the contrary, they desired it, insisting only that it must be in their behalf. They wanted the government to intervene, with troops if necessary, to break the strike; they would also have welcomed the use of an injunction against the strikers for interfering with interstate commerce. Belying his reputation for impulsiveness, TR did not move until after the press had suggested both compulsory arbitration and government ownership of the mines and the New York Democrats had called for the latter in state convention. Then, on October 1, he startled the conservatives by asking both Mitchell and the operators to meet with him in Washington.

TR conducted the ensuing negotiations from a wheelchair. On September 3 he had been seriously injured upon being thrown out of his carriage when an electric car ran into it in Pittsfield, Massachusetts. His face badly swollen, Roosevelt had continued his speaking tour, but in Indianapolis he had been forced to undergo an operation on an injured leg. He opened the discussion by admitting frankly that he had no legal authority to settle the strike, then appealed to both sides in the interest of the public welfare. Mitchell again offered to accept arbitration, but the operators, stubbornly intransigent, insulted both him and the president, and the meeting adjourned without results.

Roosevelt made tentative plans to have the army seize the mines, but before this could be done Root appealed to J. P. Morgan, who persuaded the operators to accept what amounted essentially to Mitchell's plan of arbitration. The settlement was held up for a time by their refusal to allow a representative of labor to serve on the arbitration board, but Roosevelt got around that by appointing E. E. Clark, grand chief of the Order of Railway Conductors, and calling him the "eminent sociologist" who had been asked for! In the settlement effected, the miners secured some but by no means all of their aims, and on October 23 they returned to work.

Roosevelt often gave the impression that he regarded the building of the Panama Canal as his greatest achievement. The canal was not completed until 1914, but the controversial actions that led up to it belong to TR's first administration. These have occasioned some of the severest criticism ever directed against him, and the United States government may now be said to have accepted an anti-Roosevelt view. To compensate Colombia for the secession of Panama and soothe its wounded feelings, Wilson's State Department negotiated a treaty under which she was to receive our "sincere regret" and twenty-five million dollars, but it was not until 1921, under a Republican administration, and with the approval of TR's great friend, Henry Cabot Lodge, that American need or desire for Colombian oil brought about the ratification of a modified agreement, and during the Carter administration a new treaty was negotiated.

TR himself never admitted that any apology was called for by what either he or his country had done in Panama. Everything had been effected "in accordance with the highest principles of national, international, and private morality." His Colombian opponents had been so untrustworthy that negotiating with them was like trying to nail currant jelly to the wall. Exercising "the undoubted ethical right of international domain," he wrought and achieved greatly. The watchful dispatch of American forces southward after the Panama revolt had prevented not only a corrupt and tyrannical government's reconquering a liberty-loving people but also an orgy of bloodshed. Finally, since French interests were involved, the move might even be credited with having headed off intervention by a foreign power, which would have been in violation of the Monroe Doctrine and might well have had serious consequences not only for Colombia but also for the United States.

In his more prima donna–like moods, Roosevelt did not always do justice to the complexities of the situation he faced. When he cried, "I took the Canal Zone," he handled himself as roughly as his severest critics could have asked: "I took the Canal Zone and let Congress debate and while the debate goes on the Canal does too." Consequently, "instead of discussing the Canal before it was built, which would have been harmful, they merely discuss me—a discussion which I regard with benign interest."

The story of American negotiations with Colombia and their failure, of the Panama revolt, and the part the United States played therein cannot be told in detail here. The fact that in 1898 it had taken the *Oregon* seventy-one days to travel from San Francisco to the Caribbean had dramatized the need for a canal, and Congress created the Isthmian Canal Commission in 1899. The Hay–Paunceforte Treaty with Great Britain gave the United States the right to build the canal alone. The negotiations which followed involved payments to both Colombia and the French company that had tried to build the canal and failed. The Hay–Herran Treaty with Colombia was ratified by the United States Senate on March 17, 1903, but on August 19 Colombia turned it down.

Roosevelt regarded President Marroquin as a corrupt usurper and "villainous little monkey," and he may have been right in his belief that the Colombian Senate was merely rubber-stamping Marroquin's actions and trying to hold up the United States for all it was worth. Nevertheless neither he nor Secretary of State John Hay would ever have dreamed of handling a strong nation as they handled Colombia, and Roosevelt's statement to Congress in January 1904 does not reinforce his reputation as a moralist: "In our anxiety to be fair, we had gone to the very verge of yielding to a weak nation's demands which that nation was helplessly unable to enforce from us against our will."

There is no evidence that either Roosevelt or his government was involved in the Panamanian revolt. Since the president was perfectly familiar with the activities of Philippe Bunau-Varilla and William Nelson Cromwell, there was no need for that. But unofficially both must have known that once Panama had seceded, the United States would recognize the fait accompli. This she did with indecent haste, meanwhile taking steps to prevent Colombia from quelling the revolt. TR could have supported Colombia instead of Panama, but that would have meant bloodshed, and besides it was not in our interest. Or he could have stayed his hand altogether, though it must be admitted that this too would have cost blood. All in all, he may be said to have built the canal by vigorous frontier methods; indeed, he later told William Roscoe Thayer that, "if they had not revolted, I should have recommended Congress to take possession of the Isthmus." Following his star and his faith in his own intuitive moral judgment, he felt that "we are certainly justified in morals and therefore justified in law." In his feeling that the end result was beneficent—for America and for the world—he may well have been right, but he was wrong when he claimed that the canal could have been built in no other way. If he and Hay had been more patient, an agreement with Colombia might still have been reached or, failing that, we could have chosen the Nicaraguan route, which, until recently, TR himself had favored.

There were no other Panamas while Theodore Roosevelt was in the White House, but there were other indications of "strong" foreign policy. In 1902 Germany, Britain, and Italy, moving to collect their just debts from defaulting Venezuela, established a "peaceful blockade" of that country. Regarding Germany as the principal aggressor, TR sent Dewey to maneuver in Caribbean waters and, at the same time, if his own account is accurate, notified the kaiser that, should Venezuelan territory be seized, the United States would be forced to intervene. Rejecting the kaiser's suggestion that he himself serve as arbiter, he moved instead to refer the matter to the Hague Tribunal, which was done. Because of the absence of conclusive, positive documentary evidence, many historians have doubted Roosevelt's account, but it would have been like him to avoid creating a crisis by conducting the negotiations in such a delicate matter in deep secrecy.

Another potentially dangerous situation arose in Santo Domingo at the very end of Roosevelt's first administration; this time TR, without consulting Congress, persuaded the Santo Domingans to establish a receivership under which an American comptroller collected and dispersed its revenues, and when Joseph Bucklin Bishop said he hoped that the United States was not planning to annex the island, Roosevelt replied that he had about the same desire to do this "as a gorged boa constrictor might have to swallow a porcupine the wrong end to. Is that strong enough?"

He had been less conciliatory, however, in connection with an Alaskan boundary dispute in 1903, which was settled by a tribunal representing English, Canadian, and American interests. Not only were the American negotiators—Root, Lodge, and ex-Senator George Turner—far from being the "eminent jurists" they were called, but the president had announced beforehand that, should negotiations fail, he would occupy the disputed territory and run the line on his own "hook." In Roosevelt's defense it may be argued that the Canadian claim was clearly inadmissible, that he had tried without success to get two Supreme Court justices to serve, and that the presence of the senators was probably helpful in getting the resultant agreement approved by the Senate. Lord Alverstone, the sole English member of the tribunal, who cast the deciding vote in favor of the American position, always said that he had decided the case strictly upon its merits, and Lord Charnwood, in his book on Roosevelt, says frankly, "I do not want to be dogmatic, but I think it perhaps significant that I began to study this point with feelings of intense indignation against Roosevelt, and that I end with the absolute conviction that he did both a very able and most right and friendly thing."

If Roosevelt sometimes gave the impression of relishing a fight for its own sake, this never surfaced in his dealings with the legislative branch. He consulted with reactionary leaders in both chambers, though he was always capable of standing up to them if the issue was important enough and he thought he could win. His civil service and other appointments were excellent where he had a free hand, but he disappointed reformers by making some "judicious" appointments even on the cabinet level. He appointed the first Jew, Oscar Straus, to a cabinet position and tried to treat other minorities sympathetically, though seldom to the extent of incurring a political risk.

For all his magnificent zest for life, there was a curious vein of melancholy in Roosevelt's temperament. He was fond of talking about facing our fate and going down "into the everlasting darkness," and, in view of the financial panic that hit the country in the summer of 1903 (which was wrongly blamed upon his administration policies rather than on economic conditions and business mismanagement), it was quite in character that he should have become sufficiently panicky about his chances in November to hold off from further trust-busting and even make various overtures to the business community.

It was no secret that many businessmen would have preferred Hanna as the Republican candidate in 1904, and Hanna had refused all overtures toward endorsing Roosevelt's candidacy in advance. In May 1903 the other Ohio senator, Joseph B. Foraker, forced Hanna's hand by making such endorsement, not because he loved Roosevelt but merely out of opposition to Hanna. Hanna thereupon issued a statement disavowing his own candidacy but reiterating and publicizing his opposition to precommitment. Then, obviously uneasy, he telegraphed Roosevelt, who was in Seattle:

> The issue which has been forced upon me in the matter of our State Convention this year endorsing you for the Republican nomination next year has come in a way which makes it necessary for me to oppose such a resolution. When you know all the facts I am sure you will approve my course.

In one of the cruelest and most politically astute moves of his career, Roosevelt replied, at the same time giving his reply to the press:

> Your telegram received. I have not asked any man for his support. I had nothing whatever to do with raising this issue. Inasmuch as it has been raised of course those who favor my administration and my nomination will favor endorsing both and those who do not will oppose.

Between them, Roosevelt and Foraker had driven Hanna into a corner, and he capitulated at once. As it turned out, it was all unnecessary: he died of typhoid fever on February 14, 1904. This left the Republican convention to be enlivened mainly by the reading of the spread-eagle telegram John Hay had sent to Morocco, where an American citizen, Ion Perdicaris, had been kidnapped by a bandit chief: "We want Perdicaris alive or Raisuli dead." "It is curious," remarked the secretary cynically, "how a concise impropriety hits the public."

Declining to risk a third consecutive defeat with Bryan, the Democrats nominated Judge Alton B. Parker of New York. Except for 1924, when they nominated John W. Davis, it was their most conservative nomination during the twentieth century. Though the platform was silent on the gold standard, Parker declared for it, but big business preferred the Republican party, even with a liberal candidate, to the Democratic party with a conservative one. The size of the Republican war chest led to severe criticism of the national chairman Cortelyou, in which some writers have included the president himself. The evidence here is inconclusive and the more extreme charges improbable, but it seems unlikely that TR can have been completely ignorant of what was going on. He made a grandstand play of returning Standard Oil's $100,000 contribution two weeks before the election but was discreetly silent about other contributions, including Morgan's $150,000.

In the public mind, certainly, the charges did not stick. The Republicans won their greatest victory since the Civil War, with even Missouri and West Virginia moving over into the Republican column. On election night, Roosevelt burned his bridges behind him. "The wise custom which limits the President to two terms," he formally declared, "regards the substance and not the form, and under no circumstances will I be a candidate for or accept another nomination." This politically inexpedient move would lessen his influence in his party and the Congress and handicap his second administration notably, especially toward the end of the term. It also rose to haunt him when he was to seek a nomination against Taft in 1912. By 1910 he was busy explaining that what he had meant to disavow was two *consecutive* terms, since it was only a president in office whose self-perpetuating tendencies could be a danger to the Republic. He could not have spelled this out in 1904, since such a statement would have been taken as a bid for another nomination at some post-1908 date. This was logical enough, but there is no indication that Roosevelt had any of it in mind in 1904.

W H E N McKinley defeated Bryan in 1896, the New York *Sun* published an editorial that may well measure the high-water mark of hysteria in American journalism:

> The wretched, rattle-pated boy, posing in vapid vanity and mouthing resounding rottenness was not the real leader of that league of hell. He was only a puppet in the blood-stained hands of Altgeld, the anarchist, and Debs, the revolutionist, and other desperadoes of that stripe. But he was a willing puppet, Bryan was, willing and eager. Not one of his masters was more apt than he at lies and forgeries and blasphemies, and all the nameless iniquities of that campaign against the ten commandments. He goes down with the cause and must abide with it in the history of infamy. He had less provocation than Benedict Arnold, less intellectual force than Aaron Burr, less manliness and courage than Jefferson Davis. He was the rival of them all in deliberate wickedness and treason to the Republic. His name belongs with theirs, neither the most brilliant, nor the most hateful on the list. Good riddance to it all:—To the conspiracy, the conspirators, and to the foul menaces of repudiation and anarchy against the life of the Republic.

Bryan had made a nomination previously regarded as a joke inevitable and at the same time committed the Democrats to a silver

Representative
Figures of the Time: First Series

3

platform by a speech that reduced both men and women to tears and was remembered as one of the great emotional experiences of a lifetime: "You shall not press down upon the brow of labor this crown of thorns; you shall not crucify mankind upon a cross of gold." For him and his supporters the issue between privilege and human rights was for once clearly drawn.

Those who think of Bryan as only the rather tacky figure of 1925 whom Clarence Darrow turned into a guy when he appeared at Dayton to assist the state of Tennessee in prosecuting a high school teacher who had taught Darwinian evolution in defiance of a state statute must find it difficult to understand the appeal he made in his handsome, glamourous youth. To be sure, even then Senator Foraker compared him to the Platte River—"six inches deep and six miles wide at the mouth"—and Altgeld himself, having heard the "cross of gold" speech, asked, "What did he say anyhow?" But disparagement of what you cannot match is as old as Aesop's fox, and whatever else may be said of Bryan, he was one of the finest public speakers who ever lived. If his approach to life was simplistic and his feelings always stronger than his logical processes, it is but simple justice to credit him with having committed himself to virtually everything we now call "liberal" or "progressive" before any other political leader of anything like his influence had done so; thus, though Vachel Lindsay's reference to Roosevelt as "a young dude cowboy" who "hated Bryan, then aped his way" is not fair, it does have point. Four years as a congressman (1891–95) was the only elective office he ever held, and his two years as Wilson's secretary of state many years later would complete his official career. Yet, at the age of thirty-six, he defied Grover Cleveland, the only Democrat who had occupied the White House since the Civil War, splitting his party between Bryanites and Gold Democrats, and though thrice defeated for the presidency, he remained the number one man in his party until he yielded place to Woodrow Wilson in 1912; not until his leadership was finally repudiated in 1924 did he end a far longer period of dominance than any other twentieth-century figure has enjoyed.

Bryan was born at Salem, Illinois, on March 19, 1860, and died at Dayton, Tennessee, on July 26, 1925. His father was a Democrat, a circuit court judge, and a devout Baptist. The son was educated at Illinois College in Jacksonville and Union College of Law in Chicago. The former had been created by the Yale Band, with Edward

William Jennings Bryan

Beecher as its first president. Only the classics and mathematics were carried beyond the elementary level during Bryan's time there, but Dr. Hiram K. Jones, in whose house the young man lived, knew Emerson and William T. Harris and had lectured at Bronson Alcott's School of Philosophy in Concord. Bryan read Bancroft, de Tocqueville, and Dickens, and began his career as speaker and debater in college, graduating as the first man in his class. Until 1887 he practiced law, not very successfully, in Jacksonville, then moved to Lincoln, Nebraska, and turned gradually toward a political career. Admirers began to think of him as presidential timber from the time he made his tariff speech in Congress in 1892. He edited the Omaha *World-Herald* from 1894 to 1896 and published his own paper, the *Commoner,* from 1901 to 1923. During all his later years, much of his income was derived from Chautauqua and other lecturing, and as time passed he devoted himself increasingly to religious themes. In 1921, partly because of his wife's health, he moved from Nebraska to Miami.

The first presidential candidate nominated by a major party from any trans-Mississippi state, Bryan, with his alpaca suit, old-fashioned string tie, and turned-down collar, was the voice of the West, and especially the Middle West, with its isolation, evangelicalism, and suspicion of eastern capitalism. Willa Cather found in him all the "newness and vigor" of that region, together with "its magnitude and monotony, its richness and lack of variety, its inflammability and volubility, its strength and its crudeness, its high seriousness and self-confidence, its egotism and its nobility." Though he was not unmindful of the needs of all who toil, city laborers never took to him like the farmers, who, in his time, were struggling to adjust themselves to the new technology that was revolutionizing their way of life, to exploitation by bankers and railroad interests, and to the shrinking value of the dollar. Neither did the Commoner himself ever show much interest in or understanding of blacks. In the controversy over the *Lusitania* he could exclaim that Wilson did not seem to realize that much of America lay west of the Alleghenies; he could even speak of the East as "the enemy's country."

Until Woodrow Wilson transformed himself from a conservative to a liberal around 1910, he always spoke contemptuously of Bryan, but after the latter had rendered him an important service in the 1912 convention, he felt bound to make a place for him in his administration and finally made up his mind to offer him the portfolio of state. Bryan had created almost as great a sensation at Baltimore as that produced at Chicago in 1896 by introducing a resolution pledging the delegates to oppose "the nomination of any candidate for President who is the representative of or under obligation to J. Pierpont Morgan, Thomas F. Ryan, August Belmont, or any other member of the privilege-hunting and 'favor-seeking class." The resultant furor stopped just short of murder, but Wilson passed the acid test, and after the fourteenth ballot, Bryan, who had been regarded as a Champ Clark man, conditionally switched to him. He had had no training in international affairs, and it still seems arbitrarily assumed by many that he must have been an inept secretary of state, but Wilson's own biographer, Ray Stannard Baker, calls him "the statesman of largest calibre" among all the president's advisers.

Despite his admiration for Tolstoi, who seems also to have thought well of him, Bryan was never an out-and-out pacifist, though it still seems grotesque that he should have chosen to be buried with military honors in Arlington Cemetery. Though his enemies pictured him as an anarchist, he was in complete agreement with Theodore Roosevelt that the United States had the best government on earth; what he wanted was not to overthrow it nor even importantly modify it but merely to correct its malfunctioning. In his autobiography he wrote chauvinistically, "I was born a member of the greatest of all races—the Caucasian Race, and had mingled in my veins the blood of English, Irish, and Scotch." He was for war before McKinley, though this might well not have been the case had he known what Spain had agreed to concede. He was also pro-Boer and wanted the United States to support the Boers by all means short of war. During the Spanish war he commanded a Nebraska regiment as colonel; it is true that it never got out of Florida, but that was not his fault. After the fighting was over, the administration seemed to prefer having the regiment ravaged by malaria and typhoid to bringing it home; in fact, official feet dragged to such an extent as to raise suspicion in some quarters that the delay was prompted by a desire to keep Bryan out of the political scene! What he objected to was not the liberation of Cuba but the imperialism that developed afterward. Yet he missed his chance to defeat the treaty that decided the fate of the Philippines because he did not believe in minority rule and preferred to make the fight in behalf of the islands in the 1900 campaign, all of which, though completely in accord with his principles, did not work out as he had hoped. In later life his interest in peace grew ever stronger, but even then, though he gave us one of the most thrilling examples of devotion to principle in American political life when he quit Wilson's cabinet rather than sign the second *Lusitania* note because he thought it left Germany no choice except to continue submarine warfare, thus placing the decision to declare war in her hands instead of retaining it in our own, once the die was cast he offered to enlist as a private (at fifty-seven!) and worked for the Liberty Loan. After the war he supported Wilson's League of Nations and used what influence he had in vain to achieve accommodation between the president and his Senate opponents.

As secretary of state, Bryan's principal achievement for peace came before the outbreak of World War I with the negotiation of arbitration treaties with many nations, pledging their signatories to submit all disputes to arbitration and not resort to arms while the investigation was running its course. He encouraged recognition of the new Chinese republic in May 1913, helped weather a new crisis with Japan over discriminatory anti-Oriental laws in California, and blocked a Wall Street loan to China that would have pledged the power of the United States to guarantee China's living up to her agreement and might well have infringed her independence. Later he was to fail in an effort to keep Japan out of World War I, but he did succeed in causing her to draw back from dangerous demands upon China. In Central America, both he and Wilson strove to establish better relations with Colombia. In Haiti and Santo Domingo the record was somewhat mixed, and Bryan was not pleased with those features of a new treaty with Nicaragua that continued some of the "dollar diplomacy" aspects of the Taft years. The Mexican situation was too involved to summarize here. Wilson's "watchful waiting," which culminated in a useless limited intervention and which was complicated by the restiveness of foreign powers concerned to protect their investments, was neither militaristic nor pacifistic, but Bryan did try steadily to prevent an explosion.

After the outbreak of war in Europe, Bryan addressed his energies toward preserving American neutrality and persuading Wilson to offer his services and use his influence as mediator and bring the war to an end. Though the president frequently bypassed Bryan in favor of Colonel House (his "other self" until he broke with him) and even of Robert Lansing (who, having succeeded Bryan, would also be replaced in his turn), he never really rejected the idea, reaching for the heights in his "too proud to fight" speech after the sinking of the *Lusitania* and again in his call for "peace without victory" as late as January 1917, but neither did he ever follow through; thus he accepted the suggestion that the *Lusitania* incident be arbitrated and then recalled his suggestion to that effect after it had been cabled to Berlin.

It distressed Bryan that we should hold Germany to "strict accountability" for the crimes she committed after establishing a war zone around the British Isles but never even protest the Allied blockade of the North Sea, which aimed to starve a whole civilian population. He tried to work for relaxation of submarine warfare in return for the admission of foodstuffs into Germany, distributed under American auspices, and he hoped this might be worked out through the good offices of the friendly and pacific German ambassador, Count von Bernstorff. The legalistic Wilson, however, refused to prohibit or discourage Americans from traveling in the war zone on the ground that this was their "right." To Bryan, permitting civilians to travel in ships that carried contraband, as the *Lusitania* did, was like putting women and children in the front ranks of an advancing army; he granted the "right" of a pedestrian to cross the street in the face of a speeding automobile driven by a drunkard but considered him a fool if he exercised it. On one point, however, Bryan was as absurdly legalistic as his chief; because he thought it contrary to international law, he opposed a ban on the sale of munitions, thus giving the bloated plutocrats he had been fighting all his life a chance to grow even fatter on Europe's blood and agony.

Thus Bryan was not always either right or consistent. Though he may have defeated himself in 1900 by clinging stubbornly to free silver after it had ceased to be a viable issue, he was adept at juggling issues when it seemed expedient, accepted aid from Hearst and Tammany, dispensed patronage when he had it to "deserving Democrats," and moved with skill to cut potential rivals down to size. A lifelong teetotaler (with a Gargantuan appetite for food) who refused to serve wine even at official banquets, he never made prohibition a political issue until late in his career, when the fight was nearly won. Champ Clark never forgave him for deserting him in the 1912 convention. His employees on the *Commoner* were paid

50 percent above the prevailing wage scale for an eight-hour day; the paper refused liquor and tobacco advertisements but accepted those for patent medicines. A consistent party man, Bryan supported Parker in 1904, even though he had gone beyond the platform to proclaim adherence to the gold standard; refused the nomination of the Prohibition party in 1920, after he had failed to prevent the Democrats from naming the "wet" Cox; and voted for Morgan's lawyer, Davis, in 1924 instead of the third-party candidate La Follette, who stood for the things he had been fighting for all his life. Finally, he ended his life as an undignified barker for Florida real estate.

Bryan's appearance at Dayton in 1925 need not be considered in detail here, but one cannot write about him without trying to clear up some misconceptions concerning it. If Darrow made a fool of him, it was still preposterous that counsel for the defense should have been permitted to cross-examine counsel for the prosecution, and it should be remembered that Bryan's answers disappointed his fundamentalist admirers because they did not go far enough in the direction of biblical literalism. Since Scopes was certainly "guilty," Bryan was legally in the clear even here, though he was certainly not paying much attention to minority rights. Actually he did not object to teaching Darwinism as theory but only as established fact, and those who agreed with him about this have included some as far removed from his own fundamentalism as Bernard Shaw, who, like Bryan, disliked Darwinism both on religious grounds and because of its hard-nosed sociological corollaries. Bryan seems to have carried his basic democratic conviction that the will of the majority must prevail even to the length of believing that it applied to legislation bearing upon issues that only expert opinion can fairly judge. He believed that an education which develops only the intellectual man and ignores the moral and religious man is inadequate for the needs of a democracy. He himself had gone through a struggle with religious doubt even in pious Illinois College and had turned for counsel to Robert G. Ingersoll of all people! Bryan was not personally intolerant of differences of religious opinion, and his wife interpreted him correctly when she wrote that "he argued that if the power of the State could not be used to advance religion, it followed as a matter of course that the power of the state must not be used to attack religion"; on the other hand, Richard G. Hofstadter is as much in error when he speaks of Bryan at Dayton as a "bitter and malignant old man" as was H. L. Mencken, who reported the Scopes trial and after Bryan's death, just after it had closed, figuratively danced upon his grave and flattered himself into believing that he had helped kill him. You may degrade Bryan's impregnable sweetness of spirit, if you like, by attributing it to impenetrable egotism rather than true Christian charity, but the fact of its existence is undeniable. Scopes was *convicted* at Dayton, and there is no reason for supposing that it ever occurred to Bryan that he had failed; certainly nothing that happened there can have hurt him anything like so much as his rejection by his fellow Democrats at the 1924 convention. All in all, it would be difficult to fault Louis W. Koenig's evaluation of the whole miserable tragicomedy in Tennessee:

> If Bryan failed to meet the challenge of science, Darrow failed equally . . . to meet the challenge presented by traditional religion to modern philosophy. . . . Modernism was unrepresented at Dayton, and Darrow, after hacking and scarring the faith of millions of Fundamentalists, offered only threadbare negativism and cynicism in its place. . . . Darrow and the dramatists who have taken their cue from him have cheated posterity of knowledge of the whole man, the better man, the resolute champion of social justice who for decades prior to the Monkey Trial made religion and the Bible the foundation of an earthly kingdom of social brotherhood and justice among men and nations which today and as far into the future as the mind can see deserves the best efforts of men of goodwill.

2. *J. P. Morgan, Financier*

J. P. Morgan's cross in life was his nose, which a skin disease had made bulbous, red, and hideous. It was probably fortunate that he had those fierce, penetrating eyes on either side of it to rivet the spectator's attention. As with Cyrano de Bergerac, everybody was supposed to pretend that the disfigurement was not there, and so we have the story of the nervous hostess who, serving him, is supposed to have asked, "Mr. Morgan, do you take nose in your tea?"

Morgan's most famous photograph is the one by Edward Steichen in which the reflection of the light on the arm of the chair he grasps tightly in his left hand creates the illusion, against the very

J. P. Morgan

dark background, that he is holding a large butcher knife. During the years when it was fashionable to talk about "the robber barons," this seemed the ideal image of the great banker to all left-oriented Americans. In 1913 the Pujo committee of the House of Representatives found that he and his associates held 118 directorships in thirty-four banks and trust companies, 30 in ten insurance companies, 105 in thirty-two transportation companies, 63 in twenty-four producing and trading corporations, and 25 in twelve public utility corporations and that between them these institutions were capitalized at more than 22 billion dollars, wih J. P. Morgan and Company alone holding 72 out of the total 341 directorships. How then could anybody be blamed for finding it suitable that Morgan should have called all three of his magnificent yachts, each larger and more lavishly outfitted than its predecessor, the *Corsair*?

When Morgan died in Rome on March 31 of that same year, he left an estate of 68 million dollars plus art collections appraised at 50 million dollars but worth much more than that. His New York residence was a fine but old-fashioned brownstone, not lavish or pretentious or showy like the mansions built on Fifth Avenue by the Vanderbilts and others, but he accumulated other property in the vicinity for his children, and on East Thirty-sixth Street he erected the Italian Renaissance library, designed by Charles McKim, that is still one of the glories of New York and the world of scholarship. He had a country estate at Highland Falls on the Hudson; a thousand-acre winter camp in the Adirondacks; a furnished apartment at the Jekyll Island Club off Georgia; and a "fishing box" at Newport. His London headquarters was a large double house, crammed with art treasures, at Prince's Gate, and he had a country seat at Dover House outside the city. Special suites were set aside for him at the Bristol in Paris and the Grand Hotel in Rome, and he used the *Corsair* both to entertain guests and to provide a retreat for himself. When he returned from Europe, generally on a White Star liner, his yacht, gaily decorated, would sail out to meet the steamer and salute him. When he traveled in the United States he used a private car and sometimes a special train with the tracks cleared before him. Louis Sherry might go along to provide the cuisine, and if any member of the party was ailing, there would be a trained nurse in attendance. In his later years, after he had fallen in love with Egypt, Morgan also owned a steamer on the Nile.

John Pierpont Morgan was born in Hartford, Connecticut, on

April 17, 1837, a descendant of the Welsh Morgans who trace back to the eleventh century, some of whom were transplanted to Massachusetts in 1636. His grandfather left West Springfield for Hartford in 1817, where he began with a coffeehouse, proceeded to hotel keeping, real estate, and transportation, and became a founder of the Aetna Insurance Company. Pierpont's father moved from Hartford to Boston in 1851, where he became involved in foreign transactions, and went to London, where he became a partner in George Peabody's banking firm. The maternal grandfather was the Reverend John Pierpont, a militant abolitionist and temperance reformer who defied his own parishioners at Boston's Hollis Street Church.

The subject of this sketch studied at the English High School in Boston, at a private school in Switzerland, and at the University of Göttingen, where he manifested sufficient mathematical aptitude to be encouraged to devote his life to scholarship. His health having made him ineligible for army service in the Civil War, he sold bonds, helped the wounded and soldiers' widows and families, and kept in touch for years with the substitute for whom he had paid a bonus.

In the course of his career, Morgan reorganized numerous railroads, including the Chesapeake and Ohio, Baltimore and Ohio, Erie and Reading, Philadelphia and Reading, Northern Pacific, and Pennsylvania and New York Central. His firm financed International Harvester and the International Merchant Marine, and his was the dominant figure in the organization of United States Steel. He was an early investor in Edison stock and backed the construction of Stanford White's Madison Square Garden. He did not like haggling in business transactions, collecting, or benevolences, being always inclined to make a generous offer peremptorily on a take-it-or-leave-it basis; he once paid $100,000 for a painting by Vermeer, though he had not previously heard of the artist. The figure quoted to buy out Carnegie's steel interests was nearly a quarter of a billion dollars. Charles M. Schwab handed the figure to Morgan on a slip of paper; he glanced at it and said, "I accept." Later when he and Carnegie met on shipboard, the latter told him he regretted not having asked 100 million dollars more. "Well," replied Morgan, "you would have got it if you had."

He began his collecting with stamps and coins, autographs of bishops of the Episcopal church, and broken fragments of stained glass and proceeded to manuscripts, rare books, paintings, and objets d'art. His great means made him a formidable competitor in the international market. In collecting as in business, he enjoyed power, always had to have the best, and his natural tendency was to buy up everything in sight. Though he had no genuine scholarly understanding of the things he collected, he did care for them. Certainly he learned much more about art than he ever did about music, which despite his hymn singing always more or less defeated him, though it must be admitted that he won one triumph in this area when he bridged over a crisis in an Episcopal gathering by standing in his place and starting to sing "O Zion, haste, thy mission high fulfilling," all by himself. He was interested in the Mendelssohn Glee Club, but though he liked some of the older operas, notably *Il Trovatore,* he generally occupied his box at the Metropolitan Opera House only the first night of the season. His favorite singer was Henry Burleigh, the Negro baritone and transcriber of spirituals, who frequently sang at his parties. He once entertained Sarah Bernhardt and showed her the treasures of his library, but his interest in the theater was never very keen.

Morgan's benefactions were both personal and impersonal. Among the institutions that profited by his bounty were the Cathedral of St. John the Divine (for whose erection he was largely responsible), the Metropolitan Museum of Art (which he helped organize, of which he was president, and which ultimately received the lion's share of his art collections), the American Museum of Natural History, Cooper Union, and the American Academy in Rome (to which he gave a building). He was one of the backers of the ill-fated New Theater, served as a trustee of Columbia University, and was one of the founders of the New York Society for the Suppression of Vice. His concern for the underprivileged was shown in his erection of the Lying-In Hospital and in numerous benefactions to St. George's Church, including a Memorial House, a Deaconess House, and a Trade School, and during the coal strike of 1902, he spent a considerable sum trying to make coal available to the poor at a price they could pay. Some of his benevolences, like his gift of over a million dollars to the Wadsworth Athenaeum in his native Hartford, were connected with his personal ties and friendships. He never sought advice from others nor had "surveys" made. When he was asked to contribute to the Harvard Medical School, he entered the room where the matter was to be decided, watch in hand, announcing that he was pressed for time and asking what his visitors had to show him. When they spread their plans out on the table, he indicated three buildings—"I'll give that and that and that"—and left the room. It probably embarrassed him to be thanked; certainly he never paraded his benevolences nor tagged anything with his name, and a great many gifts to individuals went wholly unrecorded. According to his son-in-law, "Each morning at his library or office he received numerous people who asked for his help or for money. He saw almost all of them personally, and few of them went away without some measure of the service or assistance they sought." But he was curt toward those who wanted tips on the stock market.

His social life was a complicated matter. Though his appearance was robust, he was rarely without health problems. Even in his youth, he was subject to headaches and faintness, and in later years he was always coming down with heavy colds. He was restless and nervous also, as his constant traveling shows; he observed Thursday as a holiday and took frequent vacations; he could do a year's work in nine months, he said, but not in twelve. Though he seems to have had no positive malady except high blood pressure, his health failed rapidly during later years, and the last time he left for Europe he did not expect to return. By this time he was taking little or no exercise, and though he did not drink much he was a heavy eater, after the fashion of his class and day, though in view of the number of cigars he smoked it is hard to believe that he ever tasted anything. Devoted to yachting, he disliked horseracing. His games were whist and solitaire (over which he seems to have thought out many problems) but not poker. He belonged to many clubs but rarely made use of them.

His power, his formidable appearance, and his brusque manner, which was probably accentuated by his sensitiveness about his deformity, frightened many people. He was an expert at playing deaf when he did not wish to be disturbed. When he was tired of walking the deck of the *Corsair* with that restless pedestrian the kaiser, he horrified the monarch's attendants by suggesting that they sit down (they sat), and when King Edward VII wondered why he had hung a certain picture in a room whose ceiling the king thought too low, he replied, "Because I like it there, sir." But he was also capable of great tenderness, and it is clear that many people cared for him. When his daughter Louisa was a baby, he had to have her crib beside his bed so that he could look after her at night, and he was great on family holidays, playing Santa Claus at Christmas, eating the traditional Morgan Thanksgiving dinner, including four kinds of pie, and shooting off fireworks at Highland Falls on the Fourth of July. He paid careful personal attention to friends and sometimes to strangers when they were sick or in trouble and was an inveterate funeral goer. He was noted for an uncharacteristic procrastination when he had to dismiss somebody whose performance had been unsatisfactory, and he seems to have respected rather than resented people who had the courage to stand up to him; it was quite in character that he should not have allowed his resentment over TR's handling of the Northern Securities matter to interfere with his cooperating with the president in settling the coal strike. Fond of animals, he was a noted breeder of collies and blooded cattle and during his later years was often accompanied by a Pekingese. He also loved birds, including sparrows, which his servants had standing orders to feed.

Morgan's deep romanticism shows nowhere more strikingly than in his early marriage to a girl so wasted by tuberculosis that she had to be held up at her wedding. He took her abroad, dropping all business interests in a vain attempt to nurse her back to health until she died four months later. We know very little about his relations with his second wife. Because he enjoyed the company of women as well as men on his yacht and elsewhere, he was credited with many "affairs." The woman whose name has been mentioned most prominently is the actress Maxine Elliott, for whom he is popularly credited with having built a theater. His son-in-law and biographer, Herbert L. Satterlee, categorically denies this, but Miss Elliott's niece-biographer seems less definite. It is certainly true that most of Morgan's travels during later years were made without his wife, but he was generally accompanied by a sister or daughter.

Morgan's piety seems somewhat surprising in so worldly a man. He began attending St. George's Church while Stephen H. Tyng was rector, and in later years he was vestryman both there and at the Church of the Holy Innocents at Highland Falls. He had a passion for attending the triennial conferences of the Episcopal church and rubbing shoulders with bishops there, and he is said to have followed even the debates on technical points of ecclesiastical polity with rapt attention. Hymn singing he loved, not only in church but at home, especially on Sunday nights, and he was known to stop in at St. George's toward evening to worship and pray alone in silence.

His theology, however, would seem to have been more fundamentalist than might have been expected in his communion, and it is not surprising to learn that he backed the Moody and Sankey revival of 1876 and sat on the platform. His will begins by committing his soul

> into the hands of my Saviour, in full confidence that having redeemed it and washed it in His most precious blood, He will present it faultless before the throne of my Heavenly Father; and I entreat my children to maintain and defend at all hazard, and at the cost of any personal sacrifice, the blessed doctrine of the complete atonement for sin through the blood of Jesus Christ, once offered, and through that alone.

Whatever else may be said of Morgan's theology, it must at least be pronounced in harmony with his extremely conservative taste in everything else; he was the greatest art collector of his time, but he never lifted a finger to help a contemporary artist. It is all the more remarkable then that he stood by his rector, the Reverend William S. Rainsford, an advanced Social Gospeler, through thick and thin because he believed in him even when he disagreed with him and that when Rainsford, to whom he had shown great generosity in many ways, felt conscientiously bound to oppose him on a proposed change in parish administration upon which he had set his heart, he did not allow his defeat either to impair his relationship to the church or to destroy his friendship with the rector himself.

Concerning the value of the services Morgan rendered to his country in 1895, when he was instrumental in supplying the United States Treasury with 62 million dollars in gold to restore the rapidly melting gold reserve in the Treasury, building it up to a safe 100 million dollars; in 1902, when he helped to break through the impasse on the coal strike; and again at the time of the Panic of 1907, there can be no two opinions. "If others had been as fair and reasonable as Mr. Morgan was," said the leader of the miners, John Mitchell, "this strike would have been settled a long time ago." Morgan took a tremendous chance when he promised Cleveland that if his plan were adopted he would guarantee that no more specie would leave the country until the contract had been carried out and the goal reached. The negotiations were painful and protracted (for some time Morgan had to fight the president as well as the panic), and though he belonged in bed at the time, he drove himself heroically to the verge of breakdown. Obviously he could not have rendered such service single-handed, but there was nobody else who could have rallied the business and financial forces of the country as he did. All three of these crises therefore provide striking confirmation of his own view that in these matters character counts for more than even money.

By the standards of his time, the lord of the *Corsair* was far indeed from being a buccaneer. He made a great deal of money, but he made it by what were then considered legitimate means, and he did not bleed his clients. Wildcat manipulations were not for him; he had little interest in either stock market speculation or real estate investment, and he disapproved not only of pirates like Jay Gould and Jim Fiske but even of men like Edward H. Harriman and John D. Rockefeller. Though he did not consider himself a good judge of men, he preferred to do business with gentlemen; as he told the Pujo committee, "I have known a man to come into my office and I have given him a check for a million dollars and I knew that he had not a cent in the world." This was no idle boast, for he had lent Colgate Hoyt exactly that amount "on your business record in Wall Street and upon what I know your character to be," refusing all collateral because he thought Hoyt might need it elsewhere. The dangers involved through the powers he acquired are obvious, but he did not manage them without regard for the common weal. He improved railroad properties and stabilized services, increased safety and efficiency, and decreased costs to operators, shippers, and the traveling public.

Obviously the things he did in railroading and in banking ought to have been done by the Interstate Commerce Commission and the Federal Reserve; even with so strong a president as Theodore Roosevelt in the White House, the seat of government shifted, during the Panic of 1907, from Washington to Wall Street. But with the ICC ineffective and the Federal Reserve nonexistent, it is hard to see how we could have got along without Morgan in his time, and it was fortunate indeed that the influence he wielded should have fallen into the hands of a man of his character. In later years he himself perceived the need for change, but he did not feel comfortable as he confronted it; he was shocked when the government moved successfully against Northern Securities and unsuccessfully against United States Steel and even more shocked when the Pujo committee grilled him on the stand as if he had been a criminal. If he was an important part of a far from ideal system he had not created, it must still be understood that he represented that system not at its worst but at its best. He was "a regularizing and disciplining force in American industry," as Frederick Lewis Allen has said, and he was capable of taking great risks in the public interest. When he died, Theodore Roosevelt was the one who summed it up best: "We were fundamentally opposed, but I was struck by his very great power and truthfulness. Any kind of meanness and smallness were alike wholly alien to his nature."

3. *Andrew Carnegie, Industrialist*

Andrew Carnegie was born in Dunfermline, Scotland, on November 25, 1835. His father was a hand-loom weaver, his mother the daughter of Thomas Morrison, who had been a friend of Cobbett. He grew up under the spell of the abbey and the tomb of Robert Bruce, but he had more admiration for Wallace, the man of the people, for his romanticism was already taking a strong antiroyalist, antiprivilege form.

The coming of steamlooms plunged the family into want, and in 1848 they came to America, where Andrew became a bobbin boy in a cotton factory at Allegheny, Pennsylvania. A messenger boy in the Pittsburgh telegraph office, he taught himself telegraphy and rose to be secretary to Thomas A. Scott, superintendent of the Pittsburgh division of the Penn railroad. Once, in a crisis, he proved his ability by running every train in the division on his own. At his superior's suggestion, he made his first investment of $500 in Adams Express stock. When Scott became vice-president, Carnegie succeeded him as superintendent, and during the Civil War he worked under him again in military transportation.

He had gone into the iron business in a small way in 1861, and he moved up rapidly. Between 1873 and 1901 the Carnegie Company established United States supremacy in steel, producing one-fourth of American steel at an annual profit of 40 million dollars. In January 1901 Carnegie sold out to the Morgan interests for 225 million dollars, and the United States Steel Corporation was formed. The rest of his life he devoted to philanthropy and work for international peace. Though he owned a castle in Scotland, he died at Lenox, Massachusetts, on August 11, 1919.

Carnegie was a short, well-formed man, with a squarish head, covered with flaxen hair that turned white, very slim in his youth, and proud that his feet were as small as a girl's. His eyes were light blue, sometimes laughing and sparkling, sometimes cold. He talked rapidly and gesticulated freely, sometimes monopolizing the conversation and pressing his opinions upon his associates. He could sleep whenever he needed to, and he took excellent care of himself, enjoying frequent vacations and building up his business not through sweat but rather through intelligent, never-wavering direction, often exerted from afar.

He prided himself upon his optimistic nature and his ability to turn all his ducks into swans. Certainly there can be no question about his capacity for hero worship. Cleveland, Roosevelt, Taft, and Wilson, all regarded with suspicion at first, became heroes when they were in power, and he showered compliments and advices upon them all. Another great hero was the kaiser, for whom he once wrote a soliloquy on peace and war. His official biographer, Burton J. Hendrick, declares of Carnegie that "all the Celtic traits— elfin, lively, imaginative, brooding, even at times melancholic— made up his complex nature." His emotions were easily roused, he was unusually expansive and responsive to the personalities of others, and he both laughed and cried easily.

He was fond of dancing and horseback riding, but he disliked contact sports and built a lake at Princeton to encourage rowing and take the boys' minds off football. Golf he did not take up until he was sixty-three, after which he became an enthusiast. His wife says that he golfed, fished, and swam (he always had a passion for running water), sometimes all three in one day, until World War I broke his health, but he avoided hunting.

As a child, Carnegie was enthralled by Scottish legendry and *The Arabian Nights*, and in Allegheny he reveled in Colonel James Anderson's library, when he opened it to working boys. His love for Shakespeare began with the plays he saw at the Pittsburgh Theater; in his autobiography he wrote that he would not exchange literature "for all the millions that were ever amassed by man. Life would be quite intolerable without it." He apparently considered Dickens inferior to Burns, but that was a subject upon which, as a Scot, he was not unprejudiced; I find it difficult, however, to understand his disparagement of Wordsworth. He brought both Matthew and Sir Edwin Arnold to America for lecture tours; his great idol, Herbert Spencer, came too, though he would not lecture, and he must have disappointed Carnegie when he declared that six months' residence in Pittsburgh would justify suicide. In the narrower sense of the term, Carnegie had no social ambitions, but he hungered for association with intellectuals and leaders in every line of endeavor, and in the course of his career he bagged an astonishing number of them. His closest friendship was with John Morley, but he knew Gladstone and many others and even contributed campaign funds to English leaders whom he admired.

His interest in music, founded on Scottish minstrelsy, was stimulated by hearing the overture to *Lohengrin*, and he was proud that he had instinctively selected the tunes by Handel in the hymnbook of the Swedenborgian Society in Allegheny as his favorites. In one passage he crowns Palestrina king of composers, but Tchaikovsky has recorded how warmly he praised him. At Skibo Castle he was awakened by a piper and entertained by organ music ("my morning devotions") at breakfast. His appreciation of painting and sculpture began with his European trip of 1887. He admired Millet, but for him Raphael was only a copyist of Perugini and Rubens "a painter of fat, vulgar women." He advised draping the nudes on one of his library buildings to avoid giving offense to "the simplest man or woman."

Even in Scotland the Carnegies had fallen away from Calvinism. As a boy, Andrew attended the Swedenborgian church with his father. As a man, he found his religious philosophy through Spencerian evolutionism, which appealed profoundly to his optimistic temperament, and his study of comparative religion convinced him of the truth of the Bible saying that God has never left Himself without witnesses. He refused to give money for missions on the ground that "all religions are adapted to those for whom they are provided" and that "to force our religious views on others," especially under the protection of Western gunboats, is not Christian. He inclined to feel that Japan had become Westernized too quickly, and his appreciation of China's culture and probable future was remarkable for its time. He rejected vicarious atonement and eternal punishment, but though his horror of death was profound, he seems to have clung to the hope of immortality.

Until Carnegie became a working boy he had apparently never come in contact with deliberate coarseness of any kind, and those with whom he was then forced to associate tended to find him priggish. In advising young businessmen what to avoid, he coupled liquor with speculation and the endorsement of other people's notes, not finding it necessary to mention his own moderate consumption of the very choice blend of Scotch whiskey he supplied to Queen Victoria and several presidents. Tobacco he never used.

During his early years, his contacts with girls seem to have been part of his zealous campaign for self-improvement: he sought out those he could look up to. Possibly he might have married Anne Dike if she had not married Thomas Scott instead, and he is nowhere more smug than in his comment on her choice: "If anybody else in the world can win her, I don't want her."

His acquaintance with Louise Whitfield began when he was forty-five and consisted mainly at the outset of horseback rides in Central Park. In 1881 he wanted her to go with him and his mother and a party of friends to Britain; at his direction, his mother delivered the invitation to hers, taking care to do it in such fashion that it could not possibly be accepted. The two were secretly engaged in 1883; the engagement was broken off, then renewed, but it soon became clear to both that Carnegie would never marry during his mother's lifetime. She and his brother Tom both died late in 1886, when he himself lay desperately sick with typhoid fever. He married Louise on April 22, 1887, when she was twenty-eight and he fifty-one, choosing her, he says, because she alone "stood the supreme test I had applied to several fair ones in my time," and his devotion to her and their only daughter Margaret seems never to have wavered.

During his 1867 trip to Europe, Carnegie became convinced that, except for a few capitals, "everything on the Continent seems to be almost at a standstill." He was impressed by London but not by Paris, for decadent France seemed bound to be overcome by "the German element which, you know, is Anglo-Saxon and therefore has the right 'blend.' " A number of books and an endless stream of articles and letters set forth his views, and Triumphant Democracy almost absurdly trumpeted the virtues of America's "perfect" system against the Old World. At one time he owned a chain of British newspapers dedicated to preaching republicanism—the abolition of the monarchy and the Lords, the disestablishment of the Church of England and the dissolution of the Empire, home rule for Ireland, and extensive land and educational reform—and though he seemed at this time much more radical in England than in America, this did not last long. For all his admiration for Spencer, Carnegie was never really laissez-faire. At first he was for a protective tariff, patent laws, and pooling agreements to restrict competition and support prices, but later he deserted protection and advocated an income tax, sweeping governmental controls, and heavy inheritance taxes on large fortunes. He anticipated some aspects of Wilson's Federal Reserve banking system. "Whatever experience shows that the State can do best, I am in favor of the State doing." He rejected Spencer's antiphilanthropism also and advocated provision for the general welfare through legislative action. Despite some misleading statements to the contrary, Carnegie was never really a racist, and temperamentally he was averse to all theories of determinism. Because he knew that the wind bloweth where it listeth, he was sure that genius and leadership were quite as likely to come from slum dwellers as from the "best people." He admired Booker T. Washington and astonished the Edinburgh Philosophical Institute by taking Negro welfare as the subject of his lecture there, and he opposed literacy tests and nationality preference quotas for immigrants.

By the time he was twenty-eight, Carnegie was earning nearly $50,000 a year. His early interests were in sleeping cars, bridge building, and telegraphy. He stopped investing in oil when his ventures there turned out badly, but he was less absolute against speculation in the beginning than he afterward wished to believe. Until 1872 his manufacture of iron was mainly to supply the Keystone Bridge Company, which built many important bridges and of which he was very proud. "We cannot afford to have an accident to one of our bridges. . . . If we stand firm on quality we must win." His interest in the Bessemer process and in the production of steel began in the sixties, not after the 1870 trip to England, as his autobiography indicates, and the opening of the new iron ore fields in northern Michigan came at an opportune time for him. Like Mark Twain, he soon decided "to put all his eggs in one basket and then watch that basket." It was his good luck that by the time the railroads were built the need for steel beams for skyscrapers was coming in. By 1899 his company controlled thirty-four working mines to guarantee their supply of raw materials and was earning 21 million dollars a year.

Carnegie held no official position in his company, seldom attended conferences, and was often absent from Pittsburgh or out of the country, but he owned 58 percent of the stock and kept every aspect of the business under firm control. He opposed overcapitalization and held as large a share of the profits in reserve as possible instead of paying them out in dividends. Corporations he disliked because this meant consulting a board of directors before making decisions. He gave valuable men a share in the company, thus binding them to him and avoiding disputes over salaries, but disposed of them summarily when they disappointed him, and he was notorious for forming pools and breaking them when it was to his interest. Despite his humanitarian reputation, his treatment of his competitors was sometimes even more ruthless than that of Rockefeller or Henry Clay Frick. He forced the Duquesne Steel Works to sell out by circulating false rumors that their rails lacked an imaginary and undefined "homogeneity" of structure. Once he actually toyed with the idea of attempting to rouse a dangerous mass protest against the Pennsylvania Railroad because he thought he was paying too much for freight, and he was in danger of going into wasteful and competitive railroad building in alliance with the notorious Gould syndicate when Morgan bought him out. During the Panic of 1873 he allowed his old friend and benefactor, Thomas A. Scott, to go to the wall. His reasons were cogent; he seems even to have convinced himself that it was his duty not to bail Scott out. If he had attempted to do so, he would have endangered his own and his partners' investments, perhaps even without saving his friend. However all this may be, it was a melancholy end to his association with the man who had given him his start. Even Frick himself was thrown out at last, after a break so sensational that for a time it seemed likely to wreck the company, and though Frick was an unamiable man compared with Carnegie, with a much narrower range of vision, his faults were not new. Carnegie had not objected to them when they were operating in his interest, and the final decision against him seems to have been made on a cold dollars-and-cents basis.

The enlightened views expressed in his articles in the *Forum* in 1888 made Carnegie a hero to labor, but after the Homestead strike in 1892, his name, as he himself said, was "a by-word for years."

The *Forum* articles defended unions (though what he meant were company unions, not national labor unions), opposed the employment of "scab" labor, and advocated sliding wage scales, with an established minimum below which wages could not fall, as a substitute for contracts that expired and consequently entailed ever-renewed bargaining and strike threats. Carnegie was abroad when the Homestead strike occurred, and in his autobiography he indicates that the trouble would never have occurred if he had been on hand. This may well be true. Certainly he would not have brought in Pinkerton guards as Frick did in his absence, for his idea of strikebreaking was simply to shut down the works. It is true also that his partners did not want him on hand, but it is equally true that he could have been there if he had wanted to and that that was where he belonged. On July 6 battle raged along the riverfront for twelve hours, the townspeople (including women) were roused to murderous fury, and several workmen and guards were killed. The strikers remained in control of the plant for four days until the governor called out the militia. Thereafter 700 "scabs" were brought in, and men were rehired on an individual basis, provided they had not interfered "with our right to manage our business." Alexander Berkman's attempt to kill Frick on July 23 illogically helped to swing sympathy away from the strikers, yet both Benjamin Harrison and the New York *Tribune* thought the GOP lost the fall elections because of Homestead.

Unlike Huckleberry Finn (and his creator), Carnegie enjoyed the blessing of a selective memory that accommodatingly blotted out the things it was painful for him to recall. In later years he thought the Homestead workers had cabled him, "Kind master, tell us what you wish us to do and we will do it for you." But neither he nor anybody else was ever able to find the cable, and the "kind master" shows the orientation of a feudal overlord rather than the democrat Carnegie believed himself to be. Moreover, Homestead was not a solitary blot upon an otherwise stainless labor record. Theodore Roosevelt was not a disinterested witness when, annoyed by Carnegie's pacifism, he declared that if he had "employed his fortune and time in doing justice to the steelworkers who gave him his fortune, he would have accomplished a thousand times what he has accomplished nor ever can accomplish in connection with international peace," but the statement has bite and point nevertheless. Carnegie built up his fortune making good steel more cheaply than anybody else, and this generally meant a twelve-hour shift at low wages, with men working twenty-four hours at a stretch every two weeks when the changeover from the day to the night shift was made. When something had to be given, he always preferred a bonus to a salary increase because this kept the situation wholly under his control and did not commit the future. Sometimes labor spies were employed and reductions made even when business was good, and after Homestead no serious attempt was made to unionize the workers during his lifetime.

In a private memorandum of 1868, Carnegie recorded his intention to retire from business in two years, devoting the rest of his life to culture and benevolence, but he did not achieve this until 1901. In June 1899 the *North American Review* carried his famous article "Wealth," in which he declared that "the man who dies . . . rich, dies disgraced," and in 1900 this and many other pieces of kindred nature were published as *The Gospel of Wealth*.

He began by giving libraries and organs (the latter, except for his endowment of the Church Peace Union in 1914, his only gifts to churches). Medicine he left largely to John D. Rockefeller. More than 80 percent of his total giving went to education. The Carnegie Institute in Pittsburgh embraced library, art gallery, music hall, and museum. The Carnegie Institution in Washington subsidized research. The Carnegie Fund for the Advancement of Teaching set up pension funds for teachers and fathered the Teachers Insurance and Annuity Association. He built the Mount Wilson Observatory in California. His gifts to established institutions generally went to small schools with limited endowments, like Berea, Hampton, and Tuskegee. Some sectarian institutions revised their charters to qualify for his benevolences; others raised their entrance requirements. He purchased his own youthful idea of heaven on earth, the Pittencrieff Estate in Scotland, making it a public park, and contributed heavily to Scottish universities and to community welfare in his native Dunfermline. Many gifts were made quite without publicity, and many individuals were on his private pension list.

Carnegie soon discovered that giving money away was almost as hard as earning it. He received between 400 and 500 applications a day, and there were those who found as much fault with his disbursements as had been found with his accumulations. In 1911, at the suggestion of Elihu Root, he created the Carnegie Corporation of New York and transferred the bulk of his remaining fortune (125 million dollars) and the responsibility for handling it to other hands. When he died, eight years later, he had been relieved of over 350 million dollars, and of the 30 million left, two-thirds went to the corporation. Between them, he and Rockefeller had created the modern "foundation."

After 1910 Carnegie devoted nearly all his personal efforts to furthering international peace, and the disappointment of his hopes in 1914 contributed importantly toward killing him. He was not, however, a consistent pacifist. In his youth he was an ardent supporter of Lincoln, and in 1898 he supported war to free Cuba, though he opposed the imperialistic expansion that followed it.

It would have been difficult for a man who suggested so many things as Carnegie did to avoid making some suggestions that were ridiculous. Not only did he wish to see Canada joined to the United States, but he wished to see England, Scotland, Ireland, and Wales admitted as states to the federal Union! At one time he suggested we give the Philippines to Great Britain in exchange for her holdings in the West Indies and again that he be permitted to buy them for the 20 million dollars the United States had paid for them and then set them free.

He treated President Harrison to some pretty straight talk in the Chilean crisis, talked out of both sides of his mouth about Venezuela, and agonized rather pathetically about whether or not it was right for his firm to make armor plate for Cleveland's navy. He ardently supported the arbitration treaties advocated by Roosevelt, Taft, and Wilson, being particularly pleased by Taft's willingness to arbitrate even questions of "national honor." Wilson's position on Panama Canal tolls also pleased him, but he worried over his conduct of Mexican affairs. He built the Peace Palace at the Hague and the Pan-American Union Building. In 1905 and 1907 he asked for what later came to be called a League of Nations. He, Morgan, and others financed TR's African junket under the auspices of the Smithsonian, which was to be followed by his propositioning the kaiser to take the lead in moving toward European disarmament and removal of the tensions that lead to war in preparation for an international conference in England. Though Roosevelt did not refuse, he was rather doubtful about it all and, as time went on, impatient of Carnegie's needling and incessant advices, and the ill-timed death of King Edward VII made it impossible to carry out the plan as originally conceived. After the war began in 1914, Carnegie continually urged arbitration efforts upon Wilson and opposed "preparedness," but by February 1917 he had done a right-about-face and was urging him to enter the war.

The Autobiography of Andrew Carnegie, published posthumously in 1920, is a real-life Alger story, and readers of these latter days are likely to find it intolerably smug and self-satisfied; nobody, they feel, could possibly always be so right as Carnegie portrays himself as having been. Many also find difficulty in reconciling his philanthropy and his professed humanitarianism and liberalism with his activities as a tycoon; "nice guys," they argue, cannot give away 350 million dollars for the simple reason that under our system they could not possibly accumulate so much. Nevertheless, it will not do simply to dismiss Carnegie as a hypocrite; he was a far more complicated man than he ever understood himself to be. He opposed political imperialism, but surely his best biographer, Joseph Frazier Wall, is right when he remarks that it was "imperial power" that he, Frick, and Rockefeller all sought—"empires of steel, coke, and oil in which each would reign supreme"—and once he had dedicated himself to this enterprise, he found his range of choices progressively narrowing. Moreover, though he was not unaware that there were conflicts in his personality, it would be myopic to discern no bridges between his various activities. As a world figure he still displayed in many aspects the wide-eyed naiveté of the boy from Dunfermline and Allegheny, and if he built one empire with steel, he built another with philanthropy.

4. Thomas A. Edison, Inventor

Nearly 1,100 patents were issued to Edison. He was welcomed at the Paris exposition of 1889 as illustrating "the triumph of genius over matter, over ignorance, over superstition," and to the man in the street he was simply the greatest inventor who ever lived. Americans took pride in his "know-how," the ingenuity and "smartness" that, rightly or wrongly, they identified with their country, and even in the limitations which, during his later years, after he had become a sage, he revealed in the opinions he aired on a variety of subjects, which were always shrewd, often wise, occasionally foolish, and sometimes inconsistent.

Thomas A. Edison. Courtesy Edison Institute

Thomas Alva Edison was born at Milan, Ohio, on February 11, 1847, and his far from extensive schooling was partly in the hands of his mother, who was devoted to him but kept a firm hand over him. He began his career by tormenting everybody with questions they could not answer, and even as a child he had a laboratory of his own as well as an observation post in a tall tree. It has been related that, having seen a goose sitting on eggs to hatch them, he tried to do the same thing himself and that, having heard that Seidlitz powders created gas, he fed them in quantity to a companion in order to learn whether they would enable him to fly.

When he was twelve, he got a butchering commission covering the Grand Trunk Railroad between Port Huron and Detroit; he also opened periodical and vegetable stores in Port Huron and employed assistants there and on the railroad. He got permission to set up a laboratory and a printing press on the train and published a paper that achieved a circulation of 400 copies and earned a local reputation for him. When, during the Civil War, the news of the Battle of Shiloh came, he bought, largely on credit, 1,000 newspapers and sold them at various stations along the route, gradually advancing the price until at last he was getting a quarter apiece.

He learned telegraphy from James MacKenzie of Mount Clemens, Michigan, and for several years he led the life of a roving telegrapher in the central West. He drifted east to Boston, New York, and Newark, tinkering with inventions and involved in business enterprises until he established his laboratory at Menlo Park, New Jersey. He improved Christopher Sholes's typewriter, worked on the automatic telegraph, and became involved with Alexander Graham Bell's telephone. The phonograph in its earliest form came along in 1877, attracting more attention than anything he had done previously, and he continued his work on it intermittently, developing wax cylinders first and later a new phonograph with disc records. Even this, however, seemed insignificant compared to the incandescent lamp, whose capacities were demonstrated sensationally before distinguished visitors from far and near on New Year's Eve 1879, after which Edison proceeded to devise and patent a multitude of devices needed to make electric lighting practical. On September 4, 1882, the New York Herald Building was illuminated.

In 1891 came what he called the kinetograph, destined to develop into what we know as motion pictures. He worked importantly on the storage battery and did some work on wireless telegraphy and on what would become radio tubes, antennae, loudspeakers, and air conditioners but did not follow through in these fields. During World War I he tried to work with the Navy but was not comfortable with government bureaucracy. In 1929 the Golden Jubilee of Electric Light was wonderfully observed at Greenfield Village, Dearborn, Michigan, where Henry Ford had constructed an accurate reproduction of the Menlo Park laboratory and other things connected with Edison's early life. Edison died of a variety of diseases on October 18, 1931.

His most famous pronouncement is his saying that genius is 1 percent inspiration and 99 percent perspiration, but he also said that he "happened to be a pretty good guesser himself" and that "imagination supplies the ideas and technical knowledge carries them out," and certainly he must have known that, though all the inspiration in the world will not suffice a man who has not learned how to work, by the same token all the work will not accomplish great things when the 1 percent of inspiration, or whatever else you may choose to call it, is lacking.

Certainly nobody ever worked harder than he did, sixteen to twenty hours a day. He boasted that he could get along on four hours' sleep and that nobody needed more, but it is clear that he could also snatch brief naps anywhere, whenever he needed them, and in almost any position, slumbering so soundly that it was difficult to wake him up, and even work uninterruptedly for several days and nights at a stretch and then replenish his strength by sleeping for thirty consecutive hours. There are stories about his elation at the end of a long series of fruitless experiments because now he knew he had eliminated all the ways the job could *not* be done and of how, upon being asked what he would do next after he had used up 400 tumblers in one series of failures, he replied that he supposed the next thing would be to order more tumblers. He himself said that he developed 3,000 different theories while working on the electric light project, only two of which were verified by experiment.

Edison was not a trained theoretical scientist, but though many of his guesses were pretty wild, it is a mistake to think of him as driving blindly ahead, ready to try anything without direction. It is true that he had no aptitude for mathematics and no skill in keeping either his personal or his business accounts and that his mathematical operations had to be done for him. He admitted his use of empirical methods in chemistry, which he considered largely an empirical science anyway, but he insisted that he solved mechanical problems by "hard, logical thinking." When he began an experiment, he tried to familiarize himself with what had previously been done in the field and to build on the foundations that had been laid.

Edison was of medium height and weight, very slim in his youth, first stocky, then portly and out of condition during his later years, when his health deteriorated from overwork, lack of exercise, unhygienic habits, and exposure to dangerous chemicals. He had a large head, gray-blue eyes, and a prominent nose. His hair, parted on the right side, often hung down over his forehead, and his bushy eyebrows remained black after the rest of his hair had turned white. He is said not to have bathed more than once a week, and he often slept in his clothes, which, when he was at work, which was most of the time, were likely to be well worn, baggy, and stained with chemicals. People made fun of the "masculine 'Mother Hubbard' " he wore in the laboratory and his disreputable straw hat. Formal, fashionable attire he disliked, but his most pronounced idiosyncrasy about clothes was that he would not wear an overcoat; when he was cold, he put on extra sets of underwear.

Though inclined to be modest in self-appraisal, he was a good public relations man and an excellent camera subject and was never shy. He often made premature announcements of his achievements. He had few intimates and no interest in socializing except with people whom he particularly liked, and he could be brusque when he did not wish to be disturbed. He preferred motorcars, in whose development he had some share and would have liked more, to horses and apparently considered them safer, and we hear little about animals in his life. In later years he greatly enjoyed camping with Harvey Firestone and Henry Ford. He tried billiards but did not care for it, and though we hear something about Saturday-night poker games, the only indoor game he seems to have cared much for was Parcheesi, of which, we are told, he altered the rules whenever necessary to enable him to win.

He was married in 1871 to Mary G. Stilwell, who died in 1884, and the marriage does not seem to have given much satisfaction to either party, especially during the later years; certainly Edison had endless trouble with her three children. In 1886 he married Mina M. Miller, with whom he had fallen madly in love. The love endured on both sides, but Mrs. Edison soon learned that she had to adapt herself to his erratic ways. The famous story that he forgot to go home on his wedding day is apocryphal, but the reply he made to an interviewer's question is both interesting and teasing: "Ask me nothing about women. I don't understand them, and don't try to." Insofar as he needed company at all, he seems to have preferred a stag atmosphere.

Edison ate and drank very temperately, one of his wildest notions being that total abstainers were likely to be sallow and consumptive with abnormally large shoulders! Cigarettes he regarded as fatal because of the acrolein produced by the burning paper, but he consumed cheap cigars, sometimes as many as twenty a day. He also chewed tobacco, preferring the floor of his laboratory to a cuspidor because he never missed.

His relations with others were importantly influenced by his deafness, which may have been due to a mastoid infection. Two picturesque stories have been handed down concerning the source of this complaint. According to one, he was cuffed on the ears and thrown off a train with all his equipment when a car caught fire from a stick of phosphorus in his portable laboratory, while the other affirms that something snapped when he was pulled into a baggage car by the ears while trying to board a moving train. Just how deaf he was is a question, however. He said he had not heard birdsong since boyhood, but there were those who believed that he heard what he wished to hear and ignored the rest. He refused to allow aurists to try to help him on the ground that his deafness aided concentration; in the early days, he could hear the ticking of the telegraph instrument without being distracted by sounds originating in the room. He could also detect flaws in phonograph records that nobody else on his staff seemed able to hear, and he is said to have told Earnest Elmo Calkins that if his hearing were better his wife would try to talk to him all the time.

He tested his associates and employees carefully and drove them hard, expecting them to be as indifferent to time as he was himself when the occasion demanded, and he could be rough and decisive when such action seemed called for. He once squelched a demand for higher wages by peremptorily ordering the plant closed, and he would have had a hard time under present union regulations in trying to work a crew for sixty consecutive hours in order to finish a job. Nor did he have much use for potential rivals. In spite of his general patience and equability, he was not free of moods, and he could make a spectacular job of losing his temper, sometimes, one suspects, deliberately, for what he considered salutary effect. Then word would go out that "the old man is on the rampage today," and no one would go near him who could avoid it.

Edison enjoyed modern painters but not the Old Masters. He had considerably more interest in music, and in the early days he both sang and played the violin. Later he played his organ with two fingers. Puccini cherished his praise of *La Bohème,* but his favorite composer was Beethoven, for whose Ninth Symphony he felt something close to adoration. During his early years at least, he often attended the theater, enjoying Forrest and McCullough as well as Bowery melodrama, and he never lost either his taste or his gift for broad mimicry of eccentric character types.

But the printed page meant more to him than any of this, and he read extensively, both for practical purposes and for recreation. According to Francis Arthur Jones, he read French, German, and Italian in addition to English, though he could neither speak nor write the foreign tongues. Newspapers he not only read but clipped, and, for some reason best known to himself, he also read the *Police Gazette,* the *Billboard,* and the *New York Dramatic Mirror.* Like Theodore Roosevelt, he possessed the invaluable faculty of being able to take in at a glance everything on a printed page that had any relevance for him, and with this he combined a phenomenal memory.

As a child he read Hume, Gibbon, and other solid writers with his mother; as a train boy, he spent the time between runs in the Detroit Public Library. He early found great stimulus and inspiration in Faraday, his reading of whom inspired him to say that he must hustle because life was so short and he had so much to do. He expressed great admiration for Herbert Spencer, Poe, and Victor Hugo; at one period in his youth, his associates nicknamed him "Victor Hugo Edison." He had a special passion for *Evangeline* and "Enoch Arden," and he was devoted to Shakespeare, though his tribute to him took the rather odd form of being sure that he would have made a wonderful inventor. He regarded the death of Gaboriau as a personal loss, and he thought *The Count of Monte Cristo* the finest of all romances; he started to read it one evening because his wife had recommended it to him, read on through the night hours, and thought this helped him with the problem on which he was working.

The many opinions Edison expressed on public questions during his lifetime generally did credit to his humanity, but he seemed perfectly indifferent to the pollution his factory introduced into the area where it was located. He objected to capital punishment because "there are wonderful possibilities in each human soul, and I cannot endorse a method of punishment which destroys the last chance of usefulness." During his later years he favored restricting immigration and (inconsistently, in view of his fantastic notions about total abstinence) enforcing the Volstead Act; this would grow easier, he thought, as a generation unaccustomed to liquor took over. He favored the United States' joining the League of Nations "under specified conditions" and was enough of an optimist to believe that the increasing destructiveness of warfare would tend to restrain it. Thomas Paine's was a liberating influence upon his mind in the early days; later he supported the Freethinkers' Society, but at one time he also flirted with theosophy. Though he once called religion "a hopeless piece of insanity," his view of the universe seems to have been basically theistic ("science cannot reach any other conclusion than that there is a great intelligence manifested everywhere"), but his speculations about the "monoids" and "entities" of which our physical and spiritual beings were supposed to be made up do not seem greatly to have impressed anybody. On the whole, he probably did about as badly on education as anywhere, for in 1923 he declared that within a quarter of a century motion pictures would have replaced books for teaching purposes, and he also once expressed the idea that only technological education had value and that three or four centuries from now would be time enough for "literary men" and for "Latin, philosophy, and the rest of that ninny stuff," certainly an expression of barbarism worthy to stand beside, if not surpass, his friend Henry Ford's celebrated pronouncement that history was "bunk."

It is not of course correct to think of Edison as *the* inventor of all the devices upon which he worked; in some cases, different men were working upon the same problem in different countries, in ignorance of each other's existence. He made mistakes and had serious accidents, sometimes narrowly escaping disaster. For a long time he backed cylinder rather than disc phonograph records, and when he finally turned to the discs he made them so thick and heavy that they took up almost as much storage space as the cylinders themselves. His record catalogue never came within hailing distance of those of either Victor or Columbia, nor was his film company, in which he took little personal interest, ever in a class as to quality with either Biograph or Vitagraph. In the beginning he was committed to the peep show, in which a fifty-foot length of film ran continuously over spools, and indifferent to projection, and though the union of image and sound was in his mind from the beginning, we find him declaring that talking pictures would never succeed because the public preferred the silents the very year before sound began taking over the theaters. Radio too, he insisted, was a passing fad.

What made Edison "tick"? Money? Fame? The desire to serve humanity? He wanted to invent things that would enrich people's lives, and there was no cant in his statement that "the poor man with a family is the man who has my sympathy and for whom I am working." But he was industrialist as well as inventor, and he wanted his inventions to be marketable. Though he could be forbearing under provocation, he was involved in endless litigation. He attempted without success to monopolize both the phonograph and the motion picture businesses. But Robert Conot hits the nail on the head when he describes him as "a lusty, crusty, hard-driving, opportunistic, and occasionally ruthless Midwesterner, whose [Paul] Bunyanesque ambition for wealth was repeatedly subverted by his passion for invention." Edison made a lot of money, but he could surely have made more if he had exercised better financial judgment and concentrated upon moneymaking single-mindedly. He invested much time and effort in the ore mill enterprise, which never paid out as he had hoped and took a heavy toll. Actually he did not need very much money. In 1923 the New York *Times* estimated that 15 billion dollars were invested in industries based upon his inventions, yet he could say that, if it came to the worst, he could always earn seventy-five dollars a month as a telegraph operator and live on that. All in all, he probably came as close as anybody can hope to come to defining his motivation when he said that he worked for no reason except that he liked it and felt a compulsion to finish what he had begun, and I for one greatly doubt that good work can be done in any field upon any other basis.

5. William Randolph Hearst, Journalist

Hearst was born in San Francisco on April 29, 1863. His father, George Hearst, was a rough, uneducated man, a gambler, fond of liquor and tobacco but agreeable and well liked and considered honest and generous. Born in Missouri, he had come to the California mines in 1850 and made his first big strike in Nevada in 1859. He later owned the great Anaconda (Montana), Ontario (Utah), and Homestake (South Dakota) mines and had extensive oil and real estate interests. In 1880 he purchased the San Francisco *Examiner.*

His wife, Phoebe Apperson Hearst, was considerably finer-grained. Early in her married life, she established something of a salon and began entertaining artists and writers. Later her great interests were the kindergarten movement and higher education; she became a regent of the University of California and gave away something like 21 million dollars. But she spoiled her only child outrageously, and the "momism" in which she smothered him may have determined the tendency toward perpetual adolescence he seems never really to have thrown off.

As a child, Hearst was intelligent, sentimental, and affectionate but completely undisciplined; he would not work at anything that did not interest him, and he engaged in pranks rather startlingly anticipative of those later performed by the Katzenjammer Kids in his newspapers. In Europe with his mother in 1873 and again in 1879, he was fascinated by everything that was romantic and began his indiscriminate collecting (he wanted her to buy the Louvre for him). He was also greatly moved by cruelty and poverty and wanted to give away not only his money but even his clothes. Back home, he became devoted to the theater, worshiping Adelaide Neilson and suffering desolation when she died. At this time he wanted to be an actor and built an amateur theater in a stable. Later he was engaged, briefly, to both Sybil Sanderson, for whom Massenet would compose *Thaïs* and *Esclarmonde,* and Eleanor Calhoun, John C.'s granddaughter.

He was expelled from both St. Paul's School at Concord, New Hampshire, and Harvard, where he sent his instructors chamberpots with their names elegantly painted inside. Though this seems to have been the straw that broke the camel's back, it was actually one of his milder pranks in the Boston area, for he had kept an alligator named Champagne Charlie, who died of his alcoholic diet, and pelted the actors at the Howard Athenaeum with custard pies. Yet he was elected to Hasty Pudding and appeared in college theatricals, and he began his career as a journalist by putting the *Lampoon* on a paying basis.

He worked briefly as a reporter on Pulitzer's New York *World*; he was already begging his father to turn the *Examiner* over to him. In 1887 he got it, but he lost $300,000 the first year. In 1895, with his mother's backing, he invaded New York with the *Journal*, buying the whole Sunday staff away from the *World*, featuring comics and magazine-type articles on violence, scandal, and sensation and losing $100,000 before making it pay.

He married Millicent Wilson on April 28, 1903 and filled his only elective office as congressman from New York, 1903–7. In 1905 and 1909 he was defeated for mayor of New York City and in 1906 for governor of the state, but he continued to yearn for the presidency and to pull strings in behalf of what he considered the lesser available evils in that office until he reached an advanced age. At his peak he owned twenty-two daily and fifteen Sunday papers, plus seven magazines in the United States and two in England. In later years he lived mostly in California, with Marion Davies, in his castle at San Simeon and elsewhere and gave much attention to the production of motion pictures. His weight reduced to 125 pounds by a long illness, he died at Beverly Hills on August 14, 1951, at the age of eighty-eight.

Hearst was a big man, with blond hair, parted in the middle, and very light blue eyes with a disconcerting stare, which those who mistrusted him called sinister. He spoke slowly, quietly, and sparingly, in a high, weak voice. Though he had humor, he was characteristically aloof and withdrawn. Many admired him, many loathed him, but few, if any, were intimate with him. He shook hands limply, when he could not avoid it, called everybody "mister" and expected to be "mistered" in his turn. In company he was likely to lounge or sit with his hands in his pockets, betraying his nervousness only by swinging a foot or drumming with his fingers. But though he had neither gift nor inclination to be a guest, he seemed to rest under a perpetual obligation to function as a large-scale host, whether at house parties or picnics at San Simeon, to which guests might be conveyed by plane or special train or in squiring smaller groups about Europe, with all expenses paid by him, always indulging in boundless extravagance and often displaying prodigal thoughtfulness and generosity. Once he cabled home an order for Boston beans, clam chowder, and codfish, to be sent to Egypt for a New England guest and had to send a second cable to explain that he was not using code.

He spent at least 30 million dollars on San Simeon. Marion Davies's Santa Monica beach compound cost about 7 million dollars, and the "bungalow" dressing room he built for her on the MGM lot and later moved to the Warner Brothers studio contained fourteen rooms. Long after he had ceased to live with her, he spent $400,000 for a castle on Long Island as a "between seasons" abiding place for Mrs. Hearst. One Fourth of July fireworks celebration at San Simeon cost him $100,000. He refurbished the whole Criterion Theater, which he did not own, for the première of *When Knighthood Was in Flower*. As a collector, he wanted what he wanted when he wanted it, even if he had to get the dealer out of bed in the middle of the night. He secured Van Dyck's portrait of Queen Henrietta Maria, which was not for sale, by offering $375,000 for it, and though he got the Spanish cloister in Segovia, which had taken his fancy, for $40,000, it ultimately cost him about half a million, for he built twenty-one miles of railroad to carry its dismantled stones to the sea, and when they finally arrived in America, they had to be stored in a Bronx warehouse.

His benevolences were as spontaneous and impulsive as his indulgences. He had nothing of the intelligently planned enterprises of Carnegie or the Rockefellers; his only large public gifts were the Lincoln Homestead to the Illinois Chautauqua Association, the Greek theater and girls' gymnasium to the University of California, and the 400 acres and $100,000 he gave Oglethorpe University after he had been given an honorary degree. But his response to public calamity was instantaneous, and though he milked these actions for all the advertising they could give his newspapers, the sympathy behind them was genuine. When Galveston was flooded, the New York *Journal*, the Chicago *American*, and the San Francisco *Examiner* raced relief trains thither, and Winifred Sweet Black (Annie Laurie) became the first outside reporter to enter the city, where she proceeded to organize relief. The Hearst family lost a million dollars in the San Francisco earthquake, but the Hearst papers raised $200,000 for relief, nor were similar efforts lacking when disaster struck abroad, as with the eruption of Mount Pelée and of Mount Vesuvius.

But what he really liked was to relieve individual need. The cartoonist Swinnerton was threatened with tuberculosis, and Hearst sent him to Arizona. A girl stenographer who was stricken with paralysis was sent to a sanitarium, and when she recovered and married a cripple she had met there, he employed her husband and set the new family up in an apartment. Sometimes the people he helped were wholly unknown to him, as when he read in one of his Chicago papers of a destitute family about to be evicted from their attic flat and promptly telegraphed his editor there to give them $10,000 and provide a home for them. And once, when he was stopping at the Drake in Chicago, he found the hotel picketed by the CIO in a dispute with his papers. Observing one frail young picket shivering in a thin jacket, he took off his overcoat and wrapped it about him. The dispute could be settled, he said, but there was no reason why the boy should have pneumonia.

His passionate love for animals extended his sympathies to the brutes. "Animals Have the Right of Way" and "Reckless Driving Will Not Be Tolerated" were signs posted at San Simeon, where all except the dangerous animals in his private zoo (he had everything but snakes, which he loathed) were allowed to roam freely, and if one chose to block the road, arriving guests would simply have to wait until it chose to move. He would permit rats to be killed but not mice, and he once stopped in the street to beg a man not to beat a horse.

His financial management was reckless in both large affairs and small. He had no interest in accumulation for its own sake, always lived beyond his means, and even raided the tills of his newspapers when he found himself out of cash. In paying bills, he was honest but often slow. He refused to unload papers that were losing money and invested some 50 million dollars in New York real estate, on which he finally found himself paying ruinous mortgage interest. The Ritz Tower, which he took off Arthur Brisbane's hands in order to relieve his mind, is said to have lost him nearly $600,000 in 1935 alone. In 1927, 126 million dollars in debt, he was forced to relinquish financial control of his publishing empire (retaining editorial control) and to begin selling instead of buying. With great courage he weathered the crisis; ironically enough, his business improved greatly when America entered the war he opposed, and before the end he was even able to resume building operations at San Simeon.

Hearst's father was nominally Episcopalian, his mother nominally Presbyterian, but neither was sufficiently religious to bother to have him baptized; that rite was performed, on the initiative of a Catholic nurse, by a priest. As a man, Hearst never went to church but considered himself an Episcopalian. Both Mrs. Hearst and Marion Davies were Catholics. He is said to have known the Bible pretty well and to have been fond of discussing religion, and he probably had some sort of belief in the basic Christian doctrines.

Because his enemies portrayed him as a marvel of lubricity, the crusades of the Hearst papers in behalf of morality were often viewed with considerable cynicism. But the publisher's enemies were often quite as unscrupulous toward him as his newspapers were toward them; there are still people who believe the idiotic nonsense that he murdered the film producer Thomas H. Ince over Marion Davies, and there are probably more who believe that he fathered children by her. Except for his early connection with the Cambridge, Massachusetts, waitress Tessie Powers and the liaison with Miss Davies herself, which began about the time of World War I and lasted until his death, there seems to be no information available in this area. Hearst gave up both smoking and drinking liquor after the indiscretions of his college years. He did not gamble, and he disliked profanity and obscenity. He supported prohibition until bootlegging and gangsterism disillusioned him. The idea of women in barrooms disgusted him, and when it was suggested that the legal age for drinking be lowered, he declared that the result would be to bring up a generation of drunkards. It is difficult to reconcile his courtly, chivalrous, almost reverential attitude toward women with the hypothesis of coarse, promiscuous debauchery. The Hearst press exploited many scandals in which women were involved, but the erring sisters themselves were handled tenderly, and sometimes crusades were undertaken in behalf of even the unworthiest among them. Hearst was terribly depressed when his mother bribed or frightened Tessie Powers away from him when he was thirty-one, and he provided her with funds when she was poor in her old age. There can be no question whatever concerning his devotion to Marion Davies, whom he would have married if

Mrs. Hearst had been willing to give him a divorce; as he himself freely admitted, this connection was wrong because it involved infidelity to his wife ("I don't say it's right; I only say it *is*"), but in itself it was not degrading. A mediocre actress, with no more beauty than many another show girl, Marion Davies, though one of the kindest, warmest, and most generous women who ever lived, had her earthy side, with considerably more relish for cakes and ale than Hearst himself possessed, but he could not have been more worshipful toward her if he had been sixteen years old and she his first girl. He spent some 7 million dollars in a vain attempt to make her the greatest star on the screen, but when she wanted to play Sadie Thompson in *Rain*, he was horrified; he had to have her (to the consequent starvation of a natural gift for comedy), in lavish, beautiful costume dramas like *Janice Meredith* and *When Knighthood Was in Flower*, herself the loveliest jewel in a setting composed of everything that was most beautiful on earth, or at least as much of it as her lover could buy for her.

In 1918 his friend Champ Clark declared of Hearst that nothing had been proposed "for the alleviation of human beings in the last quarter of a century that he did not originate or advocate." Though this was an absurd overstatement, he did urge many progressive measures. On the San Francisco *Examiner* it was union labor, the eight-hour day, an income tax, and the popular election of United States senators. In 1902 he supported the coal strike. At various times he attacked railroad rebates and advocated municipal ownership of waterworks and street railways and federal ownership of railroads and telegraph systems, and he was consistent in his opposition to the trusts and his advocacy of better schools.

Though he remained an unpredictable maverick to the end, he did become more conservative during his later years. Having fought for the income tax, he did not like it when it bit him. Though he never cared for Hoover, he did admire Coolidge and especially his secretary of the Treasury, Andrew Mellon, who lowered taxes for the rich but not the poor. When the Depression came, he was still liberal enough to urge a huge public works program, but it was not long before the New Deal became the "Raw Deal" in the Hearst press. Badly frightened by communism, he became a notorious Red baiter in the universities and elsewhere, who fought the Newspaper Guild, expressed admiration for Mussolini, and opposed Upton

Sinclair's "End Poverty in California" crusade even to the extent of publishing a still from the film *Wild Boys of the Road* as a picture of Sinclair's supporters.

The label "warmonger" clung to Hearst from 1898, when he sported the headline "How Do You Like the Journal's War?" Frederic Remington, Richard Harding Davis, and Ralph D. Paine had been sent to Cuba before hostilities began, and when Remington, convinced that there would be no fighting, wished to return, Hearst cabled: "Please remain. You furnish the pictures and I'll furnish the war." He was sincere in believing the Cubans oppressed and in wishing the "tyrannical" Spaniards expelled from the Western Hemisphere, but his methods were utterly unscrupulous, and he reported much that had never happened. Even so, he was a shade less guilty that Pulitzer, who dragged the *World* up onto the prowar bandwagon to compete with Hearst in the circulation war, though his convictions were on the other side.

For all that, it must be understood that though Hearst was always a big navy man and given to childish flag-waving, he was not consistently militaristic. If he could generally be counted upon for a belligerent attitude toward Mexico and Japan, he did his best to keep the United States out of both world wars, even though this meant both circulation losses and cruel vilification.

Hearst was not pro-German in World War I, but it would not be unfair to call him anti-British. He understood from the beginning that the Allies were conducting an industrious propaganda campaign designed to bring America into the war, and he sought a fair presentation of the German side. His opposition to hysteria after the *Lusitania* incident contrasted refreshingly with the way he had fostered it after the sinking of the *Maine*. But even now his efforts were so capricious that genuine pacifists tended to mistrust him while many real subversives embarrassed him by rallying to his support. Opposing the sending of troops over a submarine-infested ocean, he still supported conscription. His World War II record is somewhat better, however. He began opposing it in the twenties, long before it came, planning with Kathleen Norris to enroll millions of American mothers in opposition to American involvement in another conflict, and when the United States committed the greatest single mass atrocity in history by dropping the atom bombs on Japan, he was horrified.

Though Hearst suffered many disappointments, the greatest by all means was his failure to realize his political ambitions. Nobody ever more wished to be president, but he never achieved either this or any important stepping-stone toward it. During his years in Congress, he was amazingly inept, showing no interest in anything save the measures he himself was trying to get through, alienating potential supporters, and running everything according to his own whims, just as he ran his newspapers. Yet, though no man ever backed a longer succession of losers, from Bryan in the beginning to Landon, Willkie, Dewey, and McArthur during his later years, he remained a force, a threat, and an influence in politics for many years. In a sense he may even be said to have made both Roosevelts president, for TR might never have made it without the Spanish-American War, which Hearst, more than any other single man, provoked, and if he had swung Garner's eighty-six California and Texas votes to Smith instead of FDR in the 1932 convention, Smith would have been nominated.

In 1896 the *Journal* was the only big paper in the East supporting Bryan, and in 1900 Hearst established the Chicago *American* to foster his cause in the Middle West. It is interesting that he backed him without believing in either free silver or antiimperialism because he was with him on the income tax and his opposition to the big financiers. In 1904, when Hearst himself was a candidate, Bryan might have returned the favor, but he did not, and the nomination went instead to the ultraconservative Judge Parker.

In 1906 the Democrats did nominate Hearst for governor of New York against the Republican Charles Evans Hughes, but TR squelched him by sending his secretary of state, Elihu Root, to make a speech at Utica in which Hearst's morals were attacked by insinuation, and the old charge that McKinley's assassination had been triggered by the attacks made upon him in the Hearst papers was deliberately revived "by the President's authority." In 1908 Hearst headed the Independence party, campaigning industriously for Thomas Hisgen and reading letters from the Standard Oil executive John D. Archbold, which Hearst had secured by devious means and which showed up Archbold's shady dealings with legislators. Though the Independence party polled an unimpressive vote, Senator Joseph B. Foraker and Congressman Joseph Sibley were driven from office, the movement for control of trusts and campaign contributions gained momentum, and TR declared that Hearst had "rendered a public service of high importance" and invited him to the White House.

In 1912 Hearst returned to the Democrats as a supporter of Champ Clark. His power in the convention was based upon his control of the California delegation, but finally Bryan's man, Woodrow Wilson, passed Clark, and on the forty-sixth ballot he was nominated. Standing on the corner of Ogden and Kedzie avenues in Chicago when the news came, I heard an earnest old man say to a newsboy, "So it's Wilson. Well, I'm glad of it. I am glad Hearst is defeated."

Hearst supported Wilson halfheartedly in 1916 because he had "kept us out of war." In 1918 he backed Alfred E. Smith for governor of New York, after having failed to secure the nomination for himself, but the very next year he assailed him for being too close to Tammany and the public service corporations, and when a strike cut the supply of milk in New York City he even accused him of starving babies.

In 1920 he backed Harding. In 1924 he denounced the "boozing, bootlegging and bartending faction of Tammany" (i.e., Smith) and tried to break the deadlock between Smith and McAdoo on Senator Thomas J. Walsh, but the convention chose John W. Davis. In 1928 he wanted Mellon but finally supported Hoover because he hated Smith; then, eight years later, thoroughly alienated from FDR, he astonished everybody by proposing that Smith oppose him in the convention. When FDR was renominated, he came out for Landon and thereafter backed Republicans to the end of his life.

After all is said and done, however, Hearst was primarily journalist and publisher. As a newspaperman, he showed amazing industry, ingenuity, and expertise; even at San Simeon, to which all his papers were flown daily, he would often work until four or five in the morning. It is not fair to say that the Hearst press did not employ good writers, for they probably employed more than their rivals, though there was never any suggestion that Elinor Glyn or the "sob sisters" were in any way inferior to Kipling or Mark Twain. When Hearst established the New York *Mirror* late in his career, it was announced that it would supply 10 percent news and 90 percent entertainment, and this was the formula he had followed since his San Francisco days. Hence the comics, photographs, and drawings, the screaming headlines, the chopped-up front page, sometimes decorated in color, and the many magazine features designed to appeal to women and children; hence too the emphasis upon scandal and sensation (always to the accompaniment of much pious headshaking) in news reporting itself, running to exaggeration and even fabrication when necessary. Even Hearst's personal interests could be crowded off the front page by a good murder, and I well remember how the gruesome, sensational pictures in "The American Weekly" section used to scare me stiff as a small child, though I am at once constrained to add that it was from these same lurid pages that I first learned of Joan of Arc, about whom I was to publish two books.

The Hearst press fought municipal corruption, sometimes successfully, both in San Francisco and in New York, championed the poor against unfair discrimination, and exposed many public enemies. In 1910, however, in the course of a circulation war in Chicago, both Hearst and the *Tribune* found themselves caught up embarrassingly in gang warfare. When news was scarce, Hearst made it by rescuing a fisherman from a rock in the Pacific Ocean after the Coast Guard had declared itself unable to rescue him or solving a murder mystery through tracing the sale of the oilcloth in which the remains of the victim had been wrapped to its purchaser (the oilcloth was reproduced in color in the Sunday edition). Annie Laurie "exposed" polygamy by living with the Mormons, and a reporter got himself committed to an insane asylum in order to be able to inform the public about the conditions there. Once there were scareheads on the weakness of the Brooklyn Bridge, and after it had been inspected by city engineers the *Journal* joyfully reassured its readers that it was safe without bothering to point out that only the *Journal* had ever doubted it. In 1927 too there was an "exposé" of a Mexican plot, smearing four senators, though subsequent investigation showed that the Hearst press had been either completely mendacious or else childishly naïve in accepting unverified documents.

Hearst's relations with his employees were generally good. He outpaid his competitors, especially at the beginning, and was courteous and gentle. If he sometimes drove his men as hard as he drove himself, he was generous with praise and often amazingly tolerant of shortcomings. But because of his great power and the close personal supervision he maintained over every detail, he was also feared and sometimes suspected of playing a cat-and-mouse game to keep his subordinates on their toes.

When John K. Winkler's biography of him was published, Hearst refused to read it because "if it doesn't tell the truth it will make me mad, and if it tells the truth it will make me sad." Such moments of self-scrutiny must have been rare in his life. There is no evidence that he regarded his enterprises cynically, and even though he aimed his publications at the lowest common denominator of intelligence the best guess is that he published just the kind of paper he liked. He was the Peter Pan of journalism; like the little girl in the old rhyme, when he was good he was very, very good, and when he was bad he was horrid; with him there were certainly times when what H. G. Wells called "Peterpantheism" turned sour. His youthfulness of spirit, his romanticism, his essentially stage-struck quality, yes, even his love of beauty, connected here. All his life he wanted things as a child wants them and drove ahead relentlessly to get them, no matter what stood in the way. Though never unmindful of his own interests, he was probably much less mendacious than his enemies believed, for he never lost the faculty of believing what he wished to believe. He was part of his own audience, and it was his misfortune that he always believed what he read in his own papers.

CULTURALLY the America over which Roosevelt presided was very different from our own. Nearly 17 million pupils were enrolled in elementary and secondary schools, but there were only 238,000 in college. Massachusetts had achieved a compulsory school law as far back as 1852, and by 1900 nearly all states outside the South had fallen into line, but the minimum required school year still ranged all the way from eight weeks to eight months, and the farm children often went to school only from harvest to spring planting.

Thousands who, partly to save money and partly to raise standards and make new educational resources available to them, would later find themselves being "bussed" to consolidated district schools were still attending the traditional one-room "little red schoolhouse," and the "readers" that had been compiled by William Holmes McGuffey and used to the tune of some 120 million copies almost everywhere except in New England and parts of the Pacific Coast, though pretty much "out" in the cities, were to remain in use in many smaller places well into the 1920s. Mark Sullivan is not unreasonable when he suggests that their sometimes "requiring children to believe what they knew wasn't so" may have triggered later revolt, but they certainly introduced their readers to more first-rate literature than any subsequent series. History textbooks, however, were still, for the most part, chauvinistic and far from instilling any doubts into young minds concerning either the "pa-

Of Church and School

4

triotism" of Revolutionary leaders or the "tyranny" of the British.

The Spencerian steel pen, replacing the old quill pen, had come into general use in the 1860s, and the "Spencerian Style and System of Penmanship" embraced not only elegant, legible writing but elaborate ornamentation. Penmanship was stressed not only in the common school but in the "business college," which taught short-hand and typing and prepared youngsters to work in offices in short order (Harvard's pioneering School of Business and its many imitators all postdate 1900).

The German Kindergarten idea dated back to Friedrich Froebel, who had been influenced by Pestalozzi in the 1840s. Froebel, whose ideas were afterward much more elaborately developed by John Dewey, stressed the importance in education of early childhood and of learning through play and handwork activities, the basic idea being to establish a miniature society in the classroom and develop socially helpful behavior. The introduction of manual training (woodworking) for boys and "household arts" for girls into the grades was in line with Froebel's ideas; by 1900 this had been achieved in some forty American cities, where science courses, including laboratory work in high schools, had been gaining ground steadily since the 1870s.

There were fifty state normal schools in 1900, but few of them required a high school diploma for entrance, and the average annual salary of teachers in the elementary schools was $310 in the North and $159 in the South. My own teachers ranged all the way from excellent to dreadful. I have no idea what they were paid, but my general impression is that they did a much better job than their compensation warranted, and I have no reason to believe that the more richly rewarded pedagogues in the country-club type of school now in vogue are doing much better.

In the early days what we call secondary education in this country had been confined to the upper classes and was taken care of by the "academies"; when the public high school came into being (the first was in Boston in 1821), it was designed to provide for those who could not afford to attend the academies, most of whom, it was taken for granted, would not be going on to college. In the beginning, the girls, if thought of at all, were taken care of in separate schools, but by my time coeducation was the general rule, and the public high schools often had more girls than boys.

Higher education followed a similar line of development, and

School children in St. Paul, 1904. Courtesy, Minnesota Historical Society

here, interestingly enough, so far as state-sponsored education was concerned, the South pioneered; the University of North Carolina began in 1787. As for what was then known as "the West," the Ordinance of 1787 had provided land grants for higher education in the Northwest Territory, and in 1862 the Morrill Act would look to the establishment of agricultural and mechanical colleges everywhere. The University of Michigan, established in 1841, provided a kind of pattern for western universities, but the Northeast long continued to rely on the old privately endowed, generally church-founded colleges, and the State University of New York was not born until 1948.

Higher education for women developed simultaneously in two directions—through the foundation of women's colleges (Vassar, 1856, was the first fully equipped institution in this category) and coeducation in the larger schools. Oberlin had first admitted girls in 1833, and Iowa State University was coeducational from the beginning.

Early in the new century the junior colleges began to appear, and an increasingly insistent demand was made for vocational training and guidance. Johns Hopkins University in Baltimore, Clark in Worcester, Massachusetts, and the new University of Chicago, which was as much a marvel in its way as its neighbor, the World's Columbian Exposition, had been when it was just getting started, all pioneered in encouraging the development of the graduate school. At his inaugural address in 1876, Johns Hopkins's president, Daniel Coit Gilman, had defined the university's task as embracing "the exploration of all useful knowledge," "the encouragement of research," and "the advancement of individual scholars." To be sure, even such institutions were not altogether austere. William Rainey Harper, the distinguished and high-minded Hebrew scholar who was Chicago's first president, was an enthusiast for the football team (it waited for Robert Maynard Hutchins to do away with it), and another later midwestern university president, whose name may kindly be left in the oblivion it has richly earned, once defined his task in terms of creating "a university that the football team can be proud of."

Interesting extensions and variations in educational progress were provided by the Chautauqua Institution. To many Americans "Chautauqua" indicates only the higher vaudeville provided by the tent shows that, until 1933, covered America as a kind of summer extension of the winter lyceums. None of these, however, was ever officially sponsored or controlled by the bona fide Chautauqua, New York, organization, though the latter did often cooperate with those who imitated its programs and appropriated its name.

The Chautauqua Institution proper had been founded in 1874 by John H. Vincent, later to become a Methodist bishop, and Edison's father-in-law, Lewis Miller, and the first idea was to provide an institute to improve Sunday School teaching. Ardent evangelicals made strenuous efforts to turn it into a camp meeting, but this Vincent would not have, being bound to maintain its character as an educational institution. In 1876 there was a Scientific Congress, in 1879 a School of Languages; in 1880 courses in musical theory were added. In 1883, even, Chautauqua University was chartered, but this was short-lived, though it pioneered in the development of extension courses, such as, in our period, were to be added to the curricula of many American universities. The Chautauqua Literary and Scientific Circle was directed by William Rainey Harper, who was to introduce correspondence courses at the University of Chicago also, and these reading groups were a great success; by 1940 they would have enrolled three-quarters of a million people.

Chautauqua seems to provide a natural point of transition from the discussion of education to that of religion. In 1900 the Man from Mars must surely have found all the outward aspects of American religious life both promising and prosperous. Morning service, evening service, and Wednesday night prayer meeting were being multitudinously held across the length and breadth of the land, and Sunday School was being importantly supplemented for young people by the Epworth League and Christian Endeavor societies in the churches and the YMCA and YWCA in close association with them, to say nothing of such aggressive outreach movements as the Student Volunteer Movement or the Federal Council of Churches (1908). D. L. Moody, the last great revival preacher who, despite what many regarded as his antiquated theology, still commanded a pretty general affection and allegiance, had died in 1899, and though the clownlike Billy Sunday was getting underway, he would not have his first big-city success until 1909 in Spokane, Washington. The term "prince of the pulpit" still had meaning, however, and often on a much higher than the revival level. In Boston, in 1893, the great Phillips Brooks had died in his fifty-eighth year, but across Copley Square, at the Old South, George A. Gordon, who was as great a preacher and a more impressive thinker, was addressing large audiences from his pulpit and a considerably wider one through his books and articles. The religious press too was flourishing, with periodicals numbering about 1,000.

Though American culture was still predominantly Protestant, the Roman Catholic church counted 12 million members (which would increase to 18 million by 1920), while the largest Protestant communions were the Methodists (6 million) and the Baptists (5 million). There were about one and a half million Lutherans, largely German and Scandinavian, and about the same number of Jews. Congregationalism and its offshoot Unitarianism were strong in New England and in those parts of the Middle and Far West to which New Englanders had carried them, but by 1900 the Society of Friends, with 115,000 members, had passed both Unitarians and Universalists. The "Mother Church" of Christian Science was still in the 1893 building, the great domed edifice that was so long to dominate the Boston skyline being still to come, but the genteel, yet austere, idealism of the movement was in tune with the dominant optimism of the time, and its quiet, dignified manner of propagation was proving sufficiently attractive to "refined," generally well-heeled persons in the upper middle class and above, so that Mark Twain, in one of the worst prophecies on record, saw Mrs. Eddy, who did not die until 1910, in process of establishing a tyranny over men's minds unmatched since the Middle Ages. Mormonism was considerably farther removed from the religious mainstream, but after plural marriage was abandoned in 1890 it had entered upon a period of healthy growth that endured throughout our period and, for that matter, still endures today. German Ashkenazic Jews had begun to split Reformed Judaism off from the old orthodoxy soon after the Civil War, but in the eighties their liberalism and tendencies toward assimilation provoked the reaction now known as Conservative Judaism, manned by those who feared that the reformers were losing their distinctively Judaic heritage. The newcomers from eastern Europe who began arriving in the 1880s strengthened the forces of orthodoxy, but Conservatism grew stronger among Americanized Jews in the new century. When the Zionist agitation began, Conservatives generally supported it, while the Reformists, like the great Chicago merchant Julius Rosenwald and his rabbi, the famous Emil G. Hirsch, were generally opposed.

The view from within showed a far from untroubled Christendom, however. Shifting population trends, pouring into the cities many without religious affiliation or background, including some actively hostile to religion, exerted powerful pressures, despite many earnest efforts in the direction of both Americanization and Christianization, toward making both the metropolitan and the suburban churches bastions of white-collar middle classism. It was true that though some bodies, as the Lutheran, still tended to keep pretty much to themselves, the old denominational lines were rapidly coming to seem less important. On the other hand, Protestantism was developing a deep cleavage between liberals and conservatives that cut across denominational lines, and even the Catholic church was experiencing difficulty in presenting a united front.

Catholic immigration, though strengthening the church numerically, also brought it new problems; thus, the German Catholics, committed to parochial schools in which instruction was given in their native language, tended to regard the English-speaking Irish Catholics as doctrinally lax and too much inclined toward Americanization. Such disagreements were trifling, however, compared with the life-and-death struggle with the "modernists" being waged in Rome itself, which remained unsettled until 1907–8 when Pope Pius X definitively pronounced against modernism and its leader, Alfred Loisy, was expelled from the fold. As far back as 1886 American churchmen had narrowly saved the pope from condemning the Knights of Labor, an act which would certainly have alienated many workingmen, and in 1887 Father Edward McGlynn, a supporter of Henry George, was excommunicated. In 1895 Pope Leo XIII's declaration that the separation between church and state which existed in America was not a permanently tolerable situation had been a slap in the face for American Catholics, even without the specific condemnation of "Americanism" that followed four years later, in which the pope expressed his fear "that there are some among you who conceive of and desire a church in America different from that which is in the rest of the world."

Neither Cardinal Gibbons, Archbishop Ireland, nor any of the other leaders in the attempt to "Americanize" the Catholic church was a "modernist" in Loisy's sense of the term nor in any sense in which that term was being used among Protestants; all were theological conservatives. But they did perceive clearly that their church could never come into its own in America so long as it was identified with predominantly foreign or antiquated views. Convinced democrats, sympathetic toward the common man, they understood the American temper, believed in the public schools, were inclined to be cool toward the monastic ideal, and favored dialogue with Protestants. Gibbons participated in the World Parliament of Religions in Chicago, and Bishop John J. Keane gave the Dudleian Lecture at Harvard. But Keane lost his rectorship of the Catholic University in Washington, and despite such figures as Father John A. Zahm of Notre Dame University, who espoused evolution as early as 1896, and such champions of advanced social causes as Fathers John A. Ryan and Peter E. Dietz, what he and those like-minded desired for the Catholic church did not begin to be achieved until long after under Pope John XXIII.

Foreshadowed in Unitarianism and transcendentalism in the nineteenth century and in such more orthodox thinkers as Horace Bushnell, who revived and recharactered Abelard's moral influence theory of the Atonement and stressed "Christian nurture" in place of the old cataclysmal "conversion" experience (George A. Coe's influential *Religion in Education* appeared in 1901, and the Religious Education Association was organized two years later), Liberal Christianity, or "The New Theology," developed rapidly from 1880 on, commanding most of the brains in the Protestant churches, where it was to flourish without important check until 1914, when the war put a brake on the faith in "progress" with which it had tended to identify itself.

Congregationalists, Episcopalians, and the northern Methodists and Baptists were especially receptive; the Presbyterians held out longer. As early as 1874, the great Chicago preacher David Swing, acquitted of heresy charges, had gone independent to avoid further conflict. In the nineties, Charles A. Briggs and A. C. McGiffert faced heresy trials; both left the presbytery. Even here, however, there were stalwarts like Henry van Dyke, pastor of the Brick Church on Fifth Avenue, whose fame as poet, essayist, and storyteller gave him special advantages. Chicago became extremely important for the New Theology, partly because of the leadership that emanated from the Divinity School at the University of Chicago, long presided over by Shailer Mathews; here too the Disciples were to establish what would become the most influential modern religious interdenominational journal, the *Christian Century*.

The essential task the liberals faced was that of rethinking Christian faith in terms that had meaning for modern men with modern minds, living and functioning in a modern world. What they were trying to achieve was the creation of a theology with which their contemporaries could feel as much at home as medieval men had been with the world view of Saint Thomas Aquinas or the sixteenth century with that of John Calvin. Without this, they were convinced, Christian faith must either perish or retreat to an intellectual backwater from which it could exercise no real influence upon the vital life interests of the time.

The problem began in the nineteenth century with the "new" science, first in geology, then in biology (Lyell's *Principles of Geology* appeared in 1930–33, Darwin's *Origin of Species* in 1859 and his *Descent of Man* in 1871), and with the application of new critical methods and standards to the study of the Bible. If it was no longer possible to believe with Archbishop Ussher that God had created the world during six days in the year 4,004 B.C., did that mean that the world, like Topsy, had "jes' growed" and that God had nothing to do with it, or did it mean rather, as John Fiske, Henry Ward Beecher, Lyman Abbott, and others would have it, that evolution was simply "God's way of doing things" and that, instead of losing God, modern men had simply caught the vision of a vastly greater God than men had ever conceived of before? As Fiske saw it, the journey was *Through Nature to God* (1899), though George A. Gordon preferred to think of it as *Through Man to God* (1906). Newman Smyth saw his way as leading *Through Science to Faith* (1902), and Lyman Abbott wrote boldly about *The Evolution of Christianity* (1892) and *The Theology of an·Evolutionist* (1897).

Again, if it could no longer be maintained that Moses wrote the Pentateuch and King David the Psalter, if the Old Testament on occasion attributed criminal conduct to Jehovah, and if there were contradictions in the Gospels themselves, did this mean that the Bible had lost its value as a guide to life, or must we now recognize frankly that what it gave us was a record of religious *development*, with God ever striving to achieve a progressive revelation and realization of Himself in the highest terms men could understand, and ought we rather to rejoice that, besides being a divine book, it was also a profoundly human book, and that God had honored humanity by taking men into partnership in His supreme revelation of Himself?

Never mind that, so far as the intellectuals were concerned, much of this was "old hat" by 1900; the great body of American Christians were still struggling with the questions that had been raised. Never mind, again, that men like Abbott and Gladden were "popularizers" rather than independent thinkers; they were still fulfilling a tremendously important function. Gladden's *Who Wrote the Bible?*, a bombshell in 1891, had not been defused by the fact that the figures on the calendar had changed, and his *How Much Is Left of the Old Doctrines?* (1900) seemed daring enough to most of its readers.

Important influences upon the New Theology radiated from such Victorians as Frederick Robertson, Frederick Denison Maurice, and the "Broad Church" leaders in England and from such German philosophers and theologians as Friedrich Schleiermacher, Rudolf Lotze, and Albrecht Ritschl. In 1900, in a widely read and influential book, *What is Christianity?*, Adolf von Harnack, himself a Ritschlian, declared that Christianity means "one thing and one thing only: Eternal life in the midst of time, by the strength and under the eyes of God." Few modernists can have disagreed. In the best general account of the movement that has been written, Professor William R. Hutchison has expounded the basic tenets of Protestant modernism, with special reference to the summary achieved by Shailer Mathews in *The Faith of Modernism*, in the following terms:

> The basic Christian convictions were humanity's need for salvation from sin and death; the love, fatherliness, and forgiving nature of God the creator; Christ as "the revelation in human existence of God effecting salvation"; good will as essential to the nature of God and as the foundation of human betterment; the persistence of individual human lives after death; and the centrality of the Bible as a record of God's revelation and as a guide to the religious life.

Another way to put it would be to say that liberal Christianity stressed the Immanence of God (though without denying His Transcendence) and the element of love rather than judgment in His character. Of the great historic Christian doctrines, the Incarnation, which saw God as entering into human experience in order to sanctify and redeem it, was obviously the one to which it clung with the deepest passion. "Original sin" was frankly discarded, and the importance of sacamentalism declined. The general outlook was Arminian rather than Calvinistic, but formulated creeds were played down. Though faith and works were both important, there was a general agreement on the proposition that faith without works was dead. Because man was God's child, he was neither a "vessel of wrath" nor a "worm of the dust"; all the barriers between him and God were on his side, and heavy reliance was placed upon education and the improvement of environment as means of overcoming them.

There was one thing more: The New Theology looked for the establishment of the Kingdom of God in time, through the historic process. The apocalyptic strain in Jewish and Christian thinking went into the discard as now having only a historical interest, and though supernaturalism in other aspects was not rejected it was certainly played down. Whatever might happen "in the sky, by and by," what the Social Gospelers were interested in primarily, and what they believed God expected them to work at, was the building of the Kingdom here and now.

This does not mean that all the New Theology people were Social Gospelers nor even that all who were could be given a clean bill of health from where we stand now. To us Josiah Strong, one of the great organizers of the movement and an important figure in connection with the Chicago World Parliament of Religions, looks very much like a racist jingo. Abbott, Henry van Dyke, and Henry Churchill King, president of Oberlin College and author of *Reconstruction in Theology* (1901), were all turn-of-the-century expansionists, and even Walter Rauschenbusch, whose *Christianity and the Social Crisis* (1907) was probably the most important single document of the Social Gospelers, had not yet become a pacifist at the beginning of the century. Perhaps the person who was most important as modernist and Social Gospeler both was Washington Gladden; certainly his *Tools and the Man* (1893) and *Social Salvation* (1902) were as important for one aspect of modern religion as *Who Wrote the Bible?* was for another.

The roots of the two phases intertwine, with the same influences from England and Germany being brought to bear on both. There had been American activity in the area of the Social Gospel at least as early as the 1870s, and thinkers like Henry George, Lester Ward, and Richard T. Ely, often not clergymen though devout Christians, contributed to it importantly (Ely's *Social Aspects of Christianity* appeared in 1889). In 1886, when he assumed the Plummer Professorship of Christian Morals at Harvard, Francis Greenwood Peabody became the first professor of what is now called social ethics; in 1892, at the University of Chicago, Albion W. Small became the first professor of sociology. Edward Bellamy's utopia, *Looking Backward* (1886), would have an important revival as late as the 1930s; in 1894 William Dean Howells published the first of his utopian romances, *A Traveler from Altruria;* two years later, a Topeka clergyman, Charles M. Sheldon, brought out a novel called *In His Steps,* which became one of the most widely read of all American fictions. Here a group of church members in the city of "Raymond" enter into a pact with their pastor, according to which for one year they will take no action in any sphere without first asking themselves, "What would Jesus do?" The movement spreads to nearby Chicago, where it becomes involved with settlement work, the war on the saloon, and much besides. As a novel, *In His Steps* is naïve and simplistic and quite innocent of literary quality, but it is still significant for the understanding of the Christian conscience in our period. In 1901 both Congregationalists and Episcopalians set up commissions to deal with labor issues, and in 1903 the Presbyterians formed a special mission to workingmen. And these were only straws in the wind.

Aside from all this, and in many ways opposed to it, were the "prophecy conferences" for Bible study, placing heavy stress on premillenarianism and interpreting Christian history in "dispensationalist" terms, which discouraged the tendency to work for the establishment of God's Kingdom on earth by gradualistic means, but the full development of militant "fundamentalism" did not really get underway until later. In Chicago, the Moody Bible Institute, which had not inherited the irenic spirit of its founder, trained religious workers who often became disruptive influences in the churches where they labored. After 1909 many such teachers and workers used the Scofield Reference Bible, in which Cyrus Ingerson Scofield and his successors ingeniously imposed a dispensationalist framework upon the Scriptures that many readers seemed to consider as free from error as the sacred writings themselves. The "Holiness" revival, largely Methodist in origin, became estranged from that body in the nineties, and the First Church of the Nazarene was organized in Los Angeles in 1895. Pentecostalism, which emphasized the baptism of the Holy Spirit and speaking in tongues, was both farther out and a little later; the impetus that escalated it into a worldwide movement dates from the activities of a black preacher named William J. Seymour in Los Angeles in 1906.

Most of the conservatives in the old-line churches were never willing to proceed to such lengths, and during our period their general feeling might perhaps be better described as that of a vague uncomfortableness with newness and strangeness rather than a settled and formulated opposition to it. The opposition was finally to be most intelligently expressed by Princeton's J. Gresham Machen, whose arguments impressed Walter Lippmann, if not to the extent of making a Christian of him, still sufficiently to cause him to accept Machen as Christianity's authentic spokesman. Machen's position was that the New Theology was Christian only in name and the modernists religious only in a vague, general, rather than any specifically Christian sense, and that, consequently, when they called what they believed Christianity they were only trying to smuggle a new kind of religiosity into the church under the pretense that it was something else.

This point of view was not wholly obscurantist. Though most of the New Theology people remained evangelical Christians, others seemed from time to time to be taking off into naturalistic, historical, behavioristic explanations of religion itself. This was true in Chicago of Edward Scribner Ames and, even more, of George Burman Foster, whose agonized pilgrimage of later years seems to have left him without settled assurance of even theistic belief.

The truth of the matter was that more than sadism had deserted the pulpit with the disappearance of hellfire preaching. When religious emotionalism, good humor, and Christian (or even merely human) fellowship had crowded out what the Puritans had thought of as doctrinal preaching, the tide had set also, in some areas, in the direction of antiintellectualism, and many were coming to feel dangerously at ease in Zion. In 1926 the leading modernist preacher of his time, Harry Emerson Fosdick, would observe that modernism had "left out dimensions in Christian Faith that would need to be rediscovered." True as the observation was, it constituted no indictment of modernism; neither did it cancel out the need for or the significance of the movement. It simply reminded us once more that there can be no gain in any area without some loss and that no single line of approach to anything that has real vitality can embrace the whole.

AT the turn of the century traditionalism still ruled America in all the arts. The leading architectural firm was that of Charles Follen McKim, William Rutherford Mead, and Stanford White, which was responsible, among many other things, for the base of the Farragut Monument and the Washington Arch; the New York Herald Building and Madison Square Garden; the Century, Metropolitan, Harvard, and University clubs; the Morgan Library and the Brooklyn Museum; and the Low Library at Columbia as well as the general design of the campus. At the World's Columbian Exposition they had designed both the Agricultural Building and the New York State Building; Boston was indebted to them for Symphony Hall and the Public Library; Philadelphia for the Germantown Cricket Club and the Girard Trust Company Building; and Washington for a remodeled White House, with the addition of executive offices. They had also designed many residences in Italian Renaissance, Romanesque revival, and other styles.

The architectural radicals of today scorn McKim, Mead, and White for the same reason that they hate the World's Columbian Exposition, which held back the flood of architectural ugliness for more than a generation, regarding both as imitative rather than creative. Both the exposition and the firm are generally called "classical," but the label, whether used admiringly or pejoratively, cannot properly be applied to either phenomenon without entering

The Fine Arts

5

many qualifications. Both McKim and White had worked for H. H. Richardson and been influenced by him, but their firm made use of a variety of styles and showed vast ingenuity in adapting old patterns to new needs; on the whole, they were much more successful in reconciling what T. S. Eliot called tradition with the individual talent than any of the radicals whose notion of being creative is to cut all the roots of the past, glorifying originality for originality's sake, even when it degenerates into eccentricity and ugliness. Louis Sullivan (Frank Lloyd Wright's "Lieber Meister") was certainly a very great architect, and his Transportation Building, with the gold-leafed, half-circular arches above the entrance, was one of the glories of the Chicago exhibition, but its beauty did not cancel out that of the buildings constructed in more traditional styles, and his notion that it was somehow immoral for Americans to use anything but an "American" style was just as provincial, and just about as reasonable, as it would have been to argue that they must read only American books, look only at American pictures, and listen only to American music. Moreover, Sullivan used Moorish and Egyptian motifs in his own work, and his decorations on the Carson, Pirie, Scott department store are pure art nouveau, beautiful but neither structural nor functional. On the other hand, though the waiting room in McKim, Mead, and White's now wantonly destroyed Pennsylvania Station (a structure generally admired even by those who do not care for much of their work) was modeled after the Baths of Caracalla, one could make a very strong case for both functionalism and modernism in connection with it.

William L. Shirer, who points out that the 27 million Americans who attended the World's Columbian Exposition represented more than one-third of the total population, comments rightly that what they learned from the fair was that

> there was another world beyond their own drab and circumscribed one, the world of art and architecture, of color and beauty. The fair did what our literature and art had not been able to do; it stimulated the imagination of the whole nation, not only for color and beauty but for the promise of a new age of electricity.

It also did more than anything else that had ever happened in this country to stimulate city planning. In 1902 and the years that followed, its leading architect, Daniel Burnham, in collaboration with

Frederick Law Olmsted, McKim, Saint-Gaudens, and others, revived and revised L'Enfant's plan for the city of Washington and the whole City Beautiful concept to apply it in Chicago, Cleveland, San Francisco, and elsewhere, using open spaces, vistas, and parks, connected with parkways and boulevards, as well as surrounding woodlands, all of which involved important considerations not of aesthetics alone but of conservation and ecology as well. Burnham's "Chicago Plan" was formulated in 1908–9 with the backing of the Commercial Club, and condensed into the Wacker *Manual* for use in the public schools. Though the entire plan has never been activated, it did at least succeed in giving Chicago the most magnificent "front yard," facing Lake Michigan, that any American city can boast.

Sullivan, Boston-born, studied architecture at the Massachusetts Institute of Technology and came to Chicago in 1873. It was here that the skyscraper was born out of the need to solve the weight problem in an area whose foundations were sand. The first attempted solution was the "floating foundation" of steel and concrete that Burnham and Root used in the Montauk Building in 1882, and this principle was applied again in the Monadnock Block (Root and Burnham, 1889), and the Adler and Sullivan Auditorium Hotel and Theater (1887–89) with its seventeen-story tower. Beyond that solid masonry could not well go, and in 1883 William Le Baron Jenney discovered the skeleton type of skyscraper principle when he constructed the ten-story Home Insurance Building of wrought iron to the sixth story and Bessemer steel beams above. In 1901 Holabird and Roche used a complete, riveted steel frame on the Tacoma Building, and Burnham and Root made the twenty-two-story Masonic Temple the highest building in the world.

Frank Lloyd Wright of Wisconsin joined Adler and Sullivan in 1887 and early showed his predilection for plane surfaces, overhung eaves, and cubistic forms. At the beginning of the century he was constructing "prairie-style" houses around Chicago, and especially in Oak Park and River Forest. These were low-lying, "organic" buildings, in which "form" and "function" were one. Wright's ideal was to achieve harmony not only between interior and exterior but between the building and its surroundings, so that it should seem to have grown out of the land itself. Yet his early work was not wholly untouched by classicism. Samuel M. Green calls the best of it a kind of fusion between "the desire to extend into and merge with the surroundings and the desire to enclose and seal off by abstract forms and deliberate massing" and adds that his "ordered and impressed composition" is sometimes "even arbitrarily symmetrical."

In Oak Park's Unity Church, begun in 1904, Wright used poured concrete in rectangular masses, with a pebbled surface on the exterior and a skylighted interior. When I was in high school in Oak Park, I was friendly with the pastor and some of the members of this church and twice gave programs there. Though the building, directly across the street from the Gothic First Congregational Church, was distinctly controversial, I never heard Wright's name connected with it. Even so, it was conservative compared with the Midway Gardens, which Wright built near the University of Chicago in 1914 and which was more elaborate, more highly decorated, and yet closer to abstraction. From here he would proceed to the Imperial Hotel in Tokyo (1922) and the ultimate, extreme expression of all his experimentalism in the Guggenheim Museum (1955).

In 1900 the most famous American sculptors were Augustus Saint-Gaudens and Daniel Chester French. Both were so much identified with Lincoln that their Lincoln statues threaten to swallow up all the rest of their work, which is, nevertheless, well able to stand upon its own feet. French grew up in Concord, Massachusetts, and had his first lessons from May Alcott. His fame dates from 1875, when he created The Minute Man for the centennial celebration of the Battle of Concord. He studied in France and Italy and created the gigantic Statue of The Republic for the World's Columbian Exposition. When Emerson saw French's bust of him (there is a later, splendid, seated figure in the Concord Public Library), he is said to have remarked, "Yes, Dan, that's the face I shave every morning." Though French portrayed many individuals, his works also involve symbolic or allegorical figures. He created a standing Lincoln for Lincoln, Nebraska, in 1912, and, as his crowning work, the immense figure in the Lincoln Memorial at Washington in 1922.

Paul Wayland Bartlett, New Haven-born and French-trained, won his first recognition as an animal sculptor and exhibited at Chicago in 1893 but spent much of his time in France, where he created the statue of Lafayette in the garden of the Louvre. He also worked on the pediments of the New York Stock Exchange and the House of Representatives and on the facade of the New York Public Library.

Lorado Taft hailed from Elmwood, Illinois, and though he studied in Paris, his whole career was centered in Chicago, where he taught at the Art Institute for many years. An opponent of latter-day trends, he published an authoritative *History of American Sculpture* in 1903, which was followed by an outspoken *Modern Tendencies in Sculpture* in 1921. In 1912 his *Columbus* would be unveiled in Washington, the next year his surpassingly beautiful *Fountain of the Great Lakes,* just south of the Art Institute. He did not have a chance to develop all his ideas for the Midway Plaisance at the University of Chicago, but in 1922 his crowning work, the mystical, allegorical *Fountain of Time,* an immense work portraying all types and conditions of men, was unveiled at its western end.

> Time goes, you say? Ah no,
> Alas, time stays. We go.

Two much more "modern" sculptors, George Grey Barnard and Gutzon Borglum, were active during our period, though they became much better known later. Barnard, born in Pennsylvania, studied at Chicago's Art Institute and in Paris and was influenced especially by Michelangelo and Rodin. In 1902 he was commissioned to do the sculpture for the Pennsylvania State Capitol, but many Americans would first hear of him in connection with the controversy over his unidealized Lincoln in 1917. Borglum, a native of Idaho, was also much under the spell of Rodin. He came to New York in 1903, exhibited at the Louisiana Purchase Exposition, and worked on the Cathedral of St. John the Divine. His hope of creating a colossal work at Stone Mountain, near Atlanta, was frustrated, but in the thirties he was to carve the Mount Rushmore Memorial in South Dakota, with its gigantic portraits of Washington, Jefferson, Lincoln, and Theodore Roosevelt, cut out of the solid rock.

The painters best known to Americans in the early 1900s were those who made illustrations for the magazines. Edwin Austin Abbey made his first success thus, but his fame was greatly increased when his *Holy Grail* murals were placed in the Boston Public Library in 1902. Of the ranking painters of the time, probably the one most revered today is Winslow Homer, but John Singer Sargent was much more highly regarded then, and probably many would have placed Henry Adams's friend John La Farge ahead of Homer.

La Farge was born in New York of French parents, studied with Couture in Paris and William Morris Hunt in Newport and began painting in the manner of the Barbizon school. In the 1870s he decorated Boston's Trinity Church, reviving Renaissance techniques in murals and stained glass; later he traveled to the South Seas and painted what he found there. Homer, who died in 1910, first became known for his Civil War drawings in *Harper's Weekly*. During the war he began painting, first military pictures, then country life, with considerable attention to children. He used watercolors as well as oils and shows little influence from other artists; the resemblances that have been discerned between his use of light and color and that of the French Impressionists seem to have been accidental. His interest in marine subjects having been importantly awakened during a sojourn in England, he settled in 1883 at Prout's Neck, Maine, and devoted himself to painting the sea and the men associated with it. Fishing and hunting trips in the Adirondacks brought him other rugged materials, and by our time he was also noted for his vivid Floridian and West Indian watercolors.

Somewhat akin to Homer in spirit, though using different subject matter, was the Philadelphian Thomas Eakins. Eakins studied in France under Gérôme and others and discovered Velásquez in Spain but always retained his own individuality and independence; in 1870 he returned to Philadelphia, where he became director of the Pennsylvania Academy of Fine Arts, and never went abroad again. Eakins always had strong scientific and mathematical interests. He began by painting pictures of his family and friends and shocked his contemporaries by insisting that his students work from the completely nude model, even in mixed classes, and by painting pictures of clinics and operations. Recognition came late; he did not begin to become popular until just after 1900.

If Eakins was independent and unworldly in his attitude toward his art, Albert Pinkham Ryder was far more so. Born in New Bedford of a seagoing family, he was largely self-taught. He began with landscape painting, and the visionary, even religious, quality in his work appeared early. He is never merely naturalistic and reproductive; even when he draws his subjects from literature or from Wagner's *Ring,* he paints his own impressions and interpretations, often employing imagery that seems to well up from the region of the subconscious. Childe Hassam, born in Dorchester, Massachusetts, shows French Impressionist influence and exhibited with "the Ten" —Edmund Tarvell, Frank W. Benson, John Twachtman, and others. His landscapes and street scenes, largely of Boston and New York, are still admired. Impressionist too was Mary Cassatt, Pittsburgh-born but largely expatriate, who was influenced by and shows an affinity of spirit with Degas and who, for the most part, painted women and children. Eye trouble, beginning about 1908, ended her painting career in 1914, though she lived a dozen years longer.

The unclassifiable James McNeill Whistler was born in Lowell, Massachusetts, but went abroad in 1855 and never returned to America. He was influenced by English, French, and Japanese artists —does he belong to American, English, European, or international painting? Whatever the answer, he was famous as a "character" and a gamin long before he was accepted as an artist. During the eighties and nineties he at last achieved serious recognition; he died in 1903. Even his portraits are conceived primarily in compositional terms, sometimes bordering upon abstraction. Tone and mood are all-important, and the viewer is expected to concern himself more with the painting itself than with the subject.

"The Eight," as they came to be called after their first exhibition in 1908, laid the groundwork for their revolt against the American Academy of Design toward the close of our period, but their real vogue came later. They were Robert Henri, George Luks, John Sloan, William J. Glackens, Everett Shinn, Arthur B. Davies, Maurice Prendergast, and Ernest Lawson. Because they painted genre pictures, in anything but a smooth and finished style, of many of the coarser aspects of American city life, Henri, Luks, Sloan, Shinn, and Glackens were often spoken of as "ashcan" painters. Davies and Prendergast, though equally opposed to conventionality, followed their own vision. Davies painted a dream world, and Prendergast produced impressionist fantasies in terms of patterned dots and dabs of colors, arranged in something resembling a mosaic style.

By 1900, too, photography was competing with painting in both landscapes and portraits. Beginning about 1840, it was included in salon exhibitions before 1875, and in 1891 the Vienna Camera Club had put on the first international exhibition. In 1900 the four outstanding American photographers were Alfred Stieglitz, Edward Steichen, Rudolf Eickemeyer, and F. Holland Day; the last named organized a great exhibition at the Boston Museum of Fine Arts in

1900. Both Stieglitz and Steichen were pictorialists at the outset, and ultimately both would go over to modernism, though Steichen was never as extreme as Stieglitz. Steichen's accepting commissions for commercial photography in the twenties would mean a bitter break with Stieglitz, who considered this a shameful prostitution of an artist's talent.

I N Theodore Roosevelt's time, music would seem to have been considerably more pervasive in America than art. New York, Boston, Philadelphia, Chicago, Cincinnati, St. Louis, Minneapolis, and San Francisco were among the American cities that could boast symphony orchestras in 1900, and the New England Conservatory of Music and Chicago Musical College were prominent among music schools. Harvard had established a Department of Music in 1872, but its first Ph.D. in music was not awarded until 1905 when Louis A. Coerne picked it up.

German influence dominated in all phases of serious American music, and the composers who will be mentioned here studied either in Germany or Austria or under those who had been trained there. The beginnings of German influence go back at least to the coming of the Germania Orchestra to New York in 1848, and Carl Bergmann and Theodore Thomas strengthened it notably. Thomas played with the New York Philharmonic in midcentury but achieved his greatest success with the new Chicago Symphony in the Auditorium beginning in 1891. Orchestra Hall was built for him, but unfortunately he died just after it had been opened in December 1904 and was succeeded by his assistant, Frederick Stock, who was to remain in charge for nearly forty years. German too were all the early conductors of the Boston Symphony (1881 ff.), and in New York the Damrosch family was comparably influential.

Music's Sweet Compulsion

6

For all that, non-Germanic influences also appeared. Edward Mac-Dowell's work shows Celtic and Norwegian as well as German influences. Henry F. Gilbert was inspired to become a composer by hearing Charpentier's *Louise* and was also greatly interested in Negro spirituals.

In 1900 the best-known serious American composers were John Knowles Paine, Edward MacDowell, Arthur W. Foote, Horatio W. Parker, George W. Chadwick, Louis A. Coerne, Frederick S. Converse, and Henry K. Hadley. This was an interwoven group, for a number of them had studied with one or more of the others, and they were both versatile and prolific, embracing a wide variety of forms, including opera, oratorio, song, orchestral, chamber, and piano music. Paine, much the oldest, was the undisputed dean, but MacDowell was the most important.

From 1873 at Harvard, Paine occupied the first chair of music in any American university and also served as the college organist. The earliest American composer of symphonic music to attract real attention, he composed music for both the Philadelphia and the Chicago expositions, and some of his symphonic poems were inspired by Shakespeare. Arthur W. Foote, organist of the First Unitarian Church in Boston for thirty-two years from 1878 and one of the founders of the American Guild of Organists, was played regularly by the Boston Symphony. Horatio W. Parker became professor of music at Yale in 1894 and proceeded to make the university the center of New Haven's musical life. He also put in a period as organist and director of music at Boston's Trinity Church. He first won fame with the oratorio *Hora Novissima,* which was successful both in England and in America, and in 1912 the Metropolitan would produce his *Mona.* Chadwick was the head of the New England Conservatory from 1897 until he died in 1931. He was also a choral conductor and church organist in Boston and a widely esteemed teacher, and he directed the Worcester, Massachusetts, festival. Best known today for his many songs, he composed an *Ode* for the Chicago exposition, and his opera *Judith* dates from 1900.

Coerne, a native of Boston and a composer with more than 500 works in various forms to his credit, taught not only at Harvard and Smith but also at the University of Wisconsin. Converse, who was born in Newton, Massachusetts, lived in New England all his life, teaching at Harvard and the New England Conservatory, of which he finally became dean. His opera, *The Pipe of Desire,* first heard in Boston in 1906, would in 1910 become the first opera by an American composer given at the Met. Among his many other works are a dramatic narrative, *Hagar in the Desert* for Schumann-Heink and incidental music for Percy MacKaye's play, *Jeanne d'Arc*. Hadley studied under Chadwick before going abroad, but most of his achievements postdate our period, which is even more true of Charles Ives and Charles Griffes, in whom there is probably more interest today than in any of the other composers I have named.

In the light-opera field, the kings were Victor Herbert and Reginald De Koven. Herbert, an Irishman, was German-trained also and married a Viennese prima donna, Therese Foerster, who brought him to the Met as a cellist when she came to sing there. He played under Theodore Thomas, composed an oratorio for the Worcester festival, and conducted the Pittsburgh Symphony from 1898 to 1904. But though he composed orchestral works and other things, he did not come into his widest fame until he produced a light opera for the Bostonians in 1894, after which he continued in the same delightful vein until he died in 1924. His two serious operas—*Natoma* (Philadelphia-Chicago Company, 1911) and *Madeleine* (Metropolitan, 1914)—were less warmly received. De Koven, who was almost equally known as music critic (Chicago *Evening Post, Harper's Weekly*, and New York *World*) and composer, continued turning out light operas until 1913 (he died in 1920, having also produced more than 400 songs and much incidental music), but none of his later works achieved the popularity of *Robin Hood* (1890), of which the ubiquitous wedding song, "Oh, Promise Me," is a part.

Concertizing during the early years of the century was much more the domain of celebrity singers and much less that of famous instrumentalists than is the case today, and the same thing is true of recording. Paderewski began touring America in 1891 (the Metropolitan mounted his opera *Manru* in 1902), and the violinist Maud Powell, born in Peoria, Illinois, but trained and launched in Europe, had made her American debut under Thomas even earlier. But Fritz Kreisler, though first heard here in 1888, did not reappear until 1900, after an interval devoted largely to nonmusical interests, while Mischa Elman did not come until 1908, Rachmaninoff until 1909, and Efrem Zimbalist until 1911. The Columbia Phonograph Company began in 1887 and the Victor Talking Machine Company in 1901; both specialized for many years, so far as their quality records were concerned, in operatic artists. And opera, during most of our period, meant mainly the Metropolitan.

When the year 1900 dawned, Maurice Grau was in his second season in the "yellow brick brewery" at Broadway and Thirty-ninth Street—as Colonel Mapleson of the old Academy of Music scornfully called it—which was to be the home of the Met until 1966. When it was opened in 1883, the names engraved on the proscenium arch were Gluck, Mozart, Gounod, Verdi, Wagner, and Beethoven; it was of course too early for Strauss and Puccini. In 1887 the critic W. J. Henderson called the Met the *Faustspielhaus*, for Gounod's *Faust* had already opened three seasons there and his *Romeo et Juliette* six.

Grau's was a company of great "stars." They chose their own costumes, selected their own roles, sang encores whenever they felt like it, took any liberties they pleased with the score, and conducted themselves in a manner no impresario would tolerate today. Grau paid Jean de Reszke $2,500 a performance during his last season, and never mind if the fiddlers and the chorus did not earn a living wage. Ensemble too was a matter of little consequence, and even so intelligent a singer as Emma Eames could speak of the orchestra as "the accompaniment" for the singers.

Eames sang her first Aïda at the Met on January 3, 1900, in beautiful costumes designed by her artist husband, Julian Story. Three days later, Johanna Gadski made her debut as Senta in *The Flying Dutchman*, and on January 27 Milka Ternina came in as Isolde. March 30 brought one of Grau's greatest productions, Mozart's *Magic Flute*, in Italian, as *Il Flauto Magico*, with a tremendous cast, headed by Eames, Marcella Sembrich, Pol Plançon, Zelie de Lussan, Giuseppe Campanari, and Andreas Dippel; Eames and Plançon were judged the stars of the occasion.

Eames and Sembrich were both away during the 1900–1 season, but Louise Homer, Marcel Journet, Charles Gilibert, and Fritzi Scheff were all making their first appearances with the company. Puccini came into the repertoire with *La Bohème* on December 26 and *Tosca* on February 4. Henry Krehbiel thought the subject matter of *La Bohème* "foul" and its music "futile," and Henderson could see no prospect of success for the work. *Tosca* fared somewhat better; though the subject was "hideous" and "repulsive," both the music and the singers were admired.

This was the last Metropolitan season for the great Polish tenor Jean de Reszke, the reigning idol before Caruso. During the season he sang thirty times, appearing in most of his great roles; his farewell was made on April 29 in the second act of *Tristan und Isolde*, with Nordica, Ernestine Schumann-Heink, and his brother, the baritone Edouard de Reszke.

The 1901–2 season began late (December 23) and went badly, and the 1902–3 season was Grau's last; in fact he resigned before it was over, making way for Heinrich Conried, whose training had been in German-language theaters.

Conried's first complete season (1903–4) was handicapped by the absence of Nordica, Eames, Melba, and Schumann-Heink; it was also Ternina's last season, for the throat problem that was cruelly to abort her great career and drive her to spend the rest of her life teaching was already manifesting itself. Calvé was considered to have behaved self-indulgently when she returned in *Carmen* on February 1 and *Cavalleria Rusticana* on February 12 and 17, and she walked out of the theater and Metropolitan history when Felix Mottl refused to transpose some songs for her at a concert on April 24. Gadski too left, less spectacularly, at the end of the season, because "vocal artists cannot be bullied, driven or whipped in getting around for a 8 a.m. rehearsal like the little German artists of Conried's little German theater." Unlike Calvé, she would return after two seasons.

Nobody has ever claimed that Conried either knew much about music or had any tact. Nevertheless, his first season had its achievements. For this there were four reasons, and they were named Caruso, Fremstad, *Parsifal*, and Otto H. Kahn, the New York banker who now became a member of the board and was to prove himself the greatest and most intelligent Maecenas in Metropolitan history.

Enrico Caruso made the first of his 607 Metropolitan appearances as the Duke in *Rigoletto* on November 23, with Sembrich, Homer, and Scotti. He was to open every season for seventeen years, except in 1906, when Geraldine Farrar made her American debut. His reception at the outset was not enthusiastic; apparently he was not at his best. As the season advanced, enthusiasm mounted through *Aïda, Tosca, Pagliacci, Lucia,* and *L'Elisir d'Amore,* heard first in the house on January 23. Naturally his popularity led to a growing emphasis upon the Italian repertoire. Olive Fremstad made her first appearance as Sieglinde on November 25, following it with Elisabeth in *Tannhäuser* on December 4. Willa Cather, who judged her the singer who, above all her contemporaries, was scaling the frozen heights, found in her career the inspiration for *The Song of the Lark*, perhaps the best novel ever written about an opera singer. When she read it, Fremstad is said to have exclaimed, "I can't tell where I end and you begin!"

Conried's defiance of the lightning from Bayreuth to produce *Parsifal* on Christmas Eve 1903 was, however, the most sensational event of the season. Cosima Wagner went to court and lost, but the idiots who thought the work sacrilegious, especially on Christmas Eve, were not so easily silenced. At least there could be no doubt that the "show" was a success. Prices were doubled to a ten-dollar top, and the opera was not given on the subscription series. During its first season, it is supposed to have netted some $100,000 in profits.

Conried's second season (1904–5) opened with Caruso, Eames, Scotti, and Edyth Walker in *Aïda*. The great new tenor was heard for the first time in *La Gioconda, Lucrezia Borgia, Les Huguenots* (in Italian), and *The Masked Ball*. On February 16, *Die Fledermaus* was given at advanced prices for Conried's benefit.

In the 1905–6 season, Karl Goldmark's idea of *The Queen of Sheba*, presented on November 22, 1905, was notable not for any great success of its own nor for that of the leading soprano Marie Rappold but rather because she was the first American to appear in a leading role at the opera house without European training. Three days later, Humperdinck's enchanting *Hänsel und Gretel* received its first performance and was subjected to serious analysis by the critics.

On January 3, Caruso sang his first French opera in New York, *Faust*, in which he seems to have been handicapped by unfortunate costuming; at any rate he was better liked in *Carmen* on March 5. The *Faust* was turned into a freak performance by a strike of the choristers, whose average wage on this occasion was to have been something under two dollars each, in contrast to $1,500 for Eames, $1,344 for Caruso, $600 for Scotti, and $500 for Plançon. On January 5, *Tristan und Isolde* would stagger along under similar handicaps, but next day the choristers, denied the support of Samuel Gompers, accepted Conried's compromise offer and returned to work.

One of the season's presentations of the *Ring*, with Nordica, Fremstad, and Heinrich Knote, was achieved between December 25 and 29, and *The Gypsy Baron* of Johann Strauss was heard on February 15, with most of the big stars singing interpolated arias in act 3. The New York season ended with a profit of over $100,000, which was wiped out by the San Francisco earthquake and fire, which not only burned up the scenery and costumes on tour but made it necessary to refund the money paid for admission to all the cancelled performances. The company honored all claims, whether tickets could be presented or not, and found its faith in human nature strengthened when the demands matched recorded receipts almost to the penny.

The first night of the 1906–7 season (November 26) was one of the most memorable in Metropolitan history, for it marked the American debut of a beautiful twenty-four-year-old Melrose, Massachusetts, girl who was destined to become Caruso's only equal as a box-office attraction and the most beloved prima donna America has ever had. A pupil of the great Lilli Lehmann, Geraldine Farrar had made her first appearance in opera, at nineteen, as Marguerite in *Faust*, at the Royal Opera in Berlin, where she had speedily become the darling of both the public and the royal family. Now, after five years of triumph, there and in Monte Carlo, Stockholm, and elsewhere, she was back in her own country.

Dark, vivacious, and girlish in a period when most prima donnas inclined toward the ponderous, Miss Farrar came with every advantage. As her Mozart records and her singing of Micaëla's air in *Carmen* remain to testify, she had in her youth a voice of great purity and beauty, capable in climaxes of all the power she needed, and making up what it lacked in sheer animal force by its thrillingly sympathetic timbre. She combined tremendous *élan vital* with both common sense and idealism, but her power was more spiritual than physical, for her throat was delicate, and she always had to husband her resources carefully. Intensely independent, she was also reasonable, fair, and generous; she worked like a horse; her word was as good as her bond; and her loyalties were unquestioning. Above all else, she had a brain, and she applied it to everything she did. If, at the outset, some of the critics were inclined to hem and haw over her, the public was wiser. They frankly adored her, and their loyalty knew no wavering, not only to the end of her Metropolitan career, which came in 1922 because she had made up her mind at the outset that she would quit the opera at forty, but to the end of the chapter. Until she died, at eighty-five, in 1967, she was deluged every year with birthday greetings, not only from her old admirers but even from youngsters who had never heard her in a theater but only learned to love her through her records.

She had wished to make her American debut as Elisabeth, for she fancied herself much more in this spiritual role and as the Goose Girl in Humperdinck's fairy opera, *Königskinder*, which she was to create in 1910, than in her more flamboyant manifestations, but the management insisted upon Gounod's *Romeo et Juliette*. During her first season she was heard also as Marguerite in both *Faust* and *The Damnation of Faust*, as Mimi in *La Bohème* and Cio-Cio-San in *Madama Butterfly*, and as Nedda in *Pagliacci*.

Cio-Cio-San of course was the great triumph. It was the first performance of the Puccini opera in America, and she shared the great night with Caruso, Scotti, and Homer; fortunately all the highlights have been preserved on still available records. It retained a permanent place in her repertoire; as Florence Nash put it in a charming poetic tribute, "There is no Butterfly that is not you." "And when she sang," wrote Richard Watson Gilder, "I knew love's height and depth / And passion and despair." A decade later she herself was to write:

> Ah! Adorable, unforgettable blossom of Japan! Thanks to your gentle ways, that night I placed my foot on the rung of the ladder that leads to the firmament of stars! When I don your silken draperies and voice your sweet faith in the haunting melodies that envelop you, then are all eyes dim and hearts attune to your every appeal for sympathy.

But not even such a triumph can come without a price tag attached, and Butterfly's very popularity tended to keep Miss Farrar from some of the other things she would have liked to do—Eva, Elsa, Sieglinde, Pamina, Papagena, the Countess in *Figaro*, and Desdemona, none of which she was ever allowed to sing.

Two nights after Miss Farrar's debut came one of the most critical in Caruso's career; he was making his first appearance after having been arrested in the Monkey House at Central Park at the instigation of a woman who claimed he had insulted her. There does not seem to have been anything in it (his accuser gave a false address and failed to appear at the hearing), but both he and the Metropolitan management were terrified; fortunately the audience left no doubt in anybody's mind where their sympathies lay.

Though the great tenor sang *L'Africaine* on January 11, he was principally concerned with Italian opera this season.

The great "frost" of the season was Richard Strauss's brilliant *Salome*. Both the composer and the management had wanted Farrar to do it—possibly for her debut—and when she wisely refused, knowing it for a voice wrecker, it went to Olive Fremstad. But it got only an open dress rehearsal on Sunday, January 22, and one regular performance two nights later, after which moral hysterics caused the Board of Directors to ban repetition. J. P. Morgan is said to have felt so strongly on the subject that he offered to refund the cost of production.

Both the great Russian basso Feodor Chaliapin and the great composer-conductor Gustav Mahler came to the Metropolitan during the 1907–8 season, but Chaliapin departed almost as soon as he had come. He made his debut in Boito's *Mefistofele* on November 20, with Farrar and the fine American tenor Riccardo Martin, who was also making his debut, and went on to reveal his immensely amusing Dr. Bartolo in *The Barber* and his heroic Mephistopheles in *Faust*, but though he was already the great artist who would conquer America in the early twenties, the sharp break he made with "refined" operatic tradition in his naturalistic acting shocked both critics and public while his self-indulgent and childish pranks annoyed his colleagues. Mahler's production of *Don Giovanni* on January 23 with Eames, Gadski, Sembrich, Chaliapin, and Alessandro Bonci was such an integrated production as New York had hardly seen before. Conried gave Farrar *La Traviata*, which had been part of her European repertoire, for a birthday present on February 28; she repeated it twice during the season but was never permitted to do it in New York again. On March 6 she sang her first Metropolitan Mignon, with Bonci, Plançon, and Bessie Abott.

On November 14, 1908, Caruso and Farrar sang *Faust* at the Brooklyn Academy of Music, but the official Metropolitan opening came two nights later, with Toscanini conducting one of the most sumptuous productions in Metropolitan history, the *Aïda* in which the great Czech soprano Emmy Destinn made her Metropolitan debut with Caruso, Scotti, and Homer. Destinn was not photogenic, but she could sing almost anything, and she had eighty operas in her repertoire, most of which the Metropolitan never mounted; hers was a combination of dark vocal splendor and blazing dramatic force seldom seen in any operatic generation. Pasquale Amato was admired upon his debut in *La Traviata* on November 20, from which he proceeded to Amfortas and many Italian roles, but Frances Alda, soon to become the wife of the new general manager, Giulio Gatti-Casazza, was coldly received by the critics upon her debut in *Rigoletto* on December 7.

This was of course Gatti-Casazza's first season. He had come from Milan, bringing Toscanini with him, and he would remain for many years, but Toscanini would depart abruptly in 1915 for reasons that have never been made known. The relationship between the newcomers and the managerial functions of Andreas Dippel, who had been important under the Conried regime, had not been properly defined, and the result was dissatisfaction among the singers. Both Sembrich and Eames left the company at the end of their seasons, and Farrar, who quarreled violently with Toscanini after their first joint *Butterfly*, would have followed them if he had not unexpectedly made peace with her during an April performance of the opera in Chicago. On December 3 she sang Micaëla to the earthy Carmen of Maria Gay, on January 13 she assumed Cherubino in Mahler's second great Mozart production, *The Marriage of Figaro*, and on February 3 she sang her first Metropolitan Manon.

But the Metropolitan no longer had a monopoly of opera in New York. On December 3, 1906, Oscar Hammerstein opened his new Manhattan Opera House in West Thirty-fourth Street, with excellent acoustics, more intimacy than at the Metropolitan, and the focus upon the stage, not the boxes. Hammerstein owed his success to his excellent productions and casts; to his musical director, Cleofonte Campanini, later so long and successfully associated with the Chicago Opera Company, and to Conried's failure to exercise his option on Luisa Tetrazzini or reserve rights to the new French operas that would become the special stock-in-trade of the new house. This last, however, was not for the first season. During the first two weeks such familiar works as *I Puritani, Rigoletto, Faust,* and *Don Giovanni* drew disappointing business. Society did not really capitulate until January 2, when Melba, who had not sung in opera in New York since 1904, appeared in *La Traviata*, which was followed by *Rigoletto, Lucia, Faust,* and *La Bohème,* the last in the face of legal complications with the Metropolitan, which claimed exclusive American production rights. G. Mario Sammarco also found favor upon his debut in *Pagliacci,* and with Melba gone,

Hammerstein played another trump card with Emma Calvé, who came on March 3 and remained to do five Carmens, two Santuzzas, and two Anitas in Massenet's *La Navarraise*. At the end of the season, Hammerstein claimed a profit of $100,000 as against a Metropolitan deficit of nearly $85,000.

Hammerstein's second season (1907–8) started with the threat of financial disaster, but at the end he claimed a profit of a quarter of a million. What made the difference was two women, Luisa Tetrazzini and Mary Garden.

Campanini's sister-in-law Tetrazzini came comparatively late in the season, on January 15. She had been singing for nearly fifteen years in Italy and South America, and San Francisco had heard her with a Mexican company in 1904, but it was not until this season, at Covent Garden, that she had inspired the kind of hysteria that, it seems, only coloraturas can command in operatic circles. This was now to be equaled if not surpassed in New York, where her advance sales exceeded the capacity of the building and where she sang twenty-three times in *La Traviata, Lucia, Rigoletto,* and other operas.

Tetrazzini was the traditional, old-fashioned prima donna with a well-padded figure, and though she was praised for her capacity to infuse her trills and roulades with real human and dramatic feeling, her principal reliance was still upon orthodox vocal gymnastics. Nobody could possibly have presented a greater contrast to Mary Garden.

Miss Garden was a native of Aberdeen, Scotland, who had spent part of her youth in Chicago and won her operatic laurels in Paris, where she had been befriended in adversity by Sybil Sanderson and created Mélisande in the greatest of modern French operas in close collaboration with Debussy himself. She was one of the most original and creative artists in operatic history, and it was her interest in modern French opera that would enable both the Manhattan and later the Chicago Opera Company to make their most distinctive contributions to American musical life.

Each of Mary Garden's characterizations was a rounded, perfected whole in which singing, acting, and plastic pose were so perfectly blended as to defy disentanglement. Her range of sympathetic understanding was very wide, and she created an astonishing variety of characters. In *Thaïs*, in which she made her American debut on November 25, 1907, under the handicap of illness, she was first the perfect courtesan, then the saint; on January 3, 1908, as the Parisian working girl in Charpentier's *Louise,* she was startlingly plain and "modern" by operatic standards; as Mélisande, on February 20, in Debussy's *Pélleas et Mélisande* she offered one of the most hauntingly beautiful impersonations that anybody now living can remember.

Only a part of Hammerstein's sensational 1908–9 season falls within our chronological range. It opened on November 9, with Maria Labia, Zenatello, and Renaud in *Tosca,* followed rapidly by, among others, *Samson and Delilah,* which had rarely been heard in New York as an opera, with Dalmorès and a memorably seductive Delilah by Jeanne Gerville-Réache, and Tetrazzini's first *Barber.* During the summer Hammerstein had built a second opera house in Philadelphia, to be operated simultaneously with the Manhattan, using the same artists and productions, and he opened this on November 17, with Labia, Dalmorès, and Andrés de Segurola in *Carmen.*

On November 27, Mary Garden made her first appearance as Jean in Massenet's medieval miracle-play opera, *Le Jongleur de Notre Dame.* The role had been written for a tenor, and it is said to have been Maurice Renaud who urged Hammerstein to give it to Garden. On March 6, just beyond our period, she would do Louise one afternoon and the juggler the same evening.

But of course her most sensational appearance of the season was that made on January 28 as Salome, in French instead of German, with Dalmorès and Hector Dufranne. Unlike either Destinn, who had sung the role in Berlin or Fremstad at the Met, she could really make herself look like a delinquent adolescent, and she broke with tradition by doing the Dance of the Seven Veils herself. This time New York endured ten performances without complete moral destruction.

It must not be supposed, however, that the American people, during Theodore Roosevelt's time, were exclusively preoccupied with operatic music. Many more persons were concerned with the popular songs being sent out from what is still known as Tin Pan Alley, that is Twenty-eighth Street between Fifth Avenue and Broadway, the headquarters of popular music publishers from about 1900 until sometime after World War I.

So far as such things can be pinned down to a date, it all began in 1892 with the quite unexpected whirlwind success of Charles K.

Harris's ballad, "After the Ball," with its maudlin, commonplace story line and its magical, haunting refrain. The Oliver Ditson Company in Boston is said to have ordered 75,000 copies a few days after publication, and John Philip Sousa made it what we would now call the "theme song" of the World's Columbian Exposition by having his band play it every day, a circumstance that took on a note of bitter irony from the financial panic which developed after the fair had closed. The total sale ran to 5 million copies, and Harris had another great success with his Spanish-American War song, "Break the News to Mother." In 1902 Harry von Tilzer, who claimed to have published 2,000 songs in the course of his career, hit the jackpot with "A Bird in a Gilded Cage," and by 1910 several songs had sold 5 million each and almost a hundred had sold 1 million each.

Whatever may have been true of "After the Ball," there was nothing accidental about the success of the others. Tin Pan Alley established assembly-line composing and embraced far more drunkenness, debauchery, illiteracy, and dishonesty in appropriating material than musical intelligence, but it did understand two things: how to write songs about what people were interested in and how to make them aware of the songs' existence. George Gershwin, Irving Berlin, Ernest R. Ball, and many others got their start there. Even when the lyrics were imbecilic, which was a good share of the time, the tunes might be unforgettable, and even today audiences at the "Pops" concerts of the Boston Symphony Orchestra and elsewhere put their whole heart into "sing-ins" that include such numbers as Harry von Tilzer's "Wait 'Til the Sun Shines, Nellie" or Egbert van Alstyne's "In the Shade of the Old Apple Tree" (both 1905); George Evans's "In the Good Old Summertime" (1902); and "Shine On, Harvest Moon" (1908), which became the theme song of Nora Bayes and Jack Norworth.

Harry Armstrong's "Sweet Adeline" (1903) is generally thought of today as a barbershop quartette song, but in 1906 President Kennedy's grandfather, John F. ("Honey Fitz") Fitzgerald, made it his mayoralty campaign song in Boston (much later, a greater political figure, Alfred E. Smith, would pick up a song of the nineties, "The Sidewalks of New York"). Ernest R. Ball, whose talent was far above the usual Tin Pan Alley level, clicked in 1905 with "Will You Love Me in December as You Do in May?" to lyrics by a future playboy mayor of New York, Jimmy Walker, and followed it in 1906 with

"Love Me and the World Is Mine," but Ball's greatest successes were to fall between 1910 and 1914 with "Mother Machree," "When Irish Eyes Are Smiling," and "A Little Bit of Heaven," all so prominently associated with both Chauncey Olcott and the greatest Irish tenor of all, John McCormack. As a boy, Gus Edwards was hired to sit in the balconies of theaters and join in singing sentimental ballads. In 1907 came his greatest hit, "School Days," composed for his "kid" revue in vaudeville and still universally familiar, and the year 1909 brought both his "By the Light of the Silvery Moon" and Percy Wenrich's "Put on Your Old Gray Bonnet."

Though Scott Joplin's "Oriental Rag" and Joe E. Howard's "Hello, My Baby" (both 1899) are called the first piano rag and the first important ragtime song, rag did not really become a craze until around 1910, the year the "coon shouter" Sophie Tucker found the song of her life in Shelton Brooks's "Some of These Days," which she first sang at White City in Chicago. "Under the Bamboo Tree," sung by Marie Cahill in a 1902 show called *Sally*, was an important early ragtime song, but Irving Berlin's "Alexander's Ragtime Band" (1911), though often called the first great ragtime tune, actually has little syncopation in it.

The most effective way to get a song established was to persuade some star to sing it in vaudeville or a musical show, and what was afterward called "payola" may have begun when Harris gave J. Aldrich Libbey $500 and a share of royalties to sing "After the Ball" in *A Trip to Chinatown*. By 1905 large sums were being paid out; after 1916 the publishers made a determined effort to stop the practice. But songs were sung not only in the theaters but in saloons, beer halls, and restaurants, some of which had orchestras and singers who became locally famous (the enchanting "Daisy Bell," generally called "A Bicycle Built for Two," was established in the nineties by Jessie Lindsay at the Atlantic Gardens on the Bowery), and no one of these outlets was overlooked by the "pluggers," who not only lay in wait for potential customers on Thirty-eighth Street itself but appeared at sports events, at Coney Island and Atlantic City, and sometimes even performed from trucks and sold the sheet music to those who had gathered about. Dime stores often had demonstrators who would play any song a customer handed to them, and after the nickleodeons came in, "illustrated songs" often accompanied the films; in the beginning the slides were sometimes furnished free as a form of plugging.

Except that it took care to avoid the highest reaches, Tin Pan Alley's range was as wide as American life. Indian songs had a run in 1903, and in 1908 Nora Bayes gave Albert von Tilzer's "Take Me Out to the Ball Game" a vogue it has never lost. Railroads, sky-scrapers, dime stores, and automobiles were much in evidence (as in "Come, Josephine, in My Flying Machine" in 1903 and "In My Merry Oldsmobile" in 1905), and even crimes, scandals, and dis-asters inspired songs. Children might be treated playfully, as in H. W. Petrie's "I Don't Want to Play in Your Yard," or tearfully, as in Harris's "Hello, Central, Give Me Heaven," in which a little girl tries to reach her dead mother by telephone. There were Irish and German dialect songs and nonsense songs, notably "Ta-Ra-Ra-Boom-Der-Ray," which began in a Saint Louis brothel, reached Tin Pan Alley in 1891, and was sung at Koster and Bial's Music Hall. "A Hot Time in the Old Town Tonight," which had a similar origin, was adopted as a marching song by soldiers in the Spanish War, and Kerry Mills's "Meet Me in St. Louis, Louis" was to the St. Louis exposition what "After the Ball" had been to Chicago.

Tin Pan Alley had its tragedies. John Stromberg committed sui-cide before Lillian Russell had a chance to sing "Come Down Ma Evenin' Star" (1902), and Theodore Dreiser's brother, Paul Dresser, down on his luck despite his early success with "On the Banks of the Wabash," died forlornly in 1906, before Louise Dresser's use of "My Gal Sal" in vaudeville had had a chance to catapult its sales into the millions. And of course there were mistakes, like that made by Maude Nugent, who sold "Sweet Rosie O'Grady" for $100 and never got another penny out of it. But the unlovelier aspects of life in Tin Pan Alley seldom found their way into its songs. Such titles as "My Wife's Gone to the Country, Hurrah! Hurrah!" and "I Won-der Who's Kissing Her Now" and such a line as "I love my wife, but oh! you kid" in "Meet Me on the Boardwalk" were about as far as they strayed from the straight and narrow.

Among those who attempted more serious, and especially more "refined," types of song than those sponsored by Tin Pan Alley, the greatest popularity was probably achieved by Ethelbert Nevin and Carrie Jacobs-Bond. Nevin, who died at thirty-eight in 1901, was greatly admired by Willa Cather. John McCormack and other great singers sang his songs, and Mark Sullivan devoted a whole chapter to him in *Our Times*. By all means his greatest success was the vaguely religious "The Rosary," whose echoes once filled the length and breadth of the land, but "Oh, That We Too Were Maying," "Little Boy Blue," and others were also widely used. Mrs. Bond, who lived until 1946, was considerably less of a musician, but in 1903 she began a phenomenally successful career as a composer of songs that she published herself. Her greatest successes were "I Love You Truly," "Just a-Wearyin' for You," and, above all, "A Perfect Day," the silliness of whose lyric even Tin Pan Alley never surpassed.

THERE was no shortage of important or sensational news events in 1906, of which two will be considered here—the San Francisco earthquake and fire and the murder of Stanford White. The first was a public catastrophe. The second was a matter of purely private passions and interests, yet important social considerations came to be involved with it.

About a quarter after five on the morning of Wednesday, April 18, a section of the San Andreas Fault, which underlies the Pacific Coast, shuddered slightly, like a dog stretching himself, over an area extending some 200 miles from Salinas in the south to Fort Bragg in the north and between twenty and forty miles wide. San Francisco, which lies to one side of the main break, was not the only city affected but merely the largest one. No deaths were reported in Berkeley, but five persons were killed in Oakland when a wall fell through the roof of a ten-cent theater. The new Stanford University at Palo Alto was hard hit. The tower of the memorial church crashed through the roof, and the upper front of the mosaic-decorated building was shaved off. In the Santa Cruz Mountains, wooded areas slipped into the valleys, splintering the great redwoods.

The tremor lasted forty seconds, ceased for ten, then resumed for another twenty-five. Others followed, more frightening than destructive. The terrible noise was only less terrifying than the motion. Survivors compared it to rumbling, creaking, grinding, rasping,

Public Calamity
and Private Passion in 1906

7

the sound of a great wind, and the breaking of waves against a cliff, and it was followed by an equally terrible unearthly silence.

It is not true, as "disaster films" would have it, that great pits opened in the streets of San Francisco into which vehicles, animals, and human beings tumbled, to be closed in forever. It is true, however, that great cracks appeared in streets and roads, pavements bulged and heaved, water mains turned into geysers, and railroad tracks buckled and in some cases slid into ravines. Some buildings collapsed to rubble; others were opened up like dollhouses; still others adjusted themselves at crazy angles. The walls of the City Hall collapsed, and its columns tumbled into the street. Long Wharf gave out under the weight of the coal stored there. The Valencia Hotel caved in and caught fire before the wreckage could be cleared away or the number of the dead ascertained. The roof of the Majestic Theater fell into the gallery. Gas mains broke; wires came down; transportation was paralyzed. All the hospitals were damaged.

Arnold Genthe, whose photographic activities were then San Francisco–based, retained vivid memories of what he had seen, as terrified people, fearful of further shocks, fled into the streets,

> mothers and children in their nightgowns, men in pajamas and dinner coats, women scantily dressed with evening wraps hastily thrown over them. Many ludicrous sights met the eye: an old lady carrying a large bird cage with four kittens inside, while the original occupant, the parrot, perched on her hand; a man tenderly holding a pot of calla lilies, muttering to himself; a scrub woman, in one hand a broom and in the other a large black hat with ostrich plumes; a man in an old-fashioned nightshirt and swallow tails, being startled when a friendly policeman spoke to him, "Say, Mister, I guess you better put on some pants."

The diva Olive Fremstad carried the roses she had received at the theater the night before and gave them away, one by one, to homeless people, while Caruso clutched a large, autographed photograph of President Roosevelt, which once at least got him through lines he could not otherwise have penetrated. When he had got hold of himself, Genthe secured a camera and made some of the most magnificent photographs that have ever been taken anywhere, among them two spectacular moonlit scenes, one showing what

"San Francisco, April 18, 1906," photographed by Arnold Genthe.
Courtesy, The Bancroft Library

alone remained of the Towne mansion, "Portals of the Past" (they still stand in Golden Gate Park), and another, "Steps That Lead to Nowhere."

In her hotel bedroom, the great contralto Louise Homer saw the wardrobe containing all her belongings plunge across the room and fall upon its face in the middle of it. Since she could not turn it over, she was forced to flee in her nightgown, afterward putting on an extra suit that her husband fortunately had with him. Another prima donna, Emma Eames, sleeping in a four-poster canopied bed in a private house, felt it shaken out into the center of the room but remained in it, burying her face for fear of "being maimed by the crashing glass and the things that were hurled about the room at each shock," and Edyth Walker learned that her guardian angel was on the job when her trunk landed in the middle of her bed just after she had vacated it.

The Metropolitan Opera Company had opened its San Francisco engagement on April 16 with Goldmark's *Queen of Sheba*, which San Francisco seems not to have liked. On the second night, Fremstad, Caruso, Journet, and Abott appeared in *Carmen*; Caruso met with his customary reception, but Fremstad and Abott were coldly received. The great tenor nevertheless swore that he would never set foot in San Francisco again, and he kept his word.

Pol Plançon, the great French basso, cried out in terror when a "horrible bête" sniffed at his feet while he was sleeping in the park, but Madame Eames saved him by flicking the cow away with her handkerchief. The conductor Alfred Hertz, awakened by the roaring of the big cats in the nearby zoo, wondered in his confusion whether he had wandered "into the jungle." Eames herself went through the ordeal with her customary unruffled calm, which she attributed later to shock, and her chapter on the experience in her autobiography is one of the best accounts of those days that we have. The one member of the company who really suffered was Homer, who was pregnant and who had to be taken from the train when it reached Chicago and rushed to Wesley Hospital, where she lost her baby. The only other agony endured by a theatrical figure seems to have been that of John Barrymore, who was playing in *The Dictator*. When he got out into the streets, he was put to work piling bricks, which prompted his uncle John Drew to remark that it required a convulsion of nature to get him out of bed and the United States Army to make him work.

San Franciscans like better to talk about "the fire" than "the earthquake." It ought to be the other way round. If they had any responsibility, it was for the fire, for there had not been a bad quake since 1868, but everybody knew that the fire-fighting equipment was inadequate. Considering what they had to work with, both firemen and policemen performed valiantly, even though the fire chief was dead from the very beginning, and so did the Post Office, which carried all outgoing mail, whether it was stamped or not, and boasted that none was lost.

The fires began almost at once and continued till nearly the end of the week. Close to 500 blocks covering over 2,800 acres were burned, wiping out the business district and three-fifths of the homes, including the mansions of the railroad kings. Libraries, courts, jails, theaters, and restaurants were burned. Thirty schools were destroyed and eighty churches and convents. One of the worst conflagrations was the so-called ham-and-eggs fire, which was caused by a woman trying to cook breakfast when her chimney flue had been damaged. This was the kind of thing that led to the requirement, which remained in force until all chimneys had been inspected, that cooking must be done out of doors, an edict that, like the prohibition of alcohol, was wise, even if, like many other emergency measures, probably not strictly legal.

The *Call* building burned from the top, one floor at a time, and the American flag on the roof of the Palace Hotel waved stubbornly for hours, as if gallantly determined to withstand the fire on its own. On Wednesday night some thought the flames a mile high, and it was said that one might read a newspaper at midnight fifty miles away; on Thursday the thick clouds of smoke were estimated to have mounted two miles high. Those whose aesthetic sense had survived the shock were enthralled by the color combinations the flames and smoke achieved. More than 450 dead were counted in a probably incomplete tally, but the figure would have been much higher if the catastrophe had struck later in the day. The property loss was estimated as somewhere between 350 and 500 millions.

The framework of government and business survived, however, and 150,000 people lived in parts of the city that had not been touched. Technically San Francisco was never under martial law, but practically the military were in control in many areas; General Funston had acted even without waiting for authorization from Washington. Mayor Eugene Schmitz and his ally, the boss Abe

Ruef, both had bad reputations, and though they rose to their finest hour during the crisis, neither was able to withstand the strain of the temptations that came with rebuilding. By Christmas both had been indicted; subsequently they were convicted of accepting bribes, and Ruef went to prison. There were varying reports, and there are still differences of opinion, as to the conduct of the troops, but it seems generally agreed that much of the dynamiting intended to check the spread of the fires was done by amateurs and produced more harm than good. Since calamity brings out both the best and the worst in human nature, there must have been outrages committed, but such information as we have gives us far more to praise than to blame. Jack London, on Wednesday night, saw "no hysteria, no disorder," and "no shouting or yelling." "Never, in all San Francisco's history," he thought, had people been "so kind and courteous."

Congress appropriated two and one-half million dollars for relief (TR refused to accept help from abroad), and much larger sums came in from private sources, first from Oakland, Los Angeles, and other California cities, later from farther away. Sarah Bernhardt gave benefit performances in Chicago and Berkeley; Arnold Genthe has an amusing account of how her lively imagination later persuaded her that she had been exposed to dangers that never came near her. In Wall Street, George M. Cohan sold papers for as much as $1,000 each, and in Los Angeles Jim Jeffries peddled expensive oranges.

In the beginning 300,000 people were sleeping out of doors, in tents when they were available; come fall, the building of about 6,000 refugee shacks had begun, some of which still stand. No food was sold in shops; rich and poor alike stood in line side by side at the relief stations, cooked on outdoor stoves or improvisations, and received rationed water for drinking and cooking only. The use of indoor plumbing was prohibited. Between May and October, the hot-food stations served some one and a half million meals. But by July the worst was over. Life went on somehow. Churches held outdoor services, and there was an outdoor theatrical performance eight days after the fire. Babies were born in doorways and in Golden Gate Park; one man claimed to have delivered six in a day. The marriage license bureau resumed functioning while the fires were still raging, and the newspapers began publishing again within a week. Within six weeks, banks were operating, and though twelve

insurance companies failed or threw in the sponge, others faced up
to the crisis bravely. An outbreak of typhoid in September killed
seventy-seven, and bubonic plague appeared briefly in 1907, but
there was no real epidemic. Many persons indeed found their health
improved by outdoor living, hard work, and enforced abstention
from alcohol and overeating.

Exactly two months and one week after the earthquake struck,
on the night of June 25, during the performance of a mediocre new
musical, *Mamzelle Champagne,* on the roof of the Madison Square
Garden, across the continent in New York, Harry Kendall Thaw, a
rich young Pittsburgh wastrel, with a bad history of eccentricity and
depravity, walked up to the table where Stanford White, who had
built the Garden and half the other beautiful buildings in New
York, was sitting alone and fired three bullets into him at such close
range that the face of the corpse was unrecognizable.

What thus began remained until 1924, when Thaw finally gained
his freedom, the most notorious of all American murder scandals.
Crime connoisseurs have sometimes professed lack of interest in
the Thaw–White case on the ground that there was no mystery in
it, and it is true that the killing was done in a public place and that
the killer's motives were only too clear. For all that, the case is
rich in the deeper mysteries of human character. Was Thaw a lunatic and therefore not responsible for his act? Was White the monster
of lust that the Thaws and sensational newspapers and sentimen-
talists invoking "the unwritten law" tried to make him out? And
above all did Evelyn Nesbit, the show girl and artist's model whom
Thaw had married, tell the truth when, in the most sensational
testimony American newspapers had reported up to this time, she
related how White had drugged and violated her as a teenaged virgin, or was she lying to save her husband's neck?

"The trial of the century" opened on January 27, 1907, and it
took until February 4 to select a jury. The prosecution was conducted by the highly respected reform district attorney, William
Travers Jerome. The large battery of defense lawyers was headed by
"the Napoleon of the Pacific Bar," Delphin Michael Delmas, an
eccentric, a "character," an orator of the old school, and a wholesale "corn" merchant, who might, had he so chosen, have made a
name for himself in the ten-twenty-thirty melodrama theaters.

Irvin S. Cobb, who covered the trial, thought Evelyn Nesbit "the
most exquisitely lovely human being I ever looked at." She began

her testimony on February 7, and Delmas turned her over to the prosecution on February 11. Jerome grilled her mercilessly; few women in American history have ever been subjected to such public humiliation, but he was not able to shake her story. She divided the country into pro-Evelyn and anti-Evelyn factions. If she was acting, she acted superbly, and one can only wonder why she was never able to equal her performance in the theater.

It is doubtful that any crime or scandal can ever again create such a sensation as did the Thaw–White case. The press coverage was vast. William Dean Howells wrote that his wife was conducting the trial herself and living "only from the morning to the evening editions of the papers." And though Mrs. Howells had a built-in interest in the case through her relationship to White's partner Mead, hers was not an idiosyncratic reaction. President Roosevelt speculated about the possibility of excluding the newspapers that reported Evelyn's testimony from the mails. Laura Jean Libbey conducted a public debate with herself as to whether girls would be more likely to be warned or corrupted by reading it, and as late as 1909 young Mary Pickford, seeking work in the movies, was frightened by the use of the word "studio" to indicate the places where they were made. As for me, the Thaw-White case was about the first thing I was ever conscious of the newspapers covering. I was too young to read anything but the comics, but I did look at the pictures, and I heard my elders talking about the case. I sensed both that there was something very wicked about it all (though, except for the killing, I had no idea what it was) and that there was considerable difference of opinion as to who was most to blame. I remember too that Evelyn Nesbit Thaw, as she was always called in those days, was the first person I had ever heard spoken of by three names, and though I had four myself, it seemed to me somehow that this made her a very great lady indeed, probably almost as grand as Alice Roosevelt.

The case went to the jury on April 10; after having been out forty-eight hours, they reported that they were hopelessly deadlocked —seven for first-degree murder, five for acquittal—and were discharged. The second trial began January 8, 1908. Delmas was gone, but Evelyn once again faced Jerome. Night sessions speeded up the trial; on February 1, after twenty-five hours of deliberation, the jury found Thaw not guilty by reason of insanity, and he was committed to the state asylum for the criminally insane at Matteawan.

But that was only the end of an act in a play that threatened to become the longest in dramatic history. Between Thaw's commitment and his escape from Matteawan and flight to Canada on August 17, 1913, there were four attempts to set him free through the use of a writ of habeas corpus, one application for transfer to a homeopathic hospital, and one demand for a jury trial to determine his sanity. All were turned down, though the last was appealed clear to the Supreme Court. In 1912 a lawyer was convicted and imprisoned for having accepted $25,000 to conspire for Thaw's release, and the actual escape, effected by his calmly walking through the gates while the milk was being delivered, involved the cooperation of a Tammany crook and of Alfred Henry Lewis, a writer for the Hearst papers, now championing Thaw's cause. The murderer had been allowed to have his dinners sent in from Delmonico's even while he was in the Tombs awaiting trial, and in Matteawan he had lived in luxury and even been permitted outside excursions in the company of his guards.

Jerome went to Canada to get Thaw returned to New York; his deportation in September was followed by a stay in New Hampshire, and New York only got him back for a Christmas present in 1914. Meanwhile crowds hailed him as a hero, evidently bent upon proving that idiocy was endemic on both sides of the border, and feeling against Jerome was so strong that he had difficulty in getting service and once was actually arrested for having taken a hand, in his boredom, in a crap game!

In January 1915, having been indicted for conspiracy in connection with his escape from Matteawan, Thaw was committed to prison, but in summer he finally succeeded in getting the sanity hearing he had long demanded, and on July 16 he was released; thousands of New Yorkers joined the Canadian and New Hampshire lunatics by cheering him as he emerged from the courthouse. "In all this nauseous business," said the *Sun*, "we don't know which makes the gorge rise more, the pervert buying his way out, or the perverted idiots who hail him with wild hurras."

He was not out long. Early in 1917 he was arrested and tried again for having kidnapped and whipped a boy. He had always been subject to sadistic impulses, but apparently this was the first time he had satisfied them upon one of his own sex. At this point even his mother finally got it through her head that he was a menace to public safety and acquiesced in his commitment to a Philadelphia asylum, where he stayed until 1924. His mother was dead by this time; Evelyn, now divorced, fought his release with all she had and lost. From then until his death in February 1947, he was in and out of the news in frivolous or disgusting connections, but the fires were dying down, and he managed to keep out of prison.

The vilification campaign against Stanford White, cunningly designed to transform him from victim to monster and make his murderer a Sir Galahad defending the purity of every girl in New York, was callously manipulated by the Thaws and generously aided and abetted by a horde of cheap journalists and clergymen who ought to have known better. Thaw, whose maniacal hatred of White had even antedated his own acquaintance with Evelyn, had at one point enlisted the cooperation of Anthony Comstock, and this notorious smuthound, who spent his life digging up dirt about decent people, believed that Thaw's motives were pure and White a "human monster." "I know that White made a business of ruining young girls," he said, to which he added one of the most glaring non sequiturs on record: "I know of at least one specific instance." But obviously he did not have such evidence even of that as to be able to move against him.

It is not necessary to believe that Stanford White was a saint to perceive that he was shamefully smeared. Though he was certainly acquainted with show girls, we *know* almost nothing about his relations with them. The famous story, industriously circulated by the Hearst press, about the near-naked girl who popped out of a pie at a stag dinner is rather more than seriously suspect, nor is there any evidence that he continued to pursue Evelyn Nesbit after her marriage. Yet, though he knew virtually everybody in New York who was at all prominent in the cultural life of the city, few voices were raised in his behalf when he was dead and defenseless. Foremost among these was that of Richard Harding Davis, who wrote in *Collier's* (August 4, 1906) that White had been "a most kindhearted, most considerate, gentle and manly man, who could no more have done the things attributed to him than he could have roasted a baby on a spit." There was much more, and it was all very much to the point. A prep school headmaster thereupon branded Davis a "depraved romancer," and his books were thrown out of a public library in New Jersey, but Saint-Gaudens backed him up in a letter to *Collier's* in which he spoke of White's "almost feminine tenderness to his friends in suffering and his generosity to those in trouble or want."

It must not be forgotten that at the trial Evelyn was not permitted to tell what had happened between her and White but only *what she told Thaw had happened,* and though she never formally retracted her testimony afterward, she was not wholly consistent. In the 1956 film, *The Girl in the Red Velvet Swing,* which was made with her as adviser, she is represented as having sought out Mrs. White during the trial to tell her that this was not the way it was but only the way Harry's sick mind had interpreted it. Not long before she died, she called White the only man she had ever loved, and even on the stand she had declared that outside of "this one terrible thing" he did, White was "a very grand man. . . . He was kind and considerate and exceedingly thoughtful—much more thoughtful than most people. . . . People liked him very much. He made a great many friends and kept them."

None of this means, however, that it is necessary, or even possible, to accept the view of her extreme detractors that Evelyn played off one lover against another and deliberately goaded Thaw on to killing White. Whatever else she may have been, she was no vampire woman. Dorothy Dix wrote during the trial that a stronger or wiser person than "poor, weak, silly, vain Evelyn" would not have told her husband about her relations with White, but it is difficult to believe that this would have been possible. Thaw had the depraved man's fetish on virginity, and a modern psychiatrist has argued suggestively that he considered himself "chosen to be a protector of girls being ravaged by perverts" and that this delusion was "nature's method of assuaging his unconscious guilt."

The most incredible thing in Evelyn Nesbit's career was not her relationship with White, whatever it may have been, but the fact that she should have married Thaw, knowing as she did what he was. Either she was deliberately selling herself for a rich husband or else she must have been really moved by the love he professed for her and his indignation over the "fall" she had suffered. We do not know how much White loved her; we do know that he never considered breaking with his wife to marry her. In *The Girl in the Red Velvet Swing,* he was made to ask Evelyn, when he heard of her contemplated marriage to Thaw, whether that mother of hers was planning to sell her for so much a pound. It was a good question. Whatever her or her mother's motives, it was a bad bargain, for she did not weigh much, and little was ever paid.

Her long life after the trials and her divorce from Thaw was checkered, and it would take Omniscience to decide whether her own weakness or the position in which her notoriety had placed her was primarily responsible for such mistakes as she may have made. "Stanny was the lucky one," she once said bitterly. "He died. I lived." In 1910 she gave birth to a son; she named him Russell William Thaw, but Thaw never acknowledged him, though in later years he seems to have taken some interest in him. In her own view, Evelyn's relations with Russell made up the most satisfying part of her life, which is hardly surprising, for her love for children and animals had always amounted to a passion. When Russell was growing up, she set her heart upon making him a doctor, but he was fascinated by aviation, and there was nothing for her to do but yield.

She had a period of prosperity as a dancer in vaudeville (she was briefly married to her dancing partner, Jack Clifford), and she had some success as a film star, but Mother Thaw, as if determined neither to support her nor to permit her to support herself, vainly went to court to bar her appearance on the stage on the ground that "ragtime dancing" was immoral, and the film moguls could not think of anything better to do with her than put her into such masterpieces as *Her Mistake, The Woman Gave,* and *I Want to Forget,* all of which made it impossible for either her or the public to do just that. For the rest, it was trying to manage a tearoom or singing in nightclubs.

The last years were better; she spent them in Los Angeles working at ceramic sculpture. Finally, after having suffered a stroke, she died at Santa Monica on January 17, 1967, in her eighty-third year. She had been reported from time to time as interested in theosophy and the study of world religions, but she was buried with the rites of the Catholic church. Life had taught her, she said, that what happens to a human being depends upon whether he has the character needed to meet the temptations encountered and that in the end nothing matters but the love of God and compassion for everything that lives.

Some of the interest engendered by the Thaw case was quite impersonally psychological and sociological. It must have been one of the first trials in which alienists played a large role. The word *brainstorm* became a part of the American language, but Delmas's "dementia Americana" to indicate the rage of a virtuous husband, maddened by an assault upon his wife's honor, did not fare so well. The sociological considerations were more important. In Eugene Walter's play, *The Easiest Way*, the old-time booking agent, Jim Weston, disgusted by the corruption he sees all about him in the theater, tells Laura Murdock that he would like to make away with some of the rich stage-door johnnies who prey on poor show girls but that he would restrain himself because they were not worth the job of sitting on the throne in Sing Sing and he was too poor to go to Matteawan. Of course there was class feeling in America before the Thaw case, but the blatant efforts of the family to use their money to circumvent justice certainly contributed to its growth.

To be sure, the great mansions built for the wealthy on Fifth Avenue and at Newport, Palm Beach, and elsewhere were not all waste. Beauty was created as well as vanity; some of the Newport "cottages," on which the wealthy spent millions to occupy during six or seven weeks during the summer and squander perhaps $100,000 on one "affair," have survived to serve more useful functions, and it would be hard to argue that the appearance of Fifth Avenue has been improved by tearing down the mansions of the Vanderbilts and others and replacing them by whatever you wish to call what stands there now. It is worth remembering too that Gifford Pinchot served as director of forestry at George W. Vanderbilt's 203-square-mile estate at Asheville, North Carolina, and there gave "the first practical demonstration of forest management on a large scale in America."

The French novelist Paul Bourget was impressed by the decorum and sexual decency he found at Newport, and he may well have been right; it is hard to see how people who worked harder at "entertaining" than anybody has ever worked at anything useful and apparently ate more food than anybody else has ever been able to consume could have had much energy left over for other indulgences. Yet the waste, the bad taste, and the vulgar display that prevailed in these gilded revels were beyond belief. "I'm glad there is a Newport," said Mr. Dooley. "It's th' exhaust pipe. . . . I wish it was bigger." And indeed, Palm Beach, where the season began after Christmas and ended with the Washington's Birthday Ball, became a kind of winter Newport.

The marriages between rich American girls and titled Europeans were another scandal. The pioneers were Jennie Jerome and Lord Randolph Churchill, and by late 1903 a popular magazine was able to tote up fifty-seven such unions. Often the husband was bought like a piece of merchandise. The Vanderbilts set aside two and a half millions to unite Consuelo with the Duke of Marlborough, and it was not worth it, as she later revealed frankly in *The Glitter and the Gold.* Nothing could have been more appropriate than that the Thaws themselves should have been involved in one of the least dignified of these transactions. They bought the Earl of Yarmouth for their daughter Alice, but when he was arrested for debt on the morning of the wedding he raised his price, and the ceremony was delayed for forty-five minutes while the details were being worked out. The marriage was later annulled on the ground that the groom had been unable to consummate it.

THE commissioned history of the National Biscuit Company is called *Out of the Cracker Barrel*. There could have been no better title. But crackers were not the only things that were being brought out of barrels and bins and placed in labeled packages during our period. If Americans were learning to ask for Uneeda Biscuit instead of soda crackers, they were also asking for Heinz's 57 Varieties instead of fishing pickles out of the brine, drinking Coca-Cola instead of sarsaparilla or soda pop, and reaching for a Hershey bar instead of an unwrapped piece of candy, while Campbell's were bringing them soups in cans that they had previously only been able to prepare laboriously at home and Kellogg's were offering them new, ready-to-eat breakfast foods. It would take a book considerably larger than this one to tell the whole story of the food revolution in America, but the firms I have named here and their products may be used as representative of the trend.

Henry J. Heinz was born in Pittsburgh on October 11, 1844, of German ancestry and was originally intended for the Lutheran ministry. He began his career in the food business with neither pickles nor ketchup but horseradish. He was still a boy when he began bottling and selling it, and when in 1869, the year of his marriage to an Irish girl, he joined with L. C. Noble in bottling Anchor Brand food products, using the Heinz homestead and its environs as their headquarters, this relish again came first. Though

New Patterns in the Food Industries

8

they established branches in Chicago and St. Louis and won a first prize at the Cincinnati exposition, they went bankrupt in 1875. The next year Heinz started all over again with two brothers as F. & J. Heinz Company, but he did not achieve full solvency until 1879. The company turned out a variety of products—chili sauce, tomato sauce, fruit butters, mincemeat, piccalilli, baked beans, macaroni and spaghetti with cheese, currant jelly, preserved cherries, pineapple preserves, Worcestershire sauce, mustard dressing, and other preparations. In 1888 the firm name was changed to H. J. Heinz Company, and moved toward building the great complex at Allegheny City, Pennsylvania.

It is amusing that the famous "57 Varieties" slogan was taken out of the air, having been suggested to Heinz by the "21 Styles" he saw advertised by a shoe manufacturer in a streetcar. It has been deemphasized of recent years because there never were literally fifty-seven varieties, and there are now about 1,250 (there were already 200 at the beginning of the century).

Like the National Biscuit Company, the Heinz Company distributed their products in their own brightly painted wagons (the first electric was added in 1899, the first gasoline truck in 1910), but they also owned freight cars, painted a bright yellow and decorated with the pickle emblem, and from 1894 they shipped vinegar and pickles over the rails in their own cars. Their advertising went into newspapers and magazines (but never on Sundays) and into streetcars and show cards and a variety of souvenirs, to say nothing of innumerable "demonstrations" at fairs, expositions, and markets.

At the World's Columbian Exposition, the Heinz Company had more space in the Agricultural Building than any other food manufacturer, with a beautiful pavilion and pretty girls to give out the samples. Unfortunately it was placed on the gallery floor, to which foot-weary visitors did not care to climb in great numbers. Heinz thereupon blanketed the fair grounds with little cards that could be exchanged at the Heinz booth for a "free souvenir," and after that the visitors were so numerous that the authorities began to fear the floor might give way. The souvenir was a green gutta-percha pickle labeled "Heinz," which could be worn as a charm or on a watch chain, and it turned out to be one of the most fantastically successful gimmicks in the history of advertising. One million were given away at the fair; later the thing also became a pin, and millions more were distributed.

The H. J. Heinz Factory

More spectacular than any of this was the Heinz Ocean Pier at Atlantic City—"The Crystal Palace by the Sea" and "The Sea Shore Home of the 57 Varieties"—which was established in 1898. The visitor passed through a triumphal arch to a glass-enclosed Sun Parlor, equipped with numerous comforts, and a demonstration kitchen with hot and cold samples of Heinz products. From here he might, if he chose, proceed 900 feet out into the ocean to the Glass Pavilion, which was surmounted by an electric sign bearing the mystic number "57," seventy feet tall. Inside was a lecture hall, in which stereoptican slides provided a kind of extension tour of the Heinz factory, a display of Heinz products, an art gallery, and an exhibition showing the endless variety of Heinz's collections. In later years concerts were also given at the Pavilion, but the 1944 hurricane wrecked the trestle and cast the "7" of the "57" into the sea.

The Heinz complex itself was also exploited to the full for its advertising value. The first building was completed in 1889, and the enterprise was crowned in 1908 by the palatial Administration Building. For many years, however, the pride of the group was the ornate little Time Office, "a combination of elegance, splendor and beauty," surmounted by an eagle-decorated dome, where everybody checked in and out. Like the Shredded Wheat Company at Niagara Falls, the Heinz Company encouraged visitors, and by 1900, 20,000 people, including many celebrities, were inspecting every department in the plant annually.

The company was one of the first industrial employers of women, largely immigrant girls from the Pittsburgh area, first German and Bohemian, then Polish, then Italian, as the ethnic patterns in the area shifted. By contemporary standards, the hours were, at the outset, fantastically long and the wages fantastically low, but there were many fringe benefits. In a day when others were toiling in unsanitary sweatshops, Heinz girls were working in a spotless factory, spotlessly clean themselves. Their physical and moral welfare was carefully guarded; they were supplied with cultural and recreational facilities; and the company picked up their medical and dental bills. The Paris 1900 medal was awarded not only for the quality of Heinz products but also "for the policy of the firm tending to the improvement of factory conditions."

H. J. Heinz ran a strictly paternalistic show; there were no unions in his plant during his lifetime, and there was no strike until long after his death in 1919. He resolutely set his face against all forms of dissipation and refused to tolerate it among his employees. For a great industrialist, he left a small fortune—three and a half millions plus another half million in real estate. After his wife's death in 1894 he never remarried. Perhaps his greatest virtue and the most convincing testimony to his insight was that, unlike many of his contemporaries and successors, he knew that folly is often indistinguishable from evil and that one does not build up a great business by killing off the customers. So he set his face steadily against preservatives, additives, and adulterants, and he held up Dr. Wiley's arms in the Pure Food fight so enthusiastically that many other processers regarded him as a traitor to his class. As late as 1924 Wiley declared that he thought he would have lost the battle without Heinz's backing.

During his later years, Heinz was more interested in his collecting, social service activities in Pittsburgh, worldwide Sunday School work, and traveling than he was in business. His collections included antique watches, European pottery and porcelain, Chinese temple paintings, jades and crystals, old Bibles, and many other things—some valuable in themselves, others only to him because of his interest in them. After his death, his heirs hoped that his conservatory and the land adjoining would be accepted by the city of Pittsburgh as Heinz Park, but the necessary vision was lacking. Finally the conservatory, the new Oriental Museum, and the Heinz mansion were razed, and Heinz's collections sold at auction—a familiar American story.

Ginger ale began to be bottled in America in the 1880s, and Hires Root Beer was featured at the Philadelphia Centennial Exposition, but the former was never identified with any one particular brand name, and for many years the latter was promoted mainly for home brewing and bottling. The first batch of Coca-Cola syrup was cooked up by John S. Pemberton, a wholesale druggist and chemist, in the backyard of a house on Marietta Street in Atlanta in the spring of 1886, placed on sale at the soda fountain in Jacobs' Pharmacy, and first advertised in the Atlanta *Daily Journal* on May 29. When Pemberton died in 1888, Asa G. Candler acquired rights to the product and did well enough so that in 1890 he sold out his other interests to devote himself entirely to the promotion of the new drink. The company was incorporated in 1892, but before 1894 the product was sold only at fountains. Many branch offices were opened between 1894 and 1898, when the Coca-Cola Company built its own first building in Atlanta. Candler remained head of the firm until 1916, when he resigned, having accumulated a fortune of 50 million dollars; thereafter he became mayor of Atlanta and the great benefactor of Emory University.

The first bottler was Joseph A. Biedenharn of Vicksburg, Mississippi; by 1909 there were 379 bottling plants. In 1919 the company was sold for 25 million dollars to a syndicate of three banks, with Ernest Woodruff as president, and it was his son, Robert Winship Woodruff, who not only developed a national sales organization but made Coca-Cola an international beverage. Woodruff began extensive advertising, developed coolers, coin-operated vending machines, premix machines, and other devices, and contributed heavily to education, research, and medicine. "Coca-Cola" in its Spencerian script form; "Coke," which the company accepted reluctantly, under pressure from informal usage, in 1933; and the hobble-shaped vending bottle are all registered trademarks, though the exclusive right to the "Cola" part of the name was lost in 1942.

The drink has been officially described as composed of sterilized water (the use of carbonated rather than ordinary water is said to have originated in the inspired blunder of a fountain clerk), granulated sugar, flavoring extracts and caramel, caffeine, and citric and phosphoric acids, and as containing "the tonic properties of the wonderful coca plant and the famous cola nut." Other analysts have found or conjectured other elements; including chocolate, cinnamon, and even glycerin, and there has been much talk about a "secret ingredient."

Originally Coca-Cola was thought of as a tonic, a patent medicine or proprietary elixir, and until 1901 was even, at times, taxed as such. At various times it was called a "specific for headache," a "nerve and brain tonic," a "remarkable therapeutic agent," and "the favorite drink for ladies when thirsty, weary, and despondent." It has also been recommended for biliousness and indigestion. This kind of advertising was toned down or abandoned after the passage of the Pure Food and Drug Act; indeed the company must have made up its mind to promote the drinking of their product as a pleasure rather than a duty as early as 1902, for in that year they sued the government for the taxes they had paid on Coca-Cola as a medicine and won the suit. But "The Pause That Refreshes" has remained the most familiar and perhaps the most effective of Coca-Cola's advertising slogans.

Alongside the medicinal claims made in behalf of Coca-Cola, there has also been much discussion of its allegedly harmful effects. The most serious of these charges was that the drink contained cocaine, and since the untreated "Erythroxylon Coca plant" that Pemberton's formula called for does contain a minute amount of cocaine, this was not quite made up out of whole cloth. The fact was reported to Candler by a research chemist whom he employed to analyze the drink about 1900, after which the coca leaf was treated so that by 1905 all traces of the drug were supposed to have been removed. Controversy as to how much caffeine is contained in Coca-Cola and whether or not this is harmful has continued, however, and by 1963 the company had become sufficiently mindful of the weight-watchers and of the claim of a competitor that their product was a lighter, smarter, and younger drink to produce the sugarless Tab. But the current war on saccharin and other artificial sweeteners can hardly be expected to help Tab, and there are people who find all drinks containing carbonated water hard on the stomach.

The most determined enemy of the Coca-Cola people was Dr. Harvey W. Wiley, who considered them "dope peddlers" and "poisoners" and who moved against them in 1909 under the Pure Food Act, accusing them of adulteration and false advertising and charging that they added caffeine to their product and had no right to their name since the drink contained no coca and very little cola. The case dragged on for many years, involved the Supreme Court, and was finally settled by a compromise.

The Coca-Cola people have been involved in a great deal of other litigation, generally in the interest of protecting their name. They took the Koke Company to court in 1909 and won their suit in 1920, when Supreme Court Justice Oliver Wendell Holmes defined Coca-Cola as a "single thing coming from a single source and well known to the community," but they were not so fortunate with Pepsi-Cola, which was developed by a North Carolina pharmacist, Caleb Bradham, in 1898 and its trademark registered in 1903. Twice bankrupt, Pepsi-Cola gave Coca-Cola no serious trouble for many years, and the Coca-Cola interests made two serious mistakes in connection with it. They might have bought their rivals out for a song when the latter were in financial difficulties but refused to do so, and when Coca-Cola refused to sell syrup at a reduced price to the fountains in the Loft's candy stores, Loft's acquired Pepsi-Cola, dispensed it in all their stores, and built it up into Coca-Cola's most formidable competitor.

In the early 1900s the Coca-Cola Company also briefly manufactured cigars, razor blades, and chewing gum. The first two items were never important (Gillette had first marketed the double-edged safety blade in 1903), but the chewing gum was manufactured from about 1908 until 1916. Coca-Cola's heavy advertising began between 1902 and 1904. In 1908 there was a pioneer animated sign on the main line of the Penn railroad between Philadelphia and New York, the next year a dirigible with "Coca-Cola" painted on it flew over Washington, and the Associated Advertising Clubs of America called the beverage "the best advertised article in America." Madame Nordica posed for the 1903 calendar; later, movie stars were used both here and in other forms of advertising. But Coca-Cola's most enchanting girls, often, after 1921, in bathing suits but always, in advertising issued by the company itself, in excellent taste, have certainly brightened the American landscape, and in 1931 Haddon Sundblom began painting what is probably the jolliest and most lovable Santa Claus that has ever been seen.

The company is one of the heaviest of all advertisers, spending between 70 and 100 millions a year, and their contribution to advertising art is second in importance only to their product. The extraordinary variety of the advertising devices they have employed has made them very important to collectors. Undoubtedly the prize item is the Tiffany-type Coca-Cola chandelier, dating from about 1905; this sometimes brings as much as $2,000.

The most amazing among the stories we have to deal with in this chapter is that of the development of ready-to-eat breakfast foods. Around the middle of the nineteenth century, Mrs. Ellen Gould Harmon White (1827–1915), the dynamic and dictatorial leader of the Seventh-Day Adventists, made Battle Creek, Michigan, the Adventist world capital. Mrs. White had a private line to the Almighty; she experienced some 2,000 visions and revelations in the course of her life and published more than fifty books. But whatever may be thought of her peculiar religious tenets, her notions about healthful eating habits, child-centered education, slavery (Battle Creek was an important station on the Underground Rail-

road), temperance, and peace were of value. Adventists are vege-
tarians, and they are as much convinced that sensible eating is
part of the Lord's business as Christian Scientists are of His interest
in healing. Here of course is the point at which Adventism ties up
with the food industry, though in later years there was estrangement between Mrs. White and her allies, the Kelloggs. This was
partly ideational (Dr. John Harvey Kellogg had not only expressed
heretical ideas but had also shown himself restive under denominational control) and partly a power struggle. In 1903 the church
headquarters were removed to Takoma Park, a suburb of Washington, and both Dr. Kellogg and his brother W. K. Kellogg were
dropped from membership.

It is not surprising that the Battle Creek atmosphere should also
have attracted mesmerists, phrenologists, spiritualists, theosophists,
New Thoughters, antivivisectionists, hydropathists, Bloomerites,
and what-have-you. Bernarr Macfadden was there for a time, manufacturing a breakfast food called Strengtho (which turned rancid)
and presiding over the Macfadden Health Home, which stressed
massage, deep breathing, and the posing of "Living Statues" on
Friday nights by the proprietor, but his Battle Creek enterprise collapsed in 1907, when he was convicted for having published what
the Post Office considered an obscene article in *Physical Culture.*

Cooked oatmeal had become America's favorite breakfast cereal
in the 1870s, and Dr. Kellogg's basic idea was to "displace the half-
cooked, pasty, dyspepsia-producing breakfast mush" by applying
dry heat to the cereal grains before they reached the breakfast table.
His was neither the first nor the only prepared breakfast food,
however; W. K. Kellogg counted forty-four breakfast food concerns
in Battle Creek alone during the early 1900s and six firms making
health drinks. Dr. Kellogg seems himself to have devised some
eighty food products. He also established the Battle Creek Sanitarium, which Gerald Carson describes as a kind of combination
"medical boarding-house, hospital, religious retreat, country club,
tent Chautauqua, [and] spa" and which flourished from the early
1900s until it went bankrupt in 1933. There was a Battle Creek
College to train nurses, therapists, and dieticians, and from 1893
to 1908, when it was absorbed into the University of Illinois, there
was even a medical school in Chicago. Dr. Kellogg was a skilled
surgeon, who maintained sound medical standing. He displayed
an appetite for power, however, and his relations with his younger

brother do not add to the charm of either man. But the scientific aspects of his work always interested him far more than the commercial, and Kellogg's Corn Flakes never became a great commercial success until WK had taken it over.

Shredded Wheat had been developed by Henry D. Perky at Denver in the 1880s. Following brief stops at Boston and Worcester, it was located in a model factory at Niagara Falls. As the Coca-Cola Company missed their chance to buy out Pepsi-Cola, so Dr. Kellogg lived to regret that he did not buy Shredded Wheat when he had the chance (in years to come the Kellogg Company would win the right to manufacture their own shredded wheat as a competing product, but that was only after litigation and after they had lost their own suit against Quaker Oats to prevent that company from making corn flakes). Dr. Kellogg's own first experiments with flakes had been made not with corn but with wheat, but the first considerable sale of wheat flakes was not his but that of the Battle Creek Pure Food Company's Malta Vita, whose business collapsed when the product became moldy. Another wheat flake was Force, made by Edward Ellsworth at Buffalo and exploited with pictures of a Yankee Doodle–like character called Sunny Jim, who went through many adventures in the newspaper and magazine advertisements. If you were a child, you could even get Sunny Jim stamped in brilliant colors on cloth, so that your mother could cut him out, sew him together, and stuff him with cotton for you to play with, along with Aunt Jemima and Uncle Jerry, and their pickaninnies and similar treasures. The Kelloggs' first successful corn flake was achieved in 1902, with a secret formula for malt flavoring, but by this time they were facing serious competition from Charles W. Post.

Post had come to Battle Creek as a patient in 1891, after a somewhat rough and rugged career. When the sanitarium failed to cure him, he withdrew, studied Christian Science and other forms of mental and spiritual healing, and after Dr. Kellogg had refused to join him in promoting a health drink called Minute Brew, established himself at La Vita Inn in Battle Creek, where, as he said, he "simply treated patients by mental therapeutics." At the beginning of 1895 he began to market Postum Cereal Food Coffee, which had "the deep seal brown of coffee and a flavor very like the melded brands of Java." This was followed in 1898 by Grape Nuts and in 1906 by the corn flakes that Post first called Elijah's Manna, and then, because he could not register a biblical trade name in England, Post Toasties. In 1901 he cleared nearly a million dollars and became a mighty builder in Battle Creek. In the early days Post Toasties was a heavier flake than Kellogg's and resisted sogginess in milk rather better. In 1906 Post began expanding into land operations, hotel building, and other activities in Texas. He also became an art collector and maintained homes from Washington to Santa Barbara.

In 1906 the Kellogg corn flake business was placed in charge of the younger brother WK, who made his attractive package, decorated with a picture of "The Sweetheart of the Corn," as posed by a Kellogg stenographer, Fanny Bryant ("None genuine without this signature—W. K. Kellogg") familiar to every human being in America. This did not end the rivalry between the brothers, however, and it was not until 1911 that Dr. Kellogg, after litigation, was wholly eliminated from the company.

Dr. Wiley, the great enemy of Coca-Cola, was not precisely enthusiastic about prepared breakfast foods either; he tended to feel that the only advantage of flaking and rolling was that a large bulk could be filled with light weight (it was the exact opposite of the condensed soup operation) and that "while there may be no intention of deception, there exists the general impression of receiving more than one gets." The manufacturers came triumphantly through all tests for suspected adulteration, but in the early days there was some false advertising. Apeteizo, for example, was a "physiologic food" that was supposed to make red blood (all I remember of it is that it was advertised with a little picture of a boy's armored head, which, for some reason, I found enchanting and which, since I was too little to say Apeteizo, I called "The Dady Boy"), and whatever may legitimately be said against coffee drinking, Post's talk about "coffee neuralgia" and coffee as a cause of blindness was hardly scientific. Grape Nuts too was supposed to be a good brain food and to cure consumption, malaria, and even an inflamed appendix! "There a Reason" proclaimed the package, a cryptic utterance which, so far as I was concerned, quite backfired. Grape Nuts was then a hard, crisp, chewy substance, and it was marketed in very small packages. If there was a reason why you should eat only a little of it, which was what they seemed to be saying, my childish mind drew the conclusion that it must be a very dangerous food; perhaps it might be safer still not to eat it at all! Despite any disadvantages, however, convenience, palatability, intensive advertising, and a variety of premiums appealing especially to the younger fry enabled the new foods to carry all before them, though, as for me, they never wholly succeeded in ousting from my affections the cooked cereal called Pettijohn's, which I loved both for its flavor and for the picture of the bear on the package.

So far as the great figures were concerned however, triumph was not wholly unmixed with tragedy. Both the Kelloggs went into their ninety-second year, but, as we have already seen, Dr. Kellogg lost his pet enterprise, the sanitarium, and WK lost his eyesight, a calamity that interfered surprisingly little with his conduct of affairs. He gave 50 million dollars to the establishment of the Kellogg Foundation, which has been important especially in medical research, and he is said to have expended some three millions more in unrecorded gifts to persons in need. C. W. Post's second wife, who long outlived him, also carried out many benefactions after his death, but Post's own fate was the saddest of all. His interest in healing and in health foods proceeded originally from his need to heal himself, and in this he at last failed utterly. In 1914, his health finally wrecked, he was overcome by melancholia and took his own life at the age of sixty. Eleven years later his firm joined Jell-O in what was to become the General Foods Corporation.

There has been nobody named Campbell associated with the Campbell Soup Company since 1894, and that was three years before the formula for condensed soup was devised. When Joseph Campbell formed his partnership with Abram Anderson in 1869 at Camden, New Jersey, where the Campbell Company still has its headquarters, they were interested in canning vegetables, preserves, salad dressing, and ketchup. The first successful canning process had been developed in 1809 by François Appert, who used glass jars sealed with cork. In 1810 Peter Durand patented the first "tin can," actually an iron can coated with tin. But cans had to be made by hand until about 1850, and until the early 1900s a hole was left in the top for filling, after which a cap was soldered on, and long after that, mass production still waited on the development of the retort, the continuous cooker, and other devices.

The Campbell Company began the production of canned soup in 1897 after achieving condensation through reducing bulk by largely eliminating the water content of the materials and thus making storage and shipping more practicable. The famous red and white label, said to have been borrowed from the Cornell colors, was adopted in 1898, and the gold medallion was added after a medal had been won at the Paris exposition in 1900. In 1899 the first Campbell advertisements appeared in New York streetcars, and the first magazine ad, in *Good Housekeeping* in 1905, proclaimed "21 Kinds of Campbell's Soups—16 million cans sold in 1904." That was a banner year on more than one count. The first cans of Campbell's Pork and Beans were sold then, and Grace Debbie Drayton created the chubby "Campbell Kids" who have been helping to market the Campbell products ever since.

Whether "21 Kinds" had actually been developed as early as 1905 I cannot say; certainly for many years a great many Americans thought of Campbell's primarily in connection with tomato soup, with vegetable soup as a bad second, and even today, when the company boasts over 400 varieties of food—soups, juices, bean and pasta products, frozen foods, baked goods, candies, desserts, snack and cracker items, and pet foods—the tomato is still king, and much of the firm's effort still centers around it. Improved varieties, more tasty, more resistant to disease, and better adapted to climatic conditions in the various areas where they are grown, have been developed, and recent experimenters have even created a hothouse effect out of doors by covering the beds with a veil of plastic. Highlights beyond our period have included the introduction of tomato juice in 1932, the acquisition of "V-8" vegetable cocktail in 1948, the entry into the frozen food market in 1955, and the production of "Chunky" ready-to-serve soups in 1970, to say nothing of Franco-American, Pepperidge Farm, and other products. Sales first hit the hundred million mark in 1942, were five times that in 1958, reached a billion in 1971 and a billion and a half in 1975. The company has been importantly involved in urban renewal and rehabilitation projects in Camden and has shown concern for ecological considerations; it has also taken an interest in and contributed to vocational education. Nor should one fail to mention the establishment in 1970 of the Campbell Museum, whose magnificent collection of silver and ceramic soup tureens and related utensils has been shown at leading museums.

Ship biscuits or hardtack were baked at Newburyport, Massachusetts, as early as 1792, and what we call crackers at Milton from the beginning of the nineteenth century. By the 1840s several kinds of crackers or biscuits were being made, all being retailed from open barrels in general stores, along with raisins, prunes, pickles, molasses, sugar, and many other products including kerosene; even paper bags were not widely used before the Civil War.

Adolphus W. Green, the man who was to change all this, was born in Boston of Irish Catholic ancestry in 1843. Having attended Boston Latin School and Harvard University, he removed to New York and, after a time, became a lawyer. After the great fire of 1871 he came to Chicago, where he was soon associating with the leading merchants and civic leaders of the rapidly growing, rebuilt city.

The New York Biscuit Company, organized in Chicago in 1890, brought together twenty-three bakeries in ten eastern states. That same year, Green organized a number of midwestern firms into the American Biscuit and Manufacturing Company. A price war followed, in the course of which American even invaded enemy country by building a factory in New York City, but in 1898, under Green's leadership, the two rivals united to form the National Biscuit Company (NBC). The packer Philip D. Armour and Frank O. Lowden, future governor of Illinois, were important in effecting the merger, which the Chicago *Tribune* described as "the biggest financial deal in Chicago's history."

Planning concentration on the soda cracker, Green closed down thirty-one bakeries the first year and dropped many products. Hundreds of brand names were considered, including some as farfetched as Pherenice, Veronese, and Trim (out of *Tristram Shandy*), but in December "Uneeda Biscuit" was registered with the Patent Office.

Frank M. Peters designed the "In-Er-Seal" waxed paper wrapper to keep the crackers fresh. The device, involving a double cross intersecting with an oval within which "In-Er Seal" was printed and which became the company's first trademark, was derived from an old Venetian printer's mark, and the design for the package, which was purple with white lettering, the name Uneeda Biscuit being printed in purple letters within a white panel, came from a sixteenth-century Grolier volume. Frederic Goudy, a young Chicago artist on his way to becoming one of the leading type designers of the world, lettered the words "National Biscuit Company."

Green insisted that Uneeda Biscuit must sell for five cents and that the package must be small enough so that the family would empty it before the crackers had a chance to become stale or soggy. This meant a very slim margin of profit, for which he hoped to make up through mass sales. He planned to sell direct to retailers without the intermediary of jobbers, and this necessitated covering the country with brightly colored, easily identifiable delivery wagons. The ultimate goal was to have no town in America more than an overnight trip from the nearest company bakery, and goods that had been allowed to get stale on the shelves were always removed and destroyed. During its first decade the company spent 7 million dollars on advertising, and its outdoor signs were kept as fresh as its product. Gordon Stiles, the five-year-old nephew of an advertising writer, posed for the picture of the yellow slicker–clad boy clutching a package of Uneeda Biscuit that became universally familiar. By 1900 10 million packages a month were being sold, and in 1907 company profits were 4 million dollars. By that time the firm had begun moving to New York, where their complex was the biggest baking center in the world and where a visitors' center was established as part of the exploitation process.

Of course NBC was more than Uneeda Biscuit, though Green was always careful not to scatter his energies too widely. Not only did he drop many products that the bakeries he absorbed had turned out, but new products that failed to catch on had a very short life. Nevertheless, by 1908 there were about forty-four varieties, including Fig Newtons, a cookie filled with a fig jam preserve; ZuZu Ginger Snaps; sugar wafers known as Nabiscos; Graham crackers; Premium soda crackers or Saltines; a sweet biscuit called Social Tea Biscuit; oyster crackers, which, like Uneeda Biscuit, had a distinctive shape of their own and a name, Oysterettes; Animal Crackers for children, in a gay package representing a Barnum circus wagon; Arrowroot crackers; Zwieback; and others added beyond our period. The name "Nabisco" had an interesting history. It had originally been suggested for Uneeda Biscuits themselves, but its first actual use was for sugar wafers. Later when the company was obliged to share the key letters NBC, which it had been using in its trademark to identify all its products, with the National Broadcasting Company, it dropped NBC and tagged all its products "Nabisco," thus depriving the sugar wafers of any distinctive name of their own. It was the ZuZu Ginger Snaps that received the most colorful and imaginative advertising, however, in the form of pictures of brightly colored little clowns engaged in a variety of delightful activities and postures. When I was a child in Chicago, I did not like ginger snaps, but I adored the clowns, and their blossoming out in brilliant posters all over the platforms on the elevated was as inescapable a sign of spring as the blossoming of the yellow dandelions against the green grass and to me quite as welcome.

It must not be supposed that NBC did away with bulk sales. As late as 1922, two-thirds of their products were still being sold in bulk, not out of barrels, however, but from neat, clean, square metal containers with glass window panels. Nevertheless, the trend toward packaging had been established, and the service to sanitation was great, quite aside from the tremendous impetus it gave to the establishment of brand names.

Of course everything NBC did was imitated—name, trademark, packaging; by 1906 the company had won 249 infringement suits. In that year too the passage of the federal Pure Food and Drug Act cut its way through the conflicting morass of state food laws that until then had cruelly handicapped merchandising, leaving Green nothing to worry about but the continuing difficulty of bringing production into line with demand.

Personally Green was a martinet, fussy in matters of detail, who insisted on keeping every aspect of the business under his personal control. Noted for his integrity, decency, and stability, he created sanitary working conditions, refused to employ child labor, encouraged stock purchases by employees, and served them a hot lunch for eleven cents, but none of this meant high wages or toleration for newfangled ideas about unions. Two bakers defected as early as 1903 to form the Loose-Wiles firm, later Sunshine, which would give NBC sharp competition in later years, and there were many other defections before Green's death, at seventy-four, in 1917. In the post-Green era, Uneeda Biscuit itself would be deemphasized though not dropped, and many new products were introduced, including pretzels, dog food, ice cream cones, and much besides. NBC bought Cream of Wheat and Holland Rusk and established the National Bread Company as a subsidiary. As the thirties approached, the company found itself losing business to competitors who had taken up modern methods of merchandising with greater zeal but scored a tremendous success with a new salted cracker called Ritz, which still retains its popularity. There was a three-month strike in 1935, and a pretty general overhauling followed the inauguration of George H. Coppers as president in 1946.

The Hershey success story concerns the building not only of an industrial empire but of a pioneer planned community and cultural center. Milton S. Hershey was born near Hockersville, Pennsylvania, in 1857, of Swiss-German Mennonite stock. After an abortive attempt to work on a German-English newspaper, he was apprenticed to a confectioner in Lancaster, and in the year of the Centennial Exposition he tried unsuccessfully to make candy independently in Philadelphia. Further experiments followed in Denver, Chicago, and New York, where, in 1883, he was first employed by Huyler's and then opened a small shop on Sixth Avenue, which failed. His first break came through a candy importer who undertook to introduce his caramels to England, and by 1894 he was firmly established.

At the World's Columbian Exposition he had seen J. M. Lehmann's German chocolate-making machinery and made up his mind that he would make his own chocolate instead of buying it. His milk chocolate bar, almond bar, cocoa, and baking chocolate were all first sold in 1895, and in 1900 he disposed of his caramel factory and general candy business for one million dollars and, like Carnegie with steel, decided to put all his eggs into one basket. "Chocolate is a food as well as a confection. It ought to have a big future in the United States." With this in mind, he decided to build a factory in a cornfield in Derry Township (which was renamed Hershey), Dauphin County, on his native heath, and build a town around it. Ground was broken in March 1903, and production began late in 1904.

Though "Hershey bar" was to become almost a generic term for a milk chocolate bar, Milton Hershey did not originate either the form or the process; neither did he monopolize them. Chocolate had been brought to Spain from Mexico and the Caribbean by Columbus and Cortez but was thought too bitter to eat until sugar and vanilla had been added. It first became a favorite drink in Spain, from which it spread to other countries. Daniel Peter made milk chocolate bars in Switzerland in the 1870s, and Hershey, who had already learned how to add milk to caramels while he was in Denver, visited milk chocolate factories both there and in Germany; nevertheless, he did not hire or steal or borrow anybody else's formula but made, through experimentation, his own. Not all his milk chocolate went into bars, however, for the firm also turned out bulk chocolate, "kisses," syrup, and baking chips.

In building his town, Hershey steered clear of both standardization and regimentation, taking care to avoid the errors that George Pullman had made in Illinois. The houses he built were varied in style, and those who could afford it might buy their own. Moreover, transportation was provided so that nobody need live in Hershey if he preferred to locate elsewhere. New schools were built, churches were helped to pay off their mortgages; there was also a bank and what Hershey hoped would be a cooperative store.

His benevolences began in 1909, when he established what became the Milton Hershey School for orphaned (or semiorphaned) boys, and strictly speaking, this was the only one of his expanding activities that reached back to our period. The Hersheys had no children, and though they lived well, they had no taste for the extravagances that ate up the fortunes of many rich men. The school opened with four boys in the farmhouse where the founder was born and grew until it became a well-equipped institution for 1,100 boys, stressing vocational training, closeness to the soil, and nonsectarian religious instruction. Later, after buying a sugar mill in Cuba, Hershey repeated this enterprise, on a smaller scale, there.

Hershey died, at eighty-eight, in 1945, and the greatest Hershey benefaction did not begin until 1963, when the corporation gave 50 million dollars to Penn State University to establish a new medical center, which now has 300 students and assets of about 70 million. But Hershey himself had shown astonishing courage and vision during the Great Depression. The company had gone through a dangerous financial crisis in 1920, but in 1921 the net income was three million and the entire business was reorganized. Then, in 1930, he tried his hand at breaking the back of the Depression singlehanded by starting a great building enterprise—community building, luxury hotel, school, sports arena, stadium. "If I don't provide work for them I'll have to feed them," he declared. "And since building materials are now at their lowest cost levels, I'm going to build and give them jobs." He afterward pointed out that no jobs had been lost and no salaries cut in Hershey on account of the Depression.

Today the Hershey Chocolate Corporation has become the Hershey Foods Corporation, with nine divisions and annual sales of over 500 million dollars. No longer are all the eggs in one basket. In 1963 the H. B. Reese Candy Company, which made "The Original Peanut Butter Cup," was acquired, and there have been other varied acquisitions since. Hershey, Pennsylvania, has theater, music, and sports, hotel, motor lodge, and campgrounds. It is a convention center and a golf capital and the headquarters of the Antique

Automobile Club of America. There are a famous rose garden, an arboretum containing more than 120,000 plants of various kinds, a zoo, and an amusement park, which, like the Disney enterprises, emphasizes historical and cultural themes; there are also annual exhibitions of many aspects of Pennsylvania Dutch culture. And of recent years Hershey's Chocolate World, which can accommodate 18,000 visitors daily, has been exhibiting the whole process of chocolate making from the growing of the cocoa bean in the tropics to the production of the finished confection—or, perhaps Hershey would prefer to say, food.

1. Lyman Abbott, Clergyman

THE American religious community was sufficiently fragmented during Theodore Roosevelt's time to make it difficult to choose any one figure as in all respects representative, but none, surely, has a better claim than Lyman Abbott. He was TR's close friend too, though their most intimate association did not begin until after the end of Roosevelt's second administration, when the ex-president served for several years as contributing editor of Abbott's *Outlook*. When Abbott himself died, a leading religious journal would declare that "many a minister in England and America, hearing the news of his translation, must have felt as the young prophet felt when Elijah was taken away: 'My father, my father, the chariots of Israel and the horsemen thereof!' "

Lyman Abbott was born at Roxbury, Massachusetts, on December 18, 1835. Graduating from New York University in 1853, he was admitted to the bar, but under the influence of Henry Ward Beecher and the Revival of 1858, he decided to become a clergyman and served his first charge at Terre Haute, Indiana, during the Civil War.

After his return to the East, he began, in 1870, to supply the Presbyterian church at Cornwall-on-Hudson, where he had established his residence, and in 1876 became Beecher's second-in-command on the *Christian Union*, which in 1893 was renamed the *Outlook* and

Representative Figures
of the Time: Second Series

9

which he would mold into one of the most influential journals of its time.

When Beecher died in 1887, Abbott succeeded him in the Plymouth pulpit, first as stated supply, then as temporary pastor, and finally in full charge. Until his resignation in 1898 he preached to between 1,500 and 2,000 persons every Sunday. Thereafter he carried on his ministry through his books, his contributions to the *Outlook,* much preaching, especially on college campuses, and innumerable "letters to unknown friends." It is interesting that during the years when his influence was at its height he had no pulpit of his own. He died in New York on October 22, 1922.

The irregularity was, in a sense, characteristic of him. He was a self-trained clergyman who made his own theological seminary. He once remarked of his associate on the *Outlook,* Hamilton Wright Mabie, that "he thought more highly of the institutions of religion than I do and attached more value to its historic creeds." Religion itself he thought of as the "life of God in the soul of man"; theology, which was merely "what men have thought about that life," interested him much less. When a friend told him that he was not an orthodox Trinitarian but a "Modalistic Monarchian," he was not frightened, but neither was he greatly interested or impressed. His God was not "a great first cause" but "an eternal and perpetual cause," but he still insisted that what Herbert Spencer had described as the Infinite and Eternal Energy from which all things proceed was "an energy that thinks, and feels, that purposes and does; and is thinking and feeling and purposing and doing as a conscious life, of which ours is but a poor and broken reflection." His Christ was "the image of God, the reflection of God, God manifest in the flesh; that is, such a manifestation of God as is possible in human life."

The author of *The Theology of an Evolutionist,* Abbott is usually thought of first of all in connection with his service in bridging the gulf between the old faith and the new science, and his efforts in this direction were very important. Nobody will ever know how many of his contemporaries he assisted to readjust and thus retain their faith. But to think of him only in this connection would be grossly inadequate. John Fiske too did that, and Fiske was not an evangelical Christian. Abbott, for all the headshaking he sometimes inspired among the conservative brethren, was. He rejected both naturalism and Unitarianism, and if he saw religion in terms of growth, he also regarded it as a gift. Though he neither affirmed nor denied the Virgin Birth, he believed in Inspiration, Incarnation, Atonement, and Regeneration. The Bible he accepted as *a* but not the only Word of God, agreeing with the Quakers that its teachings must be checked against the criterion of the believer's spiritual consciousness, which, like the Bible itself, derives from God, "who is not an embalmed God, in a dead book." He rejected both the substitutionary and the governmental theories of the Atonement: Christ came to save men from sin, not merely to remit the punishment for sin, and his death changed man, not God. As to the supernaturalism in the Bible, Abbott's tendency was to consider each miracle recorded on its own merits, but the only one that was very important to him, apparently because it occurred against the expectation of Christ's followers and became the rock on which the church was built, was the Resurrection, which he accepted, without attempting to define its nature exactly, as one of the best-attested facts in ancient history. Faith in immortality was very important to him, and *The Other Room* (1903) was by all means his best-selling book. Declining to set boundaries to God's mercy, in this world or another, he was sure all men were "elected" to salvation, but he stopped short of dogmatically asserting universal salvation because he could not be sure that all would ratify their election. If any were to be left out of God's Kingdom at last, he thought annihilation preferable to eternal punishment. "I could endure the thought of endless suffering, but not of sin growing ever deeper, darker, more awful." Since he agreed with St. Augustine that there were Christians before Christ, he regarded such questions as whether or not the "heathen" were "saved" as so much barbarous nonsense. But even eternal life was primarily significant to him not for its extent but for its quality; the regenerated Christian enters upon his immortality here and now. "The Christian religion consists in such a perception of the Infinite as manifested in the life and character of Jesus Christ, that the perception is able to promote in man Christ-likeness of character."

In his maturity, Abbott gave the impression of complete self-possession and inner certitude, but this was a conquest, not an inheritance. He was a lean, birdlike man who had been a frail child, and he inherited a nervous, if not neurotic, temperament. Though he did an immense amount of work, he was always obliged to husband his resources carefully, resting or recreating in the afternoon and retiring early. Moreover, he made careful choice of what he would do, choosing that which interested him and called forth his powers, and he had the great good fortune of being married to a woman who lifted from his shoulders all the domestic burdens he did not understand. Indeed, he was in all respects what Chaucer called "a man of greet auctoritee," and though nobody has suggested that he was hard to work with, both the sons who were associated with him on the *Outlook* testified that they never resisted him in anything for the simple reason that it never occurred to them. Nor was he in the least overawed by Theodore Roosevelt, much as he admired him, when the ex-president joined the *Outlook* staff.

Abbott was not, nor did he ever pretend to be, a scholar; in later years he said that he would not now be able to enter the freshman class of the college from which he had graduated with honors. He dabbled in a number of languages but read none but his own with ease. For one who respected the claims of science as much as he did, he had surprisingly little interest in it. He read widely in several literatures, but outside of fiction and biography, he says he seldom read a book through. He thought Browning England's greatest poet since Shakespeare, and, oddly for a religious leader, he enjoyed Wordsworth and Byron more than Dante or Milton. Scott and Dickens he loved, and he himself wrote one novel and joined in the writing of two more. Except for this, music was the only art he ever practiced, and he seems to have played both the organ and the piano reasonably well. I should think that, though he published a pamphlet on *Parsifal,* he was probably indifferent to opera; Jenny Lind is the only singer he mentions, and this is in connection with oratorio. Indeed he did not even care for program music: "Music is the interpretation of a life which can never be interpreted in any other way. If the printed program tells you what the music means, . . . you have second-class music." For that matter, he did not care much for imitation in any art: "a man who can simply portray a falling leaf or a silk dress . . . is a skilled artisan and nothing more." In early life he seems greatly to have enjoyed the theater; when his interest in religion deepened, he turnd for a time toward the extreme Puritan suspicion of dramatic art, but this was soon outgrown, and though he always tended to approach the theater rather gingerly, he probably shocked some of his admirers by the prominence he gave Barnum and Edwin Booth, late in life, in his *Silhouettes of My Contemporaries.*

No prima donna ever nursed her high C's more carefully than Abbott prepared for his platform appearances. To secure complete concentration he slept in his study on Saturday nights, and his family did not see him on Sunday morning until they went to church. He regarded Henry Ward Beecher as the greatest preacher he ever heard—"a man to whom I owe the greatest debt one soul can owe to another—the debt of love for spiritual nurture"—but he never imitated Beecher's florid, oratorical style. When he preached on college campuses, he would arrive a day or two beforehand and spend the time conferring with students and faculty to learn "what are the conditions of college life . . . that the sermon may be adapted to the present needs." Afterward he would hold group conferences and talk individually with anyone who wished to consult him. Though he generally avoided direct exhortation—the effective application, he thought, was the one the listener made to himself—he distinguished sharply between sermon and essay. Thus his sermons were begotten and born between preacher and congregation, and unless they met the needs of his listeners, so far as he was concerned, they were nought.

This kind of thing was what Abbott really meant by the "pastoral work" he said he preferred even to preaching. Of the kind of pastoral work most pastors have to do he seems to have done very little, for there are stories about his being so preoccupied that he failed to notice visitors in his own house until Mrs. Abbott would say, "Lyman, here is Mrs. ——— come to visit us." His books sold between five and ten thousand each, and the circulation of the *Outlook*, at its height, was 125,000; one observer thought that he had more influence than the combined faculty of any theological seminary in the land. How many thousands of letters he wrote in reply to requests for counsel I have no idea, but the number must have been very large, for nobody seems to have had any hesitation about approaching him, and he encouraged them by replying in detail.

Though Abbott was less distinguished as an exponent of the Social Gospel than Washington Gladden, he was well aware that Christianity demanded a social as well as a personal application. His politics and his economics were as pragmatic as his theology; he always opposed *laissez faire* economics and was a broad constructionist of the Constitution. He considered himself an independent rather than a party man, and he supported Roosevelt in 1912, thus dealing the *Outlook* a body blow, particularly in New England where it had been particularly strong, from which it never really recovered. Otherwise, he was far more Republican than Democratic, making little of any one of the three great Democratic leaders of his time—Cleveland, Bryan, and Wilson. He did not support Gladden in the "tainted money" controversy, and he was comparatively cool toward the "muckrakers." He did not give much support to the Pullman strikers, though he realized that their employers had provoked their excesses; neither did he speak out, as Howells did, in defense of the Chicago anarchists. On the other hand, he advocated much that the Republican Bourbons opposed, including some things they have not accepted to this day. Though he preferred to have private enterprise do what it could, he believed that the state "should assume the administration of those industries, the organization and uniform direction of which are important, if not essential, to its welfare." At one time or another he advocated the direct primary, tariff reduction, civil service reform, the income tax, and the establishment of a national board of arbitration. He also believed that income from investments should be more heavily taxed than wages. The materialistic, deterministic side of socialism repelled him. Though he recognized the power of circumstances, he was like Roosevelt in that the Puritan–Protestant tradition was too important to him for him to be able even to seem to deny that man was morally responsible for his own destiny; moreover, he feared that socialism would achieve nothing save a change in mastership while still leaving society divided. Himself he proposed to steer a path between Scylla and Charybdis by setting up a system of "industrial democracy" under which the "tool users" would themselves become the "tool owners," thus developing an economically classless society.

Like most good men in his time, he was inclined to be timid about sex, and he comes closer to biblical literalism in what he wrote about marriage and divorce than he does anywhere else. He displeased many church people by not coming out for national prohibition, but he had no objection to prohibition on the local level, and the liquor interests cannot have derived much satisfaction from anything he wrote about their concerns. Personally I feel that his most serious shortcoming as a Christian leader manifested itself in connection with the issues of war and peace, and it may well be that this was due to his weakness in philosophy. He is quite unsatisfactory on the relationship between God and nature, both identifying the two and distinguishing between them, and he never really faces up to the problem of evil. "I have no solution to the problem of evil," he says: "the why and wherefore of it. A much more important question seems to me to be this: How shall I meet the evil that comes into my world and get good out of it for myself and for others?" From a commonsense point of view, this is excellent practical advice, but it hardly argues philosophical depth.

Early in life, Abbott thought that the Civil War had taught him that justice is better than peace, and he never really changed his mind about this. Since war does not secure justice, what he poses is of course a false alternative, suggesting Theodore Roosevelt's famous "If I must choose between righteousness and peace, I choose righteousness," which begs the whole question of the ethical standing ground of war itself. It is true that once the Civil War was over, Abbott stood for conciliation, and from then until nearly the end of the century his record is fairly clear. He was conciliatory during both the Chilean and the Venezuelan crises, but on March 13, 1898, he came out for war with Spain and was hailed by Hearst as an ally! Between then and World War I, his utterances, though uneven, seemed weighted more toward peace than war; when he reviewed Senator Hoar's autobiography, he even found it impossible to decide whether Hoar or McKinley had been right in 1898 and referred the question to the future. He condemned British imperialism, favored the return of the Boxer indemnity, and wanted a world court to arbitrate even disputes involving "national honor," yet he supported "preparedness," defended Oriental exclusion laws, and stood behind Wilson's bungling intervention in Mexico, even suggesting that we might occupy the country for two or three generations until we had trained the natives in self-government! When World War I came, he jettisoned neutrality at an early stage, though as late as March 19, 1916, the *Outlook* declared against America's entering the war "because we do not believe that this would be the best thing she could do to promote the cause of liberty and justice which we have at heart." Abbott appeared in J. Stuart Blackton's notorious propaganda film, *The Battle Cry of Peace*, and once we had entered the war, it became a holy crusade in which Christ himself was the commander. Now the use of force became legitimate for men of good will; indeed, Jesus himself might have led an armed revolution in Palestine had such action been practicable in his time! The war, for that matter, was not a war but a *posse comitatus* against a band of brigands, and Christ's prayer upon the cross for his enemies did not apply to the Germans, who knew only too well what they were doing. From here it was only a step to defending such rape of American liberties as was committed by those who supported the Espionage and Sedition Acts and such imbecilities as banning German music, while as for the League of Nations, the *Outlook* first supported it, then shifted its support to a world court.

2. Booker T. Washington, Educator

In TR's America, Booker Taliaferro Washington's was one of the great American success stories; he was by all means the most distinguished and influential Negro before Martin Luther King, Jr. He was born a slave near Hale's Ford, Franklin County, Virginia, on April 4, 1856. His father was a white man on a neighboring plantation, with whom neither he nor his elder brother ever had any contact. His mother was the cook on a plantation where the slaves were not abused, but her home was a small log cabin with a dirt floor, which had no glass in what passed for windows and where the door did not close properly even in winter. As a child he wore only a flax shirt, slept in a bundle of filthy rags on the ground, and had no schooling. After emancipation, the black man whom his mother had by this time married sent for the family to come to him at Malden, West Virginia, and they made the three-week journey on foot, sleeping largely in the open. In Malden the children went to work in the salt and coal mines, sometimes beginning as early as four o'clock in the morning.

Fascinated by the story of Moses, who had delivered his people from bondage, Booker determined to learn to read; somehow his mother, whom he revered and loved, got hold of a copy of Webster's blue-backed speller. There was a school for Negroes in Malden, but Booker's desire to go there had to contend against his stepfather's greed for the pittance he could earn in the mines, and much of his early schooling was given at night or by teachers who knew very little more than he did himself. He called himself Washington because he had learned that all the other children in school had a last name.

Finally he heard of Hampton Normal and Agricultural Institute in Virginia, which was presided over by General Samuel C. Armstrong, whom, as long as he lived, he considered the greatest man he had ever met. In the fall of 1872 he set out, traveling most of the 500 miles on foot. Because he was black, he could not get lodging even when he was able to pay for it; he never forgot sleeping under a wooden sidewalk. In Richmond he earned a little money by helping to unload a cargo of pig iron, but he arrived at Hampton with fifty cents in his pocket.

A percipient teacher accepted him and made him janitor, which covered much of the expense of his schooling. By various expedients, he secured clothing and the remainder. But he had to learn everything, not only book learning but the proper use of bathtub, toothbrush, sheets on the bed, tablecloth and napkins at meals. He read the Bible, learned how to address an audience, and graduated in 1875 as a commencement speaker. From here he went to teach a Negro school in Malden, where he opened night classes for those who had to work by day; he also set up a reading room and a debating society, taught in two Sunday schools, and did tutoring.

In the summer of 1879 Armstrong invited him to return to Hampton to teach and study. He took charge of the night school and became "house father" to a group of American Indians, now admitted to Hampton for the first time. Two years later, when he was asked to recommend a white man to take charge of a normal school for Negroes to be opened at Tuskegee, Alabama, Armstrong replied that he had no white man available and recommended Booker instead, who was accepted.

The sole asset of the Tuskegee school was an annual appropriation of $2,000 by the state legislature. The thirty students, many nearly forty years old, who appeared when it opened on July 1, 1881, met at first in a deserted old church and shanty, where an umbrella had to be held over the teacher's head when it rained. From the church Washington moved to a neighboring plantation with cabin, kitchen, stable, and henhouse, which he purchased for $500 of borrowed money.

What followed proved that the age of miracles is not past and will not be until there are no more wonder-workers among us. In the early days there were cold nights when a group of students sat around a single fire wrapped in one blanket. But by the time President McKinley visited in 1898, there were forty buildings (of which all but four had been erected by student labor) on 2,300 acres. In addition to academic and religious instruction, Tuskegee had

Theodore Roosevelt and Booker T. Washington at Tuskegee Institute.
Courtesy, Tuskegee Institute

twenty-eight industrial departments. There were 1,100 students and eighty-six officers and instructors. The property was valued at more than one million dollars. By the time Washington died in 1915, the annual budget was nearly three million dollars, the property value about a million and a half and the endowment two million.

Unlike Hampton's, Tuskegee's faculty was all black, and at least one member, the saintly plant wizard, George Washington Carver, was an undoubted genius. Carver became so famous that he could probably have had a position anywhere upon his own terms, but his loyalty to Tuskegee never wavered.

The institution's enterprises developed in response to need. Brick-making and carpentry were established because bricks and lumber were needed to build dormitories, cabinet- and mattress-making because they needed to be furnished. Printing, wheelwrighting and wagon-building, tinsmithing, metal-working, harness- and shoe-making, and much more followed. The Alabama legislature increased its appropriation. The Slater, Peabody, and other funds were drawn upon. John Wanamaker, Julius Rosenwald, Andrew Carnegie, Collis Huntington, Henry H. Rogers, the Phelps-Stokes family, and others were interested. In 1889 a fund-raising in Madison Square Garden was attended by J. P. Morgan, John D. Rockefeller, August Belmont, Jacob H. Schiff, Walter Hines Page, Carl Schurz, Nicholas Murray Butler, Lyman Abbott, and other influential persons. But what was done on campus was only a part of the Tuskegee achievement. The dispensary opened in 1902 became a $50,000 hospital. The National Negro Business League and National Negro Health Week, the Negro Rural School Fund, and the Movable School Farm Demonstration all fanned out from Tuskegee.

It was Washington's address to the National Education Association at Madison, Wisconsin, in 1884 that marked the beginning of his important career as a public speaker. He once traveled from Boston to Atlanta and back to speak for five minutes at an international meeting of Christian workers because he "knew that the audience would be largely composed of the most influential class of white men and women, and that it would be a rare opportunity for me to let them know what we were trying to do at Tuskegee, as well as to speak to them about the relations of the races." In the spring of 1885 he went to Washington with a company of influential Georgians to help persuade a congressional committee to provide funds for the Cotton States and International Exposition to be held at Atlanta in September, and this led to an invitation to speak at the opening of the exposition, where he created a sensation. His national reputation dates from this event; the next spring Harvard made him the first Negro to receive an honorary degree, and his autobiography, *Up from Slavery*, serialized in the *Outlook* in 1900 and published as a book in 1901, was read avidly, both here and abroad. On the very day he assumed the presidency, Theodore Roosevelt wrote Washington, inviting him to the White House to consult with him about southern and Negro problems; thereafter both TR and Taft habitually consulted him; on occasion he even reviewed speeches and messages in manuscript and suggested changes.

Washington was thrice married. His first wife was Fannie N. Smith, whom he married in the summer of 1882; she bore him one daughter and died in 1884. The second was Olivia Davidson, who married him in 1885 and died in 1889, soon after bearing her second son. In 1893 he was married to Margaret J. Murray, who outlived him. All three women labored as diligently and effectively for Tuskegee as he did himself. Late in October 1915, suffering from diabetes, arteriosclerosis, and nervous exhaustion, he collapsed in New York. By sheer strength of will, he returned to Tuskegee, where he arrived on the evening of November 13 and died the next morning.

Except for hunting, fishing, and riding, sports did not exist for Washington and games not at all. He liked everything connected with agriculture and found that an afternoon in the woods greatly refreshed him. When friends sent him and his wife to Europe for a much-needed rest, he made up his mind to enter no palace, gallery, or cathedral ("I find markets more instructive than museums"); what really interested him abroad were the Danish cooperatives. He supplied his children with good books and gave his daughter musical training in Europe, but Shakespeare and the Bible seem to have satisfied his own appetite for literature. He read biography and the newspaper avidly but disliked fiction.

The appeal of the Bible was of course primarily religious, and Washington and his family lived in an atmosphere of prayer and Bible reading. Theology did not interest him much, however, and forms and ceremonies not at all. He early resolved "that I would permit no man . . . to narrow and degrade my soul by making me hate him." Though he enjoyed the feeling of power that public speaking gave him, he refused to use his considerable gift for private gain, speaking only for Tuskegee and ploughing back everything he received into the work there.

There was certainly a simplistic element in Washington's personality. To be sure, his chapel talks on such subjects as "Helping Others," "Have You Done Your Best?" and "Keeping Your Word" struck just the right note for his hearers. But the same thing shows up elsewhere. It appears, for example, in his inability to use a name in *Up from Slavery*, even in the dedication, without putting a "Mr.," "Mrs.," or "Miss" in front of it; here evidently is a man who has not yet got quite used to being "mistered" himself. Washington's charity toward and understanding of his students was boundless, and though he could ship off a reject when necessary, his intuition for discerning promise in what anybody else must have regarded as hopeless material was very great and often brilliantly justified in the event. On the other hand, the rein he kept over his faculty was so tight that many regarded it as tyrannical, and the endless barrage of comments and criticisms to which he subjected everybody was old-womanish and picayune. Nothing was safe from his intrusion, and nothing got by; even such details as lukewarm coffee or stale flowers on the table drew instant, sometimes severe rebuke.

For all his skill in meeting people on their own ground, Washington was a perfectionist, and, oddly enough, what now seems his rather easy optimism reinforced this tendency. He tended to accept the faith of his time in automatic, irresistible progress. He was a good Republican also, remaining loyal to Taft in 1912, despite both his own close personal relations with Roosevelt and the dissatisfaction many Negroes felt with Taft's policies. Undoubtedly his conservatism helped him win support for Tuskegee. Partly because of their tendency to outlaw blacks, he was never friendly to labor unions; he had kind words for the rich, and his gracious acceptance of small gifts often drew out larger ones. He also participated in the rejoicing that followed the Spanish-American War, and I am not aware that he ever criticized America's burgeoning imperialism.

Such things as these help to explain why Washington is not a great hero to the Negroes of today. It is only fair to admit, however, that all criticisms are not of recent origin; some date back to the

Atlanta address. His most effective critic in his own time was the Massachusetts-born author of *The Souls of Black Folk,* W. E. Burghardt Du Bois, Harvard- and German-trained professor at Atlanta University. Intellectual, bitter, aloof, and painfully race-conscious, Du Bois was friendly toward Washington at the outset but soon came to feel that he was too conciliatory toward the South and toward white Americans in general and lukewarm on civil rights. Urban in his sympathies as against Washington's rural bias, and much less religious, Du Bois denied his senior's assumption of solidarity of interest between the white South and the black South, urged blacks to move north, and did not hesitate to pit the races against each other. Washington, he charged, had developed his "gospel of Work and Money to such an extent as apparently almost completely to overshadow the higher aims of life." Moreover, he dominated the Negro press and the appointment of Negroes to federal posts and exercised his jurisdiction over the allotment of federal funds to education to the disadvantage of the liberal arts colleges. The conferences Du Bois and others called at Harpers Ferry and Niagara Falls in 1905 and 1906 demanded complete abolition of all social, political, and industrial discrimination and led directly to the formation of the National Association for the Advancement of Colored People.

One can find apparent justification in Washington's utterances for Du Bois's charges. Take the Atlanta address alone:

No race can prosper till it learns that there is as much dignity in tilling a field as in writing a poem.

In all things that are purely social we can be as separate as the fingers, yet one as the hand in all things essential to mutual progress.

The wisest among my race understand that the agitation of questions of social equality is the extremest folly, and that progress in the enjoyment of all the privileges that will come to us must be the result of severe and constant struggle rather than of artificial forcing.

Nevertheless, it should be understood that Washington was never indifferent to the considerations by which Du Bois was moved. He looked forward to the end of segregation and the achievement of full political rights by the Negro, but he did not believe that this could be imposed upon the South by the North. What he was trying to make people see was that a dependent, underprivileged race must be a menace to its oppressors as well as to itself and that "if you hold a man down in the ditch you must go down into the ditch yourself." He accepted restriction of the ballot on grounds of qualification, but he never wavered in his insistence that such restrictions must apply equally to all races. Segregation he preferred to attack first by calling attention to the fact that the accommodations provided for blacks did not currently conform to the "separate but equal" provisions of the law.

The whole approach to education at Tuskegee was determined by such convictions as these and the temperament that informed them. Believing that whites and blacks shared the problems the Civil War had left behind it in the South, Washington wanted to give his people a chance to better themselves through owning land and establishing themselves in useful and gainful occupations, and he knew that unless they seized such opportunities, nothing that anybody else could do for them would avail. It is true that his assumptions worked better in the old South than they would later in the urban, technological surroundings to which many blacks would be asked to adjust themselves, but it is not fair to blame him for beginning with the situation by which he was confronted.

Washington found that those who had been taught a trade under General Armstrong at Hampton got along much better in the world than those with whom he had associated during his year at Wayland Seminary in Washington, where the education was wholly intellectual and theoretical. He could see no future for the man who sat down in a filthy, dilapidated house to study a French grammar, for those who planted cotton only and ate their food out of cans shipped from Chicago, or for the family who bought on the installment plan organs that nobody could play and sewing machines that nobody used but had no decent table utensils, toothbrushes, or nightgowns. From the beginning therefore Tuskegee committed itself to the project method, the application of theoretical knowledge to practical problems, the integration of knowing and living. It was not for nothing that Booker T. Washington's monument at Tuskegee was to quote him as having said both that "we shall prosper in proportion as we learn to dignify and glorify labor and put brains and skill into the common occupations of life" and that "there is no defence or security for any of us except in the highest intelligence and development of all."

3. *Jane Addams, Humanitarian*

During the Depression of 1893 an unemployed shipping clerk with a dependent wife and two little children applied for help to the Hull-House relief station. Since it was the rule that such persons must exhaust all possibilities for employment before being accepted, Jane Addams told him that work was available on the Drainage Canal construction. Though he objected that he had never worked outdoors and could not endure such work in winter, he followed her instructions, worked two days, contracted pneumonia, and was dead in a week. The incident taught her "that life cannot be administered by definite rules and regulations, that wisdom to deal with a man's difficulties comes only through some knowledge of his life and habits as a whole, and that to treat an isolated episode is almost sure to invite blundering."

She never forgot the lesson, and it was this fact, above all others, that kept her free of the vices that beset reformers and "do-gooders" in general. A lifelong celibate who allowed herself no indulgences, she recognized the importance of the sexual drive both in art and in life long before it became fashionable to do so and insisted on "the very energy of existence, the craving for enjoyment, the pushing of vital forces, the very right of every citizen to be what he is without pretence or assumption of virtue." Humble people sinned often, she thought, "through weakness and passion but seldom through hardness of heart," and she wrote about both juvenile delinquency (*The Spirit of Youth and the City Streets*) and prostitution (*A New Conscience and an Ancient Evil*) without either prudery or self-righteousness. Once an associate at Hull-House remarked of one of their beneficiaries, "Look at all we have done for that girl, and she isn't even grateful." "Was that why we helped her," asked Jane Addams quietly, "because we wanted her to be grateful?" Walter Rauschenbusch was quite right when he told her she had the power to see nobility "even in the most ignoble expressions"; so too was Justice William O. Douglas when, much later, he perceived that "she saw promise in the youth who was different, and [that] she stoutly rebelled at any trend to orthodoxy

Jane Addams, with two fellow workers for woman's suffrage, Mrs. Charles Blaney and Mrs. H. M. Wilmarth, outside the Art Institute of Chicago

and conformity." And Walter Lippmann summed it up well when, in his memorial article, he described her secret as "compassion without condescension."

In 1900 she was elected to honorary membership in the DAR, but during the hysteria that prevailed during and after World War I, that organization, repelled by her failure to support the war and her insistence that even subversives must be dealt with by due process of law, expelled her. She had thought, she remarked dryly, that her election was for life, but evidently it had only been for good behavior. This was probably the sharpest thing she ever said. In 1927, partly to protest against such nonsense, her friends gave her a great testimonial dinner at the Merchandise Mart in Chicago, where she was honored, in person or by letter, by all sane public men and women in America, from those archradicals President Calvin Coolidge and Governor Alfred E. Smith on down.

> I am very grateful for the affection and interest you have brought here this evening [she said in her response]; yet in a way humiliated by what you say I am, for I know myself to be a very simple person, not at all sure I am right, and most of the time not right, though wanting to be, which I am sure we all know of ourselves.

Jane Addams was born in Cedarville, Illinois, on September 6, 1860. Her father was a miller who invested in railroads and banks, was involved in community activities, served eight terms in the Illinois Senate, and died worth a quarter of a million dollars. According to his daughter, Lincoln used to write to him as "My dear Double-D'ed Addams." She also remembered that when, as a little girl, she wondered at the contrast between the large house in which she lived and the mean little houses inhabited by many of the other people in Cedarville she made up her mind that when she grew up she would continue to live in a large house, "but it would not be built among the other large houses, but right in the midst of horrid little houses like these." It may have been so, but her famous autobiography, *Twenty Years at Hull-House,* tends, like other such documents, to dramatize and oversimplify the varied and complicated influences and motivations that, in September 1889, led her and Ellen Gates Starr to open Hull-House in the heart of a cosmopolitan slum neighborhood at Halsted and Polk streets in Chicago.

It was not of course the first or the only settlement house. The Eli Bates Settlement dated from 1876, and Jane Addams herself had certainly been influenced in some measure by what she had observed in London at Toynbee Hall. South End House in Boston and Lillian Wald's Henry Street Settlement in New York became famous; ultimately Robert Morss Lovett would count thirty-five settlement houses in Chicago alone, with both Northwestern and the University of Chicago involved in such activities. Long before that, however, by 1907, Hull-House was accommodated in thirteen buildings, with as many as seventy residents.

Revolting against such earlier sentimental evaluations of Jane Addams as "the only saint America has produced," a recent biographer has placed heavy stress on her excellent business abilities, organizational powers, capacity for accommodation, gift for publicity, and care for her public image; Hull-House, he thinks, served the residents quite as well as the community, and through it Jane Addams achieved a much richer self-fulfillment than she could have found through any other kind of work. To all this she might well have replied, "Who deniges of it, Betsey?" for she herself had said much of it before him. Her years between Rockford Seminary and Hull-House were years of wavering, dissatisfaction, and wretched health, which, even though she was often plagued by illnesses later, may well have been partly psychosomatic. She always said that she lived in the Hull-House neighborhood because she found it the most interesting part of the city, and she founded the institution in part to give young women like herself a chance to bring purpose into their lives. It was the people around her who unveiled for her "the treasure of the humble," and it was in direct contact with life itself that she developed her "newer ideals of peace." "While I receive valuable suggestions from classical literature, when I really want to learn about life, I must depend upon my neighbors."

The activities of the settlement began tentatively (almost comically in view of later developments) when the neighbors were invited to hear *Romola* read in Italian, see slides of Italian art masterpieces, and borrow pictures to take home. From here it expanded as naturally and inevitably as life itself. In the beginning, the women came more readily than the men, and when they brought their children with them it became clear that Hull-House needed a kindergarten and a day nursery. A working girls' home, boys' club, art gallery, little theater, and much more followed. People came together not only to hear what we should now call university extension lectures but to play games, dance, and sing.

Jane Addams's own aesthetic sensibilities had always been keen; a country girl, she had pitied city children first of all for the way in which their play was handicapped, "the most elaborate 'plan or chart' or 'fragment from their dream of human life' " being "sure to be rudely destroyed by the passing traffic." It was the same with the theater. "One never ceases to marvel at the power of even a mimic stage to afford to the young a magic space in which life may be lived in efflorescence, where manners may be courtly and elaborate without exciting ridicule, where the sequence of events is impressive and comprehensible." Even the "debased form of dramatic art and . . . vulgar type of music" presented in the cheap melodrama theaters in the Hull-House neighborhood during Jane Addams's early residence there, to be succeeded later by the marvelous release afforded by the early movies, served such needs, but she always wanted to build upon these foundations into the higher reaches of art, and Theodore Roosevelt was greatly impressed by a performance of *Justice* he saw at Hull-House before Galsworthy's name was at all well known in America as that of a dramatist. She recognized the importance of adolescence in human development as early as did G. Stanley Hall, who brought the word into our vocabulary in 1904, and she realized the value of craftsmanship in an age when the machine was progressively removing creative individuality from work. So there was a Labor Museum at Hull-House, which displayed and dignified the often beautiful and accomplished arts and crafts the immigrants had brought with them from home, all now in such great danger of withering here for lack of exercise and appreciation.

Besides all this, however, especially in the beginning before much machinery had been set up, there was hard physical work to do— babies to bathe and sometimes even to deliver because the midwife was not available or would not serve because the mother had disgraced the community by neglecting to provide herself with a wedding ring, frightened children to comfort, helpless old people to nurse, and others who had no particular need except just to have somebody to talk to. Once, during a smallpox epidemic, Hull-House risked infection by becoming headquarters for the inspectors; once Jane Addams herself served as garbage inspector for her ward; and unless she and her associates had been willing to do such things, they could never have been accepted in the community as they were. But they were not done without paying a price. "In spite of poignant experiences, or perhaps because of them," she wrote, "the memory of the first years at Hull-House is more or less blurred with fatigue." Later, as activities expanded and became more highly organized, there must have been much less of this kind of thing; indeed there were many periods when Jane Addams was not even in residence. Many who met her in later years noticed a kind of remoteness about her; young as I was, I myself felt this on the only occasion I ever saw and heard her, when, as a youngster, I, along with many others, sat on the stage of Orchestra Hall with her during a peace meeting at the beginning of World War I. Unfailingly kind and courteous, she radiated a kind of universal, impersonal benevolence, far removed from intimacy. This, I am sure, was partly a matter of temperament. There was a mystical side to her; she needed solitude, needed to hold the citadel of her personality inviolate. But it was also imposed upon her by the strain of her manifold activities and her way of life; if she had not learned how to do this, she could not have survived.

Perhaps all this may help to explain why, though she was essentially a domestic, even an old-fashioned woman, Jane Addams apparently never had any desire to marry and have children of her own. What she realized clearly was that we were all coming to live under conditions that made it necessary for women who wished to exercise their womanly instincts effectively to carry them into the world theater. So Hull-House became involved in varied activities in behalf of welfare legislation and attacks upon political corruption, and Jane Addams found herself writing and speaking to raise funds for and rouse interest in the many causes to which it was committed. *Hull-House Maps and Papers* (1895) was a pioneering attempt to achieve a scientific description of industrial and living conditions in a cosmopolitan neighborhood at a time when most Americans had hardly heard the word *sociology*. Illinois passed a child labor law in 1893, and Chicago set up the first juvenile court in the nation in 1899; Hull-House was involved in both these enterprises and many more. Different residents found or created their own specialties and often went on to careers elsewhere outside the settlement. Julia Lathrop, who had helped organize the court and the Immigrants' Protective League, became the first head of the

Children's Bureau in Washington; Florence Kelley, who investigated sweatshops in Chicago for the state Bureau of Labor Statistics, became the first factory inspector in Illinois; and Dr. Alice Hamilton stood almost alone as a pioneering authority on industrial diseases.

If you had listened to the lunatics who were calling Jane Addams the most dangerous woman in America after World War I, you might have thought her a reckless agitator. Actually she was always the meliorist, always for "the best possible," always preferred half a loaf to no bread at all, and displayed a genius for reconciling divergent points of view among her associates. It was this "passion for conciliation" that made her a pacifist, for to her peace was something larger than the mere absence of war. Naturally all this exposed her to criticism from those standing to both the right and the left of her, and even sometimes from her associates. An unwavering champion of the rights of organized labor, she deplored strikes and violence; seeing the settlement house as inevitably a clearinghouse for all sorts of propaganda, she steadfastly refused to commit Hull-House and herself to any particular variety.

This same temperamental bias appeared in connection with religion. Though her father called himself a Hicksite Quaker, he had no formal religious affiliation. In the intensely evangelical atmosphere of Rockford Seminary, she refused to be "converted." She seems not to have been unaffected by the doubts that beset scientifically minded young people in the wake of the Darwinian revolution (at one time she hoped to be a physician). About the time she found her lifework she joined the Presbyterian church, longing "for an outward symbol of fellowship, some bond of peace, some blessed spot where unity of spirit might claim right of way over all differences." While there is no reason to suppose that she ever regretted this step, her association with the church and formal religious exercises tended to wither over the years, nor did she ever quite make her peace with "the melodramatic coarseness of life."

It was much the same with politics, except in 1912, when she appeared at the Bull Moose convention and subsequently campaigned for TR because the new Progressive party had committed itself to most of the causes for which she and her associates had been contending down the years. In 1916 she declared for Wilson, hoping, despite some disappointing contacts with him, that he would still function effectively toward ending the European war through negotiation, in 1924 for La Follette, and in both 1928 and 1932 for Hoover, under whose Food Administration she had rendered the only effective service a pacifist was permitted in wartime. Her old age was saddened by the rise of fascism in Europe; some of FDR's early actions on the domestic front won her approval, and since she died on May 21, 1935, she was spared the agony of his shift toward war.

Her pacifism too was pragmatic. She admired both Tolstoi, whom she met, and Gandhi, whom she tried to meet, but did not wholly accept the theory or method of either. In 1915 she helped organize the Women's Peace party, which held a conference at The Hague in the spring, and thereafter, though she feared she might be on a fool's errand, visited both warring and neutral nations in the interest of mediation. Out of loyalty to the cause, she would even have gone on Henry Ford's Peace Ship, though she was sure it would not accomplish anything and might well inspire ridicule, if a serious illness had not intervened. At the Second Women's Peace Conference at Zurich in 1919, she helped found the Women's International League for Peace and Freedom, which ranks second only to Hull-House among her accomplishments. She was also involved in the beginnings of the National Association for the Advancement of Colored People in 1909 and the American Civil Liberties Union in 1920.

It is interesting that in warring Europe the women seem to have met with rather more encouragement in central Europe than among the Allies. In Austria Prime Minister Stürgkh declared that they had spoken the only sensible words that had been heard in his office for months, and in Germany Professor Hans Dulbrueck suggested that President Wilson should tell England he would embargo all shipments of war materials unless she came to the conference table, simultaneously notifying Germany that he would lift it again unless that country came too. But Wilson himself remained noncommittal. When he made his "peace without victory" statement in January 1917, which was admittedly influenced by the women's resolutions, hope flared anew, only to fade with Germany's resumption of submarine warfare. For Jane Addams, who had had contacts with representatives of all the warring nations in her own neighborhood in Chicago, the war was a civil war; by the same token, the isolation from her fellow countrymen that her convictions forced upon her was an ever-present agony. Of Wilson himself she wrote retrospectively—sadly and a little bitterly—that "it seemed to us at moments as if the President were imprisoned in his own spacious intellectuality, and had forgotten the overwhelming virtue of the deed," and when America entered the war and the world in which she had functioned crumbled, she wondered "whether any man had the right to rate his moral leadership so high that he could consider the sacrifice of the lives of thousands of his young countrymen a necessity?"

Her opposition to the food blockade that was starving the children of central Europe and her advocacy of recognition for the new regime in Russia did not help her after the war, but, as we have seen, the tides of prejudice had retreated before she died. Secretary of War Baker had known the truth about her long before that; when one fanatic called his attention to the "subversive" character of one organization whose list of sponsors was headed with her name, Baker replied coldly that Miss Addams's name dignified any list on which it might appear. On May 18, 1935, she was informed that she must have an operation and asked how soon she must be ready to be taken to the hospital. "In fifteen minutes" was the reply. That was well, she said, as it would just give her time to finish the book she was reading. Mercifully, she never learned that her complaint was inoperable cancer; more mercifully still, she died three days later.

4. Carry A. Nation, Agitator

She spelled her first name "Carry," instead of the more familiar "Carrie," and insisted upon using the middle initial "A," because the whole purpose of her life was to carry the nation for prohibition. Whenever possible, she added to her signature the words "Your Loving Home Defender," and she liked to be photographed with an open Bible in one hand and her hatchet in the other. She was a large woman, nearly six feet tall, weighing about 180 pounds, big-bosomed and wide-hipped, and she dressed in black alpaca with a big white bow at her throat and a poke bonnet on her head, her eyes peering through narrow-rimmed spectacles between heavy eyebrows and a wide, sprawling nose, with her thin, down-curving lips pressed sternly together, almost to the vanishing point. "I never saw anything that needed a rebuke, or exhortation, or warning," she says, "but that I felt it my place to

Carry Nation on the steamship Columbia, *1908*

meddle with it." Besides alcohol, she hated tobacco, lovemaking, pictures and statues of nude women, corsets, trailing skirts, and feathers on women's hats, but she tolerated horseracing. Her opponents were "rum-soaked, whisky-swilled, saturn-faced rummies" and "nicotine-soaked, beer-besmeared, whisky-bloated, red-eyed Devils." She addressed judges as "your dishonor" and called Theodore Roosevelt, who never used tobacco in any form, a "blood-thirsty, reckless, and cigarette-smoking rummy." So she stormed through the opening years of the century (she is the only one of our "representative figures" whose public activities were wholly confined to our period), wrecking saloons, snatching cigars and cigarettes out of smokers' mouths, threatening hellfire and damnation on anybody who did not do what she said, and making herself one of the few universally known women of her time and a permanent part of American folklore.

Carry Amelia Moore was born in Garrard County, Kentucky, on November 25, 1846, and died at Leavenworth, Kansas, on June 11, 1911. Her father was a planter and trader; her mother boasted relationship to Alexander Campbell, founder of the Christian, or Disciples, church, and a duke of Argyll. Financial problems and possibly an appetite for roving kept the family on the move during Carry's sickly and troubled childhood—in Kentucky, to Missouri, to Texas, and back to Missouri. Her father, whom she adored, was, in the early days, a benevolent slaveowner, and all Carry's early associations were with slaves, whom she loved and whose emotionalism, religiosity, folklore, and supernaturalism she seems clearly to have imbibed. At the age of ten, she experienced a midwestern camp-meeting type of conversion, and she continued to have hysterical, emotional religious experiences all her life, some of them attended by phenomena that cannot be easily explained.

In 1867 she contracted a disastrous marriage to Dr. Charles Gloyd, a hopeless alcoholic, who became the father of her only child, a daughter, but who speedily reduced her to such destitution and misery that her father was obliged to fetch her home again, after which Gloyd promptly drank himself to death. She attended the normal school at Warrensburg, Missouri, and taught briefly; then, in 1877, she married David A. Nation, nineteen years her senior, who tried functioning as preacher, lawyer, and editor without achieving real success in any field. With him she lived in Missouri and in Texas, where she ran two small hotels, of the first of which she was virtually the entire staff (if people could not pay, she kept them on just the same), and finally settled at Medicine Lodge, Kansas. Weary of her sensational notoriety and domineering ways, Nation divorced her for desertion in 1901, in an uncontested suit, and died in 1903.

We know that as a child Carry Nation had pilfered and lied, but what she meant by calling herself "a great lover" is speculative. "I have never seen anyone who I thought had committed more sin than I. . . . I never saw the corruption of but one life, one heart— that was mine. I was never so shocked, so disgusted, so disgraced with remorse over any life so much as my own. My heart was the foulest place I ever saw." But it is also on record that she never allowed a boy or man to touch her and that when she had a caller he had to sit on the other end of the sofa and talk about literature. She may, for all that, have had a passionate nature, whose fires were afterward sublimated in her reforming zeal. We know that she desperately loved her first husband. She did not love Nation, who came to her in answer to prayer because she felt she could no longer carry her burdens alone. "I never saw a loving husband," she says, "that I did not envy his wife."

Carry Nation became active in the work of the Woman's Christian Temperance Union in 1892 and was appointed their local "jail evangelist." It did not take her long to discover that alcohol had been an important factor in the downfall of most of the prisoners, and because her first husband had drunk with his Masonic cronies, she came to hate fraternal orders along with the liquor barons. In the summer of 1899 (just a little more than a year after the death of the founder of the WCTU, Frances Willard), she and her associates began the task of singing, praying, and exhorting out of existence the "joints" that were operating illegally in theoretically bone-dry Kansas, and so far as Medicine Lodge and, later, Barber County were concerned, they were wholly successful. The next spring Mrs. Nation went alone to Kiowa, where, for the first time, she wrecked a bar, and just after Christmas she demolished one of the most luxurious saloons in the Middle West, at the Hotel Carey in Wichita; a state temperance convention gave her a medal inscribed "To the Bravest Woman in Kansas."

She first used the hatchet that became her trademark in Wichita on January 21, 1901; up to this time, she had used stones, iron bars, and billiard balls as her instruments of destruction. Toward the end of the month she went to Topeka, where she attacked the Senate bar, favorite hangout of the state legislators, and here a man thrust some souvenir hatchets into her hands and advised her to sell them and thus raise money to pay her fines and finance her campaigns. She peddled them wherever she appeared for the rest of her life, and their sale became her main source of income. Chief of Police Stahl was friendly to her, and Topeka businessmen launched a public campaign to run out the joints. Saloon smashing spread throughout Kansas (a bill to legalize it was actually introduced into the legislature, though never passed) and, more sporadically, all over the country, and insurance companies began canceling premiums. Some smashers were men and college and theological seminary boys, and at least once Carry organized a brigade of child smashers.

Carry Nation made it difficult for her antagonists by beginning and concentrating her attack in a dry state, where her victims had no legal standing; if the authorities moved against her, they left themselves wide open to criticism for tolerating the lawbreakers she attacked. But though her position was different in officially wet states, she never completely relinquished or renounced what she called "hatchetation"; the prizefighter John L. Sullivan ran and hid from her when she visited his saloon in New York. Coney Island was not free from her ministrations even while she herself was appearing there, and she once moved against a saloon in which she had taken refuge from a mob. She interrupted the California legislature and both the House and the Senate in Washington with her harangues and tried to break up a Tammany dance. She was often arrested and jailed; she was also mobbed, abused (sometimes by rum sellers' wives), rotten-egged, whipped, and had her hair torn out. This did not greatly trouble her; she would have welcomed martyrdom as an honor and an aid to her cause. But as her tactics became more familiar, saloonkeepers armed against her wherever she appeared, and she was frequently turned back from contemplated attacks, so that many of her later confrontations degenerated to mutual screaming and scolding, with an abundance of billingsgate. Her last attempt to wreck a saloon occurred at Butte, Montana, on January 26, 1910, barely a year and a half before she died, but her most intensive smashing was confined to the years 1900 and 1901. Thereafter she was primarily a platform artist.

She was booked at first into standard lecture halls (including New York's Carnegie), but since her wholly extemporaneous discourses were made up of unorganized, highly repetitive vituperation, she was not a great success in this field of endeavor, and she rapidly descended to appearing in burlesque theaters and, as already indicated, at Coney Island. Lecturing as she did it was hardly less dangerous than saloon smashing, and she was mobbed both at Coney and at Rochester when she refused to join in the mourning for McKinley because she considered him a friend of the liquor interests. She wrote two plays that she failed to get produced, but in November 1903 she appeared at Elizabeth, New Jersey, in a new version of *Ten Nights in a Barroom* called *Hatchetation,* which was later booked into both Philadelphia and New York. It included a saloon-wrecking scene, and Carry put her heart into it almost as if she had been wrecking a real saloon. She published three short-lived antiliquor papers—the *Smasher's Mail,* the *Home Defender,* and the *Hatchet*—which except for her editorials contained mainly correspondence praising and condemning her activities, and brought out a surprisingly good autobiography, *The Use and Need of the Life of Carry A. Nation,* in 1904. She visited Canada in 1903 and England and Scotland in 1908–9. Late in life she lived briefly in Oklahoma, Arkansas, and Washington, D.C., and she established a home for the wives and mothers of drunkards in Kansas City, Kansas. Her last public appearance was as a lecturer at Eureka Springs, Arkansas, on January 13, 1911; she collapsed on the platform, and her last words were "I have done what I could."

What was she then? a saint? a lunatic? a clown? an exhibitionist? a virago? or a public nuisance? The only honest answer is that she was something of all of these. I am far from being willing to commit myself to the thesis that everybody who hears voices and sees visions is crazy (surely one would rather be mad with Blake than sane with Jones, Brown, and Robinson), but Carry Nation came of tainted stock; her mother, who believed herself to be Queen Victoria and had to be treated accordingly, came of a lunatic family, and Carry's only child, whose early afflictions make up a record too painful to read, married, bore eight children, became an alcoholic, and lost her mind. With a woman like Carry Nation, it is difficult or impossible, seventy years after the event, to tell where eccentricity shades off into actual madness. She had her moments (once she insisted upon being released from jail because she had been elected president by the Smashers' League and had to go to Washington for the inauguration), but during most of her career she was certainly sane enough to be responsible for what she was doing, and early and late she carried burdens and endured sufferings that must have crushed most of us who consider ourselves much better balanced than she.

The powerful egocentric drive which impelled her is one aspect of her personality that cannot be denied. She described herself as "a bulldog running along at the feet of Jesus, barking at what He doesn't like," and I do not question her absolute, unwavering conviction that in everything she did she was obeying the will of God. Nevertheless, it was *she* who was serving Him, and she was not so stupid as to be unaware that she transformed herself in the process from a smalltown Kansas nobody to a woman who commanded the front pages of the newspapers of the world. A timorous or modest person does not serve God by smashing other people's property and virtually inciting riot, regardless of what she may believe about God or liquor or anything else. Long before she became a public figure, Carry Nation's fellow church members had found her intolerable because she not only recognized no authority but her own but also insisted upon nobody else recognizing it, and when her own husband preached she prompted him audibly from the front row and told him to sit down when she thought he had talked long enough.

But the saint? It is impossible to withhold admiration from Carry Nation for the burdens she carried, working herself to the bone in direst poverty to provide not only for herself, her husband, her daughter, her husband's daughter, and her first husband's mother but for anybody she encountered who might need help. She was telling the truth when she said, "I can truly say there is no ill will in my heart toward a creature God has made. It is a hatred for the enemies of mankind." As Robert Lewis Taylor has said, "The simple fact is that, while she disapproved of nearly everyone, she disliked nobody. She would have found decent motives in a cannibal." Reference has already been made to her affection for Negroes. When Jews stopped at her hotel, she prepared their food for them according to Jewish dietary laws. She had good relations with Catholics at a time when many of her fellow Protestants were as un-Christian toward them as they were toward Jews, and when she was in New York she attended mass at Saint Patrick's Cathedral. Reared a Campbellite (or Disciple), she moved about freely and finally formulated her own eclectic theology, so far as she had one, only Spiritualism and Christian Science apparently lying outside the range of her sympathies. Her worst enemies never questioned her scrupulous honesty. Long before anybody had ever heard of her, she ran her own private relief agency, collecting both food and clothes for the poor, and woe betide any Scrooge who refused to contribute, and she took waifs and strays into her home as some people shelter homeless cats. After she was famous, she lived on the barest necessities, deliberately limiting herself to what the poorest of her countrymen possessed and devoting everything else to benevolent and propaganda purposes. She loved children and was successful in winning their trust and love, and when she was in jail she made friends with the derelicts, perverts, and criminals who were imprisoned with her, in some cases winning their confidence and affection and perhaps even "saving" a few of them. One of her greatest successes was a "kept" woman who had murdered her lover and who became a temperance worker and a savior of "fallen" girls. But even before Carry Nation ever began her campaigns, she had run into trouble with one of the churches to which she belonged because she insisted upon their accepting a woman who was generally regarded as a prostitute but who, in her eyes, was only a poor, unfortunate, neglected wife.

Carry Nation was right about the ravages of alcohol, which, in her day and in ours, destroys uncounted multitudes of men and women who might otherwise have lived happy and useful lives. She was right about the venality of politicians, and how right she was about tobacco we have fully learned only since her death. Her first and best biographer, Herbert Asbury, was far from being a prohibitionist, but nobody has written more convincingly of the conscienceless stupidity of the liquor interests both before and during her career. Nor must it be forgotten that, if the elected officials in dry Kansas had performed their duty, there would have been neither need nor opportunity for her to do what she did. She was the most dramatic, the most picturesque, and, in a sense, the most immediately effective of all temperance reformers, but the social pressures that produced the Eighteenth Amendment would probably have operated in very much the same way if she had never lived, and her fanatical extremism must have alienated many who might otherwise have been won to the cause. If she could hardly have been expected to understand the psychological and sociological causes of alcoholism, perhaps she ought still to have known that men cannot be dragooned into righteousness and that the only effective way to improve the habits of a human being is to improve him.

In a comparatively small way, Carry Nation used the terrorist tactics that, since her time, have been far more dangerously employed in behalf of a variety of causes, good and bad. She never killed or seriously injured anybody with her rods and hatchets, but sometimes it was only good luck that saved her. Love of destruction is deeply ingrained in human nature; it does not need encouragement from good people. Obviously Carry and her followers came to enjoy smashing and to find self-expression in it, and since their activities inspired both imitations and reprisals, their example was clearly contagious. John Alexander Dowie, the Zion City, Illinois, fanatic whose doctrines Carry once eagerly embraced and then quickly repudiated, and his followers smashed drugstores in Chicago because they disbelieved in medicine. If well-meaning people are going to set out to smash everything of which they do not approve, then surely, in a pluralistically minded society, there will soon be nothing left. Carry Nation was fond of calling herself the John Brown of the temperance movement. It seems too bad that she never had a chance to ponder what John Drinkwater made Lincoln say about Brown in his play about the Civil War president: "John Brown, did you say? Aye, John Brown. But that's not the way it's to be done. And you can't do the right thing the wrong way. That's as bad as the wrong thing, if you're going to keep the state together."

5. *Helen Keller, Prodigy*

Helen Keller was one of the most famous of all American women. She met all American presidents from Cleveland on and was admired by Victoria, Wilhelmina, and the queens of Greece and Spain. At one time or another, her path crossed those of a very high percentage of the best-known people of her time: Edison took her through his laboratory, Ford through his factory, Luther Burbank through his experimental gardens. Whittier and Oliver Wendell Holmes were kind to her, and some seventy poets wrote in her praise. She was fond of William James and Henry van Dyke and especially of Mark Twain.

She was born at Tuscumbia, near Mussel Shoals, in rural Alabama, on June 27, 1880. Through her father, she was related to Robert E. Lee, through her mother to New England intellectuals. Normal at birth, she was stricken in babyhood with an undiagnosed illness that left her deaf and blind. Her own later view was that from then until Anne Sullivan came to her in 1887 she was "an unconscious clod of earth." During this period she was what is generally called a holy terror, a wild, completely undisciplined young animal, who snatched food off other people's plates and locked them in closets when she could get hold of a key.

Dickens, Alexander Graham Bell, Samuel Gridley Howe, and Laura Bridgman joined hands for her deliverance. It was in Dickens's *American Notes* that her mother read of Howe's work at the Perkins Institute for the Blind in Boston and of Laura Bridgman, the first deaf-blind child ever taught how to communicate with the world. A Baltimore doctor made the connection with Bell, who guided the Kellers to Michael Anagnos, Howe's son-in-law and successor at Perkins, and it was he who sent Anne Sullivan, the twenty-one-year-old daughter of Boston Irish immigrants, herself a Perkins alumnus who had grown up under terrible privations, to Tuscumbia.

Helen credited "Teacher" with having brought her "out of a clod in the dark silence" and "from nothingness to human life." In the very beginning, Teacher was largely a pugilist, for she could teach nothing until she had brought the wild child into some sort of order, and William Gibson's picture of their battles, in his play, *The Miracle Worker*, is not exaggerated. She arrived on March 3, and the first real breakthrough came on April 5, when Anne pumped water over Helen's hand, at the same time spelling the word into her palm by the manual alphabet. At last the child made the connection, thus first perceiving that things had names and meanings, so that, as she said, "nothingness was blotted out." It was one of the dramatic moments in the history of education. Thereafter she wanted to know the names of everything, and her progress was rapid.

In 1888 Anne took her to Boston and the Perkins Institute, where she spent considerable time during the next three years. She first spoke in 1890, and by 1891 she was asking the meaning of such words as *phenomenon, comprise, energy, reproduction, extraordinary, perpetual,* and *mystery.* In 1893 she visited the World's Columbian Exposition in Chicago and was enthralled by the exoticism of distant lands as exhibited on the Midway. In 1896 she entered Arthur Gilman's School for Young Ladies in Cambridge to be prepared for Radcliffe as the first blind-deaf girl who had ever gone to college. She entered in 1900 and was graduated *cum laude* in 1904. Neither President Eliot nor Dean Briggs took any interest in her, but Professor William Allan Neilson learned the manual alphabet to be able to talk with her, and *The Story of My Life* was composed largely of her themes for "Copey" (Professor Charles T. Copeland). It was published, first serially, while she was still in college and translated into some fifty languages.

During her later years Helen Keller spent much time on the lecture platform, but she never became an effective speaker, able to function without Miss Sullivan's help. "There were times, I am sure, when the audience could not follow me at all." She and Teacher journeyed to Hollywood to make a film, *Deliverance*, which did not amount to much, but they were much more successful on the vaudeville circuit.

Though Helen Keller began trying to help others very early, she had no regular channel to work through until the American Federation for the Blind was established in the 1920s; thereafter her principal work was raising funds for this organization, a task that took her hither and yon across the North American continent and beyond the seas. Teacher too had been at Perkins in her youth, and her sight failed again in later years; her death in 1936 came just in time to save her from a prolonged period in darkness. By that time Polly Thomson had already been in the picture for some time, and thereafter she became Helen's chief reliance until Polly herself died in 1960. On June 1, 1968, at Westport, Connecticut, Helen Keller followed her, in her eighty-eighth year.

The process of Helen Keller's learning has been described in her own books in considerably greater detail than can be given here. For the uninitiated, the first stages are the hardest to understand; as Helen herself said, once she had learned that some apples were sweet and others bitter, it was comparatively easy to go on to think of sweet and bitter as qualities, apart from particular expressions of them. Once she had got underway, she could read people's lips by placing her fingers over them. She could also read Braille, write by hand on a grooved board, and type on either a regular typewriter or a Braille machine. When she was in college, she had Anne beside her to spell lectures into her palm as well as books not available in Braille.

Helen Keller had no patience with the notion that blind persons develop special faculties to make up for the loss of sight. She seems to have had little sense of direction and to have been less dexterous than many blind persons. What she did have were physical strength, intelligence, courage, an extraordinary memory, and dauntless determination. It is clear too that if her faculties of touch and smell were not more highly developed than other people's, they were better trained. As she says about the people who could not understand how she could describe what she had never seen, "they forget that my whole body is alive to the conditions about me." She thought she could judge character by vibration of footsteps and touch of hands and tell whether a lilac was purple or white by the feel of the petals. She knew what kind of country she was passing through, and different cities had sufficient personality for her so that she reacted to them emotionally. She recognized ethnic neighborhoods by the smell of their cooking and claimed that she always knew whether a church she passed was Catholic or Protestant and that, when the door of a house was opened, she knew what fuel was burned there, whether the family roasted their own coffee, and whether or not the house itself had been freshly decorated. Flying, she once asked the pilot whether their altitude was not 8,000 feet, and he looked at his instruments and replied that she was right.

In Hollywood Helen Keller thought herself big and awkward in contrast to the "graceful and sylphlike" actresses she met. She had a strong, well-developed body, and her movements were vigorous; seeing her on a platform with "normal" persons, Richard Cabot thought her so much the most vital of the company that he wondered whether the others might not burn themselves out if they came too near her. Thwarted as a child, she sat silent until asked what she was doing, then replied, "I am preparing to assert my independence." She never had any difficulty doing this. Georgette Leblanc was quite right in judging her "not one of the meek"; she could be willful, tempery, and stubborn, and it may be significant that in her dreams she moved about freely and possessed all her senses. She wished to be treated like a normal person and appreciated it when her professors judged her work quite as severely as that of other students, and she never ceased to resent persons who tried to "run" her. When she was a child, she tried to kiss Grover

Cleveland, and he pushed her away. "I am ashamed to confess," she says, "that I was never able to see any good in Cleveland's administration after that."

She was fond of expensive clothes and more attracted to men than to women. Unlike Anne Sullivan, she enjoyed her fling in vaudeville. She accepted the cakes and ale of life and blamed St. Paul for imposing an ascetic ideal upon the church ("human nature is against it"). "It is often said that usefulness is the end of life," she wrote, "and so it is. But happiness creates and inspires usefulness." In 1916 she wished to marry her secretary and would probably have done so if her family had not interfered, an inconceivable exercise of authority over a person who was thirty-six years old and a world celebrity. I am amazed that she yielded; it must have been the only time in her life that she behaved weakly.

Her love for dogs and horses was not destroyed by some bad experiences with them. She walked rapidly enough to tire Anne out, scrambled through underbrush, indifferent to scratches, and loved to camp, ride horseback, and be out in stormy weather. She climbed trees and shook down apples. She loved swimming, rowing, canoeing, and sailing and learned to dive and to swim under water. In winter tobogganing was a special delight. In the course of a twelve-mile ride on a tandem bicycle, she fell off three or four times and made herself lame. She tried sailing a boat and guiding a locomotive, and once she even sat at the controls of a plane. Nothing could be more indicative of her driving, aggressive nature than her participation in such activities, some of which seem more obsessive than rational for a woman in her state. Idleness seems to have been intolerable to her; when she had to stay indoors and was not at work, she would play solitaire with cards marked in Braille or checkers and chess on a specially constructed board.

She was keen on the American Civil Liberties Union and the National Association for the Advancement of Colored People from the beginning, and her socialism and feminism were developed without encouragement from Teacher, who was much more conservative than she was. Perhaps her courage is shown best in the way she spoke out not only for birth control but, with the courageous help of the editors of the Kansas City *Star* and the *Ladies' Home Journal,* to make people aware that the principal cause of blindness in children was a venereal infection that could be prevented by the now standard practice of dropping a weak solution of silver nitrate in the newborn baby's eyes. "Must we leave young girls to meet the danger in the dark because we dare not turn the light upon our social wickedness?"

For all her enthusiasm for learning, she was no scholar, being too much of an executive type and too socially oriented. Her achievements were most impressive in languages. She studied Latin, Greek, German, and French (she later added Italian), had favorite books in all these languages, and got far enough to read Schiller, Racine, and Molière with enjoyment. Greek she calls "the violin of human thought." She loved history and philosophy, reading Schopenhauer, Nietzsche, Bergson, and others during her college days, but she disliked mathematics and had little interest in science.

The worst mark against her as a reader is her swallowing the Baconian idiocy. (One of the most insensitive comments on literature anywhere on record is her dismissal of Shakespeare's wonderful girls as "pretty creatures intended to be played by boys.") Whitman, Emerson, and Thoreau were the American writers she valued most. Among her contemporaries, she accepted Robinson Jeffers but not the early T. S. Eliot, and she shied from H. L. Mencken, Sinclair Lewis, and Eugene O'Neill.

Sculpture naturally meant more to her than painting, for she could run her fingers over statues, and though she could not thus get a total impression at once, she could put the parts together in her mind. Music, to her, was largely limited to rhythm and vibration, but she could dance in time to an orchestra, and she loathed and felt a savage menace in jazz. Heifetz and Goldowsky played for her with her fingers on their instruments, and Caruso and Chaliapin sang with them on their lips. To the theater she responded more enthusiastically than one might have thought possible. Henry Irving, Ellen Terry, and Joseph Jefferson tried to show her how they acted, and in later years Katharine Cornell became a close friend. It is more difficult to understand how a blind-deaf woman could have been so enthusiastic about Chaplin and about Garbo in *Camille.*

Even as a history student in college, she felt no sympathy with military leaders, and she opposed the Spanish war. The Monroe Doctrine seemed to her arrogant and one-sided, and she made an antipreparedness tour in 1916. When Emma Goldman took her stand against conscription, Helen hailed both her and the IWW as comrades. She was a fairly consistent pacifist in World War I, even pleading for a general strike against war and preparedness; later her detestation of Hitlerism and her admiration for Franklin D. Roosevelt caused her difficulties, though she afterward felt some qualms of conscience about this.

If her pacifism wavered, her socialism did not; indeed, like all Socialists, she saw war as "the inevitable fruit of our economic system." In her college years she read Marx, Morris, Kropotkin, Wells, Shaw, and others, and her thinking was permanently affected by them. She warmly admired Debs and did not hesitate to take on the big newspapers or risk alienating friends like Carnegie by proclaiming her faith in him. "I am not a worshipper of cloth of any color, but I love the red flag and what it symbolizes to me and other Socialists."

Helen Keller began to form religious ideas later than many children, first because of her handicap, then because Anne Sullivan, a renegade Catholic, had little interest in religion. Nothing in the Bible except the life and teachings of Jesus interested Helen greatly. She found Revelation and much of the Old Testament repulsive, and Trinitarianism as ordinarily conceived seemed to her a form of polytheism.

Phillips Brooks, who taught her the Fatherhood of God and human brotherhood, was an important religious influence. Later, St. Augustine, St. Thomas Aquinas, Thomas à Kempis, Spinoza, and Boehme all helped, but the real prophet was Swedenborg, as interpreted by her friend John Hitz, first Swiss consul general in Washington, then head of the Volta Bureau. Her excellent little book, *My Religion,* makes little of Swedenborg's visions, stressing instead the way he saved her from biblical literalism and "barbarous creeds," including the notion that the "heathen" must be damned for what they could not help. From him she learned, if she had not known it before, that God is love, Christ the human expression or manifestation of God, and the Holy Spirit the Power to create and maintain goodness and happiness here. God creates because He must have something to love, and He does not condemn anyone, though His love cannot avail a man who refuses to receive it. Heaven is what all were made for and hell the spiritual condition of those who will themselves out of heaven by remaining in bondage to their own "selfish instincts and love of dominion."

She admitted that she had looked into the heart of darkness. "But I use my will, choose life and reject its opposite, nothingness." Perhaps she first felt clearly her capacity for mystical experience one day when, sitting quietly alone, it seemed to her that she had been in old Athens. So her soul was real then and independent of time and place, and space was nothing to spirit! It may even be that her blindness was an advantage here, for, as she says, to her the material world was quite as vague as the spiritual, and all the data that entered her mind had to be "synchronized into harmonious entity." When she was deprived of her physical senses, she was also delivered from their limitations, realizing more clearly than others do that we cannot really possess anything except as we are able to absorb it into our own minds.

In the last analysis, the most interesting question about Helen Keller is the one that can never be answered: What would she have been like and what would she have accomplished if she had had her five senses? Katharine Cornell said of her that she was not famous because she was deaf and blind nor because, being deaf and blind, she learned to read and write and speak but because, although she was deaf and blind, "she learned to think with a philosophical depth of understanding that reaches the minds and hearts of all, and because she learned to express these thoughts with a clarity all writers must envy." As far as it goes, this tribute is quite just. Helen Keller was no freak celebrity like the Learned Pig, nor could one say of her, as of the dancing bear, that it mattered not whether she did what she was doing well or ill, since the wonderful thing was her being able to do it at all. Yet when we ask whether she would have accomplished more or less without her handicap, we must answer frankly that we do not know. Her drive being what it was, she would certainly have worked hard; her character being what it was, she would have devoted herself to something useful for the benefit of mankind. But we simply cannot be sure that her gifts were great enough so that they must surely have won for her the celebrity that, as it was, she enjoyed. She herself admitted freely that her achievements had been built upon exceptionally generous contributions from others. "When I recollect the treasure of friendship that has been bestowed upon me I withdraw all charges against life. If much has been denied me, much, very much has been given me." There cannot be many lives that lend more support to the Bible promise that all things work together for good to them that love the Lord. Cruel as her position was, there are few human beings of whom one can say with less qualification that they fulfilled their destiny.

BETWEEN 1892 and 1914 the number of daily newspapers published in America increased from 1,650 to 2,250, with a total increase of 100 percent in circulation as against a 50 percent increase in population. After 1900 the increasing size and complexity of the newspaper business, plus the coming of large-scale financing, were powerful influences in the direction of making most papers much less the personal utterances of their editors than nineteenth-century papers had been. Nevertheless, many small papers survived, and some editors, like Atchison's Ed Howe and Emporia's William Allen White, even became known all over the country. Among papers in foreign languages, the circulation lead was still held by the New York *Staats-Zeitung* and the Chicago *Abendpost*, but increasing immigration from eastern Europe would push German papers down to about one-third of the total by 1914.

The newspaper boom was nursed by many circumstances and conditions: the occurrence of sensational news events, plus improved facilities for covering them; new dimensions in illustration, through the use of halftones, cartoons, and color printing; heavy stress upon "human interest"; a new passion for sports; the use of feature writers; the acquirement of an enlarged readership of women and children; and the breaking up of the staidness and stodginess of the old editorial page. The Associated Press and other news service chains were becoming increasingly active to serve new

The Expanding Press

10

journalistic interests, while Irving Bacheller, S. S. McClure, and others stood by to furnish syndicated material. Even the universities were being drawn in. Pennsylvania organized the first journalism curriculum in 1893, but the first four-year course was set up at Illinois in 1904, and the first separate School of Journalism was that of Missouri in 1908.

In the 1870s fewer than fifty papers were defying the pious by publishing Sunday editions, and half of these were in New York, Chicago, and Boston, where the *Herald* had pioneered in 1861. By 1880 there were 100; by 1890, 250; and they were steadily expanding and taking in more and more magazine as distinguished from strictly news features. As early as May 21, 1887, when the Revised Version of the New Testament was causing controversy, the Chicago *Tribune* printed it one Sunday in its entirety, and the same paper was giving away chromolithographic reproductions of famous paintings with its Sunday edition before 1900.

Chicago contributed to the development of "columns" with George Ade's "Stories of the Streets and of the Town," illustrated by John T. McCutcheon, in the *Record* in the midnineties; and Eugene Field's "Sharps and Flats" in the *Daily News* is still famous. Finley Peter Dunne's Mr. Dooley papers began coming out of Chicago at the time of the Spanish war, and Bert Leston Taylor's "A Line o' Type or Two" appeared in the *Tribune* in 1901 and for many a year thereafter. The newspaper rhymesters Wilbur D. Nesbit and Edgar A. Guest started in Baltimore and Detroit. Edwin Markham's social protest poem, "The Man with the Hoe," in the San Francisco *Examiner*, on January 14, 1899, made almost as great a sensation as Bryan's "Cross of Gold" speech had made, and a few years later O. Henry was publishing stories in the New York *World*.

New York papers included the *Tribune*, founded by Horace Greeley in 1841 and controlled by Whitelaw Reid as a Republican organ after 1873; the *Sun* (1833), long edited by Charles A. Dana; the *Evening Post* (1801), founded as a Federalist organ and edited by William Cullen Bryant for nearly fifty years until his death in 1878 and by Edwin Lawrence Godkin from 1883 to 1900; and, most remarkably, the *Times* (1851), whose circulation was down to 9,000 when Adolph Ochs purchased it in 1896 and threw down the gauntlet to the sensationalists with the slogan "All the News That's Fit to Print." In 1898 he cut the price from three cents to a penny; during its first quarter-century under the Ochs management, the paper,

New York newsstand, early 1900s. Courtesy, Collections of Henry Ford Museum, the Edison Institute, Dearborn, Michigan

always distinguished for its accurate and dignified reporting, cleared about 100 million dollars.

Chicago had, besides the *Tribune* (1847), controlled since 1874 by the Joseph Medill family, the *Daily News*, founded in 1875–76 by Melville E. Stone and Victor F. Lawson as an evening penny paper; the *Record*, which began as the morning edition of the *News* and had a very checkered history, involving many sales and combinations (its best period was between 1901 and 1914, when it was known as the *Record-Herald*); the *Inter-Ocean* (1872), an exceptionally handsome paper, which in 1892 presented its readers with the first color printing done on a rotary press in America and which, in the course of its history, was owned by such different persons as Herman H. Kohlsaat and the traction baron Charles T. Yerkes; and two evening papers, the *Journal* (1845–1929) and the *Post* (1893–1932), which latter was widely regarded as the Chicago paper most devoted to literature and the arts.

The *Tribune* and the *Daily News* were, however, the most important of these papers, and the *Tribune* is now the only survivor. At the beginning, the *News* placed its emphasis upon local matters, but after the Spanish war it developed an outstanding foreign news service. Though generally called conservative, the *Tribune* has always been hard to classify and full of surprises. In the course of its career, it has been both military-minded and peace-minded, and in 1910, in one of the most successful of its many crusades, it drove William Lorimer out of the Senate.

Boston had the *Advertiser* (1813), the city's first successful newspaper; the *Evening Transcript* (1830), the very embodiment of the "proper Bostonian"; the Democratic *Post* (1831), which at one time claimed the largest morning circulation in New England; the Republican *Herald* (1846), which would buy the *Traveler* in 1912, making this its afternoon edition; the liberal *Globe* (1872), the strongest paper in modern Boston; and the *Record* (1884). In 1908 the city would acquire the *Christian Science Monitor*, as genteel in its own specialized way as the *Transcript* and as able, though it never built up a large circulation in Boston itself. Both the *Advertiser* and the *Record* were swallowed up by Hearst, in 1917 and 1920, respectively, and the same fate would later overtake the *Herald-Traveler*, as it had by then become, transforming it to the *Herald-American*.

Other prominent papers at the beginning of the century included the Philadelphia *Public Ledger*, the Washington *Star*, the Springfield (Massachusetts) *Republican*, the Hartford *Courant*, the Baltimore *Sun*, the Cincinnati *Commercial Gazette*, the Louisville *Courier-Journal*, the Atlanta *Constitution*, the Kansas City *Star*, the San Francisco *Chronicle*, and the Portland *Oregonian*.

The special characteristics of the so-called yellow journalism that flourished during our period have been more fully discussed elsewhere in these pages in connection with the journalist now generally regarded as its great exponent, but William Randolph Hearst did not invent yellow. More than a decade before he bought the New York *Journal* in 1887, Joseph Pulitzer, a Hungarian-German Jew, who had begun on a German paper in St. Louis, had acquired the *World* from Jay Gould and shot up its circulation figures to 100,000. But both men had been anticipated by James Gordon Bennett, Jr., when, after his father's death in 1867, he came into control of the *Herald*.

Hearst's was not the only newspaper chain developing during this period either. Frank A. Munsey bought the New York *Daily News* in 1901, after the death of Benjamin Wood, but unloaded it three years later; he also sold the Boston *Journal* at a loss but had better luck with the Washington *Times* and the Baltimore *Evening News*. About 1890 E. W. Scripps began building up a chain of what finally became more than thirty cheap afternoon papers, aimed at a low level of reader intelligence. With all their limitations, they had some value for their crusades against bosses and utility abuses.

One feature of early twentieth-century journalism was so new and distinctive, and so important for circulation building, as to call for separate treatment; this of course was the comics.

As early as 1891 a little bear drawn by James Swinnerton was used to point up the weather forecast in the San Francisco *Examiner*, from which a series of cartoons depicting both little bears and little tigers developed. These pictures did not tell a story or contain balloon dialogue; neither were the characters individualized. The first real comic character was a revolting slum youngster—baldheaded, flap-eared, and barefoot, wearing only a long nightshirt—who appeared in Richard F. Outcault's cartoons in the New York *World* beginning May 5, 1895. In the first two the Kid's nightshirt was blue; in the third he sported red polka dots; but beginning with January 5, 1896, the experimenters with color printing settled on yellow, and he became "The Yellow Kid."

The "Hogan's Alley" pictures in which the Kid first appeared were single panels depicting multiple actions that had to be studied out as patiently as the work of Thomas Nast or the pictures Joseph Keppler and others did for such journals as *Puck, Judge,* and *Life*. Though all dealt with the slums, there was no continuity, and there were no speech balloons either, though a surrogate for them soon appeared in lettering on the Kid's shirt.

The Kid's impact is hard to understand today; apparently many must have been ready for his assault on gentility. It is a fact, however, that he not only sold papers but was widely used in advertising. And when Outcault deserted the *World* for the *Journal*, he became twins, for Pulitzer employed no less an artist than George Luks to take over the Kid for him.

On October 18, 1896, Hearst added "eight pages of polychromatic effulgence" to the *Journal*, but it was more than a year later that "The Katzenjammer Kids," based by Rudolph Dirks on the German Wilhelm Busch's "Max und Moritz," by which Hearst had been captivated as a boy in Europe, made its first appearance. There were three kids originally, but one was dropped immediately; there was also a father, and Mamma was thin, not fat. The Captain, whom many nowadays mistakenly suppose to be the father of Hans and Fritz, is a boarder; Mamma and her kids were introduced to him at the gangplank of his ship on October 31, 1902. The Inspector, a truant officer, arrived considerably later. Gradually, from the time of the Captain's coming, the action shifted from the Katzenjammer home to shipboard and distant islands until the large cast embraced pirates, cannibal kings, and other fantastic persons.

The leading comic artists passed back and forth between Hearst and Pulitzer as one publisher or the other raised the ante; Rudolph Dirks's departure from Hearst in 1912 legally established the curious principle that a cartoonist might take his characters with him but not the name of the strip, after which Dirks drew "The Captain and the Kids" for his new employer, while H. H. Knerr (and later Joe Musial) did "The Katzenjammer Kids" for Hearst. It was Dirks who established for the comics the permanent cast of characters in a sequence ordinarily of six panels to half a page, and though at the very beginning he relied wholly on pictures to tell the story, he soon found that fractured German dialect in balloons added much to his humor. As a footnote to the history of American insanity, be it recorded that during World War I some newspapers turned Hans and Fritz into "The Shenanigan Kids."

In 1899 the next founding father entered the field in the person of Frederick Burr Opper, who created "Happy Hooligan," "Alphonse and Gaston," and the saga of a mule, which he called "And Her Name Was Maud." Sometimes these appeared separately, and sometimes they were combined. Sometimes, even, they were combined with the work of other cartoonists, for there was much amalgamation in the early days, especially around the holidays, when Happy Hooligan might play Santa Claus to the Katzenjammer Kids or Foxy Grandpa preside over Fourth of July exercises attended by practically the whole Hearst stable.

Maud was a deceptively sweet-looking mule with a vicious disposition who generally ended by kicking somebody, preferably her owner, the farmer Si, out of the last panel. She was susceptible of less development than any other of Opper's ideas, and she received the least. *A priori* it might seem that Alphonse and Gaston, who made politeness a vice, could not yield much more, but Opper roamed the world in search of situations and backgrounds for them, the basic idea being that they were never able to get started on anything because they spent all their time scraping and deferring. Yet they were known to everybody in America, and even today one sometimes hears "After you, my dear Alphonse" and the inevitable response, "After you, my dear Gaston."

But the great creation was Happy Hooligan, who ran for twenty-five years. Happy had a button nose, an impossibly wide upper lip, an ear-to-ear smile; a tomato can for a hat, and the disposition of an angel; except for Krazy Kat and Denny Dimwit, no other comic character has ever so glorified sheer goodness of heart. His name was a deliberate misnomer. Because he wore rags, he is generally called a tramp; he was not a tramp, for he worked whenever work was available; it was his selfish, repellent, yellow slicker-clad brother, Gloomy Gus, the original exponent of the now popular cult of not getting "involved," who adhered to the motto that "no good ever came of working." Happy himself was the eternal fall guy, a more broadly comic variation of Don Quixote or the Fool in Christ. It was impossible for him to see distress of any kind without rushing to relieve it ("I'll help youse" was forever on his lips), but because of his own awkwardness or through sheer ill luck, something always went wrong; even the one he had tried to help would often turn against him, and the stupid Policeman, whose basic conviction was that Hooligan was "a desperate character," would rush in and cart him off to jail, leaving Gus to collect the reward when there was any. Only very occasionally, in the interest of verisimilitude, would Happy get a lucky break and Gus receive his comeuppance. Those were golden days for the strip's devotees.

In 1900 Carl Emil Schultze ("Bunny") introduced "Foxy Grandpa." Here again was a pair of mischievous boys, but this time they were lay figures; the old man occupied the center of the stage. Foxy could play any game and do any trick better than anbody else (once he even demonstrated his wrestling prowess against TR!), and when the boys tried to play a trick on him, as they did every Sunday, he had no difficulty turning the tables. In the early strips the emphasis was upon his skills; later it tended to shift to his quickness of wit. When the boys take sandwiches for themselves to their little ball game but none for him, they find that he has brought delicious blackberry jam sandwiches in his "sectional dairy lunch bat," and when they steal his fishing pole while he feigns sleep, he is quite unperturbed because he has also a "collapsible fishing pole–walking stick." Again, as with Hooligan, there is the occasional variation, as when the boys steal his clothes while he is swimming, and he has to don the woman's dress they have left him to run home in.

A Foxy Grandma made occasional appearances during the early years, but nothing was seen of her thereafter. In 1903 an Uncle Alex, who looked astonishingly like Bernard Shaw, was introduced, along with a Little Lord Fauntleroy kind of boy named Bobby; indeed the name of the strip was changed temporarily to "Foxy Grandpa and Smart Uncle Alex." It is easy to see why both Bobby and Alex were quickly dropped. As Dirks had discovered, three boys were one too many, and since Foxy was more than a match for the boys, there was nothing much for Uncle Alex to do but watch; indeed, there is at least one strip in which Foxy is reduced to playing tricks on him! Schultze soon realized that a man as clever as Foxy Grandpa can have no other handicaps if he is going to succeed in holding our sympathies; in the later cartoons we never doubt either that the boys deserve everything they get or that their grandfather loves them. The artist also progressively refined his line after going over to Hearst from the *World* until he was doing more beautiful drawings than many of his contemporaries could match. One gathers that he was well aware of this; he always refused to let speech balloons break into his drawings; instead the stilted dialogue that was his weakest feature appeared below each panel.

In 1902 R. F. Outcault, who had experimented with many things since the Yellow Kid, hit upon his happiest and most lasting creation in Buster Brown, always accompanied by his talking bulldog, Tige. "Buster Brown" ended in 1926 (Outcault died, at sixty-five, two years later), but he had appeared on the musical comedy stage and in films, his style of dress was widely copied, and Buster Brown shoes are still being sold. "Buster Brown" was one of the very few early cartoons always allowed a full page, and Outcault's drawing was elaborate and frequently beautiful. His little girls were always elegantly outfitted with lace petticoats, and his stock Irish servant girls were a joy. The setting was an upper-middle-class home, for Outcault had left the slums behind him with the Yellow Kid, though one day, in 1910, he introduced that outcast to Buster and had them exchange clothes. The mischievous-boy motif was the same as in "The Katzenjammer Kids," but it was developed without the Dirks fantasy. Buster was mischievous enough, but he had far more personality and charm than Schultze's boys, and his pranks assumed no more license on the score of probability than his medium demanded. Above all, like his creator, he was an incorrigible moralist. The last panel was always devoted to his posted "resolutions," summing up what he had learned from his current experience. He never seemed able to profit by either what had happened to him or the lesson he had drawn from it, but the moralizing itself was unexceptionable and often included references to both current events and standard literature; Outcault, for example, took a dim view of President Roosevelt's interest in hunting and did not hesitate to have Buster denounce it.

The last of the "Big Four" pioneer comic strip artists to be considered here was also the first in the field, James Swinnerton. He attempted many things, but it was with "Little Jimmy," which began in 1904 (not 1905, as sometimes stated), that he really found his stride. Unlike most of his young contemporaries in the comics, Jimmy was not a bad boy but a friendly, innocent little mite, with a round cap and a broad grin, whose difficulty was wholly with his attention span. Sent on an errand, he would hurry out with the best intentions, but if he encountered anything that interested him, he would stop to watch it and entirely forget what he had been sent to do. "Jimmy" came closer to anticipating the movies than any other comic. It was seldom accorded more than a half-page, but instead of dividing this space into the conventional six large panels, Swinnerton would use as many as fifteen small ones, often displaying an action in a series of "shots," each of which advanced the story slightly. He alone among the cartoonists of his time employed parallel action, for we needed to follow not only Jimmy's doings but the fumings of his father at home, generally introduced by a "subtitle": "And in the Mean Time." All in all, "Jimmy" was one of the most creative of the early comics and richly deserves being collected and republished. It is not surprising that Swinnerton, alone among his peers, should have become a standard painter. This happened in Arizona, whither he had been exiled upon developing tuberculosis and which he fell in love with to such an extent that he "forgot to die" until 1974, when he was nearly 100. In later years "Jimmy" too used an Arizona background, and "Canyon Kids" became a regular feature of *Good Housekeeping*.

For convenience sake, I have used the term *strip* with reference to comics in general, though strictly speaking it applies not to the Sunday colored comics, which occupied a page or a half-page, but rather to the daily cartoons, which, in the early days, stretched narrowly (say, half a dozen panels) across a page; the term did not, I believe, come into wide use until after 1907, when "Mutt and Jeff" began to appear as a daily strip. I remember, however, that while I was still very small the Chicago *Daily News* devoted part of its back page to strips, though the only one I specifically recall was that devoted to the adventures of Brainy Bowers and Drowsy Dugan, which was originated by R. W. Taylor and then taken over by Ed Carey, who drew it from 1902 to 1908. Brainy was a crafty, fat-bellied, unshaven tramp, who perpetually led his lean, long, stupid, droopy-mustached companion into scrapes and then left him holding the bag. The night before a holiday, however, all the *News* cartoonists would collaborate in one large, half-page panel, in which all their rascals joined in holiday festivities, and I used to wait for these occasions impatiently and pore over the masterpieces that resulted with endless delight.

Walt McDougall did a number of continuing strips. I remember "Fatty Felix" (1903) well by name, but I can no longer recall what it looked like. "Strange Visitors from the Land of Oz" (1904) is currently being republished in the *Baum Bugle*. "Peck's Bad Boy"

(1906), based of course on the then widely circulated book, which was a kind of subliterary equivalent of the comic strip, I think I never saw.

Since small boys are not interested in courtship, I was bored by F. M. Howarth's "The Love of Lulu and Leander," whose gimmick was to devise every possible means to prevent Leander from "popping the question." Finally, however, he did get his chance and was promptly accepted, whereupon a whole new set of difficulties had to be introduced, involving importantly one Charley Onthespot, who always happened to be on hand to rescue Lulu from whatever predicament the luckless Leander had awkwardly got her into. As I reread "Lulu and Leander" now, it seems to me much brighter than it did then, and certainly Howarth's highly individual style of drawing—his heavy draftsmanship, and his expressive figures with small bodies and huge heads—sets his work off effectively from that of other cartoonists. Like Schultze, whom he strongly influenced in his early period, he eschewed balloons. He died in 1908, in his late thirties.

Two important cartoons were added during TR's second administration—Winsor McCay's "Little Nemo in Slumberland," which made its debut in the New York *Herald* on October 15, 1905, and Bud Fisher's "Mutt and Jeff," which first appeared in the daily San Francisco *Chronicle,* as "Mr. A. Mutt Starts in to Play the Races," on November 15, 1907. "Nemo" switched to Hearst on December 3, 1911, under the title "In the Land of Wonderful Dreams," and continued until July 26, 1914. McCay revived it in the *Herald* between 1924 and 1927, and his son Robert, Nemo's original, revised and reprinted a selection from the old pages in various newspapers during 1947. Hearst had captured Bud Fisher as early as December 10, 1907, whereupon the *Chronicle* hired Russ Westover to continue "A. Mutt" until June 7, 1908, when he literally killed him off. *Mutt and Jeff Cartoons* was the title of the first collection, published in hard cover, in the shape and approximate size of the daily strip, in 1911, but "Mutt and Jeff" did not become the heading used in the newspapers until 1916, and the first Sunday color page did not appear until August 11, 1918. Meanwhile, Fisher had been seduced by the Wheeler Syndicate. At his peak he devoted himself and his weekly income of $4,600 to *la dolce vita,* leaving most of the drawing to be done first by Billy Liverpool and then by Al Smith, who began signing his own name after Fisher's death in 1954.

Two comics could hardly have been more different than "Mutt and Jeff" and "Little Nemo"; indeed "Nemo" was not, properly speaking, a "comic" at all, while "Mutt and Jeff" marks the ultimate triumph of the vulgar, lowbrow, knockdown slapstick that the comics had staked out as their province from the beginning, and the chinless, long-nosed, ill-dressed, overbearing boor with big feet and his silk-hatted, pint-sized, bewhiskered sidekick (representing between them the classical appeal to incongruity as a basic source of humor) would have been quite at home in either vaudeville or burlesque. In the beginning, when the strip appeared on the sports page, its interest was limited both by its preoccupation with horseracing and by the absence of the clarity of line and the sharp contrast of black and white by which it was later distinguished, but it began to expand when, on March 27, 1908, Mutt rescued Jeff (named for the currently popular pugilist, Jim Jeffries) from a lunatic asylum or home for the feebleminded. Jeff's business at the outset was to serve as a punching bag for Mutt, but with all his limitations he often manifested both the cunning and the preternatural wisdom of the humble and moved triumphantly, if not always quite convincingly, into the driver's seat. Beyond this it hardly seems necessary to go on describing a work both so unsubtle and so familiar. Amusing as its gags sometimes are, even now, in what are generally regarded as the days of its decline its main importance is historical. It was not, as has often been said, the first daily strip; indeed, it derived directly from Clare Briggs's "A. Piker, Clerk," which Hearst had killed because he thought it vulgar, but it was the first great success in that form, and its influence was large.

Winsor McCay lived from 1869 to 1934. In addition to "Nemo" and other comics, he drew political cartoons for Arthur Brisbane editorials, presented a cartooning act in vaudeville, and created *Gertie the Dinosaur* (1909), a pioneering animated movie cartoon. "Nemo" and George Herriman's "Krazy Kat," which did not appear until 1910 or become an independent strip until three years later, are the most honored of all comics, and "Nemo" has been exhibited at both the Metropolitan and the Louvre. The formula is as simple as that of any comic: Nemo falls asleep and has enchanting, sometimes terrifying, dreams; in the last panel he wakes up or falls out of bed. The development is something else again. A master of perspective, with a gift for color, a passion for the decorative in any form, and a taste for fantasy, romantic scenery, animals, clowns, parades, pageantry, and every conceivable kind of elaborate architecture, McCay broke up his page into any form or shape he desired, sometimes using only five panels (including the tiny one in Nemo's bedroom at the end), sometimes as many as twenty. He would devote half a page to a single picture if he chose or put a huge, circular drawing in the middle, grouping the smaller pictures around it. One installment depicts in almost cinematic terms the approach of a huge elephant who, at the end, seems about ready to swallow the viewer. Another, much greater cartoon (December 27, 1908) shows the earth shrinking with the waning year until Old Man 1908 falls off at last and Baby 1909 arrives to take possession.

Generally speaking, "Nemo" is at its best when McCay applies what James Branch Cabell called "an elaborate and unflinching naturalism" to the world of dreams. This is done very simply in the lovely piece in which Nemo, putting his Noah's Ark figures away, finds the ark and its contents expanding and the animals coming to life and swarming out and, on a much more grandiose scale, in the Thanksgiving nightmare in which his house is picked up in the bill of a giant turkey and himself spilled out and doused in a lake of cranberry sauce. McCay could descend to ineffective grotesquerie. Sometimes his inspiration flagged, and sometimes the dream motivation got lost in mere fantastic adventure, but the one great weakness in "Little Nemo" was the shadowiness of its characters. Compared to Buster Brown, for example, Nemo is not interesting in himself, for he is merely the dreamer to whom something happens, and the Princess of Slumberland, whose desire to have him for a playmate impels his journeying, is not characterized at all. The green-faced Flip, with his perpetual oversize cigar, is more vivid, but he is certainly not attractive, and though the cannibal child Impy is more lovable he has very little to do.

One other greatly inferior cartoon of the period must be mentioned as at least a harbinger: the "Hairbreadth Harry" of the German-born C. W. Kahles, a prolific but crude artist, who contributed a variety of work to both the newspapers and such magazines as *Judge* and *Puck*. "Hairbreadth Harry," which began in the Philadelphia Sunday *Press* in 1906, added a daily strip in 1923, and Kahles continued both until he died in 1931, when F. O. Alexander took it over for eight more years. It was the first cliffhanger in the comics, anticipating the movie serials, which did not really get underway until 1913–14, and pointing the way toward the adventure trend that was ultimately to rob the funny papers of most of their humor. "Harry" was intended as a burlesque of the dime novels and cheap melodramas of the time (the villain Rudolph Rassendale, with his black formal clothes and gleaming white teeth— "Curses on you, Harold Hollingsworth!"—was as stagy as he could possibly have been, and the name of the heroine, Belinda the Beautiful Boiler-Maker, was an inspired takeoff on *Bertha, the Sewing Machine Girl*), but I am sure many children took it quite as seriously as I did. Kahles was imitated by Harry Hershfield, whose "Desperate Desmond" began as a daily strip in the Hearst papers on March 11, 1910, and I used to go down to the California Avenue elevated station every summer morning and spend a penny for the Chicago *American* as soon as it came out to learn how Rosamund and Claude Eclair were faring. "Desperate Desmond" had a more catchy name than "Harry," and it seems better remembered, but it had a much shorter life; in 1912 it was turned into a kind of political allegory, and the next year it folded.

IN 1900 some 5,500 periodicals were being published in the United States, and the first generalization that needs to be made is that the general magazine was much more important to readers than it is today and counted for much more as literature. Many writers derived more income from serials than from books, and a great many addressed a far larger audience in the magazines.

The "quality group" was headed by the *Atlantic Monthly*, *Harper's Magazine*, the *Century*, and *Scribner's Magazine*. Begun in 1857 and now the property of Houghton, Mifflin and Company, the *Atlantic* had begun as the organ of the New England writers of the Golden Age, and though it had long since attempted to shed insularity (in our period it had more subscribers in Wisconsin and Michigan than in Massachusetts), it was still regarded as the conservator of their tradition. Its reputation for austerity was, at the beginning of the century, due largely to its eschewing illustrations and printing its table of contents on its plain brownish cover, but it had long nourished the local-color movement, and excellent as Mary Johnston's *To Have and to Hold* was in kind, the fact that it should have shown itself, at the beginning of Bliss Perry's editorship, the most successful serial the magazine had ever had hardly indicates a very severe taste in fiction on the part of its readership.

The end of the "old" or traditional *Atlantic* had come during the editorship (1890–1898) of the gifted Horace E. Scudder, who ran a

By the Week or the Month

11

magazine of high literary quality that sold fewer than 10,000 copies. In 1898 the iconoclastic southerner Walter Hines Page took over, reminding everybody of what lately there had been considerable tendency to overlook, that the periodical had been founded as "A Magazine of Literature, Art *and Politics.*" Though Page's tenure covered only a year, it marked a turning point. Bliss Perry, who succeeded him and remained in control until 1909, was the last man who could be expected to underplay literary quality, but neither did he forget that the magazine was part of the contemporary scene.

Though Perry had his doubts about the value of long novels in magazines, he did serialize Mary Johnston's *Audrey,* as well as novels by Sarah Orne Jewett, Robert Herrick, Mary Austin, and May Sinclair, whose contribution some readers thought indecent. There were other protests on nonmoral grounds. When President Eliot was permitted to suggest that the curriculum of the Jesuit colleges was somewhat old-fashioned, the *Atlantic* was assailed as anti-Catholic, and when Henry Dwight Sedgwick spoke sympathetically of the Church in Italy, another group was just as sure that it had gone over to Rome. John Burroughs ruffled the feathers of the "nature fakers," and Philip Churchman offended the Christian Scientists. But the most distinguished objector was the president of the United States, who complained, through Henry Cabot Lodge, of Rollo Ogden's ("Alciphron's") rather bitterly satirical "Letter to Theodore Roosevelt" in March 1905, the first of a proposed series of "Letters to Literary Statesmen." This time the publishers panicked and demanded an apology and the discontinuance of the series; instead they got Perry's resignation; they refused to accept it and agreed to the editor's terms.

James, Howells, Thomas Bailey Aldrich, Edith Wharton, and other predictables contributed short fiction, but there were also new voices like Jack London and John Buchan. James, W. C. Brownell, Alice Meynell, and others produced critical articles, and there were more scholarly pieces about European writers than any general magazine would print now. Perry did not regard his record in poetry as brilliant, but he did print Edwin Arlington Robinson and Father Tabb, and remembering that the jingo Page had had the flag on the cover during the Spanish war, he got special satisfaction out of Moody's "An Ode in Time of Hesitation." There were brilliant essays by Agnes Repplier, Samuel McChord Crothers, Woodrow Wilson, Paul Elmer More, William James, and others. Besides Burroughs, John Muir and Bradford Torrey were stalwarts in nature writing, and in Gamaliel Bradford, Perry discovered a writer whose biographical portraits were to be a prime attraction through many years beyond his own editorship. The number that contained Grover Cleveland's article, "The Independence of the Executive," sold a record 23,000 copies.

In 1908 Houghton Mifflin sold the magazine to the new Atlantic Monthly Company, of which Ellery Sedgwick was president, and Sedgwick edited it until 1938. Generally eschewing serial fiction, Sedgwick proved himself a genius at unearthing human interest narratives in unexpected places, and his devotion to letters was attested not only by his fidelity to such writers as Crothers and Miss Repplier but by his discovery, among others, of the bookish A. Edward Newton.

Harper's Magazine had begun in 1850, and its function at the outset was to "transfer" contemporary British fiction to an American magazine without the bother of having to pay for it. This was all long past in 1900, thirty-one years after Henry Mills Alden had become editor; he would continue for nineteen more. In the nineties *Harper's* had become a large, lavishly illustrated magazine, commanding such talents as Howard Pyle, Edwin Austin Abbey, W. T. Smedley, Albert Sterner, and F. C. Yohn, with the halftone engraving edging out the older and more expensive woodcut. The addition of full color came in 1900, turning Pyle in the direction of medievalism as an illustrator of the early stories of James Branch Cabell and many others, and also involving such reliable talents as those of Elizabeth Shippen Green, Jessie Willcox Smith, and William Hurd Lawrence. Pyle was never more gorgeous than when illustrating his own stories in the lavish Christmas numbers, as with "The Mysterious Chest" in 1908 and "The Salem Wolf" a year later. He also pulled out all the stops for Mark Twain's essay, "Saint Joan of Arc," in 1904, with four color plates, one of which, showing the girl of Domremy in communion with her saints, is one of his finest pictures.

In 1902 Alden still boasted of having excluded "the acutely journalistic article that used to be classed as 'timely.' " By 1910 he was to change his tune slightly; the magazine's field was now "the living present." Yet *Harper's* never did change fundamentally during Alden's tenure.

The *Century* began in 1881 as a continuation of the old *Scribner's Monthly* and was edited until his death in 1909 by the poet–reform crusader Richard Watson Gilder and from then until 1913 by Robert Underwood Johnson. The name was taken from that of the Century Club, and the new publishing company that became responsible for both it and *St. Nicholas* was called the Century Company.

Printed until 1914 by Theodore Low De Vinne at the De Vinne Press and wrapped in a beautiful cover designed by Saint-Gaudens and Stanford White, the *Century* was even handsomer than *Harper's*. It vied with the older magazine in its illustrations, and its more open type page was more inviting. The great success of the early years had been the famous series on "Battles and Leaders of the Civil War," written by the participants, which ran circulation figures up to 225,000 and earned more than a million dollars for the company, and this had been followed by an abridged version of Nicolay and Hay's *Lincoln* and much other biography and autobiography. In our period, however, circulation was running about 125,000 to 150,000.

If this suggests that the *Century* was not a literary magazine, the impression is only partly accurate. Gilder serialized *A Modern Instance* and *The Rise of Silas Lapham* for Howells, *The Bostonians* for James, and *Hugh Wynne, Free Quaker* for S. Weir Mitchell. It is true, however, that he recognized from the beginning the need for discussing "living, practical questions," and though it never really joined the muckrakers, the *Century* was more reform-minded than *Harper's*. Gilder printed articles on the Spanish-American War, reminiscences by Cleveland, and an article by Taft on the Panama Canal. Frank Sprague, who built the first trolley, described it in the *Century*; Langley wrote on astronomy and Madame Curie on radium. In March 1909 there was even a "White House Number."

The artists we have already met in *Harper's* also sometimes appeared in the *Century*. The four paintings Pyle did for his own text, "The Travels of the Soul" (December 1902), rank with his best. Joseph Pennell did a series on cathedrals. Jules Guérin seemed at home in both old France and contemporary New York, and Maxfield Parrish did equally well with Edith Wharton's Italian villas and gardens and Ray Stannard Baker's Southwest, to say nothing of his pictures for Milton's "L'Allegro" and "Il Penseroso" in the

1901 Christmas number. Sometimes, even, art work appeared without accompanying text, and Gilder's interest in the theater was directly reflected in Sigismond de Ivanowski's paintings of famous singers and actresses.

When the *Century* broke away from *Scribner's Monthly*, it was agreed that Charles Scribner's Sons would not launch another magazine for five years. In January 1887, the first issue of *Scribner's Magazine*, edited by Edwin L. Burlingame, who would remain in charge until 1916, appeared on the stands, 100,000 strong, in a cover designed by Stanford White and sensationally priced at a quarter, or ten cents under the price of its competitors. It would take a few years to achieve a steady 100,000 circulation figure, but by 1900 the magazine was outselling its rivals at 165,000, and this would go to a temporary all-time high of 215,000 in 1910, when Theodore Roosevelt's *African Game Trails*, for which the magazine had paid him $50,000, sold out on the newsstands.

In the beginning the *Scribner's* emphasis was on literature and art; later more "timely" articles appeared, though never to the same extent as in the *Century*. Art always remained important; by 1900 the department "The Field of Art" was well established, while Ernest G. Peixotto had embarked upon a long series of travel articles illustrated by himself. This interest was stimulated, among other things, by the World's Columbian Exposition, and the May 1893 number, exhibiting the leading illustrators of the time, was designed for exhibition there.

Scribner's always provided a great showcase for Scribner writers: Stevenson, Theodore Roosevelt, J. M. Barrie, Frank R. Stockton, Thomas Nelson Page, F. Hopkinson Smith, Richard Harding Davis, and later John Galsworthy, of all of whom the firm published collected editions. *The Little Shepherd of Kingdom Come*, by John Fox, Jr., was serialized in 1903 and the less impressive but not less popular *Trail of the Lonesome Pine* in 1908. In 1905 appeared the finest of Edith Wharton's early novels, *The House of Mirth*, to be followed by *Ethan Frome* in 1911. There were short stories by Katharine Fullerton Gerould, Mary Raymond Shipman Andrews, Robert Herrick ("The Master of the Inn" in December 1907), Mary Synon, Kate Douglas Wiggin, Alice Brown, and many more; poetry by Edwin Arlington Robinson, Henry van Dyke, Arthur Davison Ficke, and Katharine Lee Bates; criticism and essays by W. C. Brownell, Brander Matthews, and E. S. Martin. Ernest Thompson

Seton and William T. Hornaday wrote of animals. Perhaps the most "topical" thing *Scribner's* or any of the quality group ever did was to publish an annual "Motoring Issue" beginning in 1906. Probably this was suggested by the earlier railroads series, which had increased circulation by 25,000; it certainly tied up with the interest in travel articles that *Scribner's* shared with its competitors and which gave abundant opportunity for illustrations by both artists (especially Edward Penfield) and photographers. John La Farge's article on Puvis de Chavannes, featured in the Christmas number for 1900 with color reproductions of his paintings, created a sensation; thereafter Pyle, Parrish, Wyeth, Remington, Yohn, Arthur Rackham, and Jessie Willcox Smith were all in evidence, as were Howard Chandler Christy and Frederick Dorr Steele on a different level.

Among the other quality magazines current in 1900, the *North American Review* was the aristocratic oldster; originating in Boston in 1815, it had been edited by Lowell, Charles Eliot Norton, and Henry Adams. In 1899 George Harvey acquired it, publishing some of Mark Twain's most significant social criticism, including "To the Person Sitting in Darkness," "To My Missionary Critics," and "A Defence of General Funston," as well as some of the Christian Science material and the earliest selections to appear from the *Autobiography*, and serializing *The Ambassadors* by Henry James, *The Son of Royal Langbrith* by Howells, and *Under Western Eyes* by Joseph Conrad. Harvey made the *Review*, which he owned until 1926, a distinctly personal organ, pro-TR in 1904 and anti-TR from 1906, when he began booming Wilson. By 1916 he would turn against him too.

The *Arena* and the *Forum* were openly dedicated to controversy. The former, founded by B. O. Flower in Boston in 1889 and edited largely by him until it folded in 1909, had a leftist slant, advocating free silver, feminism, the single tax, and Populist causes. Flower discussed prostitution and advocated birth control while such subjects were generally ignored in respectable journals. At the beginning he gave considerable attention to religion, showed an interest in psychical research, and gave an early hearing to Hamlin Garland. He had a melancholy end; when he died in 1918, he was editing one of the most notorious of all American papers, the Catholic-baiting *Menace*. The trademark of the *Forum* was the symposium, not always on questions of public policy. When Frederick

Taber Cooper became editor in 1908, fiction and poetry were introduced, and the next year it was sold to Mitchell Kennerley, who made it a literary magazine. After 1916 it would move back toward the forum idea. Three university-sponsored quarterlies were beginning to be known during our period: the *Yale Review*, the *Sewanee Review*, and the *South Atlantic Quarterly*. All were destined to long life and considerable distinction, but the first would become the best known.

Two magazines were devoted entirely to literature: the *Bookman* and the *Dial*. Founded in 1895, the *Bookman* was published by Dodd, Mead and Company and edited until 1907 by the brilliant if flashy Harry Thurston Peck, who was both an excellent scholar and a topflight journalist. Though its principal interest was contemporary American literature, the *Bookman* also covered Europe and published articles on older writers. It printed poetry and drama criticism and carried some fiction serials, notably Paul Leicester Ford's *Janice Meredith*. In 1907 it had a circulation of 40,000, but this dropped to 12,000 before it was sold to George H. Doran in 1918. The *Dial* was Chicago-based, edited by Francis F. Browne and published first by A. C. McClurg and Company but after 1892 by the editor himself. Its criticism, generally conservative but very able, was written largely by scholastics. In 1916 it would move to New York, where it became a handsomely and expensively printed *avant-garde* magazine, specializing in rising contemporaries, as well as "elder statesmen" who were "modern" in their outlook, and illustrated with "far-out" art.

Two monthlies were devoted to current affairs: the *American Review of Reviews* and the *World's Work*. The former began in 1890 as the American edition of W. T. Stead's English *Review of Reviews* and was edited throughout its history by Albert Shaw. Each issue opened with a thirty-page survey of "The Progress of the World," written by Shaw, which was followed by contributed articles and a fairly comprehensive account of what was appearing elsewhere. Its general outlook was conservative and Republican, and it gave some attention to books. The *World's Work* followed a similar plan but was handsomer and less of a miscellany. It began in 1900, after its editor had left the *Atlantic* to join Frank N. Doubleday in establishing Doubleday, Page & Company. Committed to "the literature of achievement," the *World's Work* reflected the optimism of a new century in "the richest of all countries." Though Page was not incapable of criticizing abuses, his was distinctly a big-business point of view. He was interested in conservation and national parks and in the industrial development of the South.

The ranking weekly journals of news and opinion were the *Independent* (1848), the *Nation* (1865), the *Outlook* (1870), and, in a different class and with a different emphasis, the *Literary Digest* (1890). Of these, the *Independent* and the *Outlook* were in our period the most important.

Both had been founded as religious papers (Congregational), and both had enlisted the talents of Henry Ward Beecher. The *Independent* was founded by Henry C. Bowen, and both he and Theodore Tilton were important in its early history. These men, first Beecher's friends, became his accusers in the great scandal of the seventies, when circulation dropped from 75,000 to 15,000, and it is curious that when the paper was sold in 1913 its new owner, Hamilton Holt, should have been Bowen's grandson; Holt made it a well-illustrated, handsomely printed, fair-minded journal, with articles on almost everything in which intelligent people were currently interested, including literature, science, and international peace.

The *Christian Union*, later called the *Outlook*, was Beecher's paper after the termination of his connection with the *Independent*. In 1894 Lyman Abbott became editor-in-chief and remained at the helm until his death in 1922. *The Theology of an Evolutionist*, *The Life and Letters of Paul*, *Reminiscences*, and *Silhouettes of My Contemporaries* were all serialized in the *Outlook*, and there were countless "Letters to Unknown Friends" and "Knoll Papers."

From 1897 to 1917 one issue each month was an enlarged "illustrated magazine number," and Theodore Roosevelt's *Autobiography*, Booker T. Washington's *Up from Slavery*, Hamilton Wright Mabie's *William Shakespeare: Poet, Dramatist, and Man*, and Edward Everett Hale's *James Russell Lowell and His Friends* were among the magazine serials. Book reviews tended to be brief and conservative. Paul Van Dyke wrote on art and Daniel Gregory Mason on music. George Kennan was Washington correspondent from 1902, and Frederic C. Howe and Frederick M. Davenport were other standbys. In 1928 the *Outlook* would be merged with the *Independent*, but the life of the combined paper was brief.

The *Nation* had been edited from 1865 to 1881 by Edwin L. Godkin. In that year it became the weekly edition of the New York *Evening Post* and continued thus until 1914. From 1909 to 1914 it was edited by the distinguished critic Paul Elmer More. Displeased by Roosevelt's conduct in Panama, the paper supported Parker in 1904 and Taft in 1908 and was in Wilson's corner in both 1912 and 1916. Oswald Garrison Villard, son of Henry Villard, who had held a controlling interest in the *Post* for many years, came into the paper in the nineties but did not become editor until 1918, when a great, new, vigorous period would begin.

If the *Nation* was between great periods in 1900, *Harper's Weekly* was pretty well past its prime. Its early fame had rested upon its serial publication of such novels as *A Tale of Two Cities* and *The Woman in White*, Winslow Homer's Civil War pictures, and in the 1870s the powerful cartoons with which Thomas Nast sent Tweed to prison (to say nothing of the happier ones in which he created the American image of Santa Claus). In the nineties its pictures had been as splendid as those of *Harper's Magazine* itself. Its great editor, George William Curtis, died in 1892, and George Harvey came in in 1901. Harpers sold it in 1913, and Norman Hapgood proved a much less successful editor than he had been with *Collier's*.

Collier's and the *Saturday Evening Post* were weeklies of another sort. The *Post* began in 1821, printed as a newspaper but filled largely with clipped literary material for weekend reading. After many changes and vicissitudes, it found itself in 1897 with only 2,000 subscribers. Cyrus H. K. Curtis bought it and proceeded to make it the most successful of all weeklies. From 1899 to 1936 it was edited by George Horace Lorimer, who directed its appeal primarily to young men who wished to get ahead in the world. Though it lost $800,000 before it began to pay, circulation hit 1 million in 1908 and climbed rapidly thereafter. There was no radical change in its character until after the editorship of Wesley Winans Stout ended in 1942.

The general outlook of the *Post* was conservative, isolationist, and "100 percent American." It supported Wilson in 1916 because "he kept us out of war" and never forgave him for changing. Later it was pro-Hoover and anti-FDR. But it was not indifferent to the abuses of big business and could always be depended upon to support conservation. Frank Norris's *The Pit* was serialized in 1901, *The Call of the Wild* by Jack London in 1903. Lorimer's own *Let-*

ters of a Self-Made Merchant to His Son struck the authentic *Post* note. Mary Roberts Rinehart's *Tish* stories and Corra Harris's writings about *A Circuit Rider's Wife* came after the magazine had begun to reach out for women readers about 1908. Among the many other writers whose names the *Post* made household words were Booth Tarkington, Rex Beach, Emerson Hough, George Randolph Chester, Arthur Train, William Allen White, Harry Leon Wilson, P. G. Wodehouse, Peter B. Kyne, Irvin S. Cobb, Octavius Roy Cohen, Sinclair Lewis, Clarence Budington Kelland, Montague Glass, Eugene Manlove Rhodes, and Joseph Hergesheimer. Though it is part of the legend that the *Post* was indifferent to literature, the selections reprinted in *The Saturday Evening Post Treasury* hardly bear this out.

The first colored cover appeared on September 30, 1899; thereafter there was one each month until 1903, after which all covers were printed in color, though the full scale was not employed until 1936. J. C. Leyendecker began contributing his brilliant, fanciful, humorous covers in 1903; Norman Rockwell's thirty-year reign began in 1916, to the delight of all America. In 1915 motorcar advertisements were filling about one-quarter of the advertising pages, with clothes, food, cameras, insurance, patent razors, and books following in that order. The *Post* rejected advertisements for liquor, cigarettes, and patent medicines.

Collier's emerged in 1895 out of the cocoon of *Once a Week*, a small magazine sold in connection with P. F. Collier's cheap subscription sets of standard authors, and its importance dates from the assumption of the editorship by the publisher's son Robert in 1898. Norman Hapgood was in charge of the editorial page through a brilliant decade, 1902–12, and Mark Sullivan and Finley Peter Dunne were also important. The magazine did a distinguished job covering the Spanish-American and Russo-Japanese wars and brought out a famous San Francisco earthquake number in 1906.

The Eternal City by Hall Caine was serialized in 1901, and there were new Sherlock Holmes stories in 1903. Kipling, Frank Norris, Israel Zangwill, Robert W. Chambers, Stanley J. Weyman, Owen Wister, Booth Tarkington, F. Marion Crawford, and Edith Wharton were all important contributors of fiction; besides Dunne, the humorists included George Ade, Jerome K. Jerome, Oliver Herford, and Wallace Irwin ("Hashimura Togo"). After 1900 fiction declined in importance, but H. G. Wells's *Mr. Britling Sees It Through* would make a very strong impression during World War I.

The artists employed on *Collier's* included Harrison Fisher, Howard Chandler Christy, James Montgomery Flagg, J. C. Leyendecker, and, above all, Maxfield Parrish and Charles Dana Gibson. In 1903 the creator of "the Gibson girl" signed a contract to deliver 100 pictures over four years at $1,000 each, and Parrish was under exclusive contract to *Collier's* from 1904 to 1910; his great *Arabian Nights* series was a feature of 1906–7.

This was the delightsome side of *Collier's;* its great public service came in connection with its articles on public affairs and its championship of many forward-looking causes. Its attacks on patent medicines and false advertising were notable. It did valiant service against the "standpatters" in Congress and contributed importantly to the fall of Secretary of the Interior Ballinger. It clashed with Hearst, the Post cereal interests, and others.

P. F. Collier died in 1909, his son, who was not a good businessman, in 1918. He had broken with Hapgood in 1912 (Hapgood was for Wilson, Collier for Roosevelt). In 1934 the paper was sold to the Crowell interests. In 1942 it was still selling 3 million copies, and at the end of the decade there was even another big exposé campaign. But the glory was fading. Crowell folded the *American Magazine* in August 1956, and both *Collier's* and *Woman's Home Companion* soon followed.

The revolutionary development of the nineties and the early 1900s was the challenge to the quality magazines posed by the new ten- and fifteen-cent monthlies that deliberately set out to meet them on their own ground (though with more emphasis on the "timely") and built up enormous circulations which enabled them to outbid the veterans for favorite writers. Most of these were importantly involved in the "muckraking" campaigns. *Munsey's* was the pioneer. It began in 1891 but did not really catch on until the ten-cent price was adopted two years later. By all means the most important was *McClure's.*

This was founded in 1893 by S. S. McClure and John Sanborn Phillips in connection with their literary syndicate business. Its first real success came with Ida M. Tarbell's biography of Napoleon, beginning in November 1894. Miss Tarbell followed this in 1895–96 with "The Early Life of Lincoln," for which she dug out many hitherto unrecorded reminiscences and many unused pictures. Stevenson, Kipling, Tarkington, Anthony Hope, O. Henry, and many other fictionists followed. There were articles on science and technology, natural history, and exploration, and much attention was given to autobiography and interviews with living celebrities. By 1900, 375,000 copies were being printed.

The magazine's muckraking was foreshadowed in 1901, when Edwin Lefèvre wrote a series of pieces with a thin fictional veneer covering notorious doings in Wall Street and Frances Willard's tramp nephew, Josiah Frank Willard, produced a series on "The World of Graft," but the grand offensive opened with Miss Tarbell's scholarly and minutely researched history of the Standard Oil Company beginning in 1902. In January 1903 Lincoln Steffens published the first in his "Shame of the Cities" series, and Ray Stannard Baker went after union labor "rackets." Steffens's exposures touched distinguished senators, set off grand jury investigations, and elected reform administrations in the cities. In 1903 too Ernest Poole exposed the vice- and disease-breeding conditions under which New York City newsboys were compelled to live, and in 1904 there was a courageous discussion of Negro problems. After Willa Cather became a member of the staff, she contributed short stories, articles, and her first novel, *Alexander's Bridge* (she is also credited with having done the actual writing on Georgine Milmine's controversial life of Mrs. Eddy). *McClure's* boasted art features also, and the reproductions of famous paintings that accompanied La Farge's series on great artists in 1901–2 created a sensation.

McClure himself was a restless eccentric and a megalomaniac as well as a genius, and in 1906, after he had drawn up a grandiose scheme involving not only vast new publishing projects but a bank, a life insurance company, and various benevolent projects, Phillips, Steffens, Miss Tarbell, and others left him and purchased the *American Magazine*. In 1911 he sold *McClure's* to Frederick Collins and Cameron MacKenzie but remained as titular editor for two years more. Thereafter the history of the magazine was checkered and worse until it finally suspended publication in 1929.

Munsey's was more given to the glorification of big business than to muckraking, and it was always heavy on pictures of women. After Robert Hobart Davis joined the staff in 1904, it became

known for its short fiction, and in 1905 it contracted with
O. Henry for a first view of all his work. In 1921 it would become
an all-fiction pulp magazine, following in the footsteps of another
Munsey project, the *Argosy*.

Everybody's, born in 1899, achieved its first peak with Thomas
W. Lawson's articles on "Frenzied Finance" in 1904–7. The articles
were nearly as frenzied as the practices exposed, but Charles Edward Russell, Upton Sinclair, and others later conducted muckraking more responsibly. *Everybody's* serialized Hall Caine's *The
Prodigal Son*, Rex Beach's *The Spoilers*, and Jack London's *Before
Adam*, and, less predictably, published Shaw's *Pygmalion* and *Great
Catherine*. TR went after the "nature fakers" in its pages, and
Hamlin Garland explored "The Shadow World." In 1909 it was
sold to the Butterick interests, and in 1921 it too became an all-
fiction magazine, which it remained until it died in 1929.

Cosmopolitan was founded in 1886 as a general literary monthly.
In 1889 John Brisben Walker bought it and engaged distinguished
writers and editors, including, in 1892, Howells, who was to serve
as joint editor with himself, but that lasted only two months. *Cosmopolitan* was jingoistic whenever there was threat of war and
much given to grandiose plans. In 1897 Cosmopolitan University
was organized to award college degrees by correspondence, and in
1902 a world congress was proposed. Walker was greatly interested
in railroads, automobiles, subways, yachts, and planes, and he gave
much space to the great fairs. In 1906, when the circulation had
reached half a million, he sold the magazine to Hearst, who soon
doubled it by printing much the same kind of material he used in
his Sunday supplements.

Cosmopolitan got into muckraking with David Graham Phillips's 1906 series on "The Treason of the Senate," which attacked
offending senators by name. Alfred Henry Lewis did a series on
"The Owners of America," Charles Edward Russell went after election frauds and Edwin Markham after child labor, while Poultney
Bigelow exposed graft in the Canal Zone. There were symposia on
Mormonism, Christian Science, and "What Life Means to Me."
Artists like Harrison Fisher and Penrhyn Stanlaws were in heavy
demand for their portraits of beautiful women, and there were
many photographs of actresses. After 1912 muckraking would be
dropped and reliance placed upon such fictionists as Robert W.

Chambers, Elinor Glyn, and Gouverneur Morris, though Tarkington (*Penrod*) and George Ade (*Fables in Slang*) also appeared.

The *American Magazine* was an outgrowth of *Frank Leslie's Popular Monthly*. The future editor of the *Atlantic,* Ellery Sedgwick,
was in charge from 1900; the change of name occurred in 1905,
and in 1906, as already related, it was purchased by the rebels
seceding from McClure's. These began by continuing their muckraking, but the emphasis soon shifted to "human interest"; as
"David Grayson," Ray Stannard Baker symptomatically became
the purveyor of "Adventures in Contentment." The magazine continued its commitment to civic welfare, however, serializing both
La Follette's autobiography and Jane Addams's *Twenty Years at
Hull-House*. In 1915 it was sold to the Crowell Company and became a decidedly "wholesome" "success" magazine for the middle
class.

The great women's magazines of the time were the *Delineator*
(1873), the *Ladies' Home Journal* (1883), *Good Housekeeping* (1885),
McCall's and *Woman's Home Companion* (both 1897), and *Pictorial
Review* (1899). Of these the *Journal* became the most famous, especially during the years (1889–1919) it was edited by Edward W.
Bok, but *Good Housekeeping* also carved out a spectacular success
for itself along rather different lines. The *Delineator, Pictorial Review,* and *McCall's* all began in the interest of selling dress patterns. The *Delineator* pushed fashions to the back in 1903, and
from 1907 to 1910 it was in charge of Theodore Dreiser, who edited
discreetly but gave much attention to social problems and especially to underprivileged children. The best-known editor of the
Companion was Gertrude B. Lane, who came in 1911 and remained
for thirty years; Kathleen Norris, Edna Ferber, and Dorothy Can-
field were among her stalwarts. Only the *Journal, McCall's,* and
Good Housekeeping survive today, and the *Journal,* no longer published by Curtis, is nothing that Bok would recognize.

It had begun as a supplement to Curtis's *Tribune and Farmer,*
and for the first six years was edited by his wife. It was Bok who
introduced distinguished writers and added numerous departments
and services; in 1902 circulation hit a million, and by World War I
the editors were receiving and replying to a million letters a year.
In the early days, D. L. Moody had a Sunday School department
called "Moody's Bible Class"; later Lyman Abbott presented a more

modern conception of religion. Josef Hofmann edited a musical department, and compositions by distinguished composers were printed; Reginald De Koven was even commissioned to compose music for Kipling's "Recessional," whose *Just-So Stories* and *Puck of Pook's Hill* also appeared in the *Journal.* Jane Addams, Helen Keller, and Rosa Bonheur discussed their work; on the lighter side there were reminiscential and other articles by famous actresses and singers including Geraldine Farrar, Mary Garden, Maude Adams, and Mary Pickford. In 1906–7 there was a department presenting the views of the president "on those national questions which affect the vital interests of the home, by a writer intimately acquainted and in close touch with him," and at one time TR himself wrote anonymously a year's articles under the caption "Men" (when the war came the *Journal* was very proud to be the third most popular magazine with the doughboys). Children and others enjoyed Rose O'Neill's Kewpies, and there were magnificent color reproductions (the *Journal's* large page gave it an advantage over even *Harper's* and the *Century* here), not only of work by Parrish, Wyeth, and others but also of famous paintings in the museums. W. L. Taylor's Bible pictures were very popular and were afterward used by Scribners to illustrate *The Children's Bible.*

The *Journal* banned all immoral and suggestive copy in both text and advertising and all references to tobacco, alcohol, and cards. On woman suffrage Bok was conservative, but he pioneered courageously in sex education and did valiant service in campaigning against the public drinking cup and venereal diseases and helping rout the power interests at Niagara Falls. For years the magazine published plans and price scales for small homes, and it was equally useful on furniture, pictures, and interior decoration in general.

Good Housekeeping, which Hearst purchased in 1911, also achieved great success; at one time it showed a greater profit than all the publisher's other magazines together. In 1900 it set up an Experiment Station to test everything mentioned in the magazine and began offering money-back guarantees on every advertisement. In 1905 there was a "Roll of Honor for Pure Food Products." Dr. Harvey W. Wiley's aid was enlisted, and in 1909 the Good Housekeeping Seal of Approval was originated. Though these and other practices sparked controversy, sometimes involving the government and the courts, they were imitated by *McCall's, Parents' Magazine,* and *Better Homes and Gardens.*

The children had two distinguished publications of their own— the monthly *St. Nicholas* and the weekly *Youth's Companion. St. Nicholas* was founded by Roswell Smith in 1873, three years after *Scribner's Monthly,* and the author of *Hans Brinker,* Mary Mapes Dodge, was its editor until 1905. In its pages appeared *Little Lord Fauntleroy, Davy and the Goblin, Tom Sawyer Abroad* and *Captain January,* L. Frank Baum's *Queen Zixi of Ix,* Palmer Cox's Brownies, Gelett Burgess's Goops, and many other delights.

The *Youth's Companion* dated back to Boston in 1827, when it was founded by Nathaniel Parker Willis's father as a distinctly moral and religious paper. At first its contents were "selected," but original material, including fiction, began to appear early. Willis sold the paper in 1857 to a firm that published under a made-up name, Perry Mason & Company. Famous writers began to appear in the sixties, and every October there was a "Premium List Number," which was a mighty circulation builder. Most of the famous poets of the flowering of New England contributed, and distinguished men worked on the staff. Circulation remained above a half-million until 1907, after which there were numerous changes and a general decline set in.

Many more specialized magazines invite comment, but I will resist the temptation except for two: *Life* and the *Smart Set.* The latter began in 1900 and until 1911 was published by the scandal-monger Colonel William D'Alton Mann of *Town Topics.* Its tone was one of deliberate, almost desperate, sophistication, in defiance of conventional morality wherever possible; it printed mostly fiction but gave some attention to criticism and light verse. In 1911 it was sold to John Adams Thayer, and from 1914 to 1923, when they left it to establish the *American Mercury,* the editors were H. L. Mencken and George Jean Nathan, who employed a variety of tricks, including the subsidiary publication of what Mencken later called "louse magazines," to put it on its feet financially.

Life began in 1883, fathered by the enthusiasm of some young Harvard men who felt the need of a satirical illustrated weekly more sophisticated than *Judge* or *Puck. Life* was against vivisection, the protective tariff, the Chicago anarchists, James G. Blaine, Ward McAllister and the 400, and, when the war came, the kaiser; it made fun of Christian Science and defended mistreated horses, and it established a fresh air fund to send poor children to the country. From 1887 to 1907 its pages were decorated by the Gibson girl, and in the twenties, with Robert Sherwood as editor, it pioneered in serious film criticism. In 1932 it would be sold to Time, Inc., and give its name to a new picture magazine.

IN January 1900 the *Bookman* reported the six following headliners among best-selling books—all American, all written by men, all except the last works of fiction, of which four were historical romances:

Janice Meredith, Paul Leicester Ford
Richard Carvel, Winston Churchill
When Knighthood Was in Flower, Charles Major
David Harum, Edward Noyes Westcott
Via Crucis, F. Marion Crawford
Mr. Dooley in the Hearts of His Countrymen, Finley Peter Dunne

One year later, the magazine cumulated its monthly reports, noting the appearance of the following titles during 1900 on the number of monthly lists indicated (I omit works that appeared only once).

To Have and to Hold, Mary Johnston (8)
Janice Meredith; Richard Carvel; When Knighthood Was in Flower; Red Pottage, Mary Cholmondeley (6 each)
Unleavened Bread, Robert Grant; *The Redemption of David Corson*, Charles Frederic Goss (5 each)
The Reign of Law, James Lane Allen (4)
David Harum; Via Crusis; Resurrection, L. F. Tolstoi (3 each)
The Gentleman from Indiana, Booth Tarkington; *The Voice of the People*, Ellen Glasgow; *The Master Christian*, Marie Corelli; *Eben Holden*, Irving Bacheller (2 each)

The Book Parade

12

Realism seems to be gaining a little, but only a little, as do women writers. Several rising American writers have appeared. Tolstoi is the only European, and he does not seem quite at home with his companions. Parenthetically, it may be noted that Dreiser's *Sister Carrie* was published during the year, but far from becoming a best-seller, it was practically suppressed, and his second novel, *Jennie Gerhardt*, did not follow until 1911.

The tastes here reflected held pretty constant, so far as current literature was concerned, through our period. George Barr McCutcheon's lightweight Balkans romance, *Graustark*, on the 1902 lists, was to launch him upon a career of dazzling popularity that would embrace stage and screen as well as the printed page (when he tried a more realistic kind of fiction, with an unhappy ending, in *The Sherrods* of 1903, he would meet with much less success). The Canadian Sir Gilbert Parker (*The Right of Way*) would get far enough to have his work collected, as would Mrs. Humphry Ward (*Eleanor*), who had begun with *Robert Elsmere* as early as 1888. Again there was a single Continental, Edmond Rostand, with a play, *L'Aiglon*. In 1903 Alice Hegan Rice would become the first writer to have two books—Mrs. *Wiggs of the Cabbage Patch* and *Lovey Mary*—included in the *Bookman* tabulations for a single year, and in 1904 Kate Douglas Wiggin would have both *Rebecca of Sunnybrook Farm* and *The Affair at the Inn*, the latter the product of collaboration. The emergence of Jack London with *The Call of the Wild* in 1903 was perhaps a portent; so, in a different way, was Edith Wharton's *The House of Mirth* a little later, but the winds of change were as yet far from violent. Close to the end of our period, in January 1909, the *Bookman* would report these best sellers of the month:

> *The Trail of the Lonesome Pine*, John Fox, Jr.
> *Lewis Rand*, Mary Johnston
> *Peter*, F. Hopkinson Smith
> *The Testing of Diana Mallory*, Mrs. Humphry Ward
> *The Red City*, S. Weir Mitchell
> *The Man from Brodney's*, George Barr McCutcheon

All the famous American poets of the "Golden Age" had died before 1900; of the crop that was to glorify the "New Poetry" renascence of the second decade of the century, Edgar Lee Masters and Carl Sandburg had begun publishing without attracting much attention, but only Edwin Arlington Robinson and Josephine Preston Peabody had really "arrived." Robinson struck his characteristic note with his third publication, *Captain Craig* (1902), which, to the shy writer's embarrassment, roused the enthusiasm of President Roosevelt and resulted in his virtually forcing a minor appointment upon Robinson because he knew he needed the money. The charming Miss Peabody had received a brilliant press for *The Wayfarers* (1898), and when *Fortune and Men's Eyes* appeared in 1900, she was called one of the foremost living poets. But she would do even better work in *The Singing Leaves* (1903), and she did not come into her greatest fame until after her play, *The Piper*, had won the Shakespeare Festival prize at Stratford-upon-Avon in 1910. All in all, the finest living American poet was probably William Vaughn Moody, who brought out his first collection, *Gloucester Moors and Other Poems*, in 1901. In 1900 he had published the first member of the poetic trilogy he would not live to finish, *The Masque of Judgment*, which was followed by *The Fire-Bringer* in 1904, and he died, at forty-one, in 1910.

Thomas Bailey Aldrich had collected his poems before 1900, but his final winnowing came in 1906 with *A Book of Songs and Sonnets*. Bret Harte had made his first strike in 1870 with his humorous verses, but this was eclipsed by the triumph of "The Luck of Roaring Camp" and other stories of the California Argonauts that followed hard upon, and when he died in 1902, everybody thought of him as a short-story writer rather than a poet. When Roosevelt's secretary of state, John Hay, followed him in 1905, he was a statesman rather than a writer in the public mind, for his famous *Pike County Ballads* dated back to 1871, and his son would not collect his poems until 1916. On the other hand, though Eugene Field had died in 1895, his vogue was still very great, especially with school children, who learned "Little Boy Blue," "Wynken, Blynken, and Nod," "The Sugar Plum Tree," and others along with "The Village Blacksmith." Maxfield Parrish contributed to Field's vogue by illustrating *Poems of Childhood* in 1904, and the collected Sabine Edition was one of the most successful among all the sets of standard authors whose placement in thousands of American homes was an important part of the book business for both Scribners and Houghton Mifflin through many years beyond our period.

The American poet of widest appeal during our period, and until his death in 1916, was James Whitcomb Riley. Riley belonged to the "Indiana school," which also embraced Tarkington, Meredith Nicholson, and George Ade, and wrote humorous dialect poems like "Little Orphant Annie," "Out to Old Aunt Mary's," and "The Raggedy Man," with a strong dramatic quality (he was platform artist as well as poet). On the subliterary level, mention may be made of the newspaper poet and "sob sister," Ella Wheeler Wilcox, who covered Queen Victoria's funeral for Hearst and described it in "The Queen's Last Ride," Edgar A. Guest, and Sam Walter Foss, who wanted to live in a house by the side of the road and be a friend to man.

The three great American fiction writers of the late nineteenth and early twentieth centuries were of course Mark Twain, William Dean Howells, and Henry James. The last important extended work of fiction Mark Twain published during his lifetime was the pseudonymous *Personal Recollections of Joan of Arc* (1896), and there was to be no other until *The Mysterious Stranger* appeared in a greatly doctored version in 1916. During our period he published mainly fictional brevities and pronouncements upon public affairs, yet he filled the magazines, his popularity was very great, and his earlier works continued to be intensively read. Among Howells's many fictions the most important after 1900 were *The Kentons* (1902) and *The Son of Royal Langbrith* (1904), which latter is more suggestive of Hawthorne or Melville than of his own generally quiet realism. He also published *Literary Friends and Acquaintance* in 1900 and *Heroines of Fiction* in 1901; perhaps the fact that he began writing the "Editor's Easy Chair" in *Harper's Magazine* in 1900 had tended to center his energies temporarily more upon criticism than on fiction.

James, however, was a very different story. Between 1900 and 1904 he brought out not only the three novels in which he developed his own distinctive contribution to fiction to its utmost limits—*The Wings of the Dove, The Ambassadors,* and *The Golden Bowl*—but also one lesser novel, *The Sacred Fount;* two topflight collections of short stories, *The Soft Side* and *The Better Sort;* and a biography, *William Wetmore Story and His Friends.* For quantity and quality combined, I doubt that this record can be matched by any other writer. In August 1904 he returned to America from England after long absence, lecturing for the first time in his life and accumulating fresh impressions at an astonishing rate for a man of his age, though unhappily he was to live to make use of these only in *The American Scene* and one unfinished novel, *The Ivory Tower*.

Among other writers of fiction there were those like Helen Hunt Jackson (*Ramona*, 1884) and Edward Bellamy (*Looking Backward*, 1888) who had died before our period began but who, being still read, were definitely a part of men's minds; those like Frank R. Stockton, Stephen Crane, and Frank Norris who died during these years; those like James Lane Allen, F. Marion Crawford, Hamlin Garland, and S. Weir Mitchell who began before and lived through it (some by many years); and those like Jack London and Booth Tarkington who were freshly arrived. George Ade's novels about Negroes, *Artie* and *Pink Marsh*, had been enthusiastically hailed by Mark Twain and other good judges in the nineties; he was also a very successful playwright, but the general public knew him best, beginning in 1900, for his *Fables in Slang*, first published in the Chicago *Record*. Edith Wharton, Ellen Glasgow, Theodore Dreiser, and James Branch Cabell were all publishing, but all except Mrs. Wharton came into their widest recognition beyond the scope of this book. The historical novel, generally highly romantic, was at the height of its vogue, and Mary Johnston was probably its most distinguished practitioner, but her most thoughtful, though not her most "successful," work would come later. Winston Churchill wrote both historical novels, like the famous Civil War story, *The Crisis* (1904), and novels depicting modern conditions from a reformist point of view, as later, outstandingly, in *The Inside of the Cup*.

The finest local-color writer was Sarah Orne Jewett of South Berwick, Maine, whom Lowell compared to Theocritus and who was greatly admired by both Kipling and James. But though she lived until 1909, Miss Jewett had done most of her best work before 1900, notably in *Deephaven* and *The Country of the Pointed Firs*. Much more of our time were Mary E. Wilkins Freeman, who began in the 1880s and lived until 1930, and Alice Brown, who did not die until 1948. Both were best known as short-story writers, but both also published novels, to which Miss Brown added poems and plays. Both too made use of the supernatural.

Local color of course can be cultivated anywhere. Mary Hartwell Catherwood, who died in 1902, lived in Illinois and Indiana and on Mackinac Island and found her best material in the early French settlements in the Middle West. Margaret Deland was not essentially a local-color writer; her affinity of spirit was rather with

George Eliot, and her most famous novel is *The Awakening of Helena Ritchie* (1906); but her Old Chester stories about the clergyman Dr. Lavendar and his people cultivate Pennsylvanian localities. The real exotic of the period was the Irish-Greek Lafcadio Hearn, who became an American newspaperman but in 1890 went to Japan, where he married a Japanese woman, became a Japanese subject, and dedicated himself to interpreting that country to the West.

It was the South, however, that really vied with New England in exploiting local color. George W. Cable was born in New Orleans, and his early books, carefully wrought but too overloaded with dialect for the taste of these latter days, antedated our period; later he lived in New England and pioneered in working for justice to blacks and other good causes; *The Cavalier* (1901) was his most important book in our time. Joel Chandler Harris, distinguished for his studies of rural Georgia and of the Negro mind and folklore, went on publishing Uncle Remus stories right through our period. The local color cultivated by Charles Egbert Craddock (pseudonym of Mary N. Murfree) is indicated by the title of her first book, *In the Tennessee Mountains* (1884), but she also wrote many novels, and during her later years she was much preoccupied with both historical themes and contemporary American problems.

Thomas Nelson Page, lawyer, classicist, biographer of Lee and student of Dante, and American ambassador to Italy during World War I, began as a quintessential southern writer with *In Ole Virginia* in the 1880s, but he had pretty well shot his bolt in this aspect before our century began. *Gordon Keith* (1903) was probably his most important novel during the Roosevelt years. F. Hopkinson Smith in some ways shared his spirit, but as an engineer and a painter he found himself less centered upon the old plantation. Both *The Fortunes of Oliver Horn* (1902) and *The Tides of Barnegat* (1906) are delightful books. A younger adherent of the Page–Smith school, if it can be called that, was John Fox, Jr., who has already been mentioned.

In a way, the "western" (with a side-extension into Alaska) might be said to belong to the local-color movement. *The Virginian* (1902) by Owen Wister is as good as place to begin as any, and the genre has not often reached the level he set. Rex Beach, James Oliver Curwood, and Stewart Edward White, who was more naturalist than writer of westerns, are other important names here, but Zane

Grey would not make his big strike before *Riders of the Purple Sage* in 1912.

I have spoken of Crawford, Mitchell, Allen, and Garland as writers of stature who lived through our period. F. Marion Crawford was the most versatile and prolific, but little of his best work dates from our time. S. Weir Mitchell, the pioneer Philadelphia neurologist, became famous with *Hugh Wynne, Free Quaker* (1897), which was read avidly into the new century and compared with *Henry Esmond*, a comparison that time has not sustained. *Constance Trescott* came in 1905 and *The Red City* in 1907. James Lane Allen's reputation was made in the nineties with *A Kentucky Cardinal* and *The Choir Invisible*, a historical novel of the Kentucky frontier, developed in a far from conventional way. With *The Reign of Law* (1900) and *The Mettle of the Pasture* (1903) he turned to more realistic, Balzacian themes, and when in *The Bride of the Mistletoe* (1909) and *The Doctor's Christmas Eve* (1910) he was to make another turn, this time in the direction of Maeterlinckian symbolism, sometimes more essay than fiction, he lost most of the readers he had not scared away already.

Hamlin Garland had a strange career. Born in Wisconsin in 1860, he lived also in Iowa and Dakota, became a teacher in Boston, moved to Chicago, then to New York, and died in Hollywood in 1940. He was influenced by Whitman, the new science, and new, then shocking, European writers like Ibsen and Björnson, and he set forth his creed of "veritism," which was allied to naturalism, in *Crumbling Idols* in 1894. It is not true, as has often been said, that Garland's novels of the Roosevelt years all ignore either American problems or his own serious interests. *The Captain of the Grey-Horse Troop* (1902) deals with Indian problems, *Hesper* (1903) with capital and labor, and *The Tyranny of the Dark* (1905) with psychic phenomena. Others, like *Her Mountain Lover* (1901), are frankly romantic, however, and there was much headshaking on the left about Garland's having "sold out." Howells, himself a Socialist, had no sympathy with such nonsense; Garland, he insisted, had always been a romantic at heart, and in all he had written he had been true to himself.

Stephen Crane, who pioneered naturalism in *Maggie* (1893), stream-of-consciousness in *The Red Badge of Courage* (1894), and imagism in his poems, died, at twenty-nine, in 1900, and Frank Norris followed him, at thirty-two, two years later. Despite Howells's enthusiasm, *Maggie* must now be called disappointing, but *The Red Badge* is still a work of genius. Frank Norris's art was not quite so fine as Crane's, but his grasp was wider; his early death, following an appendectomy, was one of the tragedies of American letters. He published one powerful naturalistic novel, *McTeague*, in 1899; then, in 1901, he achieved flawed but unmistakable greatness with *The Octopus*. The theme is wheat farming in California, and the Octopus is the Southern Pacific Railroad, which was squeezing the farmers to death. The book was followed by *The Pit* (1903), which described the selling of the wheat at the Chicago Board of Trade and which was far more popular than *The Octopus*, though it is greatly inferior to it. There was to have been a third novel, "The Wolf," about the selling of the wheat in Europe, but this the author did not live to write.

Allied to Norris in some aspects was that hack writer of genius, Jack London, who wrote fifty books in sixteen years, earned a million dollars, addressed a world audience, some of which still remains, notably in Russia, and died under circumstances suggesting suicide in 1916. London "arrived" in January 1900, in the unlikeliest possible place, when "An Odyssey of the North" appeared in the *Atlantic*. His "red blood" cult had its ridiculous side, but he was a complicated, sensitive, self-destructive man—Socialist, Darwinian, and Nietzschean all in one—and a literary phenomenon that could hardly have existed in any other period. One of his most interesting books is the nonfiction *John Barleycorn* (1908), a record of his own alcoholism and a passionate plea for prohibition.

Roughly contemporary in emergence was a more disciplined writer and more authentic novelist, Booth Tarkington, who was influenced by Howells and Mark Twain and who admired Hardy, Conrad, and Bennett and both the realists and the romantics among French novelists. Nobody has ever doubted Tarkington's gifts, but "advanced" critics often disparaged him because, though living and working into an age of rebellion (he died in 1946), he seldom departed from "right thinking." *The Gentleman from Indiana* appeared in 1899, *Monsieur Beaucaire*, a story set in Restoration Bath, in 1900; and *The Conquest of Canaan* in 1905; but the real masterpieces came later: *Alice Adams* in 1921 and the trilogy collectively called *Growth*, which comprised *The Turmoil* (1915), *The Magnificent Ambersons* (1918), and *The Midlander* (1921). *Seventeen* (1916) and the Penrod books are in a class by themselves, coming close to contemporary folklore in their portrayal of boyhood and adolescence but without the poetry and nostalgia of Mark Twain's creations.

Kate Douglas Wiggin's *Rebecca of Sunnybrook Farm* (1903) and its pendant, *New Chronicles of Rebecca* (1907), are also books about children rather than for them. In itself this was nothing new. Dickens and Mark Twain had produced such books, but they were to thrive exceedingly in the new century. In 1908 the Canadian L. M. Montgomery would emerge with the first of a series of books about *Anne of Green Gables*, but Eleanor H. Porter's *Pollyanna* would not arrive until 1913. If, as has been argued, *Rebecca* was a popularization of New England transcendentalism, with which Mrs. Wiggin had had contacts, *Pollyanna* suggests a possible affinity to Christian Science. In 1904 Gene Stratton Porter used a boy protagonist in *Freckles*. Mrs. Wiggin had begun writing, more or less accidentally, in her kindergarten days, and *The Birds' Christmas Carol* vies with Henry van Dyke's *The Other Wise Man* as the most successful American Christmas story. But Rebecca Rowena Randall, named after both heroines of *Ivanhoe* and herself one of the most enchanting girls in literature, captured the hearts of many who might have seemed unlikely to surrender to her, Jack London among them.

Among the books of the new century designed especially *for* children, L. Frank Baum's were easily the most popular. *The Wizard of Oz*, illustrated by W. W. Denslow, was published in 1900. Baum's secret was that he had learned how to transform American materials into the stuff of wonder and create an American utopia. A prolific writer of no high literary pretensions, he had no idea at first what he had accomplished. He had produced *Mother Goose in Prose*, the first book illustrated by Maxfield Parrish, in 1897, and he showed his skill in the use of traditional fairy lore in *The Life and Adventures of Santa Claus* (1902) and *Queen Zixi of Ix* (1905). It was not until 1904 that he got around to providing the *Wizard* with a sequel, *The Land of Oz*. There were twelve more before he died in 1919, and no child's Christmas was complete without a new Oz book under the tree. Though librarians have often been snobbish about them, the Oz books seem now to have overcome the worst of the prejudice against them and even to have become a cult that embraces adults as well as children.

If we may believe the best-seller lists, Americans read more fiction than anything else during the Roosevelt years and much more by American than by foreign authors. But of course this was not anything like the whole story. Of the Boston historians of the nineteenth century, probably only Francis Parkman retained any considerable body of readers, and because it was a part of the high school curriculum, many more knew him by *The Oregon Trail* than by the great series in which he chronicled the French-English confrontation in the New World. Only specialists knew Henry Adams's definitive work on Jefferson and Madison; *Mont-Saint-Michel and Chartres,* one of the nonfiction masterpieces of American literature, was privately printed in 1904 and published in 1912, but the general reader did not discover it until *The Education of Henry Adams* had created an unexpected sensation after Adams's death in 1918 and called attention to it. John Fiske, who died in 1901, was probably the most widely read historian of the time, but all literate Americans knew President Roosevelt's *The Winning of the West,* at least by reputation.

Our fathers did better with an erudite, refined type of literature that we have nearly lost, the personal essay. Agnes Repplier had published her first collection, *Books and Men,* in 1888, and she would continue to bring out others at intervals throughout our period and until *Eight Decades* appeared in 1937. During her early years she was essentially a literary essayist, who combined basically romantic tastes with a cool, crisp intelligence and a caustic distaste for sentimental nonsense. Later she concerned herself more with public affairs, but her style was always a thing highly polished and balanced, and enriched by amazingly apt and brilliant scraps of quotation drawn from the most diverse sources and combined into a kind of tapestry effect. Samuel McChord Crothers began later with *The Gentle Reader* in 1903 and ended with *The Thought Broker* in 1928. As an essayist, though serious in purpose (he was pastor of the First Unitarian Church, on the edge of the Harvard Yard), he was essentially a humorist, and one gives him no more than his due in calling him the Oliver Wendell Holmes of his time.

Until his death in 1921, John Burroughs was the dean of American nature writers. His first book in the field was *Wake-Robin* in 1871, the last *Under the Maples* just fifty years later. In 1900 he published also the first of his four volumes of philosophical and religious studies, *The Light of Day,* and in 1902 an excellent book on *Literary Values.* In 1903 he went with TR to Yellowstone; see

Camping and Tramping with Roosevelt (1907). John Muir too was an important nature writer, though he was more important for his scientific discoveries and his services to conservation and the national parks.

Except for Mark Twain, the greatest humorist of the time was Finley Peter Dunne, the creator of Mr. Dooley, a Chicago saloon-keeper who developed into one of the great moralists of American letters. The Dooley sketches began appearing in Chicago about the time of the exposition, and in the beginning they dealt largely with local matters. They were not copyrighted or syndicated until papers in other cities began reprinting them without acknowledgment, and they did not come into widespread fame until the Spanish-American War, whose imperialistic, expansionist tendencies Mr. Dooley opposed. *Mr. Dooley in Peace and in War* was the first collection, and by 1902 four more had followed. All in all, Dunne wrote more than 700 Dooley papers, of which only about one-third were collected into eight volumes. Mark Twain, Henry Adams, Henry James, and Theodore Roosevelt all admired him.

Criticism was not so widely read in America during the Roosevelt years as it came to be in the twenties, but W. C. Brownell published *Victorian Prose Masters* in 1901 and *American Prose Masters* in 1909, and in 1904 Paul Elmer More brought out the first series of his *Shelburne Essays,* which collectively stand without parallel in kind, whether one accepts all More's standards or not. The music critic James Huneker, for whom Mencken was later so industriously to blow the horn, published *Melomaniacs* in 1902, and *Overtones, Iconoclasts, Visionaries,* and *Egoists* followed hard upon. Among academic critics, Brander Matthews was recognized as an authority on the drama and Bliss Perry on fiction. George Santayana brought out his *Interpretations of Poetry and Religion* in 1900, followed by a collection of poems, *The Hermit of Carmel,* the next year, and in 1902 William James produced one of his most influential books, *The Varieties of Religious Experience.*

But in spite of all that has been said hitherto, no adequate idea of what Americans were reading during our period can be had without some reference to what is often snobbishly called "subliterature." "For one who read Mark Twain's *Huckleberry Finn* or *Tom Sawyer,*" said George Jean Nathan, "there were ten thousand who read [Burt L.] Standish's *Frank Merriwell's Dilemma.*"

The so-called dime novel was not of course the creation of our time. The publishers Beadle and Adams began in the 1850s. In the eighties about 100 different series of dime and nickel stories were being published; after 1900 the number gradually diminished by about 25 percent.

Important as the western was in this area, the dime novels were not all westerns; if it and the detective story were staples, the sea, railroading, city life, and sports all furnished much material, and there were reprints from standard fiction as well. In the usual sense of the term, no boy was ever corrupted by reading dime novels, for their heroes were not allowed to drink, smoke, swear, or make love. But killing Indians was another matter, and the reader's nerves were battered by an unending succession of sensational incidents, dished up according to carefully prescribed formulas, with endless repetition of incident and utterly without grace of style.

After 1900 the old yellowbacks were largely replaced by the five-cent weeklies, each containing a single long story, printed in double columns on pulp paper and encased in luridly lithographed covers. These were legion; I can remember shopwindows filled with them week after week, but probably the Buffalo Bill series, the Nick Carter series, and the *Tip Top Weekly*, devoted to the adventures of Frank Merriwell and his friends, were supreme. Though they appeared serially, these publications were not, in the ordinary sense of the term, magazines but rather paperback novels published at weekly intervals.

The real Buffalo Bill (Colonel William F. Cody, who lived until 1917) was a showman in our time, but in his youth he had been a pony express rider, a scout for the Union army, and a buffalo killer for the Union Pacific when it was creeping across the plains and needed meat to feed its crews. Nick Carter began with John Russell Coryell, assisted by the editor Ormond Smith, but Frederick Van Rensselaer Dey claimed to have written more than 1,000 of these yarns. Though he was not the first detective in the dime-novel field, Nick was by all means the most successful, enjoying an international vogue and influencing *avant-garde* writers in France.

The stories about boys, mainly city boys, written by Horatio Alger, Jr., were considerably less sensational. Though the first, *Ragged Dick,* appeared in 1865, Russel B. Nye quite correctly points out that they reflect the taste of a later and more sophisticated period than the Buffalo Bill stories. Indian killing and train robbing are old-fashioned now, and an increasingly urban society is in-

creasingly preoccupied with "making good." Alger's books, in
cheap reprints, sometimes in paper covers but more often, in my
experience, in rather flimsy hard-cover bindings sold like hot cakes
in the department stores for nineteen cents each, all through my
boyhood and at least up to World War I, as did also, though to a
lesser extent, those of Edward S. Ellis, Oliver Optic (William Taylor
Adams), and the British G. A. Henty, a considerably better writer
than the others. Though the libraries scorned Alger even in my
boyhood, he has enjoyed a nostalgic revival during these latter
years; his writings are collectors' items in any edition; several books
have been written about him; and standard publishers have reissued
some of his stories at prices that would have astonished him or any
of his contemporaries.

The real challenge to all the older types of popular fiction for
boys came, however, with Burt L. Standish (Gilbert Patten), who
in 1895 began the long series of stories about Frank Merriwell that
put his publishers, Street and Smith, at the top in the popular field.
Standish resembled his predecessors only in the entire decency
of his work. His hero was a fashionable prep school and Yale College student, almost insanely athletic, whose position in society
was such that he could take "making good" for granted and devote
himself seriously to vindicating his manhood in style. Flourishing
technology was added to athletic prowess by Edward Stratemeyer,
who published his first Rover Boys books in 1899, added the Motor
Boys in 1906, and formed a syndicate that is said to have turned
out 1,000 volumes. Tom Swift probably invented more things than
Edison. There was a Boy Aviator series, and as America became
increasingly movie-conscious, a Motion Picture Boys and a Moving
Picture Girls series followed, while little children were looked after
by the Bobbsey Twins.

On the whole, juvenile pulp publishers took better care of boys
than of girls. In 1900, however, Street and Smith did establish a
weekly rather foolishly called My Queen, which chronicled the
adventures of one Marion Marlowe as nurse, actress, detective, and
what-have-you, and it should be remembered that Martha Finley's
Elsie Dinsmore books, which had begun in 1868, continued to be
written until 1905 and read long after that. Nobody who inspected
the paperbacks on the cheaper newsstands during my childhood
could avoid running into the names Bertha M. Clay and Laura Jean
Libbey again and again. The former was originally an English-

woman named Charlotte M. Braeme who wrote about the aristocracy for servant girls as early as 1884, but the pseudonym proved
far too profitable to be allowed to die with her, and it was kept
alive by a number of undeniably male hacks including, it is said,
Frederick Dey and Thomas Chalmers Harbaugh. Laura Jean Libbey
lived on until 1924 and is supposed to have sold some 15 million
books. During her later years her principal enjoyment was to sit
in the cemetery and contemplate the handsome monument she
had erected prematurely to her memory so that she might share
in posterity's enjoyment of it. Among her masterpieces are *Had
She Loved Him Less, When His Love Grew Cold, Lovers Once but
Strangers Now,* and *The Price of a Kiss.*

I N 1900 theaters advertised in the New York *Times* only in the thirty-eight-page, three-cent Sunday edition, not the fourteen-page, one-cent daily edition. On the first Sunday in January, Richard Mansfield's "farewell performances" in repertoire were announced (though his actual farewell would not be played for seven years yet). Nat C. Goodwin and his current wife Maxine Elliott were in Clyde Fitch's play, *The Cowboy and the Lady*. William Gillette was in the third month of his own play, *Sherlock Holmes*, and Annie Russell was beginning the last two weeks of Jerome K. Jerome's *Miss Hobbs*. The Bijou had *Sister Mary* with May Irwin. On Tuesday night Maude Adams would begin a revival of *The Little Minister;* it had first been produced in 1897 and had made her a star.

David Belasco was opening his own play, *Naughty Anthony*, on Monday (on March 5 he would add *Madame Butterfly* to the bill), and the Donnelly Stock Company was doing *The Wife*, which he had written some time back with Henry C. De Mille, at twenty-five, thirty-five, and fifty cents for evening performances and twenty-five cents for matinees. Daly's had Henry Arthur Jones's play, *The Manoeuvres of Jane*, the Empire H. V. Esmond's *My Lady's Lord*, and the Madison Square R. C. Carton's *Wheels within Wheels*. The spectacular *Ben-Hur*, which had opened in November with Edward J. Morgan and William S. Hart, was triumphant at the Broadway; *Way Down East*, which had first appeared in 1898 and

The Many-faceted Theater

13

was to be a perennial for many years, was in its third month at the Academy; another revival, *The Village Postmaster*, was beginning its last fortnight in Fourteenth Street. The Grand had *The Gunner's Mate*, "greatest of all naval dramas," while the Third Avenue was still exhorting its patrons to *Remember the Maine.* A German comedian named Schweichofer was at the Irving Place.

In the musical field, Anna Held was in *Papa's Wife*, with music by De Koven, and Frank Daniels was in Victor Herbert's *Ameer.* Raymond Hitchcock and Marie Cahill, not yet stars, were in *Three Little Lambs.* On Monday night the Castle Square Opera Company would revive *Iolanthe;* over in Harlem, Jefferson De Angelis was doing something called *The Jolly Musketeer.* Hammerstein's Victoria had "a new and extravagant hit," *Chris and the Wonderful Lamp*, with Edna Wallace Hopper and music by Sousa, and there was a fairy extravaganza about *Little Red Riding Hood* at the Casino. Keith's, Proctor's, and the Palace were all playing vaudeville (the Four Cohans were at Proctor's), and several music halls, museums, and burlesque houses were advertising. The Eden Musée was supplementing its regular "World in Wax" with the "Cinematograph"; tonight they were doing *The Story of Cinderella.*

Mid-January brought Lily Langtry ("What is the difference between Madame Modjeska and Mrs. Langtry?" "The one is a Pole and the other a stick") in Sydney Grundy's *The Degenerates.* Later E. H. Sothern and Virginia Harned appeared in Hauptmann's *The Sunken Bell;* Sothern had not yet united, either personally or professionally, with Julia Marlowe, who was busy with Clyde Fitch's *Barbara Frietchie.* There were also two rival dramatizations of *Quo Vadis?* But the most sensational event of the spring season was Olga Nethersole's production of Fitch's dramatization of Daudet's novel *Sapho*, which was closed by the police and the star arrested; to fill up the interval until she was acquitted, she revived two Pinero plays, thereafter returning to *Sapho.*

The most important September openings of the new season in the fall were those of Augustus Thomas's *Arizona* and James A. Herne's *Sag Harbor.* The vogue for dramatized novels continued unabated. Henrietta Crosman became a star in *Mistress Nell*, and Maude Adams assumed the Sarah Bernhardt role in *L'Aiglon.* The November sensation was the musical *Floradora.* Nobody cared much for the show itself, but the girls in the double sextette, "Tell Me, Pretty Maiden," became the toast of the town.

In 1900 Augustin Daly had just died, and Daniel Frohman's Lyceum company was about to disband. What was coming into being was a stars' theater. Maxine Elliott did not speak for herself alone when she remarked that a good actress was more important than any play; Charles Frohman, the leading producer of the time, quite agreed with her, and so did the public. People went to see players, not plays; sometimes the theater's electric sign carried only the name of the star, not bothering to mention the play. Those who had "arrived" were under contract to a producer who saw to it that they were supplied with new "vehicles" each autumn. Since there was so much more live professional theater than there is today, actors obviously had a much better chance for steady employment, but rehearsals were not paid for, and if a show flopped and disbanded somewhere in the "sticks," the actor must get back to New York on his own resources or stay where he was and starve.

It was a theater geared to entertainment, neither a clinic, an agency of social reform, nor a brothel. George Jean Nathan was never more penetrating than in his observation that when people stopped building theaters that looked like places of entertainment and began to build theaters that looked like mortuaries, the character of the plays presented in them was altered to correspond. It was also, in the boxes and orchestra, a fashionable theater; actors have spoken of the array of white shirtfronts and décolletage they witnessed when the curtain rose and of the perfume that was wafted to them over the footlights. Many persons dined before the play or supped afterward, and in New York Delmonico's, Sherry's, and, above all, Rector's were the fashionable night spots.

It was also a national theater; Broadway produced not for New York alone but for the nation. Long runs in the modern sense were the exception, and even when they were achieved, it never occurred to anybody that that was it; triumph in New York was expected to be followed by triumph on the road, and "road" meant not only the cities but innumerable one-night stands in little towns that have now forgotten they ever had a theater. John Drew played a few weeks in New York each autumn and then took to the road, playing northern and southern routes in alternate seasons, and some actors of considerable stature were only rarely seen on Broadway. Plays like *The Old Homestead, Sis Hopkins, Way Down East, In Old Kentucky, Peck's Bad Boy,* and *The Round-up* toured year after year, turning up in the big cities about once each season.

The Old Homestead depended upon Denman Thompson and *Sis Hopkins* on Rose Melville, but the others were tied to no particular personality; here if anywhere the star system languished and the play was the thing.

The leading producers included Charles Frohman, David Belasco, Klaw and Erlanger, and William A. Brady. Daniel Frohman became less important after the disbanding of his Lyceum company, and he was to give up production altogether with *Seven Sisters* in 1911. At his height, Charles Frohman controlled more than 200 theaters in the United States and five in London; he had twenty-eight stars under contract and produced about 500 plays. He preferred established, especially British, playwrights and young players whom he could mold. His first great stars were men—John Drew and William Gillette—but the most were women. He was a pudgy, uncultured, almost inarticulate man with a passion for pastry, but he inspired devotion even in J. M. Barrie, whom he turned from prose fiction to playwriting. Nobody ever questioned his word and some worked for him without a contract; Marie Doro says she never even asked him what he was going to pay her. He went down with the *Lusitania* in 1915, quoting Peter Pan's statement that death must be a beautiful adventure.

The only blot on Frohman's fame is his connection with the theatrical syndicate in which the dominating figure was Abraham Erlanger. This enterprise began in 1896 to standardize booking and achieve efficiency in routing touring companies but developed into a theatrical monopoly that by 1906 controlled 600 theaters and barred all attractions that would not meet its almost ruinous terms. Belasco, Mrs. Fiske, Richard Mansfield, the aging Joseph Jefferson, and others revolted, but only Mrs. Fiske had the courage to keep her banner flying to the end; at the height of the controversy she and Sarah Bernhardt were playing in tents and skating rinks. The power of the syndicate was finally broken by the rising rival firm of the Shuberts, who in time would establish a very nice monopoly of their own. There were three brothers, sons of a Jewish peddler in Syracuse, but Sam, the most gifted among them, died horribly in a train wreck, in 1905, just as they were coming into their success. His brothers named all their theaters Sam S. Shubert Memorial Theater, and his photograph still hangs in the lobbies of those that survive.

Henry Arthur Jones and Arthur Wing Pinero were the favorite

contemporary British playwrights on the American stage; the outstanding Americans were Clyde Fitch and Augustus Thomas. The
pioneer of realism, James A. Herne, died in 1900, and Bronson
Howard, whose *Shenandoah* (1888) had helped launch Charles Frohman's career, was inactive. William Gillette, who wrote plays largely,
though not entirely, for his own interpretation, also had his best
achievements in playwriting behind him, though he continued to
act almost until he died in 1937 and last revived his *Sherlock
Holmes* at seventy-four. But Fitch, who was reputed to earn a
quarter of a million a year, was outstandingly the "success." In
the course of a short career (appendicitis killed him at forty-four
in 1909), he turned out sixty plays, of which thirty-eight were origi-
nals. He had five plays running on Broadway simultaneously; once
he had two openings on the same night. Though such early plays
as *Nathan Hale* and *Barbara Frietchie* were highly romantic, he
was essentially a realist and social satirist, with a keen eye for the
foibles of upper-class women. Fitch made enemies. He was something of a fop, who lived in a miniature palace and was probably
homosexual, but he was the exception among the playwrights of
his time in directing his own plays with intelligence and meticu-
lous care. He wrote rapidly and was capable of superficiality, but
a careless fecundity is the mark of a certain kind of genius, especially in youth, and Fitch was still growing when he died; his last
play, *The City*, posthumously produced, marks a milestone in
American theater realism.

Richard Mansfield was probably the most distinguished actor of
the time, with the richest and most varied list of accomplishments
to his credit. His idealism matched his ego, and his tantrums harmed
himself rather than others; he established his own unemployment
insurance long before the government had dreamed of such a
thing. Another idealist, E. H. Sothern, a gentleman with no idio-
syncrasies except an excessive addiction to work, had graduated
from the farces in which he had acted at the Lyceum into the
romantic drama, but his great achievements as producer and interpreter of Shakespeare were just beginning. Robert B. Mantell, who,
through many years, was to be the only Shakespearean as well
known as Sothern and Marlowe, was also settling down to the Bard
to whom he would devote the rest of his long career. Compared
with Sothern, Mantell was a comparatively rough and unfinished
actor, who carried ragged productions and a second-rate company,

but at his best he was also an actor of genius, and there were moments in his King Lear when one understood what Kean's contemporaries meant by saying that to see him act was like reading Shakespeare by flashes of lightning. William Faversham and James K. Hackett were more spectacular, and John Drew, after more varied fare during his years with Daly, now seemed quite satisfied with the comparatively light drawing-room comedies with which Frohman supplied him, and which he acted with incomparable finesse, but Otis Skinner, an intelligent actor of varied gifts, never lacked either force or finesse and succeeded as well as anybody in blending the best elements of the old theater and the new.

On the distaff side, Sarah Bernhardt was, by common consent, "the greatest actress in the world," but Bernhardt was an exotic, the only foreign visitor who attracted Americans in droves to plays of which they could understand no word, and her reputed eccentricities, of whose publicity value she was shrewdly aware, were quite as valuable a part of her endowments as her undoubted genius. Among the Americans, Mrs. Fiske was the most admired among the realists and Julia Marlowe among the romantics, while Maude Adams was the most dearly loved.

Mrs. Fiske's devotion to serious plays (she pioneered in the presentation of Ibsen and appeared in adaptations from Thackeray and Hardy) is as undeniable as her idealism as producer and her humanitarianism. To her admirers she was the greatest actress of her time, and they committed themselves to an unblushing snob appeal by proclaiming that stupid people always disliked her; others insisted that she always played herself. She was a brittle, almost unemotional actress, whose staccato utterance muffed half her lines, yet at her best she created moving, illuminating effects. Like Mansfield and Henry Irving, she triumphed over great limitations.

Julia Marlowe had beauty, intelligence, and (except for Bernhardt's) the most beautiful voice that has been heard in the theater of our time. She hated realistic and indecent plays and always knew that what she wanted was to play the heroines of Shakespeare. She was a star from the beginning to the end, but there were a number of years when she had to devote herself to such plays as *When Knighthood Was in Flower*. In E. H. Sothern she found at last the perfect partner, whose gifts and whose ideals perfectly matched her own. Neither was given to playing for points or to outbursts of passion; the pleasure of seeing them was that of having everything done absolutely right, with every element completely adjusted to all the others.

Maude Adams was never seen in public except upon the stage, and the theatergoing public felt about her very much as the larger movie public would later feel about Mary Pickford. If her emotional range was comparatively narrow, nobody cared; Barrie must have been thinking of her when he wrote in *What Every Woman Knows* that if a woman has charm she needs nothing else and that if she lacks it nothing else makes any difference. One wonders a little why she so far outstripped two other Frohman stars also well endowed with this quality—Billie Burke and Marie Doro, and if one disqualifies Billie Burke on the score that her charm, which awakened a wide response of its own, was that of piquancy rather than the fey quality that distinguished Maude Adams, one can hardly dispose thus of the almost unearthly delicacy of Marie Doro.

There were two ladies in the musical field whose fame filled America—Lillian Russell and Anna Held. They were the kind of actress that cigars are named after, and they were as familiar to Americans as contemporary baseball players or prizefighters. Anna Held was the incarnation of everything Americans thought of as "Frenchy," and Ziegfeld flooded the newspapers with cock-and-bull stories about her jewels and her milk or champagne baths. She probably had little real talent, and such songs as "I Just Can't Make My Eyes Behave" and "Won't You Come and Play wiz Me?" were as trashy as we should probably now find them innocent, but when she sang them her audiences read wonderful meanings into them. Lillian Russell, however, was as American as corn on the cob, which she was reputed to be able to consume on a scale matching that of her (almost certainly Platonic) companion, "Diamond Jim" Brady, one of the legendary trenchermen of all time. It is not surprising that she developed a well-upholstered figure; her famous portrait as Lady Teazle is one of the standard exhibits on the taste of the time. She had a phenomenal natural voice (Melba warned her that she would ruin it if she continued to toss off as many high C's in an evening as a prima donna would venture in a week), and she could probably have succeeded in opera if she had cared to submit to the necessary discipline. Her early marriages were disasters; her fourth, successful marriage was to Alexander P. Moore, publisher and ambassador, and President Harding crowned her career when he appointed her special commissioner of immigration and sent her off to Europe to study the problem! She was a down-to-earth (but not disreputable), kindly, generous woman, and she must be one of the few great stars who ever managed to swing a big career without ever quarreling with anybody.

Ethel Barrymore, David Warfield, and William Faversham became stars in 1901—in Fitch's *Captain Jinks of the Horse Marines*, *The Auctioneer*, and *A Royal Rival*, respectively—and many famous players appeared in dramatizations of popular romantic novels. Mrs. Leslie Carter had a great success in *Du Barry*, Maude Adams was beautifully accommodated in *Quality Street*, and Sothern made the popular hit of his career in *If I Were King*, which he later revived and which would become a musical, *The Vagabond King*, in 1925. There were brilliant new productions of *Uncle Tom's Cabin* by William A. Brady and of Sardou's *Diplomacy* by Charles Frohman, and George Henry Boker's *Francesca da Rimini*, one of the best American plays of the nineteenth century, was seen again, this time with Otis Skinner as Lanciotto.

The year 1902 was more noted for revivals than for new plays. Mansfield mounted *Julius Caesar*, and Henrietta Crosman as Rosalind established a record of sixty performances, which stood until Katharine Hepburn broke it in 1950. Mrs. Fiske turned to Germany for Paul Heyse's *Mary of Magdala*, Eleonora Duse came in three D'Annunzio plays, and Edith Wynne Matthison reached back to the fifteenth century for her American debut in *Everyman*, directed by Ben Greet.

In 1903 more than a quarter of the shows were musicals. Victor Herbert had two, *Babes in Toyland* and *Babette;* with the latter Fritzi Scheff moved from the Metropolitan to Broadway. *The Wizard of Oz* was the highly successful first joint starring vehicle of David Montgomery and Fred Stone. *Mr. Bluebeard*, with Eddie Foy, first performed in New York on January 31, was to become sadly memorable as the attraction at the Iroquois Theater in Chicago at the time of the fire on December 30 that killed some 600 people, including many children. *Life* published a cartoon showing trapped victims beating against doors that would not open while Death looked on, under a caption reading "Messrs. Klaw and Erlanger present Mr. Bluebeard." The producers sued for libel and lost; the jury was out less than five minutes.

Richard Mansfield made a hit in *Old Heidelberg*, later to become

The Student Prince, and the name of the central character in *Raffles, The Amateur Cracksman* became a household word. Mary Shaw revived Ibsen's *Ghosts,* and Mrs. Fiske did her first *Hedda Gabler,* to be followed in 1904 by Nance O'Neil and in 1906 by Nazimova.

In 1904 David Warfield found his play of plays in Charles Klein's *The Music Master;* other triumphs of the popular theater were *Mrs. Wiggs of the Cabbage Patch* and *The Virginian.* Fitch gave Mrs. G. H. Gilbert, the grand old lady of Daly's Theater, her only starring vehicle in *Granny* (she died, at eighty-three, in Chicago on December 2, four days after it had opened there), and George Ade turned out his most durable comedy in *The College Widow.* Frohman assigned Barrie's *Little Mary* to Marie Doro and revived *The Little Minister* for Maude Adams. There was a notable revival of *The Two Orphans,* with Grace George and Margaret Illington, in which Clara Morris played her farewell to the stage as Sister Genevieve. George M. Cohan had his first starring vehicle in *Little Johnny Jones,* produced by the new firm of Cohan and Harris, and Julian Eltinge began his career as a female impersonator.

What was most notable about 1904, however, was the extraordinary resurgence of interest in Shakespeare, which involved not only the ever-faithful Robert B. Mantell but Viola Allen, Otis Skinner, Forbes-Robertson (doing his first New York Hamlet), Edith Wynne Matthison with the Ben Greet Players, and, above all, Sothern and Marlowe, who joined forces this year, though they were not to marry until 1911. It was a big year for both. In January Frohman had presented Virginia Harned in Sothern's play, *The Light That Lies in Women's Eyes,* and in May Miss Marlowe had given a special matinee of one of her very first successes, *Ingomar the Barbarian.* They first acted together in *Romeo and Juliet* in Chicago on September 19; in October and November they brought the Veronese lovers, *Hamlet,* and *Much Ado about Nothing* to New York. Thereafter, with intervals, they would carry Shakespeare's banner triumphantly through the land until 1924.

Nine of the shows mounted in January 1905 achieved substantial runs; one, surprisingly, was Arnold Daly's production of *You Never Can Tell;* Shaw had at last "arrived" on Broadway. Later Daly put on two months of Shaw repertoire, including *Mrs. Warren's Profession,* which landed both him and Mary Shaw in police court, and Robert Lorraine gave *Man and Superman* its first American production.

Charles Klein's *The Lion and the Mouse* not only ran for two years in New York but generated road companies and stock productions. An undistinguished play about trust-busting, it was significant as registering the theater's increasing awareness of contemporary problems. Two "westerns"—Belasco's *The Girl of the Golden West* and Edwin Milton Royle's *The Squaw Man*—were also destined to long and varied lives.

The happiest event of the year was Frohman's production of Barrie's *Peter Pan* on November 6, carrying the Maude Adams vogue to its height and giving the modern theater one of its few really enduring and enchanting plays. Nearly fifty years later, Mary Martin enjoyed great success in a musical version, as did Sandy Duncan at the beginning of the 1980s. In 1924, too, Herbert Brenon would triumphantly transfer the play to celluloid, with Barrie's hand-picked, seventeen-year-old Betty Bronson as an ideal Peter. On Christmas night, Ethel Barrymore opened in another Barrie play, *Alice-Sit-by-the-Fire;* other holiday offerings included Victor Herbert's *Mlle. Modiste,* with Fritzi Scheff singing "Kiss Me Again."

The most significant new plays of 1906 were William Vaughn Moody's *The Great Divide,* generally regarded as marking a milestone in the development of literate realistic drama in the modern American theater, with Henry Miller and Margaret Anglin, and Langdon Mitchell's *The New York Idea* with Mrs. Fiske, George Arliss, and John Mason. George M. Cohan had a banner year in *Forty-five Minutes from Broadway* and *George Washington, Jr.* Lillian Russell appeared in her first play without music, *Barbara's Millions,* and the vaudeville star Elsie Janis found her first Broadway vehicle in *The Vanderbilt Cup.* Other great successes were *The Man of the Hour* and *The Road to Yesterday,* a superbly titled and richly theatrical and atmospheric drama about reincarnation by Beulah Marie Dix and Evelyn Greenleaf Sutherland which shifted back and forth between the seventeenth century and the present. In the musical field, Victor Herbert gave Montgomery and Stone one of his—and their—best in *The Red Mill.*

The outstanding hit of 1907 was the American production of Franz Lehár's *The Merry Widow,* with Ethel Jackson and Donald Brian. Viennese operetta "never had it so good" over here. The

Merry Widow Waltz was sung and danced everywhere, while Merry Widow hats and everything else became the subjects of newspaper cartooning. The year also witnessed the first edition of Florenz Ziegfeld, Jr.'s long-successful attempt to "glorify the American girl" in his *Follies* and the first American appearance of the great Scottish comedian, Harry Lauder.

In February, Richard Mansfield opened his last engagement in New York, presenting his newest virtuoso performance in *Peer Gynt* plus selections from his familiar repertoire; on August 30, he died at the age of fifty. Sothern and Marlowe added three non-Shakespearean items to their repertoire—Percy MacKaye's *Jeanne d'Arc*, Sudermann's *John the Baptist*, and Hauptmann's *The Sunken Bell*. Ellen Terry gave her last performances in New York in *Captain Brassbound's Conversion* and other plays and Billie Burke her first, as John Drew's leading woman in *My Wife*. Mabel Taliaferro had a success in *Polly of the Circus*, and Belasco's production of *The Warrens of Virginia* marked the first appearance of the name Mary Pickford on a playbill, though Gladys Smith had been on the stage since early childhood. Considering the popularity of Sir Gilbert Parker's novel, *The Right of Way* had a surprisingly short run, but it was to survive long in stock. It was even more surprising, in view of its later popularity, that the initial engagement of Edmund Day's *The Round-up* should have ended after 155 showings. The most distinguished new American play was Augustus Thomas's study of telepathy, *The Witching Hour*. John Galsworthy's *The Silver Box*, with Ethel Barrymore doing outstanding work in an unglamorous role, was not a box-office success, but it did introduce an important new playwright. Fitch's *The Truth*, one of his best plays, was a failure, and when its star, Clara Bloodgood, probably his favorite actress, took it on the road in the fall to give it another chance, she killed herself in Baltimore, for reasons that are still unknown.

In 1908 came Charles Rann Kennedy's modern morality play, *The Servant in the House*, with Edith Wynne Matthison, the elder Tyrone Power, and Walter Hampden as the Christ figure. Mrs. Fiske put on *Salvation Nell* by a new, young American playwright, Edward Sheldon, who was to be a power in the theater up to and beyond his tragic disablement, and Eugene Walter achieved his first success with *Paid in Full*. On August 18, George Arliss and Edwin Stevens appeared in rival productions of Molnar's *The Devil*.

Sothern and Marlowe were not appearing together this season. Sothern was in a repertoire comprising *The Fool Hath Said in His Heart There Is No God*, which was Laurence Irving's idea of *Crime and Punishment;* Paul Kester's *Don Quixote;* and a revival of his father E. A. Sothern's signature play, *Our American Cousin*, which had been the bill at Ford's Theater the night Lincoln was killed, as well as his more familiar *Hamlet* and *If I Were King.* Miss Marlowe was appearing less ambitiously in James Fagan's *Gloria*, which the public did not care for but in which she intensely believed. Maude Adams had another perfect Barrie vehicle, *What Every Woman Knows*, and Otis Skinner found scope for flamboyant romanticism in *The Honor of the Family*. Musicals continued popular; in one, *Three Twins*, Bessie McCoy won the heart of Richard Harding Davis as the Yama Yama Girl (Grace Duffie Boylan's *Yama Yama Land*, a successful juvenile of the period, has been strangely forgotten). All in all, though 1908 did not blaze new trails, it did have its share of successes.

Our period includes only the opening months of 1909, which were full of promise. If Julia Marlowe had only a *succès d'estime* in *The Goddess of Reason*, a poetic excursion into the French Revolution via Mary Johnston's only play, Frances Starr and Eleanor Robson found more enduring theater fare in Eugene Walter's *The Easiest Way* and Frances Hodgson Burnett's *The Dawn of a Tomorrow*, respectively, and, among the musical comedy stars, Elsie Janis scored in *The Fair Co-ed*, for which George Ade furnished the book. *The Dawn of a Tomorrow*, a play of spiritual aspiration, with a Christian Science–like affirmation of the power of mind and spirit, in a slum setting, marked Miss Robson's farewell to the stage, preceding her marriage to August Belmont and her long years of service as a patron of the Metropolitan Opera, and *The Easiest Way*, an intensely moral play about immoral people, which was banned in Boston, was hailed by Burns Mantle as "the first bold denial of the happy ending in modern drama."

The history of the American theater outside New York has been recorded in less detail than that of the metropolis. Much has gone beyond recall; the rest must be pieced together from local newspapers and personal reminiscences. The history is many-sided. Aside from vaudeville and burlesque, it embraces the touring versions of Broadway shows, with or without the original casts; the ten-twenty-thirty circuits, devoted mainly to blood-and-thunder and domestic melodrama; innumerable resident stock companies, presenting second-run productions of popular plays, generally for a week at a time and at very low prices, plus whatever they might choose to excavate from the older drama; tent shows, showboats, and of course the circus.

How many stock companies there were in America during the Roosevelt days I have no idea; I remember once hearing Barrett H. Clark say that in 1910 there were 2,500. They were manned by players, many of them extremely able, who were famous locally and elsewhere unknown; they began dying out with the competition of the movies, and by the 1930s their race was about run. Chicago, in the days of my youth, had the People's on the West Side, the College on the North Side, and the National on the South Side, and in my semiautobiography, *As Far as Yesterday,* I have tried to describe how the People's, and especially its remarkable leading woman Marie Nelson served me nobly as a means of introduction to the wonderland of theater. For it was there that I saw *Fanchon the Cricket, The Road to Yesterday* (both among my most enchanted memories), *The Heart of Chicago, Eben Holden, Shore Acres, Old Heidelberg,* and heaven knows how many other forgotten delights. My first *Romeo and Juliet* I encountered later, however, through the stock company at the Imperial on West Madison Street, which was headed by Eda von Luke.

Probably the most illustrious figure in the history of American stock was Jessie Bonstelle. She began her career in a touring company, presenting *Bertha, the Sewing Machine Girl,* and also appeared with Janauschek and Daly and in William Vaughn Moody's *The Faith Healer,* but she really began to find her way when she was in charge of a Shubert-backed stock company in Rochester from 1900 to 1905. From 1906 she was at the Star in Buffalo and from 1910 at the Garrick there; both theaters were controlled by Dr. Peter Cornell, whose daughter Katharine became Miss Bonstelle's most distinguished alumna. In 1925 she opened the Bonstelle Playhouse in Detroit, which became the Civic Theater and which she managed until she died in 1932. Winifred Lenihan, William Powell, Frank Morgan, and James Rennie all worked for her, and Guthrie McClintic, Katharine Cornell's husband-and-director-to-be, was one of her lieutenants.

Unfortunately, Jessie Bonstelle left no autobiography. Sarah Truax did, and it sheds considerable light on the period. Miss

Truax studied under Anna Morgan and others at the Chicago Conservatory of Dramatic Art, where she became a pupil–teacher, and
at Chicago Musical College. Her first three seasons were with Otis
Skinner, and George Tyler used her in the road company of *The
Eternal City* and in his all-star revival of *The Two Orphans*. Essentially, however, she was a stock actress, employed almost continuously, winter and summer, in Denver, Salt Lake City, Butte, Chicago (the Great Northern and the Bush Temple), Syracuse, Detroit,
Minneapolis and St. Paul, San Francisco, Spokane, Buffalo, Baltimore, Pittsburgh, and elsewhere. In Pittsburgh she played twelve
performances a week in a theater that generally changed the bill
every Monday night, with rehearsals for the next play beginning
at ten on Tuesday morning. The layman's wonder over the giants
there were in those days must be increased when he reads that the
actor never received the manuscript of a play but only the thirty
to a hundred or more "sides" that contained his own lines with
their cues and that, if the play was unfamiliar to him, he did not
know the plot until it emerged at rehearsal. No wonder the author,
who listed about 150 plays in which she had enacted the leading
feminine role, could write: "I am not sure I could have named the
President. Except for the drama page, the newspaper might almost
as well not have been printed, as far as I was concerned. The theater
was my life, a full, various, and demanding life," to which she adds
that she "knew scarcely a woman who was not contributing in
part, if not wholly, to the support of a mother, father, brother—
some relative, perhaps a husband." Fortunately she had the wit to
understand that the work she was doing, despite its drudgery, was
important: "After all, as a stock actress, I was able to perform outside of New York and bring New York successes to the people
there. They could afford the very reasonable prices of admission,
and I enjoyed enormously being able to help in offering theatrical
fare which they eagerly welcomed."

For the popular melodramas we may well turn to Owen Davis
and Charles A. Taylor. When the Harvard-trained Davis tried to sell
producers a play about the Wars of the Roses, they suggested that
he go see *The Great Train Robbery* and tell them whether he
thought he could do something like that. He reported that he
thought anybody could but could not understand why anybody
would want to; however, when he was assured that he could earn
$500 by doing it, he changed his mind. In his autobiography, *I'd*

Like to Do It Again, he is vague and contradictory on the number of plays he wrote according to formula, citing the number variously as 150, between 200 and 300, and "literally hundreds." He tells us that during one five-year period he turned out thirty-eight melodramas, two farces, a number of vaudeville pieces, and a Hippodrome show and that during another five years he did fifty-odd plays for Al Woods. He put his version of *Under Two Flags* on the stage five days after picking up Ouida's novel for ten cents from a tray of secondhand books, and he sometimes got ready a play about a murder of current interest before the murderer had been identified. For eight years he had seven to thirteen plays each year on the Stair and Havlin circuit, and *Nellie, the Beautiful Cloak Model* brought $4,000 a week into the box office for a solid year. Whatever the exact figures may be, there can be no question that he did an immense amount of work, putting Hero, Heroine, Heavy Man, Heavy Woman, Soubrette, Comedian, Light Comedy Boy, and Second Heavy, supplemented by two or three utility actors to play such "walking parts" as the plot required, into each set of four acts. Davis insisted that he never wrote down to an audience and never wrote a "dirty" play. He was honestly and deeply moved by Nellie's misfortunes himself; otherwise he could not have moved his audiences. If he knew it was unrealistic to insist that the virtuous heroine must always be rewarded both spiritually and materially, it still seemed to him that it made "pretty good sense." For his humble audience, the theater

> meant not life as it was but life as they wanted it to be, and the young girl in our audiences who thrilled for an hour over the wealth and luxury and the ideal love that always came to the fictitious character she had for a time exchanged places with had little chance of remaining in this fairyland for too long.

All this continued until about 1910, when Davis saw the handwriting on the wall and tried to break away from the treadmill, ultimately achieving such serious successes as *The Detour* and *Icebound,* which won the Pulitzer Prize.

Unlike Owen Davis, Charles Taylor never graduated from melodrama; if he was an even more remarkable man, he can hardly be credited with comparable character and stability. The portrait of him sketched in an utterly charming book by his son Dwight, called

Blood-and-Thunder, is altogether winning, but his daughter sees him less glamorously and probably more realistically in her biography of his wife. Although Taylor had a number of shows on Broadway as early as 1898 and half a dozen companies on tour, with royalties of $1,250 a week coming in, he now owes most of his fame to the fact that in 1901, when he was thirty-six, he took as his third wife the sixteen-year-old Loretta Cooney, toward whom his attitude and behavior seem to have been composed of a curious mixture of callousness and sentimentality.

From 1905 to 1907 Charles and Laurette Taylor made their headquarters in Seattle, and Dwight lists twenty-seven plays they offered there between May 19 and December 21 of the last-named year. In them Laurette Taylor was "tied to sawmills, thrown to wolves, hoisted to railroad trestles, shot from horses, burned at the stake, and chased by Chinese butchers beneath the streets of San Francisco." Finally tiring of these activities, she left for the East and a milder type of theater. Later she married J. Hartley Manners, who wrote *Peg o' My Heart* and other plays for her, but she carried the name of her first husband through all her distinguished though checkered career.

The old melodramas lived on in tent shows and showboats after they had died out of the metropolitan theater. Tent shows were largely a midwestern, southern, and southwestern phenomenon, and they confined themselves mainly to rural areas. They began in the middle of the nineteenth century, but there were still about 400 of them as late as 1925. William Chapman's is supposed to have been the first showboat in 1831. This trade, which involved both regular plays and vaudeville, developed its own aristocracy: there were floating palaces, and there were barges that were not much more than floating saloons. By 1938 there were only three showboats left.

Uncle Tom's Cabin played the tents and the boats of course, but it also played everywhere else—in stock and on Broadway. "Uncle Tomming" became a career in itself; there were actors who began as Little Harry, went on to Marks or Shelby or Simon Legree, and ended as Tom. It is said that from 1853 to 1931 the play was never off the boards; it supplied many Americans with their only contact with the theater and served importantly to break down the idea that playacting belonged to the devil. My father once told me that it was the first play he ever saw, at the Academy on Halsted Street, when that was still a respectable Chicago theater area, and that he went about for days afterward lost in a world of wonder. From 1903 on it was several times filmed. Its last great triumph in the theater came in the twenties in the form of a musical comedy, *Topsy and Eva,* in which the Duncan Sisters starred, afterward continuing to play the name characters in vaudeville and nightclub engagements until Rosetta was killed in a traffic accident in 1959.

Motion pictures did not give live theater any real competition during Roosevelt's administrations (even toward the end they were more a portent than a present threat), and the president himself apparently never developed any interest in them. Indeed, he did not even make a phonograph record before the 1912 campaign; when Henry Cabot Lodge suggested it in 1904, he sarcastically inquired whether Lodge did not also wish him to do a dance for the Kinetoscope.

This was not because of any actual lack of film. Edison had established the first American motion picture studio, the Kinetographic Theater, or "Black Maria," a box-like affair, mounted on a pivot so that it could be swung about to catch the sun, in 1891, and by 1900, when Edwin S. Porter came to work for his company at the Twenty-first Street studio, they had copyrighted some 500 pictures. The Biograph catalogue of November 1902 listed nearly 2,500 subjects.

Such of these films as have survived, often through having been deposited as paper rolls for copyright purposes in the Library of Congress, are of great interest to film historians, but few have any aesthetic interest or value. In the beginning the miracle of movement in a picture was the essential thing, and the nature of the movement was immaterial. Dance acts and prizefights were popular because they accommodated themselves comfortably to the then fixed and narrow camera range.

The idea of making something happen for the purpose of photographing it came later and took at the outset very primitive forms. There is not much to Edison's *Washday Troubles* (1895) but a mischievous brat upsetting his mother's tub. Film men covered the coronation of King Edward VII, the Pan-American Exposition, and President Roosevelt's 1903 visit to San Francisco; in that same year Edison made an advertising film for the Lackawanna Railroad, showing Phoebe Snow riding "The Road of Anthracite" in gleaming white, in order to prove how clean travel by railroad had been made. When a news event could not be photographed, it was often faked; thus the line of demarcation between fact and fiction was not absolute. Joseph Jefferson seems to have been the first top-flight stage celebrity to succumb to the films when he did some scenes from *Rip Van Winkle* for Biograph, but he had been pre-ceded by such personalities as Buffalo Bill, Annie Oakley, and Sandow the strong man. In 1904 Mark Twain cooperated with Vita-graph in filming *A Curious Dream*, and he is said to have made a brief introductory appearance in Edison's one-reel version of *The Prince and the Pauper* in 1906.

The Edison, Biograph, and Lumière projectors were all demon-strated on Broadway, and in the 1896 presidential campaign both candidates appeared before the motion picture camera for the first time. Films were used as a part of vaudeville programs, very suc-cessfully at first, then, as development lagged, interest waned and threatened to die out. "Kinetoscope parlors," equipped with peep-show machines, began springing up in the midnineties in down-town areas and amusement parks. Some of the early nickelodeons were specially constructed, but more were only converted stores or halls, hastily fitted up with booth, screen, and seats; sometimes the posters were even displayed in what had been the store win-dows. Many were called Electric or Family Electric theaters. The term *nickelodeon* may have been first used by the theater that Harris and Davis opened in Pittsburgh on Thanksgiving Day 1905, but Tally's Electric Theater in Los Angeles dated back to 1902, and there may well have been other, less durable establishments earlier. By 1907 there were some 3,000 such theaters in America, and by 1910 there would be 10,000.

In the early days, France dominated the world film trade, and the leading firm was Pathé, whose beautiful red-rooster trademark was known everywhere. The first picture theater the present writer ever attended showed only Pathé films. But the most creative spirit in the early French cinema was George Méliès, a magician and theatrical producer, the maker of "Star Films." "Artificially ar-ranged scenes" he called them, and he has a reasonable claim to be called the first artist in world cinema. Méliès wrote his films, directed them, and acted in them; he even painted the scenery. He had begun, like others, by photographing actualities, and it is said that he achieved his first transformation when his camera jammed one day while he was photographing a street scene, so that when the film was developed, a bus seemed to have been transformed into a hearse. His pictures were composed of "scenes" in the theater sense; he did not use intercutting or novel camera angles, but he did employ double exposure, stop motion, and many other devices to do on the screen what could not be done in any other medium. As opposed to the dominant naturalistic trend of film making, Méliès used the camera to create a world of wonder, and he exploited this angle more successfully than anybody else has ever been able to do it except for Walt Disney and the makers of the great German "studio" films after World War I. Though it was not his most elaborate production, *A Trip to the Moon* (1902) was by all means the best known in America; it is still being shown.

Unlike Méliès, Edwin S. Porter was very much in the naturalistic trend, and his is the most important American name before that of D. W. Griffith. Porter is a somewhat puzzling figure; he was capable of alternating coventionality and creativity to such an extent that one sometimes wonders whether he ever quite realized what he had achieved. His most important contributions to screen history, from the point of view of influence, were *The Life of an American Fireman* (1902) and *The Great Train Robbery* (1903), but both were far and away surpassed in the dazzling virtuosity of *The Dream of a Rarebit Fiend* (1906), obviously suggested by the Winsor McCay comic, in which he used the camera to let the audience see the world through the drunken man's eyes as brilliantly as F. W. Murnau was to do it in *The Last Laugh* in 1925, when he was hailed for having created something startlingly new. Other Porter films—*The Ex-convict* and *The Kleptomaniac*, the latter contrasting the sympathetic treatment accorded a wealthy woman shoplifter with the brutal handling of a poor woman who had stolen a loaf of bread—are interesting for their social consciousness.

Another favorite emerging type was the chase film, and here again was something that could have been done in no other medium. Mack Sennett, who afterward made such good use of the chase in his Keystone farces, generally credited the inspiration for his "slapstick" to the Pathé craftsmen. He might quite as reasonably have cited such pre-Griffith Biographs as *Personal*, *The Escaped Lunatic*, and *The Lost Child* (all 1904), three years before Émile Cohl's charming French film, *The Pumpkin Race*. In *The Lost Child* a mother puts her baby out in the yard to play, where he crawls into the dog kennel and falls asleep. When she cannot find him, she concludes that he has been kidnapped by the passing stranger who is putting something into a basket. The frightened man flees from the enraged woman, who picks up a weird assortment of companions in the ensuing chase. When the "kidnapper" is finally overtaken, a close shot reveals the "child" in his basket as a guinea pig. Modern viewers of *The Lost Child* are generally horrified by the presence in the procession of a one-legged boy hobbling along on his crutch, and those who read the Biograph bulletin that announced it get another shock from its reference to a different pursuer as "a dago pushing a junk cart."

New companies sprang up during TR's second administration, and production, which had at first been an eastern matter, began to fan out. Selig and Essanay were Chicago-based, and both pioneered in California production, the former late in 1907, the latter in 1908, when the "A" of the combine, Gilbert M. Anderson (or Max Aronson), who had appeared briefly and unheroically in *The Great Train Robbery*, established a base of operations at Niles, and through a long series of one-reelers made himself famous as "Broncho Billy," the first cowboy hero of the screen. Against their will and at their expense, the Kalem Company became the means of establishing the principle, till then unformulated, that copyright protected a writer's work against unauthorized film adaptation. When in 1907 they came out with a one-reel *Ben-Hur*, they were sued by the author's estate, his publishers, and Klaw and Erlanger, who controlled the stage play. They appealed clear to the United States Supreme Court, lost, and in 1911 were forced to pay $25,000.

Perhaps at this point the establishment of the motion picture business upon a sound financial basis was more significant than aesthetic achievement. The patents companies certainly thought so. In the beginning the Edison interests claimed a monopoly, but in 1907 they began to make peace with some of their competitors, and the next year the Motion Picture Patents Company, popularly known as "the trust," was formed. This finally consisted of Edison, Biograph, Vitagraph, Essanay, Selig, Lubin, Kalem, and the American branches of Méliès and Pathé and involved an alliance with the film exchange man George Kleine of Chicago. From 1910 on the "trust" would distribute its product through General Film Company exchanges, which also imported Gaumont and Urban-Eclipse films from France. They collected a license fee of two dollars a week from all exhibitors who showed their films and refused their customers permission to exhibit anything produced by the independent companies. However immoral all this may have been, there is no denying that for a few years the patents companies produced better films than most of their competitors.

But the most important event in the early history of the cinema was the beginning of the directorial career of David Wark Griffith. His first film, *The Adventures of Dollie*, a simple but still oddly charming little picture about a child who is kidnapped for revenge by gypsies and recovered after having been floated down the river in a barrel, was released on July 14, 1908, and before he left Biograph late in 1913, Griffith had directed some 450 films, mostly one-reelers. A romantic and idealistic Kentuckian, the son of a Confederate officer, Griffith had knocked about the country as an undistinguished actor and aspiring playwright and had himself acted in films, first for Edison (*Rescued from an Eagle's Nest*, 1907), then for Biograph. It is hardly too much to say that during his Biograph years he created the syntax of the motion picture. This is not because nobody else had ever used "the large or close-up figures, distant views . . . , the 'switchback,' sustained suspense, the 'fade out,' and restrained expression" which have been claimed for him; far too many early films have perished to permit us to be dogmatic about "firsts." But priority is not what counts in art; Shakespeare wrote not the first English plays but merely the best. By what seems like a Providential miracle, almost all Griffith's early films have survived, and their sophistication and intelligence bury most of the work of his competitors fathoms deep. Nor is his preeminence due merely to technical virtuosity. The director's humanity, his powerful dramatic vitality, his quivering sensitiveness to the life around him, plus his great skill as a teacher of acting—all this added up to a cinematic achievement unparalleled in kind and still impressive after the lapse of considerably more than half a century.

But if the film did not come into its own during the Roosevelt years, the circus, like vaudeville and burlesque, was a very different story. The circus is of course a highly specialized branch of show business, which, in its way, demands as much expertise as opera. Its modern history is generally dated from Philip Astley's London enterprise of 1768. In America animal shows go back to colonial times, and in 1792 John Bill Ricketts presented a horse show in Philadelphia, to which he later added other attractions. P. T. Barnum was introduced to circus business by William Cameron Coup and Dan Castello, who wanted the lure of his name, in 1871. But Barnum's heart was never in it, and from 1887 James A. Bailey was in actual command of the Barnum and Bailey show. He died in 1906, and the next year Ringling Brothers bought the show, operating it apart from their own until 1919, when the two were combined. From then on the Ringlings were the undisputed monarchs of the circus business, but the Depression created problems for them as well as for lesser circus men, and by the 1940s hardly any of the other big circuses that had been operating for a generation were still going concerns. Then, on July 16, 1944, at Hartford, the Ringlings themselves suffered a body blow when, during a performance, their tent caught fire and 168 persons died in the worst disaster in circus history. Insurance claims, manslaughter charges, even prison sentences followed, and though tent operations were resumed in 1946, by 1965 the Ringlings had decided to give them up altogether, since when they have performed only indoors, in large city auditoriums.

In Roosevelt's time the circus was well into its great period, bringing color, drama, and ballyhoo to "children of all ages," as some announcements boasted. Till 1870 circuses traveled by wagon; thereafter all except the "mud shows," which played the smallest towns, took to the rails; the Ringling entourage, at its height, used 147 cars. In 1904 the St. Louis exposition gave circus business a shot in the arm and also inspired specialization. There spectators saw a fire-fighting show put on by Fire Chief George C. Hale, a Boer War show, the Mulhall Wild West performance, which became the 101 Ranch Wild West Show, and the Karl Hagenbeck Wild Animal Show. The great German zoo man never came to America in person, but, to his grief, he allowed his show to go on the road in 1905, and after he withdrew from the enterprise, his partners sold his name to a disreputable showman and the American courts allowed Hagenbeck no redress.

If there was anything more complex, highly organized, and exciting than "The Greatest Show on Earth" itself, it was the fact that it could be carried, often for one-night stands, anywhere in America. During a performance, you might see three wild animal acts in progress simultaneously in three rings, while aerialists flew about overhead and clowns paraded about the track. Butchers peddled candy and every variety of junk to the spectators, and sideshows exhibited such animals as could not be taught to perform, along with every variety of freak, including, on occasion, giraffe-necked women from Burma and Ubangi savages with distended lips, advertised as "The Greatest Educational Attraction the World Has Ever Known." And every year there were new thrill acts, like a man being shot out of a cannon or an automobile that turned somersaults in the air. There were even freak animals, like "Tinymite, the World's Smallest Hippopotamus" in the John Robinson show, or Ringling's "Pawah, the Sacred White Elephant of Burma." And on occasion there were gorgeous, elaborate production numbers like "The Durbar of Delhi" (Ringling) or "Adam Forepaugh's Spectacular Pyrotechnic Pageant," showing "Lallah Rookh's Welcome."

In the smaller towns and cities especially, an important part of the show was free—the circus parade, which heralded the arrival of the troupe. Here was where the elephants, the most popular of all the circus animals, shone, and here too might be seen the wonderful circus wagons, carved as elaborately as any ship's figurehead or carousel. If all this was given away, it was not wholly for love, since it was much better advertising than any the circus could buy.

The parade was not the first herald of the circus in American towns, however; that honor belonged to the posters, which in their heyday covered every wall and fence in the vicinity. If there was anything better than the circus itself, it was the posters, if only because the animals pictured there were so much fiercer and more vital than their often tired, bored counterparts in the circus ring. There have been many more artistic posters than those that announced the circus, but surely none ever more unerringly achieved their purpose. There is a great collection of them in the Circus World Museum at Baraboo, Wisconsin, and many of them have been generously reproduced in a delightful book by Charles Philip Fox and Tom Parkinson called *The Circus in America*.

The Wild West show began with Buffalo Bill's engagement at a rodeo in North Platte, Nebraska, on July 4, 1882. Next year he organized his own show, which lasted until 1913 and spawned many imitators. Exhibitions of riding and shooting, by Cody himself, Annie Oakley, and others, formed the heart of the show. Tents were not used as the poles and riggings would have got in the way of the riders; instead, a canopy was stretched over the spectators; and there were Indians (Chief Sitting Bull himself during one season), buffalo hunts, Indian attacks, and other shenanigans, all of which was at least as popular in Europe as it was here.

As a child I loved the circus, especially the clowns, who, to my way of thinking, were far more beautiful than any other humans and of whom I could never get enough; I would gladly have turned the whole show over to them if it had been in my power. Sometimes they were allowed to preempt a main ring and put on a brief act, but usually they merely traveled around the track, and they were always gone far too quickly to suit me. Nowadays I do not go to the circus because I will not be a consenting party to having aerialists who perform without nets risk their lives to entertain me, and I love animals far too much to wish to have them carted over the country in the discomfort that, in spite of the best intentions, must prevail under the conditions of circus life. Animals can be made comfortable in zoos, I believe, though I know they sometimes are not, and as man, the master predator, extends his depredations farther and farther, and even against himself, many creatures may well survive finally only in captivity. But the life of a touring animal is something else again.

Vaudeville and (to a lesser extent) burlesque were also an important part of the theatrical life of the time, but the amorphous, inconsequential, often topical character of their material makes them more difficult to consider than the "legitimate" drama. Both originated in the variety shows given in saloons, beer halls, and honky-tonks, but as time passed vaudeville took the high road toward family entertainment and burlesque the low road toward bawdry presented for a "stag" audience.

"Vaudeville" originally meant light French plays interspersed with music, while "burlesque" indicated pieces like The Beggar's Opera or The Critic in which serious works of art were parodied or ridiculed. Such entertainment requires considerable intellectual sophistication as well as knowledge of the original. This element survived up to a point in The Black Crook (1866) and some of the shows presented thereafter by such troupes as Lydia Thompson and her British Blondes, but here the story, like everything else, was only an excuse for the display of hefty women in tights. Weber and Fields also parodied plays in their famous music hall at the turn of the century, but though both had had experience in burlesque, their productions came closer to vaudeville.

The first big name in American vaudeville is Tony Pastor, who started as a saloon singer and circus performer. In Civil War times he began developing variety shows, which he cleaned up to attract family audiences. In 1881 he established his Fourteenth Street Theater, where he sang topical songs and gave the ladies door prizes ranging from dress patterns to dresses and hats to sewing machines. In the 1880s, two New Englanders, Benjamin Franklin Keith and Edward F. Albee, joined forces and built a vaudeville empire. Backed by funds from the Roman Catholic diocese of Boston, they established strict censorship over materials (performers called Keith-Albee "the Sunday School circuit"); put on continuous performances; and built palatial theaters, anticipating the movie palaces of the 1920s. The opening of their Colonial in Boston in 1894 marked the beginning of the golden age of vaudeville; another highlight came in 1904 with Willie Hammerstein's Victoria on West Forty-second Street in New York. The climax was in 1913 when Martin Beck built the Palace, and the sun went down when motion pictures took over that temple of entertainment in 1932.

How many theaters there were presenting vaudeville at the height of its vogue would be hard to say. People talked about "small-time, medium small-time, big small-time, little big-time, medium big-time, and big-time." It was two-a-day in the big-time, increasing sometimes to as many as six at the bottom of the pyramid, and after the movies came in, many five- and ten-cent theaters presented vaudeville, especially on weekends, along with the pictures. At such theaters as the Majestic in Chicago and the Orpheum in Brooklyn and San Francisco, families held weekly reservations year after year, while show business inns and restaurants stretched across the country to provide small-timers with homes away from home. It was a hard life, for the vast majority never made either big-time or very much money, but they dwelt in a world apart, which they would not have dreamed of exchanging for another, and when it was over they lived on their memories.

Not satisfied with their chain of theaters, Keith and Albee formed the United Booking Office (UBO). Establishing tyrannical control over the performers, extending in some cases to espionage, they not only fixed salaries at their own discretion but collected a 10 percent commission besides! Recalcitrants were blacklisted, and headliners were required to take expensive advertisements in theater programs. In 1900 there was an abortive strike by rebels who had attempted to organize a union known as the White Rats; Sime Silverman's Variety, founded in 1906, valiantly supported them, but in 1916 Albee organized his own company union, the National Vaudeville Association (NVA). William Morris tried to interest Klaw and Erlanger in starting a chain to compete with Keith-Albee, but they stayed with him only long enough to sell out to Albee at a handsome profit, and Morris was kept afloat mainly through the honorable loyalty of Harry Lauder, whom he was bringing to America just as Klaw and Erlanger were double-crossing him. Morris was not Albee's only competitor, however. Albee bought out F. F. Proctor, but the Connecticut impresario Sylvester J. Poli remained independent. The Orpheum circuit, with headquarters in Chicago, was controlled by Martin Beck, and Alexander Pantages operated, though less impressively, on the Pacific Coast. But when Beck audaciously invaded Keith-Albee territory to build the Palace, Albee secretly bought stock in it, and when it opened Beck found himself holding only a minority interest.

What did the shows present? Almost everything. There were stars of the stage, taking a fling between seasons. Sarah Bernhardt was one of them, and Ethel Barrymore used Barrie's *The Twelve-Pound Look* whenever she felt vaudeville calling. There were opera singers (I once heard Johanna Gadski give a miniature recital at the Majestic in Chicago) and ballet dancers. There were one-act plays without stars, generally comic but sometimes very serious and sentimental, and in the big theaters even what we learned later to call production numbers. There were trained animals, acrobats, jugglers, contortionists, tightrope walkers, weightlifters, even bicycle riders and swimmers (notably Annette Kellerman, who was most at home at the Hippodrome, where the stage was big enough for her tank). No "gag" or "gimmick" was too simple to build an act around. I remember one girl whose only stock in trade, besides her legs, was to be drawn up to the proscenium by a bit she held between her teeth, another who was said to have a trick of making herself so heavy that no man in the audience could lift her, and (in a different category) a pretty, red-haired girl named Cecile Gordon, who merely sat, dressed for a journey, upon a wicker suitcase and sang while her dog, beside her, howled an accompaniment.

There were monologists galore, ventriloquists, hypnotists, mind readers, impersonators, magicians, and stunt men, among whom the escape artist Houdini created the greatest sensation. There were even transvestites, and I remember with horror a fantastic creature in a ten-cent movie theater who would come out in a hideous makeup including a cherry on his nose, wearing a long skirt slit to the waist and sing "Mary Is a Grand Old Name" in countertenor, after which he would jerk off his wig, revealing his own short black hair, and retreat hastily from the stage. There were sister acts and family acts (the Cohans, the Foys, and the Keatons), and of course there were song-and-dance acts galore, single or duo. Hammerstein sent Gertrude Hoffman to London to observe Maude Allen's Salome dance, after which she came back and did it for him; it ran twenty-two weeks and inspired an epidemic of imitations.

There was also an abundance of ethnic humor—Irish, German, Italian, Yiddish. Leo Carillo told Chinese dialect stories, and Bert Williams, a sensitive man who suffered much from the indignities inflicted in those days upon touring artists of his race, became the first Negro headliner. I remember many acts made up of a dialogue between a white "straight man," impeccably dressed and straw-hatted, and a tramplike comedian in blackface who served as his butt, and one Yiddish dialect playlet called *The End of the World*, in which the devil was a character and I heard "Oi vay!" for the first time. Ethnic humor was not always unfriendly, however, and the reaction that later set in against it, though well intentioned, has sometimes been a little hysterical.

Hammerstein made a feature of "stunt" and "freak" acts. A "stunt" act might consist of, say, assembling an automobile on the stage in record time. "Freak" act does not at all imply that the people who appeared were freaks but merely that the public was curious to see them not because of any abilities they might or might not possess but because of the fame or notoriety they had acquired. In this sense, Helen Keller was a "freak" act. Hammerstein brought out a fake Carmencita, years. after the death of that dancer, and Dr. Cook was allowed to tell his side of the Cook versus Peary North Pole controversy. But the manager's great success in this area was Evelyn Nesbit, whom he built into a headliner after the Thaw trials.

Yet, though Bernhardt and Barrymore and Nazimova lent "class" to vaudeville, probably the biggest drawing cards were those that vaudeville developed for itself. Nora Bayes popularized a number of top hit songs, married five times, lived with insane extravagance, died broke or very close to it, and was buried with a Christian Science funeral. There is a tendency among writers about vaude-

ville to regard Eva Tanguay as the quintessential vaudeville performer (at her height she collected $3,500 a week). This was not
because of her talent, for she had little. What she did was to prance
about the stage like a woman possessed in what was then considered very suggestive undress, screaming out songs like "I Don't
Care" and thus affronting all the reticences of the time. Some
sympathetic observers thought they detected a wistfulness beneath
all the bravura, and they may have been right, for there was an
almost prescient inner uncertainty about Tanguay, who was to
lose all her money in the stock market crash and spend her last
years as a victim of arthritis.

Vaudeville programs were built with extreme care, opening perhaps with a "dumb act," such as animals or acrobats, to give the
audience a chance to settle down; using the forestage, backed by a
curtain showing a city street and often containing advertisements
by local merchants, while the stagehands were setting up a more
elaborate act behind it; and building steadily to one or more climaxes. About ten minutes were allotted to the lesser acts, but
headliners got twenty to thirty minutes. Trifling as the material
was, the technique was highly expert.

As for burlesque specifically, women in tights had posed as
"living statuary" (which was supposed to be "refined") in New
York as early as the 1840s, but the real inspiration for the "girl
show" that burlesque became dates, as already indicated, from
The Black Crook, and the first full-blown example is supposed to
have been Mme. Rentz's Female Minstrels, presented by M. B.
Leavitt in 1870. Sam T. Jack, later a notorious burlesque operator
both in New York and in Chicago, started as a manager with the
Rentz-Santley shows, and May Howard, rated the first big burlesque "queen," who married Paul Dresser, also began with them.
In the nineties taste began to shift toward less ponderous women,
and "Little Egypt" introduced the "cootch" or belly dance, featuring
erotic movement, at the World's Columbian Exposition. Millie de
Leon, the great burlesque star of the early twentieth century, had
Eva Tanguay's frenetic movement but went much further because
she both established physical contact with her audiences and ridiculed those who had yielded to her blandishments. Arrested in
Brooklyn in 1903, she learned how to exploit such incidents for
their publicity value, as well as how to publicize her alleged affairs

of the heart and spurn the "advances" she claimed had been made to her. Long before bare legs had been accepted on the stage, she sometimes "forgot" to put on her tights.

In 1915 a theatrical press agent described 90 percent of the burlesque presented up to 1900 as "a conglomeration of filthy dialog, libidinous scenes and licentious songs and' dances with cheap, tawdry, garish and scant scenery and costumes," presented in theaters that were "dirty and unkempt, dismally lighted, and with no attempt at ventilation." But now the "wheels" were moving to standardize bookings for burlesque in the manner of Klaw and Erlanger and Keith and Albee in other areas and simultaneously to clean it up and make it acceptable to respectable people. Samuel Scribner's Eastern or Columbia Wheel and the Western or Empire Circuit were both influential; the terms are a little misleading since neither reached beyond the Middle West. Scribner at least strove valiantly to realize his ideals, but in the long run less successfully than Keith and Albee. By 1906, 2,000 performers were playing a thirty-week season; in 1908 the Star and Garter opened in Chicago, advertising "Censored Burlesque" and "Clean Entertainment for Self-Respecting People"; and in 1910 the Columbia in New York was opened with fanfare and the presence of dignitaries.

Yet burlesque had two problems that in the end proved insoluble. First, it was continually being drained of its best talent as a "feeder" for vaudeville and musical comedy; thus, while Weber and Fields, Bert Lahr, W. C. Fields, Red Skelton, Sophie Tucker, Fanny Brice, and many others all appeared in burlesque, they moved out as soon as possible. Second, as standards changed or were abandoned and the other branches of show business began to do what until now only burlesque had done, the latter was forced to increase the pressure or else get out of the race altogether, and this went on until, in the 1920s, burlesque found its own "thing" with the striptease. By the time the Depression came, burlesque was more prosperous than vaudeville itself, and it virtually took over Times Square until the law put the lid on it in the late thirties.

The "amusement park" was another characteristic institution of the Roosevelt years—an enclosed area embracing a "shoot-the-chutes," a carousel, a variety of roller coaster and boat rides, a Ferris wheel, a dance hall, and every kind of show from the cheapest carnival exhibitions to large-scale depictions of such events as the destruction of Pompeii, the Chicago fire, and the battle of the

Monitor and the *Merrimac*, to say nothing of photograph galleries, peep shows, and "fun parlors," and roadside stands supplying popcorn, candy, balloons, and much besides. Coney Island, in the borough of Brooklyn, off the south coast of Long Island, was the home base, and there were three separate parks there—Steeplechase Park (1897–1964), Luna Park (1903–49), and Dreamland (1904–11)—as well as individual attractions outside them.

Architecturally, amusement parks went in for the fantastic and the rococo. By all accounts, Luna Park was the most imaginative. It was supposed to have cost three and one-half million dollars and was equipped to accommodate 750,000 visitors. It had promenades, plazas, and lagoons, all brooded over by a tower 375 feet high and modeled on a Spanish original. In a day when many of its visitors had no electric light in their homes, it spent $4,000 a week to illuminate its million light bulbs, of which 100,000 were in the tower. If you approached it by night from the water, "a fantastic city of fire" suddenly rose

> from the ocean into the sky. Thousands of ruddy sparks glimmer in the darkness, limning in fine, sensitive outline on the black background of the sky shapely towers of miraculous castles, palaces, and temples. Golden gossamer threads tremble in the air. They intertwine in transparent flaming patterns, which flutter and melt away, in love with their own beauty mirrored in the waters. Fabulous beyond conceiving, ineffably beautiful, is this fiery scintillation.

And who was it who was thus impressed? Ella Wheeler Wilcox? Nay, it was Maxim Gorki.

Coney Island had been an amusement center long before the establishment of the three great parks. The first roller coaster in America was built there in the 1880s, and James V. Lafferty built a hotel and bazaar facing the ocean across Surf Avenue in the form of an elephant 122 feet high. His glass eyes glittered at night, and his howdah was an observation platform. Rooms could be engaged at will (so long as they were available) in different parts of his anatomy, including the trunk. Later John Y. McKane, who afterward went to prison, made the place a center for gambling, prizefighting, horseracing, and political corruption. Jeffries and Sharkey fought at Coney in 1899, and in May 1900 Jeffries fought Corbett, just before prizefights were outlawed in New York State.

Steeplechase, built by George Tillyou, took its name from the mechanical horses that people who knew no better paid to ride; among its other original attractions were a Ferris wheel, imitated from the original at the World's Columbian Exposition, a Grand Canal with naphtha launches, and a miniature steam railway. After the Buffalo exposition of 1901, Tillyou brought to Steeplechase a cyclorama called "A Trip to the Moon" and also a giant seesaw. Dreamland had a scenic railway through the Alps, gondolas to glide through the canals of Venice, and at one time the aviator Santos-Dumont to take the really daring out over the water.

One might suppose that the roller coasters, scenic railways, and other contraptions that took people up in the air on flimsy wooden structures and sent them flying about at breakneck speed would have killed half those who rode on them, but as a matter of fact, the safety record, at Coney and elsewhere, was very good. Fire was another matter. Dreamland burned just before the opening of the 1911 season, Luna, after a long period of decline, in 1949. Steeplechase had anticipated both in 1907, but the indefatigable Tillyou rebuilt it, first charging ten cents to view the ruins, and in 1964 it was not fire but the bulldozers that razed it for a housing project. Peter Lyon called Tillyou the greatest of all Coney Island showmen because only he devised schemes for causing the customers themselves to put on the show and be amused by their own discomforts and humiliations. His were the Wedding Ring (or Razzle Dazzle or Hoop-La), the Human Whirlpool, and the Barrel of Love, all such devices as Reginald Marsh loved to paint, which blew up skirts, whirled people about, and threw them on top of each other, with much other idiocy to the same effect. It is said that operators developed an uncanny ability to "spot" the customers who would not tolerate such treatment.

My own interest in amusement parks did not survive my childhood, but I cannot deny that it was keen. I lived in Chicago, and the first park I ever visited was a small and short-lived one on the West Side called The Chutes, which would be important to me, even if for no other reason, because it was there I saw my first motion picture. There, too, my mother and I had two terrifying adventures: one when a ride we had supposed to be a variety of carousel turned out to be an "airship" in which we were swung off the platform and into the air, and the other in one of the "fun houses" then in vogue. I was entertained beyond measure by distorting mirrors that showed me elongated and compressed into every conceivable shape, but I was not entertained by darkness, wind, and swaying floors, especially when these things were sprung upon me in a building called the Katzenjammer Castle and decorated exteriorly with beautiful, larger than life-sized colored statutes of comic strip characters; if ever hopeful promises were betrayed, it was there! One summer too The Chutes had a "mermaid" called Helter, whose picture, with beautiful yellow hair, decorated the elevated platforms all over the city. When I saw Helter, alas, the glamour faded, for the hair was short and black and the figure unmistakably male; indeed I am not sure that "she" was not the same bruiser who rode down the chutes on a motorcycle and plunged into the water through a flaming hoop.

Chicago's greater and longer-lived amusement parks were Riverview, the largest in the Middle West, on the northwest side, and White City, which borrowed its name from the World's Columbian Exposition and was located appropriately not far from the University of Chicago. It was a comparatively small enclosed area, laid out in the shape of a court and with a great tower, modeled, I imagine, on Dreamland's. My own most cherished memory of White City is "A Trip to Venice" that I took there; the boat traveled, in its narrow channel, through enchanting sets, bathed in a wonderful golden light. The dance hall survived the other attractions, but the tower burned in 1927, though the enterprise as a whole was not condemned until 1939. Riverview was to survive into the sixties, when it, like Steeplechase Park, yielded to a housing project.

Riverview, though within the city limits, was more spacious, more rustic, more German than White City and seemed less sophisticated. It had trees and its name was not a cheat, for it was built on a riverbank. I was never very enthusiastic about the chutes, probably because the first time I went down I bit my tongue when the boat hit the water, but as a child I reveled in the roller coaster, which I would not ride for money today. If the carousel ride itself was nothing much, the carved, prancing, revolving, highly colored animals were enchanting. Having seen my first film at The Chutes, I heard my first phonograph record at Riverview, a squeaky cylinder to which you listened through earphones after having put a coin in the slot. At the time, however, I was much more interested in the peep machines. So far as I recall, I never encountered an Edison

Kinetoscope, in which a film revolved continuously over spools; the pictures I saw were on cards, as in the Biograph Mutoscope, so that, as you turned the crank, they flipped over and the illusion of motion was achieved. There was also a rarer type consisting of large, colored, still pictures viewed through stereoscopic lenses.

One night at Riverview, for the only time in my life, I saw life-sized puppets, which flopped about the stage in a rather terrifying manner and seemed to me to have something sinister about them. For many years I was told that I must have dreamed or imagined this, for there never were any such puppets. Finally I told my story to an authority on puppetry. When was it? he wanted to know, and I told him as well as I could remember. Yes, he replied, I had seen them, for there was one Italian troupe that did use such puppets, and they were touring America during those years. Thus the wisdom of childhood was vindicated once more.

What I liked best at Riverview, however, was the big spectacles, especially "The Creation," which was presented in a building designed especially for it, with a huge plaster angel holding it up, the gigantic wings outstretched across the whole width of the edifice. This, like the other shows of its kind, was a real-life motion-picture-in-the-round, similar, I imagine, to those that Steele Mac-Kaye had designed to be presented in Chicago in 1893. It depicted the six days of Creation to the accompaniment of a narrated Bible text, and in those pre–movie-spectacular days it was something to see. Adam and Eve were both attired in pink union suits, and even I knew that they were both women. I knew too that the waves were made of cloth, which was made to ripple by mechanical means, but no art is possible unless you are willing to lend yourself to an illusion.

The great expositions or "world fairs" to which the early twentieth century was so addicted were much more serious and important than the amusement parks, but they had their affinities with them, and consideration of two of them—the Pan-American Exposition at Buffalo from May 1 to November 1, 1901, and the Louisiana Purchase Exposition at St. Louis from April 30 to December 1, 1904—may well conclude our survey here.

When the Pan-American Exposition was planned, the 1893 triumph at Chicago was still fresh in everybody's mind, and the Buffalo organizers set out therefore to differentiate their show as clearly as possible from its predecessor. They decided that they would concentrate on the resources and achievements of the Western Hemisphere and that, instead of duplicating the dazzling brilliance of the White City, their emphasis must fall on color. As a compliment to Latin America, they chose Spanish Renaissance as the general architectural style, and since the proximity of Niagara Falls supplied them with abundant waterpower, they stressed electricity and electrical progress, including telephone and telegraph, X rays, and many articles for domestic use. The Electric Tower rose 409 feet and was flanked on either side by seventy-five-foot colonnades, forming a semicircular space opening toward the two-acre Court of Fountains, which was surmounted by Herbert Adams's sculptured figure of the nude Goddess of Light dominating the fair.

The exposition occupied 250 acres, embracing a portion of Delaware Park, with its irregular-shaped lake, and with a solid wall of foliage enclosing the grounds. The general plan was that of an inverted T, with the cross line as the Esplanade, around which the principal buildings were arranged in courts covering about thirty-three acres. The Manufactures, Liberal Arts, Machinery, Transportation, Agriculture, and Electricity buildings were grouped about the Court of Fountains. Southeast of the main group were the state and foreign buildings; southwest lay the Music Gardens. The national government exhibits were housed in three structures at the eastern end of the Esplanade. The middle building had a dome rising 250 feet above the floor and crowned by a figure of Victory. There was a separate building for colonial possessions. The Midway occupied thirty acres to the west. There was also a stadium for athletic events, seating 12,000.

The agricultural exhibit stressed progress through recent inventions; its aim was to make the farmer aware of the resources available. There were extensive exhibits of nursery stock and a profusion of trees and flowers throughout the grounds.

The national government exhibited ordnance, Post Office, and State Department. There was a coin press in operation. Coins of all nations were shown, with a complete set of government medals and currency. The workings of lighthouses and of quarantine and lifesaving stations were demonstrated. The National Museum Exhibition, under the auspices of the Smithsonian, displayed the resources of North and South America. Architectural treasures going back to the mound builders, the Aztecs, and the Indians were shown. Education was stressed in the Liberal Arts Building, and there was a special section on food production in South America. "Progress" was the magic word everywhere, for it had not yet occurred to many that that dame might turn out to be a harridan. Even the fine arts exhibit concentrated on the last quarter-century and especially the last decade.

The Temple of Music had an organ created by Emmons Howard of Westfield, Massachusetts. There were daily organ recitals, as well as concerts by Sousa and the Mexican Government Mounted Band and choral and orchestral productions. Those who desired livelier entertainment might go to the Midway, where there was a giant teeter-totter called the Thompson Aero-Cycle, each end of which supported four cars hung in a wheel, which, when raised, revolved 275 feet up in the air. Here too were cycloramas, spectatoriums, and panopticons, including "Darkness and Dawn," "a realistic representation of the experience of a departed spirit whose conduct on earth has not been exemplary"! The visitor also had the privilege of visiting the streets of Mexico; a Bedouin encampment, with natives from the Sahara; a southern plantation; old Nuremberg; an Eskimo or African village; or an "Indian congress." Again, he might wander in the maze of "Dreamland," and if he craved more excitement, there were "The Captive Balloon" from the Paris exposition or "The House Upside Down," which was billed as an improvement on the French "Topsy-Turvy House." Obviously Chicago was not the only place Buffalo did not hesitate to take on.

There was no regional emphasis in the Louisiana Purchase Exposition. As at Buffalo, there was heavy stress on water and electricity; as at Chicago, the prevailing color was white and the dominating architecture classical with Beaux Arts ornamentation. It was an enormous exhibition, covering 1,240 acres (two miles long and one wide), with about 500 buildings in all (including some that belonged to Washington University), 128 acres of exhibition space, thirty-five miles of roadway, an intramural railroad covering six miles, and a mile of waterways, all of which, according to H. Phillips Fletcher, a British architect who wrote a book about the fair, added up to more than the area of the Chicago, Paris, and Buffalo fairs combined. Fletcher, who was by no means an unsympathetic observer, complained that the show was too big, pointing out that, to inspect all the exhibits in the Agricultural Building alone, a visitor would be obliged to walk nine miles.

The central edifice was Festival Hall, a domed erection 250 feet high, standing on an elevation and flanked on either side by fifty-foot colonnades reaching to pavilions used as restaurants. Along the colonnades were ranged heroic statues representing the fourteen states that were carved out of the Louisiana Purchase. In front of the combined structure, cascades using 90,000 gallons of water a minute and elaborately illuminated at night descended over a succession of grand terraces, flanked by groups of statuary. The main exhibition palaces radiated like the leaves of a fan on broad avenues with stretches of water between.

Scientific and industrial progress was exhibited and illustrated much as at Chicago and Buffalo, and it was both characteristic and ominous that the War Department and the Navy should have had 15,061 square feet each in the Government Building while Justice got 2,019 and Library 2,161. The stadium was larger than at Buffalo, seating 25,000 and programming many events, including the Third Olympics. But there were other highly individual features that visitors must have remembered as belonging to this fair alone.

Louisiana's Cabildo reproduced the building where the transfer of Louisiana territory to the United States took place. Massachusetts, Connecticut, and Rhode Island were all represented by colonial buildings, Maine by a log cabin. New Jersey reproduced Ford's Tavern, which had served as Washington's headquarters at Morristown; Virginia, Jefferson's Monticello; Tennessee, Andrew Jackson's Hermitage; Mississippi, Jefferson Davis's Beauvoir. California had a replica of the Santa Barbara Mission; Colorado, one of its state capital. South Dakota's structure was made of corn, and Alaska's had a totem pole at each end. The French headquarters, prominently placed both because of France's connection with Louisiana and in recognition of her importance as a Continental republic, copied the Grand Trianon, with a section of its gardens.

The United States exhibited the Declaration of Independence; Britain, Queen Victoria's Jubilee gifts. There was a large Indian exhibit, showing various tribes in surroundings suggesting their native habitat, with well-known chiefs in attendance, and similar exhibitions of Philippine villages. John McCormack, not yet famous, and his wife-to-be, Lily Foley, were singing at the Irish Village, and another coming celebrity, Will Rogers, was in the Wild West show. Twelve acres were devoted to a reproduction of a California mining gulch of 1849, with a placer gold mine in operation, and there was a ten-acre map showing the crops raised in various

American states, with graveled walks to mark the states' boundaries. There was also a floral clock, with a dial 120 feet in diameter.

Pike being an old Missouri term, the St. Louis equivalent of Chicago's Midway was inevitably called that. It was a mile long and 600 feet wide. Here one might visit Jerusalem or the Tyrolean Alps. The many shows included Hagenbeck's trained animals. "The Creation" began here, and the St. Louis fire chief George C. Hale exhibited "Hale's Tours," travel pictures photographed from the platform of a moving train and shown in tiny theaters like railroad coaches, which spread out into other American cities, as did Kerry Mills's song, "Meet Me in St. Louis, Louis," just as Charles K. Harris's "After the Ball" had done from Chicago. But perhaps the most enduring monument of the St. Louis exhibition was the ice cream cone, which originated there.

My old teacher, Professor Albert H. Tolman of the University of Chicago, used to enjoy telling on himself how every year he would ask his classes how many had attended the Columbian Exposition. Every year fewer hands went up, and at last it dawned on him that the fair was twenty-five years behind him and that hardly anybody in his class was over twenty! The Columbian Exposition took on special glamour for me from hearing my parents talk about it, and I have always been inclined to regret that I did not come into the world in time to see it. With both Buffalo and St. Louis, however, I felt I had achieved a kind of connection by remote control. An aunt and uncle of mine were arriving at Buffalo just as President McKinley was being carried out, and my father made a business trip to St. Louis, probably in the interest of the Temple Pump Company, by whom he was employed. I still remember his returning home one night after I had gone to bed, and I can hear my four-year-old self asking him a perfect Rube Goldberg foolish question when he came into my room and bent over my bed to kiss me: "Did you get home?"

HE was one of those rare writers whose personalities are as important as their work—and, for that matter, of that even rarer breed whose personalities do not crowd out or obscure their work. "Mark Twain." The very name provokes an affectionate smile—and an image: an old man by 1900, with his great shock of once red hair now as white as the suits he unconventionally insisted upon wearing, drifting through and brooding above a land that was surely almost as much his as President Roosevelt's. Surely this could be said of none of his writing contemporaries, nor even, I think, with anything like equal emphasis of his contemporaries in any other pursuit. Edison? Perhaps we felt equally grateful to him. But his lineaments as an individual were far less vivid in the public mind.

It was always "Mark Twain" in those days, never "Twain." That linguistic outrage was reserved for later scholars and critics with no sensitiveness to language. *Mark twain* was a Mississippi River term, indicating safe water; it is a unit and should not be divided. He had his days of piloting on the great river behind him now; and beyond that his uninhibited Tom Sawyer–Huckleberry Finn boyhood on the southwestern frontier (he was born in Florida, Monroe County, Missouri, on November 30, 1835, and grew up in Hannibal); and on this side his adventures as a successful journalist and unsuccessful miner in San Francisco and on the Comstock

Representative Figures of the Time: Third Series

14

Lode; and his wanderings, first in the Sandwich (Hawaiian) Islands, then in Europe and the Holy Land, which produced the most influential of all American travel books, *The Innocents Abroad*, in 1869; and his marriage to the wealthy, delicate, high-minded Olivia Langdon, of Elmira, New York, their settlement at Hartford, and the joys and sorrows of their devoted family life; and the heart-crushing, agonizing death of his most beloved daughter Susy, just at the conclusion of the triumphant lecture tour of the world he had undertaken to avoid bankruptcy and honorably meet the debts he had incurred through the failure of the Paige typesetter and other unwise investments, to be followed by that of the devoted Livy herself, in Florence, in 1904; and his successes with the books about Huck and Tom and *Life on the Mississippi* and *The Prince and the Pauper* and *A Connecticut Yankee in King Arthur's Court* and his later travel books and "The Man That Corrupted Hadleyburg" and scores of lesser pieces, to say nothing of the ambitious historical novel, *Personal Recollections of Joan of Arc*, which he regarded as his masterpiece and in which he paid his tribute to the girl whom he considered to have incarnated the moral and spiritual ideal of humanity; and the widening social and intellectual horizons that produced the increasingly trenchant social criticism of his later years. He was to die at Redding, Connecticut, on April 21, 1910, when Halley's comet, which had ushered him into the world nearly seventy-five years before, returned to usher him out, as he had foretold it would. Shakespeare's Calpurnia says,

> When beggars die there are no comets seen.
> The heavens themselves blaze forth the death of princes.

Princes and Mark Twain!

He had begun as a "Phunny Phellow," first impinging upon the eastern consciousness with a mining-camp yarn about a Jumping Frog, which he himself called "a villainous backwoods sketch" but which is actually a most sophisticated piece of narrative art, and except among very literary people, he is still generally thought of first of all in this aspect, so that "as Mark Twain says" provokes a smile even before the listener knows what is coming. This deeply disturbs those who have been most impressed by the "pessimism" of *The Mysterious Stranger* and the soul-wilting determinism of *What Is Man?* but though there is truth in their objections, it is not the whole truth. Mark Twain said some of the bitterest things any

Mark Twain in the open-air study at Quarry Farm, 1903. Courtesy, Mark Twain Memorial, Hartford, Connecticut

American has ever uttered, yet he often turned despair itself to laughter; it has taken scholars a generation and more to correct the solemn, doctrinaire overemphasis of Van Wyck Brooks's brilliantly and seductively wrongheaded book, *The Ordeal of Mark Twain*. He was far too volatile, contradictory, and many-sided to cleave consistently to any philosophical position, and there was too much vitality in him to permit him to turn against life altogether. A pessimist one day, he might be an optimist the next; only a few months before his death, sick in body and crushed by his last great sorrow, the death of his daughter Jean, he could write, "I am happy—few are so happy." Nor did the contempt he frequently expressed for humanity in general ever keep him from loving individual specimens of it, and if his mind had been convinced that man was a machine and free will a delusion, his heart continued to make him indignant over wrongdoing and passionately moved by those who lived nobly and unselfishly. Moreover, though it cannot be claimed that he ever achieved a settled or satisfying religious faith, neither did he ever throw off the religious conditioning of his youth (after all, Calvinism too was brutally deterministic). God, Satan, Adam and Eve, and the angels haunted his imagination always, and Captain Stormfield learns that the worlds Christ died to save are as the sands of the sea in number.

Few men can have been more thoroughly committed than he was to the Christian moral outlook; nothing in *The Mysterious Stranger* is more moving than the author's bitter indignation against the "Christian" warriors who have only learned how to kill more effectively than their "heathen" predecessors. "I believe in God," he wrote in the most formal attempt he ever made to sum up his beliefs; even when he seemed to hate Him, he paid Him this compliment, for one can hardly hate what does not exist. Contrary to what many believe, he was not even unsympathetic toward Christian Science as a religion; he merely denounced what he considered Mrs. Eddy's cupidity and lust for power. Always too, clear to the end, he was capable of finding happiness in simple, innocent things, especially the cats and kittens he loved so passionately all his life and the small girls in whose society he delighted; the pains he took to entertain his little friends when they came to visit him are amazing in so impatient and absentminded a man.

Life groomed him for authorship as it has groomed few Americans and supplied him with rich and varied materials for it. "The

Lincoln of our literature" his friend William Dean Howells called him, and this seems as inevitably right as Ben Jonson's tribute to Shakespeare: "He was not of an age but for all time." Nor is this wholly because both he and Lincoln had their roots in that Middle West that has often been called the most American part of America. That Lincoln hailed from Illinois and Mark Twain from Missouri cuts no ice (after all the Lincoln log cabin is in Kentucky, and Springfield itself is partly a southern town). Nor would it be fair to Mark Twain to overstress the thoroughly Anglo-Saxon character of the world out of which he came; though his name was Samuel Langhorne Clemens, he was in no sense a "WASP." In his youth, to be sure, he was comparatively insensitive to Indian abuses and briefly seduced by Know-Nothingism, but these were false notes struck off in his finger exercises. He loved blacks (as his portraits of "Nigger" Jim, Roxy in *Pudd'nhead Wilson*, and Aunt Rachel in "A True Story" eloquently testify), admired Frederick Douglass and had a picture of the pioneer antisegregationist Prudence Crandall in his billiard room, put a Negro through college as part of the "reparation due from every white man to every black man," wrote "The United States of Lyncherdom," and blasted King Leopold II of Belgium for his atrocities in the Congo (Mrs. Clemens was more than a humorist when she suggested that he might save himself much wear and tear in the way of indignation if he would only consider every man colored until he was proved white). He consistently championed Jews against Christian prejudices and oppression, and he practically began his career of social protest by defending the Chinese in California. Though he would disapprove of and refuse to accept much of what we have to live with in twentieth-century America, he would never have turned against the melting pot.

In a country of such vast, cosmopolitan variety as now prevails in the United States, it no doubt becomes increasingly difficult to define just what "Americanism" is, but if the word means anything it surely must indicate an adherence to the ideals of ordered freedom upon which this nation was founded, and where in literature does this survive more eloquently than in his pages? (Part of his despair in his old age was prompted by fear that his land was turning into a dictatorship.) His use of folklore materials is by no means the only thing that has led critics to find a bardic element in him, gathering up in himself, "almost unconsciously," as Gamaliel Bradford once wrote, "the life and spirit of a whole nation" and pouring it out again "more as a voice, an instrument, than a deliberate artist." The frontier tradition he inherited was that of the oral improviser or raconteur; his platform work was therefore no arbitrary addition to his art but a vital part of it. To be sure, his careful literary workmanship, even in the traditional sense, as witness the abundant source material he wove into even such a seemingly spontaneous book as *Huckleberry Finn*, has now been more fully documented than was the case in Bradford's time. He was a master of the art that conceals art, and he was often most deliberately literary in his calculated spontaneities, but his representative, assimilative character remains.

If all the books upon which Mark Twain's primary reputation rests had already appeared before 1900, his fame as a public figure reached its height during our period. It is not true that his social consciousness awakened late, for he was "The Moralist of the Main" even while he was still "The Wild Humorist of the Western Slope." Beyond any other book, *The Gilded Age* named and characterized and excoriated a corrupt period in our history, and *A Connecticut Yankee* is so far from having escaped from the problems of the present by retreating into a romantic past that it carried all those problems with it, being as much concerned with the threats posed by our metastisizing technology as was Henry Adams himself. Mark Twain's was a love–hate relationship to science; if it promised to save men from ancient superstitions and lift the curse of backbreaking labor from their shoulders, it was no more exempt from the dangers of prostitution than man's life in any other aspect. As he surveyed the world of the early twentieth century, he could not feel that man's moral development had kept pace with his technological development, and unless somehow morality could be made to catch up, he feared that Caliban, not Prospero, might well rule the island and destroy it.

As he grew older, Mark Twain became more and more concerned with such things. Quicksilverish, temperamental, and unpredictable, he was completely consistent in nothing, not even pacifism; he carried no union card for any ideology. Hating violence, he still hoped for a revolution in czarist Russia; friendly to organized labor, he shied from even the mild socialism of his friend Howells and was under no delusions about laboring men and their leaders' using their increasing powers unselfishly. If he was taken in by the Span-

ish-American War at the outset, when the theater of conflict shifted
to the Philippines and the United States itself became the aggressor,
committing atrocities as unpardonable as any that had been attributed to the Spaniards, he thought that if we wanted the flag to
represent us accurately it might now be time to have the white
stripes painted black and the stars replaced by a skull and cross-
bones. When the calendar changed, he greeted a new century by
presenting

> the stately matron named Christendom, returning, bedraggled,
> besmirched, and dishonored, from pirate raids in Kiao-Chou,
> Manchuria, South Africa, and the Philippines, with her soul
> full of meanness, her pocket full of boodle, and her mouth
> full of pious hypocrisies. Give her soap and a towel, but hide
> the looking-glass.

Even the missionaries, much as he had admired their work in
Hawaii, now seemed to him tied up with imperialism, and he
shocked his more pious readers by attacking them savagely in "To
the Person Sitting in Darkness" and "To My Missionary Critics."
The bitter description of how a nation can be dragged into war
in Chapter 9 of *The Mysterious Stranger* and of the intolerance
toward dissenters that follows was fulfilled to the letter within a
year of the book's publication and frequently quoted a quarter of
a century later by those then resisting FDR's interventionism. Elizabeth Wallace, who knew Mark Twain in his old age and produced
a charming book about him called *Mark Twain and the Happy
Island*, wrote me that she was sure he would be desperately unhappy in what had been made of America and was glad that he
was at rest. What would he have said about Hiroshima? about Viet-
nam and Cambodia? about Watergate? And how desperately we
needed him to say it!

If he produced no important long books during his last decade,
it was not for lack of trying. He wrote continually, leaving probably more aborted manuscripts than any other writer of his eminence, and they are all being published at last by the University
of California Press in the Mark Twain Papers series. It was natural
that he should have done this, for he was less the possessor of an
imagination than its possessed (even his finest characters are evoked
rather than constructed), and it is well that we should have them,
for though none of them is wholly successful, he is the man of

genius, fitfully at least, in most of them. Like that of all really great writers, his art was a combination of realistic and romantic elements. If *Tom Sawyer* is, as he said, "simply a hymn, put into prose to give it a worldly air," the greater *Huckleberry Finn* is a serious, comprehensive picture of the whole Mississippi frontier, from its aristocracy to its scum, and it made the backwoods vernacular in which Huck speaks the wholly adequate vehicle of great art. Yet it gains a valuable added dimension through the folklore and superstition imposed upon its realism, and in *Joan of Arc* some of this Mississippi material is transported into medieval France, while in *The Mysterious Stranger* the Austrian village of Eseldorf (Assville or Donkeyton) is Hannibal with a Christmas-book coloring; indeed in one version of the story Hannibal is openly the scene. In *Pudd'nhead Wilson* he employs the folklore motif of the Wicked Nurse who exchanges the babies in their cradles, daringly combining it with such ultramodern stuff as identification through fingerprints, and it was not until I had assembled what I considered Mark Twain's finest short stories for a collection published by the Limited Editions Club that I fully realized to what extent fables, apologues, fairy tales, allegories, and exempla predominate in them. Even "The Man That Corrupted Hadleyburg" is only a fairy tale disguised, with the hoax replacing the test offered or the tasks set by a supernatural being in the older forms of literature.

Mark Twain was, in some respects, "a man with the bark on," and his work is generally taken as representative of a revolt against the Genteel Tradition, yet he himself greatly admired and respected the older, "classical" New England writers, and he showed amazing sensitivity in many ways. In his published writings, he was far more squeamish about sex than the much more polished James and Howells, and at least one of his biographers, Dixon Wecter, thought that he came through the whole mining-camp and Mississippi steamboating world a virgin. Like Huck Finn, he was tormented by a hypersensitive conscience that took up more room than all the rest of his insides but had no more sense than a yellow dog, since it went after him just as hard after he had done right as when he did wrong. Was it any wonder that Huck should finally have decided to "go to hell" rather than do his duty to society, as he saw it, by turning in the runaway "Nigger" Jim or that in *The Mysterious Stranger* the Moral Sense should emerge at last as the root of all evil?

2. *John Singer Sargent, Painter*

Henry James, Augustus Saint-Gaudens, Stanford White, and John Singer Sargent were the high priests of the Long Afternoon of American Culture that lasted until World War I. They were all acquainted, with close relationships between James and Sargent and between Saint-Gaudens and White. Contemporaries called Sargent "the finest portrait painter since Reynolds and Gainsborough" and mentioned him in the same breath with Velásquez, Frans Hals, Holbein, and Van Dyck. However this may be, there can be no question that he was the representative painter of his time; nobody who was anybody would have preferred to be painted by another when his brush was available. "His very name," writes Alexander Eliot, "whispers of the gilt frames, plush draperies, chandeliers, fringed bellpulls, spats, bowler hats, and potted palms that furnished the Victorian and Edwardian ages." Yet most of these properties meant very little to him. During his early years indeed, he was something of a rebel, and it took the Royal Academy, whose presidency he at last refused, a long time to swallow him. Long before the end he had become heartily sick of what he was contemptuously calling "paughtraits" and had virtually dropped them for watercolors and murals.

Sargent's paternal ancestors were merchants and shipowners of Gloucester, Massachusetts, but the fortunes of the family declined in the days of the painter's grandfather, who moved his family to Philadelphia. John's father, Dr. FitzWilliam Sargent, a physician and surgeon of some standing, gave up his work to follow his restless wife through a nomadic life in Europe, and the artist, born in Florence in 1856, grew up multilingually in a cosmopolitan atmosphere. His father looked after his early education and religious training, but his interest in both painting and music came from his mother. Though he always insisted he was an American, on this ground refusing a knighthood from King Edward VII, Sargent did not visit America until he was twenty, when his mother brought him and his sister to the Centennial Exposition at Philadelphia.

His most important teacher was Carolus-Duran in Paris; he first

"The Daughters of Edward D. Boit" by John Singer Sargent. Courtesy, Museum of Fine Arts, Boston. Gift of Mary Louisa, Florence D., Jane Hubbard, and Julia Overing Boit, in memory of their father

exhibited at the Salon in 1877, and two years later a portrait of his teacher graced the cover of *L'Illustration*. In 1882 came the superbly theatrical *El Jaleo*, the fruit of a visit to Spain and Morocco, now so effectively placed at the Isabella Stewart Gardner Museum in Boston, and the famous picture of the four little daughters of the Boston painter Edward D. Boit, which is one of the treasures of the Museum of Fine Arts. The sensation and scandal created in 1884 by his *Madame X* are now rather difficult to understand; were they caused by the notoriety of the model, Mme Pierre Gautreau, a native of Louisiana, by what contemporaries chose to regard as a provocative pose, or by the weird lavender coloring of her skin? Commissions falling off, Sargent decided to remove himself to London, but here too he was, at the outset, considered too far out, even by an art critic named Bernard Shaw, of all people.

In 1887 he made his second trip to America to paint Mrs. Henry Marquand, and it was here, especially in Boston, that he achieved his first real acceptance. He exhibited at the St. Botolph Club in 1888 and, on a larger scale, at Copley Hall in 1889, and in 1890 he began work on the complicated and richly symbolic series of murals in the Boston Public Library, depicting the progress of religious thought and belief from early Oriental polytheism to what Sargent regarded as its climax, through Judaism, in Christianity, that would absorb him more and more until completed in 1919. Though he went to France in 1918 to paint a war picture for the British Ministry of Information, he spent almost as much time in Boston as in London during his later years, and in 1916 he began work on another important set of murals in the dome and ceiling of the Museum of Fine Arts, which had to be rebuilt to accommodate his designs. These decorations, in paint and in relief, deal with subjects drawn from classical mythology and are much lighter both in spirit and in coloring than the library murals. He was on the verge of sailing again for America to see the last of them placed when he died in his sleep at London on April 15, 1925.

In his early years, Sargent was described as "very tall, almost slight of build, of erect carriage, and wearing a dark, roundish beard —the picture of a handsome attractive young man, rather awkward and shy, but withal possessing the indescribable charm of a fresh, winning personality." The slightness disappeared as he grew older, and the figure acquired a bulk that in later years some thought overwhelming. His gray-blue eyes were large and prominent and opened wide, and his complexion, never pale, became more ruddy. He was well groomed and dressed well but not dudishly; nobody ever thought he "looked like an artist"; some said a lawyer or a businessman, but at least one saw in him "a superior mechanic." His manner was quiet, dignified, sedate, and a little withdrawn.

Sargent's was the eclecticism of a highly cultured cosmopolitan painter who had encountered, sensitively responded to, and in a measure subsumed many widely varied, even generally considered disparate, kinds of art; the library murals reflect and combine Egyptian, Assyrian, Gothic, Byzantine, Renaissance, and modern influences, and his response to the cultures he first encountered in later years was remarkable for a man of his age. It has been the fashion to stress the influence upon him of what Barbara Novak calls Velásquez's "subtle control of values within an atmospheric space," as shown so notably in his study of the Boit children. He encountered the Spaniard in a big way at the Prado in 1879, going on to Frans Hals at Haarlem, but he had been enthralled by the Japanese exhibit at the Centennial Exposition when he was twenty, and the impact made upon him by Monet and the Impressionists also predates his encounter with Velásquez. Once at least he placed Rembrandt, Titian, Tintoretto, and Raphael ahead of the Spaniard, finding that supreme technician deficient in spiritual power, and in 1914 he said that Raphael, El Greco, and Ingres were now his "admiration."

Art remained remarkably fresh for him as long as he lived. Even as a portrait painter he shows great variety. Dogmatic as he was in matters of pose and costume, he did not, at his best, subject the sitter to his "method"; instead he devised whatever he thought needful to express what was before him. In later years he seemed to care more for the rougher, less conventional landscapes than for his smoother, more finished style, and still more for the murals that seem so different from his other pictures and the watercolors in which, as E. P. Richardson says, "everything flows and swims in the vibration of dazzling summer light" and for which he sought and found his inspiration in the Rockies, Florida, Switzerland, Venice, and the Near East. It is true that the watercolors tremble at times on the verge of a romantic abstraction, so that it seems as if he would paint painting and never mind the subject matter, yet he never actually does this. He admired Gauguin's use of color but deplored his sacrifice of everything else to it, and he did not care for the later Turner. In 1910 he refused to sponsor an art show that would include Picasso, Matisse, and Derain, and when, despite his refusal, Roger Fry publicly proclaimed him a champion of such painters, he set aside his otherwise consistent refusal to be drawn into controversy and blasted Fry in the *Nation*. As a matter of fact, he disapproved even of Monet's later tendency to permit form to disappear from his work. If Sargent himself was never quite "regular" from the academic point of view, he nevertheless respected tradition and sought to preserve its continuity, ensuring its vitality by drawing enough from new progressive, even radical, tendencies into the mainstream to keep it fresh and alive but never permitting it to be overwhelmed by these things. From impressionism as from the academics themselves he drew what he needed for his own highly individual art, expressive of his own vision, neither more nor less.

The dazzling expertise that Sargent achieved almost from the beginning awakened qualms for his future in the admiring Henry James ("Yes, but what is left?"), but though Sargent's methods were largely instinctive (this was at least one reason why he disdained elaborate theory and chatter in relation to art), he was never merely an improviser; some of his most apparently spontaneous effects were the fruit of much scraping out and beginning again. To be sure, he worked rapidly, pacing the floor and mumbling to himself and his sitter; he once computed that he walked four miles a day in his studio. He also had the gift of seizing upon what James called "the suddenly determined absolute of perception," as when Theodore Roosevelt swirled suddenly and half-angrily while mounting the stairs to stand grasping the newel post and Sargent recognized at once that they had found the pose they had been seeking so long. On the other hand, he did not succeed with Mrs. Gardner until the ninth try, and *Madame X* cost him almost as much pain. Sometimes too, for no discernible reason, he would be frustrated by something that came with ease at another try, though he said that only "once in a great, *great* while" did he succeed in pleasing himself.

Sargent has often been considered a "psychological" painter, but he himself had no patience with this kind of talk. "I paint what is before me, using my brains and my feelings." And again: "I don't dig beneath the surface for things that don't appear before my eyes." And finally: "I do not judge. I only chronicle."

Perhaps there has been some exaggeration here on both sides, and perhaps the contradiction is less absolute than it appears. Caro-lus-Duran had stressed the importance of painting what you see, but he had also insisted on the importance of understanding your model. Sargent himself admits that he used brains and feelings as well as, in the narrower sense, eyes, and he must have known too that he made some use of his own set of values. Shakespeare's—or King Duncan's—notion that "there's no art to find the mind's con-struction in the face" is adequate for a writer, but it will not do for a portrait painter who is not content to limit himself to super-ficialities.

Obviously, like other artists Sargent must sometimes have failed in his "seeing." He did that, as he was well aware, with Speaker Thomas B. Reed, whom he respected and found delightful but whose corporeal being was hopelessly unflattering and unpictorial. "His exterior does not somehow correspond with his spirit, and what is a painter to do?" On the other hand, he got an impression of saintliness from both John D. Rockefeller and Sir Henry Irving, and because Mary Hunter's photographs do not show "half the radiance or the beguiling look" that Sargent caught in his portrait of her, Charles Merrill Mount concluded that the difference was indicative of his attitude toward her. He was pleased when Mrs. Van Renssaelaer responded to the tenderness expressed in his por-trait of little Beatrice Goelet, "for very few give me credit for insides," and surely neither Vernon Lee nor Mary Duclaux erred in seeing his most enchanting canvas, Carnation, Lily, Lily, Rose, in terms of "an altar-piece, those Barnard children in pinafores becoming more than Botticellian angels lighting up the shrine of an invisible Madonna, a Madonna immanent in the roses and lilies and the fading summer afternoon." Moreover, if there is a subjec-tive element in the painter's seeing, the same must be true of that of the viewer. Henry Adams and others have seen something sin-ister in Sargent's portrait of Asher Wertheimer, but the painter seems to have liked him and all his family; he did twelve canvases of them, including one of an ill-fated son whom he did his best to help and advise.

Sargent was almost completely indifferent to everything relating to politics, business, and public affairs; perhaps this is the reason he steered clear of painting royalty and even managed to decline an invitation to dine with the king and queen of England (he did do a picture of Edward VII on his bier). Nor does he seem to have cared any more for presidents. His portrait of TR, brilliant as it is on its own terms, proceeded under difficulties and was rather skimped at the end; he said that Roosevelt made him feel like a rabbit in the presence of a boa constrictor. Wilson he found agreeable but uninteresting, and he refused Coolidge altogether. He had so little interest in World War I that Henry James, who rather lost his head over it, was tempted to be annoyed with him. At the front, when he went there on request to paint, he showed neither fear nor any other emotion and betrayed a complete inability to grasp the distinctions in military rank. His big war picture *Gassed* might be called good peace propaganda of a cool, unemotional kind. He was frankly bored by the group picture he did of British generals (especially their boots), and surely the World War I murals in the Widener Library at Harvard are as undistinguished as anything a painter of his eminence ever did.

From time to time we hear of Sargent's dancing, fishing, swimming, mountain climbing, and playing tennis; the swimming seems to have meant the most to him, but he did more riding than might have been expected of a man with his gift for falling off the horse. He was also a poor sailor. His only important indoor amusement seems to have been chess.

He was well read but better in Continental than in English literature, especially French poetry, which he could reel off in great quantities. He was an industrious theatergoer and painted Ada Rehan, Ellen Terry (as Lady Macbeth) and others. When Nijinsky was in Boston, he liked to come to Sargent's studio to watch him paint, and Sargent himself was devoted to Chaplin, whose early films he and Mrs. Gardner devoured together.

Outside painting, however, his great passion was music; when, after his early failure in Paris, he was discouraged enough to think of giving up art, he talked about going into music instead. He liked Wagner but apparently cared little for Mozart, and he did not respond to *Pelléas et Mélisande*. He was fond of Grieg and above all of Fauré. Both C. M. Loeffler and Percy Grainger vouched for his musical knowledge and know-how. At one time he tried to collect folk music in Spain for Vernon Lee, and he often rested his sitters (and no doubt himself) with piano playing when they were tired of sitting.

He went into society more than might have been expected of a man with his disinclination to small talk. Public speaking was probably the thing in life he hated most, and the stories of his choking and sputtering on the rare occasions when it was forced upon him are comical and pitiable. But though he talked to his sitters freely to put them at ease, words did not come easily to him even in friendly conversation, and it is said that when he met the equally tongue-tied Field Marshal Haig, he began and Haig ended every sentence in dumb show. He was considered reserved, even inscrutable, sometimes blunt toward persons not on his wave length, and there were those who were afraid of him even in his youth. Sometimes he gave "arty" questions a frivolous answer by reference to which the interlocutor might mislead himself if he chose. With intimates, on the other hand, he could be boyish, simple, and capable of high spirits and skillful mimicry. There is one amazing story of his deliberately seeking out and thrashing a man who had insulted him, and when Henry James had been booed on the first night of *Guy Domville* he amazed his friends with a startlingly eloquent and uncharacteristic outburst of picturesquely varied profanity that must have been worthy of Mark Twain.

Except for his immoderate eating and smoking, he seems to have steered clear of dissipation even during his youth in the art student's Paris. As to love, his name has been connected with Judith Gautier, who had been one of Wagner's flames; with the half-barbaric Spanish dancer Carmencita; and later with Mary Hunter, sister of the composer Ethyl Smyth, but we know nothing about his relations with them. Carmencita was definitely out of character for him, and if he had any serious interest in her, it did not last long. Mrs. Hunter, on the other hand, seemed well qualified to make him a suitable wife, and after her husband's death, many wondered whether he would marry her. He did not, and it is possible that she may have been more interested in him than he was in her. As his relations with his own family show, Sargent was a deeply emotional man, capable, despite a somewhat gruff exterior, of genuine tenderness, but he did not wear his heart upon his sleeve, and it seems to have been difficult for him to express affection or perhaps to accept it. There is therefore a strong suggestion of something unfulfilled about him (like what Henry James, in one of his most teasing phrases, called "the starved romance of my life"), and we get hints during the later years especially, that he poured everything he had into his work because he knew no other depository. Once when the elevator man at the Pope Building in Boston, where he kept a studio, asked him if he never took a holiday, he countered with another query: "What would I do for recreation?"

But if he was starved for love, he was rich in friendship and eminently worthy of it. He "boomed" both musicians and painters whom he liked, used his influence to secure commissions for them, gave generously of his means, and extended a helping hand wherever it was needed, even at times lending his brush and his skill to the work of others. His criticism, though frank, was kind and considerate, and he always took pains not to wound anybody who was making a respectworthy effort. All in all, he was an honest, unpretentious man, and there is no recorded instance of meanness, jealousy, or smallness in the history of his life.

3. Augustus Saint-Gaudens, Sculptor

"Augustus Saint-Gaudens" (thus President Eliot upon the occasion of conferring Harvard's LL.D. upon him), "a sculptor whose art follows but ennobles nature, confers fame and lasting remembrance, and does not count the years it takes to mold immortal fame."

He was by common consent the greatest American sculptor of his time, but though he spent much more of his life in this country than Sargent did, he differed from him in not coming of American parentage. He was born in Dublin on March 1, 1848; his father was a French shoemaker, his mother Irish. The potato famine drove the family to New York while Augustus was still a baby, and he was put to work at thirteen, choosing to be apprenticed to the then popular trade of cameo cutting because he already knew that he wanted to be an artist. His most important early art education was received in night classes at Cooper Institute and the National Academy of Design. In 1867 he went to Paris and thence to Rome. He studied under François Jouffroy and Jean Baptiste Guillaume, and in 1873 he met Augusta Homer—then an art student from Roxbury, Massachusetts, and a relative of both Sidney Homer the composer and the painter Winslow Homer—whom he married in 1877. After returning to America, he gained much from his association with John La Farge and Stanford White; in his characteristic, large-hearted way, the dynamic, restless White devoted himself to Saint-Gaudens's interests almost as industriously as to his own and often designed the pedestals and settings for his monuments.

Saint-Gaudens's first big commission was for the statue of Admiral Farragut in Central Park in 1881. Among the many distinguished works that followed were the standing (1887) and the seated (1907) Lincoln, both in Chicago; the memorial to Deacon Samuel Chapin, generally called *The Puritan*, in Springfield, Massachusetts (1887); the unnamed monument at the grave of Mrs. Henry Adams in Rock Creek Cemetery, Washington (1891); the nude, bronze Diana atop White's Madison Square Garden from 1892 until the building was pulled down in 1925; the famous memorial to Colonel Robert Gould Shaw and the Fifty-fourth Massachusetts Regiment, across the street from the State House in Boston, and the General Logan in Grant Park on Chicago's lakefront (both 1897); the General Sherman at the entrance to Central Park (1903); and the Phillips Brooks memorial beside his Trinity Church (1907). Among his many bas-reliefs, the Bastien-Lepage, the Children of Joseph H. Schiff, and the William Dean Howells and his daughter Mildred are among the most famous. He designed a medal for the World's Columbian Exposition and a series of United States coins during the Roosevelt administration.

In 1885 the Saint-Gaudenses moved to the place now most closely associated with their memory, Cornish, New Hampshire. During his later years the sculptor received so many honors that he began to wonder "whether the world has gone mad or whether I am more a fool than I think I am." In 1900 he discovered that he had cancer and underwent the first of two serious operations at the Massachusetts General Hospital. He died on August 3, 1907.

Saint-Gaudens had a long, thin face, with a large nose and a pointed chin. As a baby, he was, as he said, "red-headed, whopper-jawed, and hopeful." The hair at least remained, and he, Charles McKim, and Stanford White thought and spoke of themselves as "the three redheads." Robert Louis Stevenson thought Saint-Gaudens not handsome because his eyes were too close together—"only remarkable looking and like an Italian cinque-cento medallion." In later days, Howells found his face "full of a most pathetic charm, like that of a weary lion," and thereafter encountered sculptured lions all over Europe that looked like him.

In Saint-Gaudens's youth we hear of his fencing, wrestling, swimming, fishing, and hunting. In those days at least, he did not dance. In France he was a great walker, swimmer, and frequenter of gymnasiums, but he always remained a poor sailor. He did not understand football but rejoiced in the strength and grace shown in the movement of the players. Basically, however, he was a city man until he came to Cornish, when "it dawned upon me seriously how much there was outside my little world." Thereafter, even during the agonies of his final illness, he devoted himself to both outdoor work and winter sports.

He makes something of a point of not being much of a reader, yet a reasonable number of books and writers are listed as favorites, beginning in youth with *Robinson Crusoe,* Fanny Fern, and the *New York Ledger.* Plutarch's account of Germanicus made him resolve "to be the most lovable man that ever was." He had some interest in Maeterlinck and Anatole France and a novel by Daudet once kept him up into the night, but he did not care for Henry James. Apparently his interest in literature was considerably stimulated by his contacts with Stevenson. His theatergoing went back as far as Rachel and Edwin Forrest, but he cared much more for French and Italian theater than for the English or American, and even as late as 1899 he could go to "that cheap circus at Montmartre where I laugh at the same jokes and idiotic farces I have laughed at twenty times before."

He was like Sargent, however, in his love for music, and he compares his first encounter with a Beethoven symphony to his first visit to the Sistine Chapel. As a student in Paris, he attended the Sunday Classical Concerts at the Cirque d'Hiver but scorned Offenbach, to his later regret. He loved the older French and Italian operas but never took to Wagner. In the eighties the Standard Quartette and the Philharmonic Quartette gave Sunday afternoon concerts in his studio.

He himself tried to play the flute, and I judge he must have played it well since his playing reminded Louise Homer of the basso Pol Plançon. It has been reported that as a student in Paris he split the ears of his associates with his whistling and singing, and he never really gave up delivering both songs and arias while he worked.

His humor appears both in his mimicry and in the cartoons he liked to draw. He was a good storyteller, and he acted out his stories as well as telling them, but it was only during his later years that he took to clubs. On public occasions he always tried to make himself as inconspicuous as possible. At the dedication of the Shaw memorial in Boston, he was terrified at the thought of being called upon to speak, yet he found "the great storm of applause and cheering" that greeted him "a sensation worth having. I realized what an extraordinary feeling of triumph and power must come to a successful actor." Soon, however, he forgot that he was being observed "and became the principal observer." He generally found it difficult to express his feelings, but after his father died, he took his son Homer "to the barnlike Thirty-sixth Street studio, and there, lighting one feeble gasjet, walked sobbing, back and forth, in and out of the black shadows, telling to my young, uncomprehending ears all that his father had meant to him."

As a boy growing up in a tough neighborhood, he was combative; later his studio rages, triggered especially by cold and noise, were famous. But it is interesting that he could be terrified as well as terrifying. One assistant so dominated the studio that his employer "was afraid to speak to him, afraid to discharge him, and aproached him in terror and trembling when I had anything to ask." This continued until, "in a burst of fury, I discharged him with oaths, curses, and objurgations." When the man replied quietly, "I had not the faintest idea that I was disagreeable, Mr. Saint-Gaudens," all the wind went out of the sculptor's sails, and he apologized. The two parted but ultimately became friends.

He was subject at times to intense depression. In 1899, in Paris, he felt "a complete absence of ambition, a carelessness about all that I have cared so much about before, and desire to be ended with life." In a letter of January 1901, which was after his first operation, he speaks of "my terrible mental condition, no doubt the prelude to the deeper depths of Hell I have been in since." This, he thanks God, is "now a horrible dream of the past." Yet in October 1903 he writes that for six years a horrible vision of death had hung over him until, about three months ago, "a total change in mentality came; the vision of death vanished and an entire new grip on life and health took possession of me." Certainly there can be no question about the courage with which he lived and worked through his final illness. He took philosophically the studio fire of October 1904 that destroyed four years of work and many pictures and papers he cherished. In 1903 he still feels young, and in 1905 he says, "The older I get the more I see of things to take pleasure in, and the more youth seems good to contemplate." We have his son's word for it that there was no "morbid introspection" during the last pain-wracked days.

Saint-Gaudens's marriage to Augusta Homer, which produced one son, was an up-and-down affair; the tie and the love between them endured to the end but not without strain, and Mrs. Saint-Gaudens's poor health, her deafness, and her far from easygoing temperament were not helpful factors. Though Saint-Gaudens was no rake, he did have one long-enduring affair with the model known to us only as Davida, by whom he had a child. For a long time Augusta did not know; when she found out, he exhorted her in terms that would have seemed more suitable coming from her to him, begging her not to lose sweetness, kindness, or charity, lest she should "come down from the high place you hold in my heart"!

Though reared a Catholic, Saint-Gaudens revolted against what seemed to him "the historical self-chastising doctrines" of Christianity, and only toward the end was he, according to his son, drawn to Christ "as a man, tender yet firm, suffering yet strong." But when, after the death of his friend Paul Bion in 1897, he was driven almost to despair over the hopelessness of finding any meaning in life, it came to him like a flash that whatever the nature of the unfathomable might be it must be benevolent, and this thought was "a great comfort." If life was "terribly sad and tragic," love and courage were still "the great things." If we were all "drifting in an open boat on the ocean," cheerfulness was still better than melancholy; so he flung Schopenhauer aside. And though we might be "microscopical microbes" on an "infinitesimal ball in space," it was still true "that every earnest effort toward great sincerity, or honesty, or beauty, in one's production is a drop added to the ocean of evolution, in the something higher that I suppose we are rising slowly (damned slowly) to."

Royal Cortissoz wrote of Saint-Gaudens that "he was not only our greatest sculptor, but the first to break with the old epoch of insipid ideas and hide-bound academic notions of style, giving the art a new lease of life and fixing a new standard." I have no notion of what an insipid idea may be, but it is not necessary to label or libel all Saint-Gaudens's predecessors in order to perceive the truth of the last part of this statement. As a student in Paris, he would have needed to be peculiarly insensitive not to be aware that a new and vital spirit was blowing through the art world, and in Rome his contacts with fifteenth-century sculpture, and especially Donatello, strengthened his interest in both naturalism and low relief. Among contemporary sculptors he admired Paul Dubois, J. Q. A. Ward, Daniel Chester French, and F. W. MacMonnies, but though he broke with the academicians, he always insisted upon both "construction" and a thorough knowledge of anatomy as the necessary foundation for successful work, and he had no patience with the geniuses who were above the necessity of pointing and measuring. He did not care for the later Rodin and called his Balzac "a guttering candle." He was generous in his appreciation of contemporary painting and disagreed decidedly with those who considered illustration beneath a real painter and therefore denigrated such men as Edwin Austin Abbey, Howard Pyle, and Maxfield Parrish. He knew that art was made for man, not man for art, and there was no snobbery in his attitude toward either. "I am not one of those who believe that only the few who possess marked talent should attempt to be artists."

Though he could not go along with Tolstoi's views on art, he characteristically admired his "sincerity and kindness of heart." Himself he had little use for theory, believing that what was best could never be fully analyzed or explained. "I could not answer that man," he said once, "but I know he is wrong." And again: "I'm a poor hand at argument, but if I can get my hands in some clay, I can show you what I mean." Nor was he afraid to trust his own reactions, in art or other things. In the cathedral at Saragossa, "human grandeur seemed the dominating note, not the reverence of God," and the Escurial was "a colossal, appalling, and terrible monument . . . to neurasthenia," but the Alhambra was one of the two or three "great pearls of beauty on this globe." And though he was revolted by the Spanish bullfight, he could still understand "how, like drink, notwithstanding the disgust, a man goes to it again and again."

Since nothing can ever be reproduced exactly, he thought it best to err, since err one must, "only on the side of beauty." The stock judgment is that he was much less inclined toward allegory than was French. Yet the decorations on the exedra of the Farragut monument suggest both abstraction and art nouveau, and *The Puritan* is less the portrait of a particular man than the expression of an attitude toward life. The Diana too is an ideal figure, and the image floating above Robert Shaw's head and the Victory leading General Sherman's horse make the works in which they appear a combination of realism and symbolism. Homer Saint-Gaudens says that his father longed all his life to escape from the limitations of portraiture "in order to create imaginative compositions. . . . Moreover, he constantly spoke to me and to others of his pleasure in suggesting the half-concealed." He came closest to abstractionism and expressionism in the figure at the Adams grave, which some place at the height of his achievement. To create this, he studied buddhas and strove for "something sexless and passionless, a figure for which there posed sometimes a man, sometimes a woman." He called the result "The Mystery of the Hereafter," but Henry Adams, who had commissioned it, thought of it as "The Peace of God." Speaking of it and *Silence* together, Theodore Roosevelt wrote finely:

> The strange shrouded, sitting woman, the draped woman who stands, impress the beholder with thoughts he cannot fathom, with the weird awe of unearthly things; of that horizon ever surrounding mankind, where the shadowy and the unreal veil from view whatever there is beyond, whether of splendor or of gloom.

In one of the Forsyte interludes, Galsworthy brings Soames to brood before the Adams memorial on his visit to Washington.

Saint-Gaudens's self-judgments varied from time to time. The one thing he was always sure of was that sculpture was "hard labor, in a factory." Chairs, folds in garments, legs and feet—even such commonplace things as these gave endless difficulty. Sometimes he was exultant: "I think I told you that my 'Victory' is getting on well. It's the grandest 'Victory' anybody ever made. Hooraah!" And when it was exhibited at the Salon, he became so "cocky" that he was sick of himself for three days. But of another piece he wrote earlier that he had no idea as to its merit: "At times I think it's good, then indifferent, then bad." There seems to have been gain in this area as time passed and the sense of mastery increased. "I never felt sure of anything before," he wrote in 1898. "I groped ahead. All blindness seems to have been washed away. I see my place clearly now; I know, or think I know, just where I stand." But such certitude is not for permanent possessing by mere mortals.

He was a hopeless perfectionist always and an addicted doer-over, with the result that he sometimes outspent his fee and came up with a loss and a disgruntled client to boot. "Nevertheless too much time cannot be spent on a task that is to endure for centuries." The first Diana was eighteen feet high; because they thought her too tall, Saint-Gaudens and White took her down at their own expense and replaced her by a figure five feet shorter. He took ten years on the Sherman, fourteen on the Shaw, and death beat him to completing the figures that were to have stood before the Boston Public Library. He undertook the Shaw commission as a low relief, but under his "extreme interest in it," the "rider grew almost to a statue in the round and the negroes assumed far more importance than I had originally intended." For the sixteen heads shown he modeled about forty. He also altered and realtered his American coins for a year and a half, constructing seventy models of the eagle. The original idea for the Phillips Brooks memorial was to have been an angel behind the preacher, and Saint-Gaudens sketched thirty angels before he turned instead to Christ, after which he designed two reliefs for the Savior, one low, the second almost in the round, and then constructed the whole figure as a statue.

It all meant self-realization, but it was far indeed from self-indulgence. Up to the time he did Robert Louis Stevenson, Saint-Gaudens's sitters were to him mainly "visible, tangible objects to interpret." His great admiration for Stevenson changed all that, and from then on he read books about his subjects when they were available and tried to draw them out by conversation and understand them. As a teacher at the Art Students' League, he was intolerant only toward pretense and frivolity. He rendered personal services to many artists, and there is a story about how, one day, having been fired by the sight of a piece of work by a sculptor wholly unknown to him, he jumped into a cab, sick as he was, and burst in upon the man to tell him how much he admired it. He was in on the planning of the World's Columbian Exposition, the report of the Washington Park Commission, the organizing of the Society of American Artists, and the founding of the American School of Fine Arts in Rome. Though he was unable to take general charge of the sculpture at Chicago, as Burnham had hoped he might, he suggested French for the statue of the Republic, dreamed up the scheme for the peristyle opening on Lake Michigan, advised Mary Lawrence about her statue of Columbus before the Exposition Building, and helped secure MacMonnies to do the Columbia Fountain. He called the planning conference "the greatest meeting of artists since the fifteenth century" and the Fine Arts Building "the best thing done since the Parthenon." "The days I passed there," he wrote of the exposition in retrospect, "linger in the memory like a glorious dream, and it seems impossible that such a vision can ever be recalled in its poetic grandeur and elevation." That was what he wanted America to be like, and who ever contributed more toward realizing the lovely, impossible dream?

4. Edward MacDowell, Composer

The announcement of Edward MacDowell's appointment as Columbia's first professor of music in 1896 called him "the greatest musical genius America has produced." During the Roosevelt years, until his death at forty-seven in 1908, his position was roughly equivalent to that of Elgar in England or of Sargent in painting here. The leading music critics bowed down to him, and Richard Watson Gilder toasted him in verse. In many quarters he was hailed as the peer of the great composers of Europe.

MacDowell was born in New York City on December 18, 1861, of Scottish, Irish, and English ancestry. His Quaker father, who had wished to be a painter, had been forced into business by his unsympathetic family; his mother, though not artistic herself, understood the aspirations of her son and backed them to the limit. Though the boy was a dreamer who wrote stories and colored the pictures in his fairytale books and once placed a sword between his brother and himself in bed in emulation of the romances, he also participated in "normal" boyish sports and indulged "normal" combative instincts. His first contacts with nature were made in the new Central Park, where he caught his first fish (illegally), and at his grandfather's farm at Washingtonville, New York. His first music teachers, among whom the Brazilian pianist Teresa Carreño, who later featured his music in her recitals, was the most important, were all South Americans. So far from being a boy prodigy, he hated to practice, but from the time he was taken to Europe in the 1870s he seems to have made up his mind to be a concert pianist.

In Paris he won a scholarship at the Conservatory, where Debussy, who did not impress him either then or later, was a fellow pupil, but having heard Nicholas Rubinstein in 1878, he was convinced that he could only learn to "play like that" in Germany. By this time too he was beginning to " 'make up' pieces for fun." At the Frankfort Conservatory he encountered Carl Haymann and Joachim Raff, who influenced him greatly. When Haymann retired, he recommended MacDowell as his successor, but the authorities did not see fit to employ an American youngster. He began taking private pupils, however, including Marian Nevins, whom he was to marry in 1884, and soon became head piano teacher at Darmstadt. In 1882, at Raff's suggestion, he took his first piano concerto to Liszt at Weimar, who encouraged him generously, engineered his first publications, and brought about his professional debut as composer-pianist at Zurich.

In 1888 MacDowell and his wife returned to America and settled in Boston, where he made his first professional appearance on this side of the water with the Kneisel Quartet at Chickering Hall on November 19. On March 5, 1889, he played his Second Concerto under Theodore Thomas in New York; Henry Edward Krehbiel called it a finer work than Tchaikovsky's Fifth Symphony on the same program. He appeared with the Boston Symphony and in 1891 gave a solo recital in Boston. When in 1894 he played his Second Concerto with the Philharmonic in New York, Henry T. Finck said he had had "a success, both as pianist and composer, such as no American musician has ever won before a metropolitan concert audience." W. J. Henderson found difficulty in speaking of his music "in terms of judicial calmness, for it is made of the stuff that calls for enthusiasm," and James Huneker declared that "it easily ranks with any modern work in this form."

MacDowell's appearance suggested the composer of the Norse and Keltic sonatas rather than the poet of the wild rose and the water lily. He was a comparatively large man of muscular build. His eyes were a bright blue, his skin light, his hair dark. "He seemed an out-door man," writes John Erskine in *The Memory of Certain Persons*, "full of energy and health. When he strode across the campus in his tweed suit, with his cane hooked over his arm, even the least musical passer-by looked at him twice." The first thing he told one student in whom he had taken an interest was to wash his neck and cut his hair. Some of his portraits are those of a dreamer; in others he wears a fierce or grim expression. His voice was quiet, cultured, and well modulated, but we are told that he gestured when roused and made faces when he was displeased.

Small talk he had none, and his uneasiness with strangers made him seem gauche or blunt, especially since he was a very honest man of strong and frankly expressed convictions. Even on the concert stage, where he was wholly in control of the situation, he seemed ill at ease, and a Chicago critic described him as "a singularly unhinged and awkward-appearing person [who] sways upon his seat as if all the joints in his body had been freshly oiled." When he bowed his acknowledgments, he seemed to be threatening to fall apart in the process, and after a concert he would agonize over what he had not done to his own satisfaction and ignore the rest. Restive under praise, he never discussed his own music except to express dislike of some trifling or inferior piece that had become popular.

"He was an ardent sportsman," writes Lawrence Gilman, "and he spent much of his time in the woods and fields, fishing, riding, walking, hunting. He had a special relish for gardening and for photography, and he liked to undertake laborious jobs in carpentry, at which he was quite deft." He made walking trips in the mountains and contributed to the creation of a golf course at Peterborough, New Hampshire, but though he enjoyed baseball, he seldom attended games and had no interest in exercise for its own sake. It is not surprising that a man of his general intuitive makeup should have developed a gift for water dowsing, but it is a little startling to learn that he enjoyed prizefights; we also hear of his drinking beer and smoking cigars. The most surprising thing, however, is that one who invested wildlife with the almost supernatural meaning it held for MacDowell should also have enjoyed hunting. It has been said that he only "played" at it, and Gilman says that "though an excellent shot, he never brought down game without a pang." But why did he try?

If, as often appears, musical intelligence and culture seem to bear little relationship to other areas of human interest, this was emphatically not the case with the variously gifted, even erudite MacDowell. The volume of *Critical and Historical Essays*, based on his Columbia lectures and published after his death, displays not only musical scholarship but a wide variety of intelligent reference to other disciplines. He wrote many of the lyrics for his own songs, and his book of poems, many original, some adaptations from Heine, Goethe, and others, are, if not always technically expert, at least beautifully adapted to his own musical purposes. When, as a young student in Paris, he amused himself in class one day by drawing a satirical portrait of his teacher, the master, having confiscated it, was so much impressed that, instead of being angry, he showed it to Sargent's teacher, Carolus-Duran, who offered to take MacDowell under his wing for three years, with all expenses paid, if he would give up music for painting. Gilman calls MacDowell "an omnivorous reader of poetry, an inquisitive delver in the byways of mediaeval literature, an authority in mythological detail," and Aristophanes, Herodotus, Sophocles, Livy, Virgil, Plutarch, *The Song of Roland*, Malory, Vasari, Byron, Lamartine, Schiller, Gibbon, Guizot, Erckmann-Chatrian, Emerson, and Carlyle have all been mentioned among his reading interests. Richard Jeffries, Tolstoi, Kipling, Mark Twain, Fiona Macleod, Yeats, and Maeterlinck all interested him. He loved Howells and drew upon his verses for his songs. According to Upton Sinclair, he disliked Balzac, and in his *Essays* he speaks of Horace Walpole's work (and presumably, by extension, of the "Gothicks" in general) as the product of "an unhealthy and diseased mind." He is also reputed to have read widely in history, science, and politics. About his religion I know only what may be inferred from his *Essays,* where we read that before Christianity "the soul of mankind had its roots in fear," that the religion of Israel "fostered idealism, and gave mankind something pure and noble to live for, a religion over which Christianity shed the sunshine of divine mercy and hope," and that with Christ "a God had come to live with men."

Perhaps the words that recur most often in the attempts made to describe the character of MacDowell's music are *noble* and *nobility.* He composed to express his own impression or vision of life, and this was clearly idealistic and inspirational. Except that he was sure the artist must be free, he did not think there was any "right" or "wrong" way to compose music, but he was always sure that it was not enough to please the ear: "If I really thought music a mere mixture of sound, or even a vibratory means of affecting the body, I would never dream of wasting the poor rest of my life at it." No composer ever celebrated the beauty of the earth more rapturously than he did, yet he saw it as

> the nature of the spiritual part of mankind to shrink from the earth, to aspire to something higher; a bird soaring in the blue above us has something of the ethereal; we give wings to our angels. On the other hand, a serpent impresses us as something sinister. Trees, with their strange fight against all the laws of gravity, striving upward unceasingly, bring us something of hope and faith; the sight of them cheers us.

MacDowell has no touch of the twisted, obscure, frenetic quality characteristic of so much modern music and art, yet his work does not lack force; neither is it cold.

At rare moments, MacDowell experienced touches of inspiration that seemed to him supernatural, but this was not something he could either speak of or depend on. He tended to think of different keys in terms of different colors, and his ideas often came to him while he was improvising; to keep his hand in, he always tried to write down at least a few bars every day. When a composition absorbed him, he could keep at it almost day and night, and he was always an incurable reviser. He believed in the form that is coherence, but though he continued to compose sonatas after many thought they were played out, he is said to have played his own as if they were tone poems. He inclines toward program music, as when he places verses before a composition to indicate its subject or mood, but his students often failed to guess the subjects of his pieces when he played for them. In songs he believed that the accompaniment should serve as a background for the words. "A song, if at all dramatic, should have climax, form, and plot, as does a play."

In his *Essays* he slashes about in fine style. Though Sinclair says he thought the Hymn to Joy in Beethoven's Ninth Symphony commonplace, he saw that composer as having expressed an ideal far beyond any of his predecessors; it was only with him "that the art of musical design showed anything like complete comprehension by the composer." Bach he loved, but believed that "owing to the contrapuntal tendency of the time, his feeling for *melodic* design is often overshadowed, and even rendered impossible by the complex web of his music." Except in the fugue, the material at his disposal "precluded spontaneity and confined spiritual design to very restricted limits." All in all, he accomplished his mission not by means of these conventions but in spite of them, and those who played him like mathematics, finding "a grim pleasure in it, like biting on a sore tooth," did him no service. Handel, on the other hand, MacDowell admired little, nor did he care much for Brahms. "Handel killed English music; no development after him; his scores are empty; his work is filled with quotations; he stole music from everyone." Mozart at his best was very great, but his sonatas are written "in a style of flashy harpsichord virtuosity such as Liszt never descended to, even in those of his works at which so many persons are accustomed to sneer." He recognized Wagner's greatness, but he speaks of his "materialism" and was wearied by his lack of terminal facilities. Wagner achieved "the most perfect union of painting, poetry, and music imaginable to our nineteenth-century minds," but listening to one of his operas is like watching a circus with three rings.

MacDowell admired Grieg and Rimsky-Korsakov and Tchaikovsky too, though he says his music sounded better than it really was. He is condescending toward Richard Strauss; though he grants that *Thus Spake Zarathustra* "stuns by its glorious magnificence of tone color," he adds, "I remember once hearing in London, sung in the street at night, a song that seemed to me to contain a truer germ of music," and indeed what he called "the strange twistings of ultra modern music" in general tended to repel him.

It is said that toward the end of his life MacDowell considered an Arthurian opera, suggested in part by Abbey's Holy Grail pictures in the Boston Public Library, but opera in general seems to have meant little to him, and his comments on it are not very satisfying. He thought it governed by passing fashions beyond all other musical forms. Of the eighteenth-century opera he seems to have discerned continuing vitality only in *The Magic Flute* and "less probably" in *Don Giovanni*, and he sweeps away most of the early nineteenth century too—Spontini, Rossini, most of Meyerbeer, though he granted some merit to Halévy and to *William Tell*. French opera in general he dismisses as never having "developed beyond Massenet's *Roi de Lahore* and Delibes' *Lakmé*." One does not gather that the Italians meant any more to him, and indeed all the influences and affinities of his music were with northern rather than southern Europe.

There has been much tiresome discussion about whether or not MacDowell was a really "American" composer, and in the light of his own aims and beliefs, much of it is irrelevant. His training was German; the Germanic influence, especially in his early work, is admittedly large, and the best of his songs are about all we have to set beside the *Lieder* and *mélodies* of the Old World. He himself believed that there was also a certain Celtic coloring in his work, inherited from his ancestry. He wanted a music to express "the youthful optimistic vitality and the undaunted tenacity of spirit that characterizes the American man," and he sought out Hamlin Garland after having read his literary manifesto in *Crumbling Idols*. Yet one can hardly believe that he listened with much patience to Huneker's comment on his Indian Suite—"At last we are treated to genuine American music, with roots plunged into aboriginal sources"—for he did not identify Americanism with primitivism. Indeed, he says that "so-called Russian, Bohemian, or any other national music has no place in art, for its characteristics may be duplicated by anyone who takes a fancy to do so. On the other hand the vital element in music—personality—stands alone." When the American nation, through being itself, produces musical genius, then we shall have great American music.

MacDowell had been a teacher from the beginning of his musical career. He never forced his own methods on his pupils ("you might find a better way than mine"), and he never turned away anybody he believed in because he could not pay. At Columbia he was called upon both to deliver lectures and to organize a department. Upton Sinclair found him groping for words and thought his teaching not good by academic standards; to John Erskine, on the other hand, MacDowell's was the first classroom that justified his "dreams of what a college or university could be." He worked himself beyond the bounds of his strength, but his methods were his own; even Erskine admits that he was better at demonstration than discussion and that "his teaching was most effective with students who were already well grounded." All went well enough until Seth Low was succeeded as president by Nicholas Murray Butler. Unhappy under the new regime, MacDowell made up his mind to resign, and if he had been allowed to do this quietly, there would have been no controversy. Unfortunately Butler saw fit to issue a statement that, as MacDowell saw it, misrepresented both his position and the situation. Never averse to a challenge, he virtually gave the president the lie and published a copy of the report he was making to the trustees, for which he was publicly rebuked.

His students gave him a loving cup, begged him to reconsider his resignation, and asked to be taken on as private pupils. But he would not be in a condition in which he could teach anybody for long. He worried himself into a state of nervous exhaustion and insomnia, and being knocked down by a cab did not help. Though Finck says he had feared insanity for years, MacDowell was never insane; neither was he in pain; but for the last two years of his life, his was pretty much a vegetable existence. Since the basic cause of his death, in New York on January 23, 1908, was a brain tumor, it is not correct to say that the Columbia controversy killed him, but it certainly did not lend comfort to his last years.

MacDowell may have been overestimated by his contemporaries; if so, posterity has certainly made up for it by underestimating and neglecting him. He was neither Bach nor Beethoven; neither was Mark Twain Shakespeare nor Whitman Dante; but those who think of him as only the exquisite miniaturist of the *Woodland Sketches* are obviously imperfectly acquainted with his work. His end was pathetic but not tragic, for it revealed no flaw in him, and no other American musician will ever have such a monument as Mrs. MacDowell built to him in the MacDowell Colony at Peterborough, New Hampshire, where so many creative Americans have found inspiration and support.

5. David Belasco, Playwright and Producer

Those unfortunate people who love the drama but hate the theater have always been obliged to take a dim view of David Belasco. He was theater incarnate. He lived and worked in his private museum above the Belasco Theater, and those he chose to admit there were ushered into his presence with as much ceremony as if they were visiting an emperor or a pope. Even the semiclerical attire he always wore until his last years was a costume, and it was part of the legend he developed around himself that this derived from his having lived in his youth at a monastery in Victoria, British Columbia, under the tutelage of an aged, learned, and benevolent priest. But though William Winter swallowed this story, Craig Timberlake has now shown that there was no monastery in Victoria at the time, and neither is there any record there of a Father McGuire.

He was a sensationalist and a sentimentalist, and he made scenes, sometimes no doubt to relieve his own feelings but more often to impress others. Mary Pickford tells how, during a rehearsal of *The Warrens of Virginia,* he smashed a jar of maple syrup on the stage and tramped it into the rug because the script had called for molasses, after which he came to her fourteen-year-old self, where she sat awed in a box, to tell her that he found it necessary to smash something at least once before opening night in order to keep the cast on their toes and to ask her what she had thought of his performance. George Arliss too has recorded that when a problem arose during a rehearsal, Belasco might stop and "walk up and down the stage for as long as half an hour in absolute silence," and we have another account of how he once stopped to receive a "message" from the late Charles Frohman. Obviously one as much needs toleration for the vagaries of the "artistic temperament" to relish Belasco's personality in all its aspects as one must love theatrical effects completely to accept his plays. But it does seem clear that he often failed to differentiate clearly between art and life and became a part of his own audience.

He was born in San Francisco, to which his Portuguese-Jewish parents (the name was originally Valasco) had come from England, on July 25, 1853. About 1858 the family removed to Victoria, where the father kept a store and engaged in real estate and mining operations without much success in any capacity, but in 1865 they were back in California.

Stagestruck from his poverty-stricken boyhood, Belasco worked at any odd job that could put a few dollars into the family exchequer, never neglecting a chance to "spout" recitations in halls, churches, and homes. His theatrical experience took him up and down the coast to lumber camps, mining camps, and elsewhere but also brought him in contact with such personalities as Edwin Booth, John McCullough, Adelaide Neilson, and Dion Boucicault. For a time he was connected with Piper's Opera House in Virginia City, Nevada, but his most important association was with the manager Tom Maguire at Baldwin's Academy of Music in San Francisco. William Winter's partial list of the roles he played on the coast occupies seven pages, and it ranges from supers up through Uncle Tom, Claude Melnotte, Fagin, and Armand Duval to Mercutio,

Antony, and Hamlet, to say nothing of Juliet's Nurse and Hamlet's mother; he also wrote or adapted scores of plays.

His first collaborator as a dramatist was James A. Herne, with whom he produced *The Marriage by Moonlight* for Rose Coghlan at the Baldwin. *Chums,* which they wrote for James O'Neill and Lewis Morrison, became *Hearts of Oak* when it reached Chicago in 1879, but its New York engagement was a disaster that left Belasco stranded to sleep in Union Square Park and then "bum" his way back to Frisco. He first gained a foothold in New York at the Madison Square Theater, where he was stage manager from 1882 to 1885 and where *May Blossom* in 1884 was his own first really successful play. After two years of free-lancing, he went to work for Daniel Frohman as stage manager, adviser, general assistant, and acting coach at the Lyceum Theater, all for thirty-five dollars a week. Here he began collaborating with Henry C. De Mille, father of Cecil and William, with whom he wrote *The Wife* and *Lord Chumley,* which latter was an important vehicle for young E. H. Sothern in his first phase as a light comedian.

In 1889 Caroline Louise Dudley was divorced from the prominent Chicago businessman Leslie Carter after a sensational battle in the court and the newspapers. He accused her of adultery with five men, including the actor Kyrle Bellew; she countered with charges so sensational that the newspapers could not print them. After he had won the case and the custody of their son, Mrs. Carter, now a social outcast, came to Belasco and begged him to train her for the stage. Though he had to teach her literally everything, he saw enough potentiality in her to be willing to stake his hopes of independent production upon her. Feeling against her was so strong that at first he found it difficult even to command a stage upon which she could rehearse, but he persevered, trying her out in *The Ugly Duckling* and *Miss Helyett* in 1891; she must be very nearly the only American woman who ever founded a successful career upon a scandal. After he had taken time out to write *The Girl I Left behind Me* with Franklin Fyles for the opening of the Empire Theater in 1893, he at last succeeded in getting *The Heart of Maryland* produced at the Herald Square in 1895, and with it success was won.

In 1899 he presented Mrs. Carter, to the accompaniment of much moral hysteria in the press, in his own somewhat laundered adaptation of a French play, *Zaza,* about a courtesan who redeems herself, from which they went on in 1901 to *Du Barry* and in 1905 to her last Belasco production, *Adrea,* in which she conquered even her most determined critical enemy, Winter. Mrs. Carter belonged to the furniture-breaking school of acting, and her plays were devised to give her a chance to work up to hysterical climaxes in which she could bring down the house. She was not my kind of actress, but I must admit that I saw her only during her later years and that even then she was capable of poignant moments.

By this time Belasco had acquired two other important stars—Blanche Bates and David Warfield—and he also had a theater of his own. Miss Bates began in a minor piece, *Naughty Anthony,* but her great successes were in *Madame Butterfly* (1900), *The Darling of the Gods* (1902), and *The Girl of the Golden West* (1905). Both *Butterfly* and *The Girl* were turned into operas by Puccini, and Belasco was involved in the Metropolitan productions. David Warfield, his greatest heart-interest star, came to him from the Weber and Fields music hall, making the transition easily in a Jewish dialect comedy-drama, *The Auctioneer* (1901). From here he proceeded to his greatest success as Herr Anton von Barwig in *The Music Master* (1904) and on through *A Grand Army Man* (1910) and *The Return of Peter Grimm* (1911) to what he had looked forward to as the crown of his career, his Shylock in 1922. The Republic Theater, which he rebuilt and named the Belasco, the producer leased from Oscar Hammerstein in 1902; in 1907 he built the present Belasco Theater, which until 1910 was called the Stuyvesant. For years, however, he was in great trouble on "the road," where Klaw and Erlanger would book his attractions only on extortionate terms. He paid them 50 percent on *The Auctioneer* but then decided to fight, and *Adrea* was acted in Washington at Convention Hall before a distinguished first-night audience that was obliged to hold up umbrellas for protection from the leaking roof. In 1904 Belasco allied himself with the rising power of the Shuberts, and in 1909 the Klaw and Erlanger syndicate came to terms.

In 1907 Belasco presented Frances Starr, who had had a small part in *The Music Master,* in *The Rose of the Rancho,* which was followed two years later by *The Easiest Way;* this fine and charming actress would remain with him to the end of his career, appearing in more plays than any other star. The most important star of his last years was Lenore Ulric. The cultural background of this Minnesota-born actress (originally Ulrich) was wholly German Catholic

(German was the only language she spoke as a small child), but the Spanish strain in her ancestry predominated in her dark beauty, and Belasco made her Indian in *The Heart of Wetona* (1916), French-Canadian in *Tiger Rose* (1917), Chinese in *The Son Daughter* (1919), French in *Kiki* (1921), and Negro in *Lulu Belle* (1926). She had the lead too in his last elaborate and certainly his strangest production, *Mima* (1928), an adaptation of Molnar's *The Red Mill*, in which the actors were nearly crowded off the stage by a huge property machine called a "psycho-corrupter," designed to destroy a human soul in an hour, and even sophisticated critics were embarrassed by devils leaping between the auditorium and the stage. Ina Claire and Jane Cowl also appeared less importantly for the master during his later years, but Jeanne Eagels and Katharine Cornell found that they had nothing in common with him.

Many of Belasco's later productions seemed less characteristic than what the public had come to expect of him, though *Deburau* (1920), adapted by Granville-Barker from Sacha Guitry, was hailed as one of his very finest achievements. In 1915 he and Charles Frohman marked their reconciliation after estrangement caused by syndicate battles by coproducing a revival of *A Celebrated Case*, just before Frohman's death. In 1919 he opposed the actors' strike, and Warfield and Miss Ulric stood by him in organizing the Actors' Fidelity League, which vainly opposed what became Actors' Equity. In November 1930, while rehearsing his last production, *Tonight or Never*, in Baltimore, Belasco collapsed with pneumonia. He astonished everybody by weathering the crisis, and on March 18, 1931, he was even well enough to take a curtain call with Helen Gahagan at the Belasco Theater, but on May 12 he suffered a heart attack and died two days later.

William Winter's list of Belasco's plays covers five pages of fine print, and Lise-Lone Marker gives him 123 productions on Broadway alone, including 34 of his own plays and adaptations. She adds that in the course of his career he had had a hand in the authorship of nearly 200 plays. The same tastes and themes appear in what he took from others as in what he wrote himself, which is not surprising, considering how often he revamped them. There are western Americana in *The Girl I Left Behind Me*, *The Rose of the Rancho*, and *The Girl of the Golden West*; history, exoticism, and extravaganza in *Du Barry*, *The Darling of the Gods*, and *A Good Little Devil*; domestic drama in *The Auctioneer*, *The Music Master*, and *The Return of Peter Grimm*; social realism and the demimonde in *Zaza, The Easiest Way*, and *Lulu Belle*.

It seems reasonable to suppose that the *Six Plays* he chose to include in the volume Little, Brown published in 1928 were the ones Belasco valued most highly; these are *Butterfly, Du Barry, Darling, Adrea, The Girl of the Golden West*, and *Peter Grimm*. It is a mistake to go to any Belasco play for literary quality. "A play text," says Miss Marker, "was to him primarily a starting point for directorial elaboration," and Montrose J. Moses adds that "one went to a Belasco play as one went to a crystal-gazing shop —anaesthesia already on one at the mere suggestion of going!" There was no disparagement in this, for both writers were admirers, and Belasco would not have resented their judgment. "The standards by which true literature is judged" he said, "cannot properly be applied in judging drama." And again, "My plays are written to be acted, not to be read." He was a "practical" playwright, no more concerned with "originality" than Shakespeare was, and he helped himself freely to every device that dramatic history and tradition had contrived.

What really interested him were stagecraft and acting. He preferred young, untrained actors, if possible from the humbler strata of life, whom he could mold to suit himself; hence, he ransacked "the varieties and the cheap stock companies," and night after night he would "go down on the stage of the Belasco Theater after the performance is over, and listen to recitations and readings by people who think the planets in the heavens ordained that they should act." Nothing was too insignificant to work on, and nothing was too much trouble. Lillian Gish has related how he drilled her as a child for two weeks on the word *apple* until he was sure she would say it so that the last person in the gallery would understand it. His methods were infinitely varied and adaptable. "I coax and cajole, or bulldoze and torment, according to the temperament with which I have to deal." But though his was a director's theater in the sense that he aimed at a unified effect, he was very careful not to upset the players' equilibrium or hurt their pride. He did not standardize pronunciation, and he cherished and fostered such mannerisms as were not mere awkwardness but "indexes of personality." "While the performance is in progress I never reprove." To him the director was the "unseen interpreter" who guided the players and created the atmosphere for the play, but he was never the intruder or personality crusher that Belasco often thought he saw in the productions of others that he witnessed during his last years.

Everything had to be real in a Belasco production that could possibly be shown in that way; so he built a Child's lunchroom on the stage for *The Governor's Lady* and bought the contents of a room in a cheap theatrical lodging house for *The Easiest Way*. Properties for *Du Barry* were imported from France and those for *The Darling of the Gods* from Japan. He visited hospitals, prisons, and lunatic asylums, attended a bank director's meeting, and toured opium joints under the direction of a Bowery denizen. It is said that the audience at *The First Born* could even *smell* San Francisco's Chinatown.

In all this lighting was an immensely important factor, and Belasco's lighting effects long anticipated the experiments of those who, in later years, imagined they had outgrown him; thus, he tried eliminating footlights and lighted from the balcony rail as early as 1879, when Salmi Morse's controversial *Passion Play*, with James O'Neill, was acted in San Francisco. If he was ever arrogant, it was about lighting: "It may be possible for others to copy my colors, but no one can get my feeling for them." He has described how he achieved the combination of light and color he needed to create the effect of midsummer heat in southern California in *The Rose of the Rancho* and the tedious process of experimentation he went through while trying to create the River of Souls effect at the close of *The Darling of the Gods*. This he finally discovered by accident, just as he was about to scrap the scene; yet after all, it harked back to what had been done in the illusionist "Egyptian Mystery" in San Francisco days. In *Madame Butterfly* he relied wholly upon lighting to hold the attention of the audience without words or movement through the fourteen minutes that indicated the passing of the night while Cho-Cho-San waits for Pinkerton, and in *The Return of Peter Grimm*, where David Warfield was a ghost after the first act, he was differentiated from the "living" characters solely by being lighted differently.

Though Belasco did make a limited use of framing drapes and other "in" devices in his 1922 production of *The Merchant of Venice*, he remained hostile to the end to the notion "that a few violent splotches of green upon a drapery can better express to an audience the idea of a forest than the actual reproduction in painting and in light effects of that forest," but he was also determined never to reveal on the stage what can be better *suggested*, and during his later years at least, he was sure that "the time of the overdecorated stage" was as far gone by as "the day of the cluttered and overcrowded drawing-room" and that "action" on the stage should be more mental than physical. For that matter, he had always known that scenery and accessories became an "inartistic blunder" just as soon as they were allowed to distract the attention of the audience from the play itself, and if this was not always recognized by Americans, Stanislavski's Moscow Art Theater did recognize it, for after they had visited America in 1923 Belasco, alone among American producers, was made an honorary member. Though he produced far fewer significant plays than his most celebrated Continental contemporaries, he was their peer in everything relating to stagecraft. In his works, says Lise-Lone Marker justly, "all the individual elements of a production, from text to setting, lighting, and acting," operated "as completely integrated parts subordinated to the larger realistic whole." He achieved a "harmoniously balanced ensemble" and manifested "a unique talent for the creation . . . of a pervasive mood." He also worked in harmony with Zola's conception of environment as "a conditioning element" in human life and never relied on "mere literalism or facsimile realism"; instead, his methods "were distinguished by the exercise of selectivity and suggestion."

One who knew Belasco well called him shrewd and naïve, extravagant and stingy, kind and cruel, intuitive and insensitive, humble and haughty, trusting and suspicious. If we may judge by his many photographs, his countenance gained in grace, dignity, and refinement as he grew older, and Mary Pickford speaks of "the sharpest, loveliest eyes I have ever seen on man or woman." According to Winter, his face was masklike, extraordinarily mobile and expressive, or "positively Mephistophelian," according to its owner's mood and whim. Cecil B. De Mille, as a child, found that "he had the spirit of fun that children love, and with it the rarer gift of taking children seriously, treating them as persons," and loved him so much that he forgave him even when he promised him a pony on his twelfth birthday and then forgot all about it. His relations with the children in his casts were always cordial, and his discussion of the problems involved in using children on the stage is both intelligent and humane. He was fond of showering extravagant praise upon those he cared for, and there are enough examples of his thoughtfulness and kindness so that it is not surprising to learn that his actors generally loved him as much as the smaller children did. He professed faith in God and in immortality and told how the spirit of his mother came to him in New York at the moment, as he later learned, of her death in San Francisco.

On one score at least, his withers were unwrung: he did not, as Charles Frohman said of himself, keep a department store. Unlike most of his competitors, he wrought not for money but for love of the dramatic art. This was not because he was indifferent to money, but when gain got in the way of a desired effect, it was always gain that tasted defeat. *Du Barry* cost nearly $100,000 to produce and had 147 people in the cast, and *The Darling of the Gods* was so expensive to produce that, though it played to excellent business, it earned him only $5,000 in two years.

It was often said and widely believed that in Belasco's theater the way to the stage door led through the bedroom, and it is hard to tell just how much stock to take in this. In view of the way he broke with Mrs. Carter when she married William Louis Payne, it is hard to believe that their association had been purely professional. Though he did do her some kindnesses in later years, through an intermediary, not even her pitiful, hysterical letters could persuade him ever to see or speak to her again, to say nothing of doing another play with her. On the other hand, there can be no question that he respected, and himself held the respect of, women with whom no question of an amorous connection can be raised.

I am amazed to find him speaking of the heroine of *The Easiest Way* as a "thoroughly unsympathetic" character. Since he was to say of even *Ladies of the Evening* that he had produced it to make his audiences aware of the good in "those poor little painted dolls" with which it deals, this seems quite out of character, and it was bad criticism too, for Laura Murdock, though weak, is not vicious, and it was a pity that the reformed prig of a rake who was her lover ever found out that she had lied to him, for she would have made him a good wife and saved herself in the process; indeed, she might even have saved him, who, as it was, only destroyed her. Belasco is naïve when he proclaims that he understands all women and that there is a good deal of the woman in him, but there can be no doubt as to his interest in women and his deep sympathy with them. David Warfield was his only male star, and he once said that he had met bad men but never a bad woman.

"People go to the play," he said, "to have their emotions stirred." Stirred, not harrowed. James Huneker was right when he explained that Belasco disliked Strindberg because he himself needed "the consoling veils of illusion to cover the nakedness of the human soul." His temperament goes far to explain his estrangement from many of the main currents of dramatic writing in his time. He admired Ibsen's technique but not his tone, and to him Shaw's plays were merely flippant and cynical. If, as Meredith says, the sense of women is all mixed up with their senses, Belasco's idealism was all mixed up with his showmanship. But in his own theatrical way he was an idealist for all of that.

I am no longer a political accident." Thus Theodore Roosevelt to his wife upon his election in 1904 with the greatest popular and electoral majority that had ever been achieved. "I had no conception," he said "that there was such a tide in our favor." Though he was always inclined to expect the worst from an election and never quite convinced that his popularity would last, he had this time some reason for uneasiness, for he was the first vice-president to succeed to the presidency by death whom his party either nominated or elected the next time around.

The achievements of Roosevelt's second administration included the railroad bill, the pure food legislation, and fresh victories in the battle for conservation, as well as his services in ending the Russo-Japanese War by negotiation and helping the European powers to weather the Moroccan crisis (he was awarded the Nobel Prize for Peace), and in piloting his own country through a potentially explosive crisis in its relations with Japan. There were also enlivening controversies over Brownsville, the "muckrakers," simplified spelling, the "nature fakers," and the behavior of Ambassador Storer and his wife.

The Hepburn bill relating to the regulation of shipping rates by the railroads, signed into law on June 29, 1906, represented another important stage in establishing the right of the federal government to interfere with the previously almost unchallenged

TR in His Own Right

15

right of big business to manage its affairs on Cornelius Vanderbilt's "public be damned" principle. As common carriers, the railroads were more vulnerable than many businesses because they had been granted the right of eminent domain and other privileges on the assumption that they were performing a public service.

The pioneering agitators for railroad regulation, which involved an attack upon rebates to large shippers, the lavish use of passes to win public and legislative favor, and other evils, were the Grangers in the farm states, and the first victories were won there, but state legislatures had no power to regulate traffic except intrastate. The Interstate Commerce Commission had been created in 1897, but court decisions had emasculated it sadly. TR attacked rebates as early as 1901, and in 1903 the Elkins Act was passed. This was found inadequate within a year, but the president waited until after the 1904 election to press the fight.

In his message of December 1904 he called not only for railroad regulation but for an employers' liability law, tariff relief for the Philippines, and a child labor law in the District of Columbia, but none of these suggestions had been activated by Inauguration Day. The fight for tariff reform TR never pressed, though, realizing that the tariff was the number one GOP sacred cow, he threatened to raise the issue from time to time in order to pressure Congress into giving him something he wanted more. Roosevelt's understanding of economics was rudimentary and his interest in it virtually nonexistent. This was true even on the domestic front; Mrs. Roosevelt ran all the financial affairs of the household and actually put into her husband's pocket such money as she thought he would need. Inevitably, therefore, his interest in those toward the bottom of the social pyramid proceeded from his warm human sympathy rather than from any real understanding of their economic problems. This factor even played an important role in his "abdication" in 1908. "New issues are coming up," he told Ray Stannard Baker. "I see them. People are going to discuss economic questions more and more: the tariff, currency, banks. They are hard questions, and I am not deeply interested in them; my problems are moral problems, and my teaching has been plain morality."

To achieve "just and reasonable rates" for all shippers, Roosevelt opposed special favors, including passes (which three roads discontinued on January 1, 1906, and which federal statute banned the following June), and advocated government inspection of railroad

Theodore Roosevelt

books. In contrast to Bryan and many farmers and small business-men, who were moving toward a demand for government owner-ship and operation, what TR asked for in the fight won in 1906 was power for the ICC to fix maximum rates that could be set aside, in any given case, only by court decision after formal com-plaint through legal channels. Though hysterical newspapers ac-cused the president of trying to wreck his party, destroy both personal property and states' rights, and "subvert the American tradition" and though his own great friend, Senator Henry Cabot Lodge, doubted the wisdom of any attempt at rate regulation, the Old Guard leadership, headed by Nelson Aldrich in the Senate and "Uncle Joe" Cannon in the House, knew that they could no more block all railroad legislation than King Canute could roll back the tide; their strategy therefore became that of attempting to maneuver through a bill that would provide the courts with such wide areas of review that the law would have no teeth. Wisconsin's La Follette and other progressives, on the other hand, thought that the president was not going nearly far enough. They wanted the ICC invested with the power to determine the value of the railroad property before fix-ing rates; TR rejected this suggestion because "I want to get some-thing through" this session. Breaking with tradition, the freshman senator took the floor with a two-day speech, but though he con-verted the floor leader, Jonathan P. Dolliver, only four Republicans supported his measure, and it was defeated. By 1907, however, TR would come round to La Follette's point of view.

To embarrass Roosevelt and save the faces of the Old Guard, Aldrich and Senator John C. Spooner, who were steering the Hep-burn bill through the Senate without really believing in it, man-aged to transfer floor management from themselves to "Pitchfork Ben" Tillman of South Carolina, a back-country Democrat with whom the president had clashed and with whom he was not on speaking terms! Tillman, whose allegiance was not to the railroads but to small southern farmers, strove to limit the area in which court review of ICC decisions would be permitted and even to outlaw temporary injunctions. Somewhat childishly dealing with Tillman only through an intermediary, TR agreed to go along with this, provided Tillman could secure a majority, but when it became clear that the South Carolinian was going to be four votes short, the president abandoned his uneasy allies and abruptly accepted the

Republican-sponsored Allison Amendment. The Senate passed the Hepburn bill on May 18, 1908.

Roosevelt's inheritance was all on the conservative side; he became a moderate reformer who moved steadily leftward as he grew older. He found the American government committed to the protection of the interests; he aimed to move it to an intermediate position, checking the excesses of both the right and the left and thus avoiding both "government by plutocracy and by a mob." Though he opened the doors of the White House, for the first time, to union officials as well as employers, he never accepted the "closed shop," and he always retained a certain distrust of professional agitators. He was adamant on the proposition that private profit was not the ultimate value and that it could not form the basic criterion for government policy, but he was also sure that real amelioration of the human lot must depend upon the improvement of human character. He admitted that his natural tendency to preach was accentuated by the White House having given him such a "bully pulpit," but while there is no denying that his devotion to righteousness sometimes shades off into self-righteousness, it is hard to disagree with him when he says that "the most perfect laws that could be devised would not amount to anything if the average man was not a pretty decent fellow." The only serious question is whether he really is, and upon the answer to that the future of democracy and perhaps of civilization itself must depend.

Roosevelt himself claimed that the Hepburn bill gave him all he had originally asked for, which was true, and justified his desertion of the Tillman forces on the ground that he had come to see that review questions were, after all, academic, since, in the last analysis, the courts must inevitably have the final say about all laws. This also was true, and, as a matter of fact, the Hepburn Act, which did open up the companies' books and which the courts showed no general tendency to undercut, worked pretty well and paved the way for other regulatory legislation. That Tillman really deserved the place he was awarded in TR's famous Ananias Club, after he had made his grievances public in a Senate speech, is doubtful, however. In the long run, Tillman was more generous to Roosevelt than Roosevelt ever was to him; without the president's efforts, he said, "we would not have had any bill at all." And La Follette too, who did not love TR, later credited him with having "made reform legislation respectable in the United States."

"An act for preventing the manufacture, sale or transportation [in foreign or interstate commerce] of adulterated or misbranded or poisonous or deleterious foods, drugs, medicines and liquors and for regulating traffic therein" became law on June 3, 1906. Here Roosevelt was something of a Johnny-come-lately in a battle that Dr. Harvey W. Wiley, chief chemist of the Department of Agriculture, and others had been waging for years. TR recommended action in his annual message of December 1905, but he did not push it until March 1906, after he had read Upton Sinclair's novel, *The Jungle*, with its sensational exposé of the unbelievable filth that not only existed in the Chicago Stock Yards but was actually incorporated into processed foods. By this time Samuel Hopkins Adams had attacked patent medicines in *Collier's*, the American Medical Association had enlisted in behalf of reform, and pure food legislation had passed the Senate but was stalled in the House.

Roosevelt's most effective weapon was the independent report on the packing industry that he had authorized Commissioner of Labor Charles P. Neill and a New York social worker, James B. Reynolds, to make. When the House continued to drag its feet, he sent in the first part of this damning, disgusting report and threatened to make the whole of it public if action were not forthcoming. But by this time, the industry itself, frightened by the drop in sales that followed the publication of *The Jungle*, had relaxed its opposition to any form of inspection. Compromising on minor points, Roosevelt achieved his primary objectives, including limited court review, and Representative James Wadsworth of New York, who had held up the legislation as chairman of the Committee on Agriculture, was driven from public life. It was ironical that the most disappointed man should have been Upton Sinclair, who had contributed so importantly to the victory yet so signally failed to convert his readers to socialism. He had aimed at the public conscience, said Sinclair, but he had only hit its stomach. It is hard to see, however, why saving people from being poisoned is not as worthy an aim as changing their system of government.

In at least one area of his activity, there can be no difference of opinion concerning the rightness and value of Theodore Roosevelt's policies except among those who wish so to conduct themselves that we shall become the last generation that is able to live upon this continent. Though intelligent men as different as Henry David Thoreau and James Fenimore Cooper had recognized the need for

conservation long before TR was born, if we ask what the government had accomplished in this direction before the beginning of
his administration, it would hardly be an exaggeration to answer,
"Nothing." Theoretically, to be sure, more than 23 million acres
of our territory were in government hands, but actually private
exploitation of our resources was being carried on even here, and
the law under which this was permitted was not repealed until
1906. Before Roosevelt left office, on the other hand, he had increased the acreage of our national forests to 194 million, created
five national parks (which was as many as all his predecessors together), set up sixteen national monuments, and established fifty-
one wildlife refuges, besides contributing importantly toward saving
the Grand Canyon, Niagara Falls, and other scenic wonders from
the spoilers.

Not all these achievements belonged to TR's second administration. He had sought the advice of Gifford Pinchot almost immediately after moving into the White House, and as early as November
1901 he recommended "selective cutting" in the reserves and the
creation of strategic dams, financed by the national government
when necessary, in arid regions. The next month he urged the
creation of a forest reserve in the Appalachians and supported
the Democrat-sponsored Newlands irrigation and reclamation bill
against strong Republican opposition. This became law in June
1902, the most important conservation measure adopted up to this
time, under which thirty irrigation projects, including the Roosevelt Dam, were set up. In 1903 too he saved Muscle Shoals from
falling into the hands of private developers.

During the second administration, the Forest Service was transferred from the Department of the Interior to Agriculture, and Chief
Forester Pinchot's powers were enlarged. By this time too conservation had become not only something much larger than the "scenery" for which Speaker Cannon had vowed not to spend "one cent"
of public money but even something larger than saving the forests
alone. Grazing lands; areas containing deposits of coal, minerals,
and oil; and waterpower were all now embraced in the concept.
From 1906 on the policy of fifty-year controlled leases to power
companies obtained (the electric power lobby was one of the special objects of TR's wrath during his last months in office). During
the two years beginning in June 1906, more than 50 million acres

of land suspected of containing mineral deposits were withdrawn for classification; later, 18 million more were added in Alaska.

All this meant bucking Congress every inch of the way and a great part of the West as well. If the Southwest welcomed irrigation, ranchers, mine operators, lumbermen, and power companies all wished to continue their hitherto triumphant policies of unregulated competition; this feeling was especially strong in the Pacific Northwest, where, though selective cutting won some support, many of the smaller operators thought the new regulations gave their big competitors an unfair advantage. One of Roosevelt's cleverest acts, performed with great glee, came in March 1907, when Senator Fulton of Oregon succeeded in attaching an amendment to the agricultural appropriations bill specifying that no new forest reserves should be created in Washington, Oregon, Idaho, Montana, Colorado, or Wyoming. Since the Department of Agriculture could not continue to function without funds, it was believed that Roosevelt must sign the bill. So he did, but four days before his grace period expired and the new law took effect, he used the power of executive decree to set aside 16 million more acres in the six states involved. That same month he appointed an Inland Waterways Commission, whose findings he presented before a conference of governors in May 1908, upon whom he urged the formulation of a "coherent plan" for the development, utilization, and conservation of our national resources. The resolution adopted affirmed both the interdependence of the states and the necessity for cooperation between them in the conservation cause, and forty-one states formed conservation commissions shortly thereafter. In conducting these negotiations, Roosevelt was a model of tact and charm, and his determined enemies on the ultraconservative New York *Sun* struck one of the few sour notes in the nearly universal chorus of praise that greeted him.

By any standard, the Russo-Japanese adventure was one of TR's great achievements, but it needs to be considered in connection with his foreign policy in general and his relationship to the growing importance of the United States as a world power.

Roosevelt was an imperialist and expansionist during his early public life; during his presidency, however, though he might occasionally speak rashly, he nearly always acted prudently. Except toward the end of his life, when he tended rather to lose his head in his indignation over Germany's conduct in World War I, his general movement was away from his early romantic attitude toward war; hence, if pacifists cannot give him a 100 percent rating, neither can they fail to credit him with important services. For all that, he never completely sloughed off his early imperialism, nor did he cease to discriminate between the "backward" nations and the more advanced. In the Orient, China, to his way of thinking, was backward and Japan was advanced. He thought China needed help from other nations, and he wished to save her from being exploited of partitioned, but he felt no such sympathy for her as he felt for Japan. When the Chinese boycotted American goods and disorders ensued, he sent the *Oregon* to the neighborhood of Hong Kong, talked about landing marines, and achieved concessions by the threat of force. In 1904 too he signed a Chinese exclusion bill; William Henry Harbaugh calls this "one of the weakest actions of his Presidential career." He was convinced that excluding Chinese laborers was an economic necessity; on the other hand, he did his best to avoid discrimination against professional people, favored the admission of qualified Chinese to citizenship, and approved the use of the Boxer indemnity payment to provide scholarships for Chinese students in American universities. Yet he pretty much gives himself away when he remarks, apropos of American relations with Japan, that we shall invite disaster "if we show that we regard the Japanese as an inferior and alien race, and try to treat them as we have treated the Chinese."

At first Roosevelt had been pleased by Russia's advance into Turkestan and Siberia, seeing it as a civilizing influence, but he was disgusted by the Jewish massacre at Kishinev in 1903 and by Russia's failure to withdraw its troops from Manchuria in accordance with the 1902 agreement. He was far more prescient in his appreciation of the future importance of both Russia and China than most statesmen were in his time, but he continued to feel that their day was far off and that any possible immediate problems must much more centrally involve Japan. He was also disposed to favor Japanese ambitions in Manchuria as a counterbalance to Russian domination there, and in 1905 Taft in Tokyo suggested privately that the United States was not averse to Japan's taking over Korea in return for a Japanese promise to keep hands off the Philippines. The same year a "gentleman's agreement" was concluded, according to which it was understood that the United

States, Britain, and Japan would act together in any far eastern crisis that might develop. This was not proposed as a formal treaty because Roosevelt knew he could not get it through the Senate, and it was kept secret because he was also aware that public opinion would be outraged. This was an early example of the secret and unconstitutional kind of commitment that has so often since placed the United States in the position of the proverbial Irishman who inquired, "Is this a private fight or can anybody get in?"

The Russo-Japanese War began in February 1904, and by 1905 Japan had been spectacularly successful. Roosevelt's sympathies were with Japan, and he later claimed to have notified both Germany and France that should either move in to support Russia the United States would support Japan, but many historians have refused to credit this statement. What is certain is that he did not believe it to be in either China's interest or that of world peace that either of the contending powers should be permitted to gain unchallenged preeminence in the Far East. It might have been in our interest, temporarily at least, that both should be allowed to bleed themselves white, but Roosevelt was too humane to give that possibility serious consideration. The alternative was to try to end the war by negotiation.

His first overtures were repulsed, but after Admiral Togo had practically destroyed the Russian fleet on May 27–28, 1905, Japan grew more friendly toward the idea of American negotiation, and Kaiser Wilhelm used his influence skillfully to bring the czar into line. With great moral courage, Roosevelt staked not only his personal prestige but that of his country on his own tact and skill in conducting what everybody knew would be cruelly difficult negotiations with the representatives of an Oriental people, the workings of whose minds few westerners at the time even pretended to understand, and those representing a Eurasian people whom we did not understand much better.

The first test came on August 5 on the presidential yacht *Mayflower,* anchored at Oyster Bay. Nations being as irrational as they are, and as puffed up with meaningless, unwarranted pride, the whole enterprise might have been wrecked on the shores of protocol. Who should enter the dining room first? Who should have the place of honor on the president's right? Which sovereign should be toasted first? TR, who addressed his letters to "Dear King Edward" and "Dear Emperor William," was equal to the occasion. Exerting all his combined force and charm, and chattering volubly in what he himself called his "Frenssh-atte-Sagamore," he ushered in the envoys companionably on either side of him, served them a buffet luncheon, and, before anybody else had had a chance to say anything, proposed "a toast to which there will be no answer and which I ask you to drink in silence, standing," to "the welfare and prosperity of the sovereigns and peoples of the two great nations" in whose behalf it was his "most earnest hope and prayer, in the interest . . . of all mankind that a just and lasting peace may speedily be concluded among them." After that, everybody ought to have known what would happen.

Which does not in the least mean, however, that the battle had been won. Working out the terms of agreement, after the conference had been moved to Portsmouth, New Hampshire, proved fiendishly difficult. The kaiser, as Roosevelt later reported, "stood by me like a trump," and at one time the president, to break a deadlock, appealed direct to the mikado, over the heads of his own envoys. In the end there was compromise. Japan backed down on its demand for indemnity; nobody got everything he wanted, but nobody was humiliated. In Japan the jingoes fumed, demonstrating against both the United States and their own government, but the bloodletting stopped and the peace was a fait accompli. Even in America there were those, like Mark Twain, who thought that if the war had been allowed to continue, Japan would have trounced Russia so completely that the Romanov tyranny would have been ended then and there, but this is doubtful, for though Japan came to the conference table flushed with victory, its war chest was empty. The president had covered himself with glory, and Pope Pius X thanked God for his courage. "The man who had been represented to us as impetuous to the point of rudeness," said one close observer, "displayed a gentleness, a kindness and a tactfulness mixed with self-control that only a truly great man can command."

This was not the end of Roosevelt's negotiations with Japan, however. The very year after he had settled the war, "the idiots in the California legislature," as he called them, proceeded to upset our relations with the Nipponese, and the San Francisco School Board committed "a crime against a friendly nation" through the "wicked absurdity" of segregating Oriental children. The problem was precipitated by the incursion of the Japanese along the Pacific

Coast, and there were anti-Oriental riots clear up to Vancouver, but it was the San Francisco action that really drew fire. Nor was it only the Hearst press which began to babble about war with Japan; at one time British International thought it imminent, and the kaiser heard that 10,000 disguised Japanese soldiers had been landed in Mexico. Roosevelt denounced the school board in his annual message, and in February 1907, in an action reminiscent of his behavior in the coal strike, he asked them to send representatives to confer with him at the White House. The result of this meeting was at least a limited success. The board agreed to allow all who knew English and were in the proper age group to attend the regular schools, and TR promised to try to exclude coolie labor. This was achieved when, in October, he sent Taft to Tokyo, where it was agreed that each nation would control the emigration of undesirables to the other.

Meanwhile, probably from mixed motives that he never spelled out, Roosevelt decided upon the most spectacular gesture of his administration, the sending of the sixteen battleships of the Great White Fleet around the world. They left on December 16, 1907, on what was at first announced as a visit to the Pacific Coast, and it was not until the following March that the country was informed they would return home through the Suez Canal.

Some Americans resented what they considered an unnecessary display of American might; some feared that Japan would attack the fleet; still others were terrified at the thought of leaving the Atlantic Coast undefended. At one point Congress refused to appropriate the needed funds, to which TR tartly replied that he had enough money to get the ships to the Pacific and that if Congress did not choose to bring them back they would just have to stay there! The determined opponent of gambling was taking a great gamble of his own, and he knew it; even now it can be argued that the happy outcome and the safe return of the fleet on February 22, 1909, came under the heading of fool's luck. False reports of dire calamity trickled in to Washington from time to time, but the lack of interest shown at the first stop, Trinidad, where the British were too busy celebrating Christmas to pay much attention, was the only real blow suffered. A Chilean cruiser kindly guided the ships through the treacherous Straits of Magellan; the Japanese turned out en fête; and nobody seemed dissatisfied except those in the places *not* visited. Except for a brawl in Rio, the gallant tars too seem to have behaved well. Roosevelt himself later went on record as believing that the cruise had represented his most signal service to peace. Nevertheless, it may well have stimulated the naval arms race.

Roosevelt's service in resolving the Moroccan crisis in 1906 may have prevented World War I from breaking out eight years earlier than it did. The British had recognized French control over Morocco in 1904 in return for recognition of their own overlordship in Egypt. This was sharply challenged by the kaiser in a speech of March 31, 1905, in which he opted for the same kind of "open door" in Morocco that the United States had championed in China. It was not unreasonable then that the kaiser should look to America for some understanding of his position.

The situation grew tense and seemed to be moving toward a showdown throughout the spring. At first reluctant to make a move both because the United States had little or no interest in Morocco and because of opposition in Congress and the country at large to international meddling, Roosevelt grew more inclined toward mediation after the sultan had called for an international conference and France had dismissed the minister responsible for its Moroccan policy. TR's proposals, through his representative at the Algeciras conference, Henry White, on February 19, 1906, favored France more than Germany, for though they accepted the open door in principle, they gave France and Spain control over the Moroccan police.

Roosevelt's attitude toward Kaiser Wilhelm II, who always professed admiration for him, was mixed. Basically he believed that the mutual fears that England and Germany entertained toward each other were unwarranted. "It is as funny a case as I have ever seen of mutual distrust and fear bringing two peoples to the verge of war." He admired the kaiser personally in some aspects, but he also regarded him as a "fuss-cat" who was given to "pipe dreams." In the Moroccan affair, it is easy to understand why TR wished to preserve good relations with France, especially in view of her relationship with England, but he must also have realized that, in spite of the unfortunate belligerence of the March speech, the kaiser's position was fundamentally just. Furthermore, His Majesty agreed in advance not only to accept an advance agenda for the conference, which the French wanted and he did not, but also to go along with whatever TR should decide upon as "the most fair and the most practical," and though he must have been disappointed in the outcome, he kept his word. It is hard to see how he could have been more reasonable and conciliatory.

Roosevelt's conduct of foreign affairs in general was highly individualistic and in a sense arbitrary; he never had any hesitation about ignoring Congress and the cabinet or bypassing both his own ambassadors and those accredited to us, but it was also cautious and responsible, and when he found it advisable to make anything approaching a threat, he was careful to do it under circumstances that would make it easy for the other party to back down without losing face. Under his administration nobody was ever allowed to talk about possible or probable enemies ("to make public statements about . . . a probable enemy is to help by just so much to turn the probable enemy into a certain enemy"), and the military were never permitted to entertain any delusions as to who was in charge of policy. For a man who praised the military virtues as much as he did, TR was surprisingly cold toward professional soldiers. When his son Ted contemplated making a career of the army, he did his utmost to dissuade him; nobody should consider going into the peacetime army, he argued, unless he had proved that he was unable to stand on his own feet in civilian life.

So far as the Western Hemisphere was concerned, however, Roosevelt not only adhered to the Monroe Doctrine but assumed that it could not be defended unless we were prepared to assume the responsibility of keeping order here when and if the smaller nations failed to do so. Root spelled it out at a South American conference, where the United States disclaimed territorial ambitions and assured her neighbors that so long as they behaved themselves they had nothing to fear but added that, if "brutal wrongdoing" occurred or such "impotence" appeared as must result "in a general loosening of the ties of civilized authority," then the northern giant must intervene. Undoubtedly there was a large element of schoolmasterish paternalism and self-righteousness in such a declaration, but during the Roosevelt administration its practical application was pretty successful.

The Venezuelan incident of 1902 and the peaceful intervention in Santo Domingo that came at the very end of TR's first administration, and whose sequelae carried over into the second, have been noted in chapter 2. So too, of course, has been the disagreement with Colombia over the Panama Canal. There was another less serious Venezuelan crisis in 1908, when Roosevelt considered sending battleships there and landing marines; this was not done, but diplomatic relations were severed until after the dictator Castro had been overthrown. In 1906 we prevented war between Guatemala and Salvador and also intervened in Cuban disorders, as we had a treaty right to do. Foreign observers generally assumed that this time we would stay, and it was TR himself who made this impossible: "I will not even consider the plan of a protectorate." When Senator Beveridge wrote him that "Tom, Dick, and Harry" thought it nonsense "to keep on setting up one Cuban Government after another," TR replied sharply "that even the most ignorant have their limitations, and that it is not safe to follow the advice even of those who know nothing about the subject." On the other hand, the Roosevelt administration did encourage American financial interests in the Caribbean and the Orient and did move toward the establishment of overseas bases, thus contributing to some of the entanglements that have cursed our own times.

Finally, though Roosevelt's general movement in military matters was from right toward left, the specific subject of disarmament was something of an exception. He no doubt would have claimed that if he did retreat here, the retreat was imposed upon him by circumstances. He dropped the arbitration negotiations he had undertaken with nine powers when the Senate insisted upon changing "special treaties" to "special agreements," which would have required Senate action before any specific dispute could be arbitrated, upon the wholly sensible ground that there was no point to an agreement that simply provided that we might arbitrate if we had a mind to, and he was to enter similar objections, on the ground of uselessness and impracticality, to those negotiated during the Taft administration, though even the *Outlook* would oppose him here. In 1908, nevertheless, something like what had previously been proposed was set up with twenty-four nations under Root's guidance.

Roosevelt was interested in an international meeting for the consideration of disarmament and the lessening of international tensions as early as 1904, and though his recommendations to the Second Hague Conference in 1907 were not radical, they turned out to be in advance of anything that could be secured. After that conference had failed to limit naval armaments, however, TR, as G. Wallace Chessman has recently expressed it, "made far more headway at building dreadnoughts than he ever had at limiting them," with the result that he "heightened the rivalry he had often deplored." He never advocated the arbitration of disputes involving the misty conception of national "honor" nor the all too solid one of national "interest," and since it is difficult to see how any nation could become involved in a dispute that embraced neither one of these concepts, this was a serious limitation. Neither did he ever give up the idea that the "civilized" nations must exercise a certain overlordship over the "barbarians."

It might have been supposed that an executive who was so often forced to contend with backward legislators and unprogressive public opinion would have found his aggressiveness sufficiently stimulated and satisfied without engaging in controversies upon unimportant or marginal issues. This was hardly the case with Theodore Roosevelt, however. Of the famous controversies in which he participated during his second administration that with the Bellamy Storers was forced upon him and the Brownsville controversy grew out of one of the few impulsive actions of his presidency, but surely the clashes over simplified spelling, the "nature fakers," and the "muckrakers" might have been avoided.

Mrs. Storer was an aunt of Nicholas Longworth, the president's son-in-law, and both she and her husband were intimate friends of the Roosevelts. A managing woman with more zeal than judgment, Mrs. Storer failed to obtain either the Navy or the War Department for her husband; neither did she succeed in getting him sent to London, Paris, or Madrid; but Roosevelt did make him ambassador to Austria-Hungary. If TR had had the kind of temper many people imagine him to have had, he would have blown up under Mrs. Storer's shameless persistence long before he did, and as things turned out, it would have been better for everybody if he had.

This much accomplished, Mrs. Storer directed her energies elsewhere. A devout Roman Catholic, she set her heart upon getting the red hat for Archbishop Ireland, and so little did she understand the temper of the American people on the subject of the separation between church and state that she actually tried to persuade Roosevelt to make such a recommendation to the Vatican.

He was not foolish enough to do that, but unfortunately he happened to be a great admirer of Archbishop Ireland, a staunch Republican, who had supported the Spanish-American War, "sound money," and other aspects of Republican policy and who was credited with an influence toward Republicanism among his predominantly Democratic coreligionists. Knowing Mrs. Storer as well as he did, it still seems incredible that Roosevelt should have written her a letter in which he expressed his admiration for Ireland and authorized her to show it "to any one you see fit."

What followed soon convinced him that he had acted imprudently, and he asked for the return of the letter and directed Storer "not to quote me to any person in any shape or way in connection with any affair of the Catholic Church." The Storers now recognized the seriousness of the situation sufficiently so that the ambassador tendered his resignation in January 1904, but when Roosevelt refused to accept it, they proved that they had not really learned anything, and in December 1905 Mrs. Storer asked the president to send her a cable she could show the pope!

This brought Roosevelt at last to the end of his patience. "You actually propose that I should use you to go to Rome to take part in what I must call an ecclesiastical intrigue—and drag the United States government into it." He added that, unless all such actions were suspended, it would be impossible for him to retain Storer as his ambassador.

This letter the Storers did not see fit to answer. With almost saintly patience, Roosevelt waited until March before cabling Storer his dismissal.

I think it must be admitted that it is difficult to deal with an ambassador who will neither obey the orders of his chief nor communicate with him, and the conduct of the Storers afterward in permitting Roosevelt's letters to them to find their way into the newspapers must surely have destroyed any faith in their good judgment any intelligent person might until now have entertained. Roosevelt added Bellamy Storer to the roll of the Ananias Club, the press had a field day, and "Dear Maria" became almost as familiar in American speech as "Ain't it awful, Mabel?" would be in 1908. Though the pope seemed at one time to have promised the red hat to Ireland, he gave it instead to Archbishop Farley, and at least one American newspaper was converted to a belief in clerical celibacy: "But the rulers of the church are far-sighted; they know human nature; they have no doubt considered the awful possibility of a Mrs. Bellamy Storer." As for that good lady, she died in the 1920s, still believing that Roosevelt had behaved like a child.

On the night of August 13, 1906, fifteen to twenty members of three all-Negro companies of soldiers, who had been stationed at Fort Brown in Texas and had had some friction with the townspeople, shot up the town of Brownsville. One man was killed and two wounded. Some shots, fired into houses, narrowly missed women and children.

TR wanted the guilty men, and when he found them shielded by a conspiracy of silence, he discharged without honor nearly all members of the three companies. Six Medal of Honor soldiers were involved and thirteen who held certificates of merit for bravery. The duty of the army, as Roosevelt saw it, was to protect Americans, not murder them. "Unless that duty is well performed, the Army becomes a mere dangerous mob" and would better be disbanded.

The president was accused of having violated traditional Anglo-Saxon codes of justice in dismissing these men without trial and punishing the innocent rather than letting the guilty go free. It does not seem unreasonable to suppose that some of those accused of shielding the guilty soldiers may have been simply ignorant. Roosevelt may have judged wrongly or acted (for once) hastily, but there is no foundation whatever for the charge of racism that some entered against him. No sane person can doubt that his action would have been exactly the same if white soldiers had been involved, and no true friend of blacks will argue that they should have larger license to commit crimes than white men.

Senator Joseph B. Foraker, who constituted himself the champion of the discharged men, had a more radical objection. He did not believe the soldiers had committed the crime of which they were accused. The argument, which is based on the kind of bullets found in the streets of Brownsville and the condition of the soldiers' guns after the raid, is very complicated, and TR found it unconvincing. The two men clashed personally when they attacked each other verbally with gusto at a Gridiron Club dinner in January 1907, though Roosevelt soon recovered his balance sufficiently to be disposed to make some excuses for his adversary. James Amos, TR's black retainer, says that Roosevelt brought some of the accused to the White House and that under his questioning they admitted the justice of the charges. He adds that, though it would have freed him of much criticism, TR did not feel at liberty to use this admission in justifying his action because he considered that it had not been made willingly "but only under the influence of his dominating personality." Recent historians do not seem to have taken this into account, but Amos was certainly a reliable man.

However all this may be, Roosevelt never admitted that he had been wrong about Brownsville, though the fact that he completely ignored the matter in his *Autobiography* would suggest that he did not regard it as one of his successes. At the very end of his administration, he compromised to the extent of setting up a military court to consider the complaints of those who had denied implication, and it may be significant that only eighty-four persons appeared before it and that of these only fourteen were reinstated.

Of the other, less serious controversies, the attack on the muckrakers is the most puzzling while the clashes over simplified spelling and the nature fakers would seem in retrospect the most unnecessary. All this, however, contributed to the public entertainment of the time and further dramatized the personality of a president who, without radio and television, managed to permeate the country and stamp his personality upon it as none of his successors have been able to do even with these aids.

The attack on the muckrakers was made first at a Gridiron Club dinner on March 17, 1906, and amplified at the laying of the cornerstone of the House of Representatives Office Building. The text came from Bunyan's figure of

> the Man with the Muckrake, the man who could look no way but downward with the muckrake in his hand; who was offered a celestial crown for his muckrake but who would neither look up nor regard the crown he was offered but continued to rake to himself the filth on the floor.

The beginnings of the muckraking movement have already been described in these pages in connection with the history of the ten- and fifteen-cent magazines in chapter 11. Generally speaking, the muckrakers rendered valiant service in attacking the same evils that Roosevelt attacked and advocating such reforms as he himself desired. Why, then, did he so suddenly seem to be turning against them?

Incidentally he also, of course, flatly misinterpreted Bunyan's meaning in *The Pilgrim's Progress,* and it is hard to believe that so well-read a man was not perfectly aware of this. In Bunyanesque terms, the real muckrakers were the "malefactors of great wealth," not those who exposed them and sought to remedy the abuses they had created.

The attack came just after David Graham Phillips had begun publishing his articles on "The Treason of the Senate" in *Cosmopolitan,* and William Henry Harbaugh conjectures that TR may well have feared that Phillips's extravagance, like that of Thomas W. Lawson and other writers, might strengthen the forces opposed to the Hepburn bill and the other reforms he was trying to secure. Roosevelt never ceased to pray to be delivered from the "lunatic fringe" among his allies. *Cosmopolitan* too was owned by William Randolph Hearst, whom Roosevelt despised and mistrusted. Nobody wanted corruptionists cleaned out of the Senate more than he did, but he did *not* want people to become so disillusioned about government that they would tend to "cop out" from all participation, as a dangerously high percentage of Americans were to do after Watergate.

Moreover, the dramatic intensity of Roosevelt's attack on muckraking provides no excuse for ignoring the careful qualifications he made: "I hail as benefactor every writer or speaker, every man who, on platform or in book, magazine or newspaper, with merciless severity, makes such attack, provided always that he in his turn remember that the attack is of use only if it is absolutely truthful." Of course the conservative papers, delighted to have found at last one statement from Roosevelt that they could wholeheartedly approve of, did ignore the qualifications, as they also ignored the fact that, in the Gridiron speech itself, he had called for federal regulation of corporations engaged in interstate commerce and a progressive inheritance tax on large fortunes.

Ray Stannard Baker was probably the muckraker to whom TR felt closest, and he came as close to determinism as he ever approached when he wrote Baker:

It seems to me one of the lessons you teach is that these railroad men are not to be treated as exceptional villains but merely as ordinary Americans, who under given conditions are by the mere force of events forced into doing much of which we complain. I want so far as I can, to free the movement for their control from all rancor and hatred.

But the moderation and charity of an unconverted moralist are even more evident here than the approach to determinism. If conduct was three-fourths of life to Matthew Arnold, it came close to being four-fourths to Roosevelt. He had only contempt for those advocates of "free enterprise" who championed the "right" of a factory girl "freely to contract to expose herself to dangers of life and limb," but the meaning of life itself was bound up for him with the conviction that men must be held accountable for their actions. He did not misrepresent his own general attitude as a reformer when, employing one of the most vivid figures he ever called into service, he told Baker that "if a room is fetid and the windows are bolted, I am perfectly willing to knock out the windows, but I would not knock a hole in the drain pipe." Baker was not convinced. After the attack on the muckrakers, he could never again, he thought, give TR his "full confidence, nor follow his leadership."

More than anything else in Roosevelt's administration, the simplified-spelling controversy was a matter of much ado about nothing, and nowhere else was he more completely routed. The war began on August 27, 1906, when he ordered the public printer to begin spelling 300 words according to the recommendations of the Simplified Spelling Board. "Though" would become "tho"; "thorough" would be changed to "thoro"; "through" would find itself transmogrified into "thru"—this last a recommendation of whose wisdom TR himself felt considerable doubt. Many of the changes were mild, such as "program" for "programme" and the dropping of the "u" from words like "honour," and a great many had already appeared in standard dictionaries as alternative spellings. In December Roosevelt sent his annual message to Congress in the new spelling.

The scholastic credentials of the Spelling Reform Association, which was headed by Columbia's Brander Matthews, were respectable, even distinguished, and Andrew Carnegie would devote a quarter of a million dollars to the cause. But the furor that ensued was such as to lead the Man from Mars to suppose that, for the first time in our history, Americans were concerned primarily with linguistic correctness. The president was accused of attacking "the

King's English" and undermining our culture, of lending himself to a conspiracy on the part of printers and publishers to get all books reprinted, and of attempting to make himself a universal dictator ("What will he do next?"). Congress decreed that the Government Printing Office must follow standard usage in printing all official documents, including the president's message, and the Supreme Court ruled that all previous decisions must be cited exactly as they had been handed down.

One need not be sympathetic toward simplified spelling to observe that when Henry Watterson suggested that the president should spell his name "Rucefelt," with "the first silabel riming with goose," he simply proved that he did not know how to pronounce "Roosevelt," and that TR was a much better scholar when he observed that simplified spelling "is not an attack on the language of Shakespeare and Milton, because it is in some instances a going-back to the forms they used, and in others merely the extension of changes which, as regards other words, have taken place since their time." The pious invocations of Noah Webster's authority too would have startled and amused that audacious innovator. But it was no use. "I could not by fighting have kept the new spelling in," Roosevelt wrote Matthews, "and it was evidently worse than useless to go into an undignified contest when I was beaten."

Since it involved a question of scientific truth, the nature-faking controversy was less trifling in itself, but though Roosevelt came out of it with the support of the scientists intact, he probably lost ground with the general public. Like John Burroughs and others, he had for some time been annoyed by writers who, as he saw it, falsified their nature reporting, and when, early in 1907, Edward B. Clark asked him, "Why don't you get after them?" he replied, "I think I will." What he had to say appeared in an interview, "Roosevelt on the Nature-Fakirs," which Clark published in June 1907 in *Everybody's Magazine*.

Roosevelt criticized Ernest Thompson Seton and Charles G. D. Roberts mildly but lashed out at Jack London for *White Fang* and at William J. Long, "the worst of the nature-writing offenders." Again, he carefully qualified his objections, and as usual the public ignored all the qualifications. He had no objection whatever to writers like Kipling and Kenneth Grahame and Joel Chandler Harris who humanized animals in stories presented as fiction or fable;

on the contrary, nobody enjoyed such writers more than he; but the presentation of fiction as fact seemed to him both immoral and a disservice to the diffusion of sound scientific knowledge.

The sympathy that went to Long, a clergyman and a private citizen whom the president had used the dignity of his great office to make the object of a personal attack, seems a bit sentimental in view of Long's reply; if his courage awakened admiration, he gave little evidence that the gentleness he thought he discerned in the heart of wild folk had rubbed off on him. Long accused TR of cowardice and venom and declared that he was neither sportsman, naturalist, nor gentleman. "I find, after careful reading of his two big books, that every time Mr. Roosevelt gets near the heart of a wild thing he invariably puts a bullet through it." Exaggerated as this was, it proved Long no mean controversialist. Deliberately or by accident, he had shifted attention from the area where he was vulnerable and appealed for support not only to those who objected to TR's hunting but also to those who were antipathetic to him on other grounds and therefore eager for any issue on which they might trip him up. Some more thoughtful persons, too, felt that Roosevelt's moralism had betrayed him into discerning a moral issue where no real one existed; as Speaker Thomas B. Reed once remarked, "If there is one thing more than another for which I admire you, Theodore, it is your original discovery of the Ten Commandments." Roosevelt himself admitted, in a letter to John Burroughs, "I know that as President, I ought not to do this, but I was having an awful time toward the end of the session and I felt I simply had to permit myself some diversion."

The most painful episode in TR's second administration, however, was the Panic of 1907, and this time, as already related, the hero who rode out the storm was J. P. Morgan, who began to scheme and plan while Roosevelt was off hunting bear! The first sharp break in the market came on March 14, 1907, and Harriman and others openly blamed Roosevelt, who tried to be reassuring but refused to alter his policies. On August 3, in Chicago, Judge Kenesaw Mountain Landis fined Standard Oil more than 29 million dollars for violating the Elkins Act on innumerable counts (the government lost on appeal). Then, on August 20, in a fighting speech at Provincetown, Massachusetts, TR declared that "certain malefactors of great wealth" were trying to throw the country into a panic in the hope of freeing business from regulation in the public interest, "so that they may enjoy unmolested the fruits of their own evil-doing."

The situation became critical when, on October 22, during a run on the bank, the Knickerbocker Trust Company, unable to pay out further moneys to its depositors, closed its doors. The Westinghouse Company went into receivership; the Pittsburgh Stock Exchange suspended operations; even the Trust Company of America was threatened with collapse. Supported by Henry Clay Frick, Edward H. Harriman, James Stillman, John D. Rockefeller, and others, Morgan prevented this in the manner that has already been described.

In November, Roosevelt received Frick and Judge Elbert H. Gary as ambassadors from United States Steel, sounding out his attitude toward the possible acquisition by that corporation of the Tennessee Coal and Iron Company, which was facing imminent collapse, as a means of preventing the financial crisis from worsening. "I answered that while of course I could not advise them to take the action proposed, I felt no public duty of mine to interpose any objection." This decision was made hastily, since if the proposed action were to achieve anything it must be taken at once, and its wisdom was long to be debated. It also had important political consequences, for the move under the Taft administration (October 27, 1911) to accuse U.S. Steel of having violated the Sherman Act ("making me," said TR, "either a fool or a knave") would contribute importantly to the Taft–Roosevelt rift and the Republican debacle in 1912. The Aldrich–Vreeland Act, which Roosevelt accepted, was not radical nor far-reaching enough to provide real reform.

As we have already seen, Roosevelt publicly committed himself to not becoming a candidate in 1908 as early as election night in 1904, and though H. H. Kohlsaat quotes him as having declared that he would cut off his hand to be able to recall that statement, there is no evidence to show that he ever reconsidered. The election of 1906, in which TR supported all the Republican candidates, even the most reactionary, reduced the party's power in the House; whether or not this influenced the president's increasing progressivism during his last two years in office is speculative, but there can be no question that the shift occurred, and it is not unreasonable to believe that the disinclination of the Congress to give him even the moderate changes he asked for must have helped to disillusion him further about the right. He grew less hostile toward Bryan and La Follette, and by 1908 he was even willing to concede that some Socialists held ideas "worthy of respect" and to speak of himself as a "radical" who was trying to lead an "ultraconservative party" toward "progressive conservatism" or "conservative radicalism."

It is no exaggeration to speak of Roosevelt's retirement in 1908–9 as an abdication; he had to fight quite as hard to prevent his own renomination as to get Taft chosen, and had he been nominated he would certainly have been elected. Nevertheless, his action was firmly grounded in everything he believed about the American government. He believed that the effective operation of the government depended upon a strong central executive, and wherever he saw an opportunity to extend the powers of the presidency, he seized upon it, not only in the interest of his immediate objective but because he believed he was setting a valuable precedent. At the same time, he was convinced that no such powers should be granted to any one man for a very long period; neither must he be permitted to use the power of his office to keep himself in power.

TR had never made a secret of the fact that he immensely enjoyed being president; he gave up his office when he did only because he thought it right to do so, and nobody except himself has ever known what it must have cost him. But though he had always felt more comfortable about being away from Washington when he could leave Secretary of War Taft—all 350 pounds of him—"sitting on the lid," Taft was not his first choice as his successor, nor did he finally come out for him until January 1908, and he did it then only because his secretary William Loeb convinced him that if he did not get behind another candidate soon the convention would be stampeded for himself.

His first choice was Elihu Root ("I would walk on my hands and knees from the White House to the Capitol to see Root made President"), but he never seriously considered backing him because he did not believe a corporation lawyer could be elected. Root served his clients, and if he were president the United States would be that client, but TR knew the electorate would never see it that way. Taft's only other real rival was Charles Evans Hughes, the "bearded iceberg" whom Roosevelt respected but did not like, though he would campaign for him against Wilson in 1916. As already related, TR had rendered important, perhaps even decisive, service to Hughes during his gubernatorial campaign. Later there was an unhappy rift between the two men, and once he had settled on Taft, Roosevelt delivered the coup de grâce to Hughes's presidential aspirations by apparently timing a sensational special message so as to keep off the front page the important policy speech Hughes delivered on the night of January 31, 1908, after the New York Republican County Committee had endorsed his candidacy.

If Roosevelt refused to use his control of the party machinery to keep himself in office, he showed no scruples about employing every trick in the book in Taft's behalf, even to the extent of hinting that "if they won't take Taft, they'll have to take me." Though at one point there was danger that the convention might get sufficiently out of hand to name Roosevelt himself, Taft was safely nominated, but both the platform and the vice-president, "Sunny Jim" Sherman of New York, were very conservative.

The Democrats turned for the last time to William Jennings Bryan, who ran on a platform that condemned the use of injunctions in labor disputes and advocated the dissolution of trusts controlling 50 percent or more of the market, federal guarantee of bank deposits, and tariff for revenue only. Since this was to go farther to the left than Roosevelt at this time thought it wise or expedient to move, there was some exaggeration in Bryan's claim that he, not Taft, represented the Roosevelt policies, but he had a point, and he was formally endorsed by Samuel Gompers and the American Federation of Labor.

Roosevelt engaged in controversy with Gompers (one would guess with a somewhat divided mind), and he rushed to Taft's defense when religious bigots attacked him on two separate fronts: he was a Unitarian, and he had been too friendly to the Catholic church in the Philippines! But it was hardly necessary. Between Roosevelt's popularity and his own empty war chest, Bryan never had a chance, and though Taft did very little to ensure his own election, he won hands down, polling 50,000 more votes than TR had polled in 1904, though his plurality over Bryan was only about half of what Roosevelt's had been over Parker.

Actually, Taft had never wanted to be president. What he did want, and what he was supremely qualified for, was the Supreme Court justiceship he finally achieved. It was Mrs. Taft who wanted to be president, and she must have felt that at last she was sitting where she belonged when, upon TR's decision to go direct to Oyster Bay after the inauguration ceremony, instead of riding back to the White House on the new president's left, she smashed precedent by seizing that place for herself. The weather was so terrible that the ceremony had to be held indoors, and Taft quipped that he had always known it would be a cold day when he became president. His mother had warned him that that office was not for him, and he must already have been beginning to realize that she was right, for he called the summer of 1908 "one of the most uncomfortable four months of my life." It is one of the ironies of American political history that his wife, who wanted to be in the White House as much as he had wanted to stay out of it, became seriously ill shortly after they had entered it, so that she could not function as they had both supposed she would.

Roosevelt's choice of Taft as his successor can hardly be considered in retrospect one of his most perspicacious acts, but at the time it did not seem unwise or unreasonable. It was not only that there was a strong personal affection between the two men; if Taft sometimes fell asleep at cabinet meetings, he had been immensely efficient in everything Roosevelt gave him to do, and he often showed more zeal in defending the Roosevelt policies than the chief himself. TR actually believed that Taft was a much more attractive man than he was: "You blessed old trump, I have always said you would be the greatest President, bar only Washington and Lincoln, and I feel mighty inclined to strike out the exceptions." During the campaign, he wavered between coaching Taft as a stage mamma might hover over her beloved offspring—"Let the audience see you smile *always*, because I feel that your nature shines out so transparently when you do smile—you big, generous, high-minded fellow"—and honestly attempting to keep himself out of the limelight. It was because he knew the danger of his dominating any scene upon which he appeared that he took himself off to Africa after the inauguration. "If I talk," he told Ray Stannard Baker, "people will say I am interfering where I have no right to interfere. If I refuse to talk, they will say my silence is disapproval."

Whether Roosevelt's later dissatisfaction with the Taft administration was foreshadowed, and if so to what extent, during the campaign or between the election and the inauguration is speculative. He must have found his patience tried by Taft's listless campaign, but it was never easy for him to admit he had made a . mistake, and he sometimes exercised his gift for not seeing what he did not wish to see. Certainly there were others who did see, or fancied they saw, unlovely handwriting upon the wall. In August Moorfield Storey was already writing Charles Francis Adams that, while publicly Taft stood committed to the Roosevelt policies, "privately he allows it to be understood that he will not carry them out," and in February Henry Adams found himself wondering "if the new president is so bent on making a clean sweep of Roosevelt's men, why did we elect him expressly to carry on the Roosevelt regime?" Being the man he was, one would think Roosevelt must have been angered by the knowledge that came to him of Taft's contemplated cabinet changes, which he made with no explanation to Roosevelt after the latter had been authorized to tell people that they would be retained. Taft certainly knew what was being whispered behind the scenes, for at one point he wrote TR, "People have attempted to represent that you and I were in some way at odds during this last two or three months, whereas you and I know that there has not been slightest difference between us." But where perfect harmony exists, it is rarely necessary to proclaim it, and one can hardly believe that TR was less sensitive to the currents of opinion around him than his successor. Nevertheless, he controlled himself admirably, and we have nothing stronger from him than his reply to Mark Sullivan, who asked him, just before Inauguration Day, how he thought Taft would make out: "He's all right, he means well, and he'll do his best. But he's weak. They'll get around him. They'll lean against him." Coming from a man with Roosevelt's gift for language, this seems mild enough, but it is a far cry from his earlier conviction that the new man would be the greatest president since Lincoln.

If Roosevelt restrained himself during the campaign, he certainly behaved like anything but a lame duck during his last months in office; indeed, when a friend remarked that the period between election and inauguration must be a period of stagnation, he replied that the stagnation "continues to rage with uninterrupted violence." His annual message of December 1907 had already recommended, among other things, inheritance and income taxes, further railroad regulation, including rate fixing based on the evaluation of railroad property, a postal savings bank, the compulsory investigation of large labor disputes, and the extension of the eight-hour day and workmen's compensation. A month later, in a special message calling for revision of the Sherman Act, he had called for federal regulation of stock market gambling, which he denounced as quite as immoral as gambling with cards, along with the "flagrant dishonesty" of such lords of "predatory wealth" as the Standard Oil and Santa Fe Railroad moguls and the abuse of labor injunctions by judges indifferent to "the abuses of the criminal rich"—all this to the accompaniment of applause from Bryan and the Democrats and from scattered liberals everywhere but to the consternation of the Republican Old Guard and conservative newspapers. The country would have to wait until the 1930s for a substantial portion of these recommendations to be acted upon.

Nor was the last annual message of December 1908 any better from the point of view of the conservatives. It stressed judicial reform, conservation, and the rights of labor and urged that telephone and telegraph be regulated by the ICC. Roosevelt now demanded a larger share of the national wealth for workingmen, for he had come to feel that if such actions as a recent court decision against the workman's compensation law were allowed to stand "we should not only have a revolution, but it would be absolutely necessary to have a revolution, because the condition of the worker would be intolerable." To this he added a denunciation of the recent action of Congress in limiting the activities of the secret service, caustically charging that Congressmen "did not wish themselves to be investigated," and on January 4, 1909, in a special message, he returned to the attack. The House voted to lay on the table that portion of the annual message that dealt with the secret service and the whole of the special message. Unabashed, TR reiterated his charges in his last message to Congress, what the newspapers called his "last whack" and "stinging rebuke for finale," sent in on the morning of Taft's inauguration. He still believed in reform, not revolution, but it was clear that he had come to believe that considerably more radical action would be required to achieve this than he had once supposed.

One of the most brilliant of the innumerable cartoons inspired by Theodore Roosevelt's career was Albert Levering's in *Puck*, February 1909, on "The Teddyfication of the White House." It showed an astonished and nonplussed Taft entering a great room in his new abiding place and finding himself overwhelmed by the fact that not only every figure in the paintings and tapestries but every rug, chairback, light fixture, and andiron, every section of the frieze, and every stuffed animal head wore the features of his predecessor. I could not but recall this when I visited the Theodore Roosevelt house in New York and found something that looked very much like his face on the back of the chair he had sat in as a little child. Obviously he had begun "Teddyfying" his surroundings very early!

In *Saint Joan* Shaw makes the point that, however we may revere the saints, we do not care to live with them; even those who have come together to honor Joan of Arc after her rehabilitation are appalled at the suggestion that she might come back. But this is true not only of saints but also of human dynamos, and when Roosevelt left Washington after Taft's inauguration, it was not only his enemies who experienced a certain sense of relief. Now that he was gone, maybe life would be a little easier, if only because they would not need to live up to what often seemed his unreasonably high expectations and requirements. After all, even the admiring John Burroughs had remarked that when he was with Roosevelt he always felt as if the Day of Judgment might come at any moment. Yet at the same time everybody also felt that life had somehow grown grayer and duller, as if a certain brightness had fallen from the air. The brilliant, sardonic, sensitive, heart-hungry Henry Adams had had mixed emotions about TR, whom he considered "never sober, only he is drunk with himself and not with rum." On another occasion Adams had written, from his home in Washington, that "the twelfth century still rages wildly here in the shape of a fiend with tusks and eyeglasses across the way," yet when he called at the White House to take his leave, this master of fine phrases could find nothing better to say than "I shall miss you," and any old cleaning woman could have said as much. Even in Europe they felt it; as Kipling was to put it to Brander Matthews: "Take care of him. He is scarce and valuable." However all this might be, one thing was certain: an era had ended. However all this might be, another thing was certain: those who had prayed for a letdown were going to get their wish.

Suggestions for Further Reading

Abbott, Lyman. *Reminiscences*. Houghton Mifflin, 1915.

Addams, Jane. *Twenty Years at Hull-House* and *The Second Twenty Years at Hull-House*. Macmillan, 1910, 1930.

Ahlstrom, Sydney E. *A Religious History of the American People*. Yale University Press, 1972.

Alberts, Robert C. *The Good Provider: H. J. Heinz and His Varieties*. Houghton Mifflin, 1973.

Allen, Frederick Lewis. *The Big Change: America Transforms Itself, 1900–1950*. Harper, 1952.

The American Heritage History of the Confident Years. American Heritage Publishing Company, n.d.

The American Heritage Pictorial History of the Presidents of the United States. Vol. 2. Simon and Schuster, 1968.

Andrist, Ralph K., and Ray Brousseau. *Looking Forward*. American Heritage Publishing Company, 1970.

Asbury, Herbert. *Carry Nation*. Knopf, 1929.

Austin, William W. *Music in the Twentieth Century*. Norton, 1966.

Beals, Carleton. *Cyclone Carry: The Story of Carry Nation*. Chilton, 1962.

Becker, Stephen. *Comic Art in America*. Simon and Schuster, 1959.

Belasco, David. *The Theatre through Its Stage Door*. Edited by Louis V. Defoe. Harper, 1919.

Birdoff, Harry. *The World's Greatest Hit—"Uncle Tom's Cabin."* S. F. Vanni, 1947.

Blum, Daniel. *Great Stars of the American Stage*. Greenberg, 1952.

———. *A Pictorial History of the American Theatre, 1860–1970*. New, 3d ed., enlarged and revised by John Willis. Crown, 1969.

The Britannica Encyclopedia of American Art. Simon and Schuster, n.d.

Bronson, William. *The Earth Shook; the Sky Burned*. Doubleday, 1959.

Brown, Ira V. *Lyman Abbott, Christian Evolutionist: A Study in Religious Liberalism*. Harvard University Press, 1953.

Bryan, William Jennings, and Mary Baird Bryan. *The Memoirs of William Jennings Bryan*. Winston, 1925.

Butterfield, Roger. *The American Past*. Simon and Schuster, 1947.

Cahn, William. *Out of the Cracker Barrel: The Nabisco Story from Animal Crackers to Zuzus*. Simon and Schuster, 1969.

Carnegie, Andrew. *The Autobiography of Andrew Carnegie*. Houghton Mifflin, 1920.

Carson, Gerald. *Cornflake Crusade*. Rinehart, 1957.

Churchill, Allen. *The Great White Way: A Re-Creation of Broadway's Golden Era of Theatrical Entertainment*. Dutton, 1962.

Clark, Ronald W. *Edison: The Man Who Made the Future*. Putnam, 1977.

Coletta, Paolo E. *William Jennings Bryan*. 3 vols. University of Nebraska Press, 1964–70.

Cone, John Frederick. *Oscar Hammerstein's Manhattan Opera Company*. University of Oklahoma Press, 1966.

Conot, Robert. *A Streak of Luck*. Seaview Books, 1979.

Cortissoz, Royal. *Augustus Saint-Gaudens*. Houghton Mifflin, 1907.

Cubberley, Elwood P. *The History of Education*. Houghton Mifflin, 1920.

Davis, Owen. *I'd Like To Do It Again*. Farrar & Rinehart, 1931.

Downes, William Howe. *John S. Sargent, His Life and Work*. Little, Brown, 1925.

Ewen, David. *The Life and Death of Tin Pan Alley: The Golden Age of American Popular Music*. Funk & Wagnalls, 1964.

The Fabulous Century, by the Editors of Time-Life Books. Vols. 1–2. Time-Life Books, 1969.

Farrar, Geraldine. *Such Sweet Compulsion: Autobiography*. Greystone Press, 1938.

Garden, Mary and Louis Biancolli. *Mary Garden's Story*. Simon and Schuster, 1951.

Genthe, Arnold. *As I Remember*. Reynal and Hitchcock, 1936.

Gilman, Lawrence. *Edward MacDowell, A Study*. John Lane, 1909.

Glad, Paul W. *The Trumpet Soundeth: William Jennings Bryan and His Democracy, 1896–1912*. University of Nebraska Press, 1960.

Green, Samuel M. *American Art: A Historical Survey*. Ronald Press, 1966.

Handy, Robert T. *A History of the Churches in the United States and Canada*. Oxford University Press, 1977.

Harbaugh, William Henry. *Power and Responsibility: The Life and Times of Theodore Roosevelt*. Farrar, Strauss and Cudahy, 1961.

Hendrick, Burton J. *The Life of Andrew Carnegie*. 2 vols. Doubleday, 1923.

Holbrook, Stewart H. *The Golden Age of Quackery*. Macmillan, 1959.

Horn, Maurice, ed. *The World Encyclopedia of Comics*. Chelsea House, 1976.

Hornblow, Arthur. *A History of the Theatre in America*. 2 vols. Lippincott, 1919.

Hutchison, William R. *The Modernist Impulse in American Protestantism*. Harvard University Press, 1976.

Jones, Howard Mumford. *The Age of Energy: Varieties of American Experience, 1865–1915*. Viking, 1971.

Kahn, E. J., Jr. *The Big Drink*. Random House, 1960.

Kasson, John F. *Amusing the Million: Coney Island at the Turn of the Century*. Hill and Wang, 1978.

Keller, Helen. *Midstream: My Later Life*. Doubleday, 1929.

———. *My Religion*. Doubleday, 1927.

———. *The Story of My Life, with Her Letters (1887–1901) and a Supplementary Account of Her Education, including Passages from the Reports and Letters of Her Teacher, Anne Mansfield Sullivan, by John Albert Macy*. New ed., with introduction by Ralph Barton Perry. Doubleday, 1954.

Koenig, Louis W. *Bryan: A Political Biography of William Jennings Bryan*. Putnam, 1971.

Kolodin, Irving. *The Metropolitan Opera, 1883–1966*. Knopf, 1966.

Langford, Gerald. *The Murder of Stanford White*. Bobbs-Merrill, 1962.

Lash, Joseph P. *Helen and Teacher: The Story of Helen Keller and Anne Sullivan Macy.* Delacorte Press/Seymour Lawrence, 1980.

Laurie, Joe, Jr. *Vaudeville: From the Honky-Tonks to the Palace.* Holt, 1953.

Lord, Walter. *The Good Years: From 1900 to the First World War.* Harper, 1960.

MacDowell, Edward. *Critical and Historical Essays.* Edited by W. J. Baltzell. Reprint ed., with introduction by Irving Lowens. Da Capo Press, 1969.

Mantle, Burns, and Garrison P. Sherwood, eds. *The Best Plays of 1899–1909* and *The Best Plays of 1909–1919.* Dodd, Mead, 1944, 1933.

Marker, Lise-Lone. *David Belasco: Naturalism in the American Theatre.* Princeton University Press, 1975.

Mathews, Basil. *Booker T. Washington, Educator and Interracial Interpreter.* Harvard University Press, 1948.

May, Ernest R., and the Editors of Life. *The Progressive Era.* The Life History of the United States, vol. 9, 1901–1917. Time, Inc., 1964.

McCullough, Edo. *Good Old Coney Island.* Scribners, 1957.

Miller, George, and Dorothy Miller. *Picture Postcards in the United States, 1893–1918.* Clarkson N. Potter, 1976.

Mooney, Michael Macdonald. *Evelyn Nesbit and Stanford White: Love and Death in the Gilded Age.* Morrow, 1976.

Mott, Frank Luther. *American Journalism: A History, 1690–1960,* 3d ed. Macmillan, 1962.

———. *A History of American Magazines.* Vols. 2–5, Harvard University Press, 1938–68.

Mount, Charles Merrill. *John Singer Sargent: A Biography.* Norton, 1955.

Mowry, George E. *The Era of Theodore Roosevelt, 1900–1912.* Harper, 1958.

Mulhern, James. *A History of Education.* Ronald Press, 1946.

Munsey, Cecil. *The Illustrated Guide to the Collectibles of Coca-Cola.* Hawthorn Books, 1972.

Nye, Russel. *The Unencumbered Muse: The Popular Arts in America.* Dial Press, 1970.

O'Connor, Richard. *The Golden Summers: An Antic History of Newport.* Putnam, 1974.

Ormond, Richard. *John Singer Sargent: Paintings, Drawings, Watercolors.* Harper and Row, 1970.

Porte, John F. *Edward MacDowell: A Great American Tone Poet, His Life and Music.* Kegan Paul, 1922.

Quinn, Arthur Hobson. *A History of the American Drama from the Civil War to the Present Day.* Appleton-Century-Crofts, 1936.

Reynolds, Quentin. *The Fiction Factory; or, From Pulp Row to Quality Street; The Story of 100 Years of Publishing at Street and Smith.* Random House, 1965.

Rhodes, James Ford. *History of the United States from the Compromise of 1850 to the End of the Roosevelt Administration.* New ed., 9 vols. Vol. 9, 1896–1909. Macmillan, 1928.

Robinson, Jerry. *The Comics.* Putnam, 1974.

Roosevelt, Theodore. *Works.* Memorial ed., 26 vols. Scribners, 1923–26.

Saint-Gaudens, Augustus. *Reminiscences*. Edited and amplified by Homer Saint-Gaudens. 2 vols. Century, 1913.

Satterlee, Herbert L. *J. Pierpont Morgan, An Intimate Portrait*. Macmillan, 1939.

Shippen, Katherine B., and Paul A. W. Wallace. *Biography of Milton S. Hershey*. Random House, 1959.

Shirer, William L. *20th Century, A Memoir of the Life and the Times: The Start, 1904–1930*. Simon and Schuster, 1976.

Speaight, George. *A History of the Circus*. A. S. Barnes, 1980.

Spencer, Samuel R., Jr. *Booker T. Washington and the Negro's Place in American Life*. Little, Brown, 1955.

Spiller, Robert E., et al., eds. *Literary History of the United States*. 2 vols. Macmillan, 1948.

Stage, Sarah. *Female Complaints: Lydia Pinkham and the Business of Women's Medicine*. Norton, 1979.

Sullivan, Mark. *Our Times: The United States, 1900–1925*. Vols. 1–4. Scribners, 1926–33.

Swanberg, W. A. *Citizen Hearst*. Scribners, 1961.

Taylor, Dwight. *Blood-and-Thunder*. Atheneum, 1962.

Taylor, Robert Lewis. *Vessel of Wrath: The Life and Times of Carry Nation*. New American Library, 1966.

Tharp, Louise Hall. *Saint-Gaudens and the Gilded Era*. Little, Brown, 1969.

Thompson, Oscar, et al., eds. *The International Cyclopedia of Music and Musicians*. 9th ed. Dodd, Mead, 1964.

Timberlake, Craig. *The Bishop of Broadway: The Life and Work of David Belasco*. Library Publishers, 1954.

Toll, Robert C. *On with the Show: The First Century of Show Business in America*. Oxford University Press, 1976.

Truax, Sarah. *A Woman of Parts: Memories of a Life on Stage*. Longmans, Green, 1949.

Wachhorst, Wyn. *Thomas Alva Edison, An American Myth*. The MIT Press, 1981.

Wagenknecht, Edward. *Cavalcade of the American Novel*. Holt, 1952.

———. *Chicago*. University of Oklahoma Press, 1964.

———. *Mark Twain, the Man and His Work*. 3d ed. University of Oklahoma Press, 1967.

———. *The Seven Worlds of Theodore Roosevelt*. Longmans, Green, 1958.

Wall, Joseph Frazier. *Andrew Carnegie*. Oxford University Press, 1970.

Washington, Booker T. *Up from Slavery: An Autobiography*. Doubleday, 1901.

Winter, William. *The Life of David Belasco*. 2 vols. Moffat, Yard, 1918.

Zeidman, Irving. *The American Burlesque Show*. Hawthorn Books, 1967.

Index